FAIRY TAIL

4

HIRO MASHIMA

CONTENTS

Chapter 23: Crime and Punishment ⊷ ⊷ ⊷ 3

Chapter 24: Second Floor ⊷ ⊷ ⊷ 23

Chapter 25: The Cursed Island ⊷ ⊷ ⊷ 43

Chapter 26: Is the Moon Out Tonight? ⊷ ⊷ ⊷ 63

Chapter 27: Deliora ⊷ ⊷ ⊷ 85

Chapter 28: Moon Drip ⊷ ⊷ ⊷ 115

Chapter 29: Gray and Lyon ⊷ ⊷ ⊷ 135

Chapter 30: The Dream Continues ⊷ ⊷ ⊷ 155

Translation Notes ⊷ ⊷ ⊷ 191

Volume 5 Preview ⊷ ⊷ ⊷ 199

FAIRY TAIL

Chapter 23: Crime and Punishment

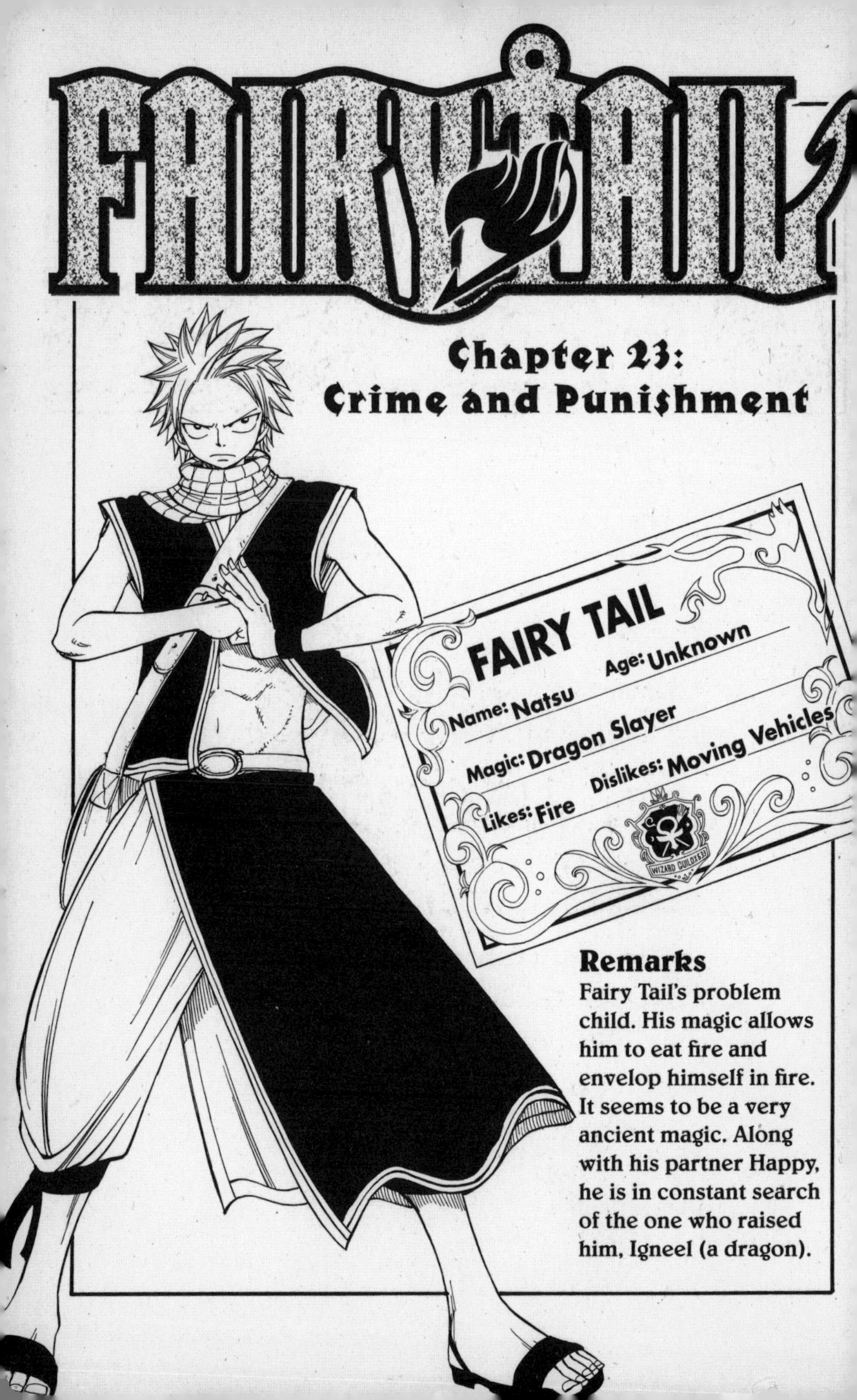
FAIRY TAIL
Age: Unknown
Name: Natsu
Magic: Dragon Slayer
Likes: Fire
Dislikes: Moving Vehicles
WIZARD GUILD

Remarks

Fairy Tail's problem child. His magic allows him to eat fire and envelop himself in fire. It seems to be a very ancient magic. Along with his partner Happy, he is in constant search of the one who raised him, Igneel (a dragon).

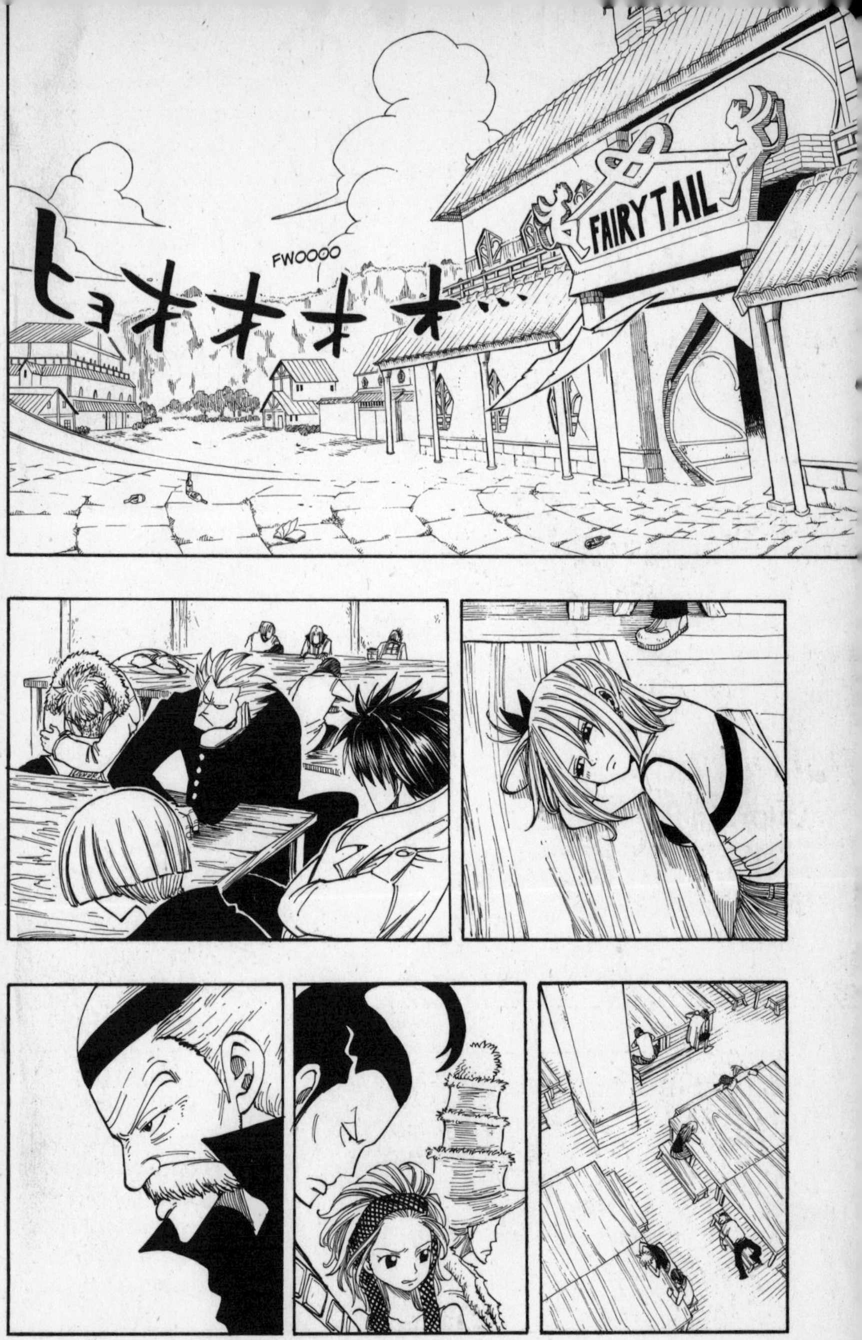

FAIRY TAIL
ヒョオオオオ…
FWOOOO

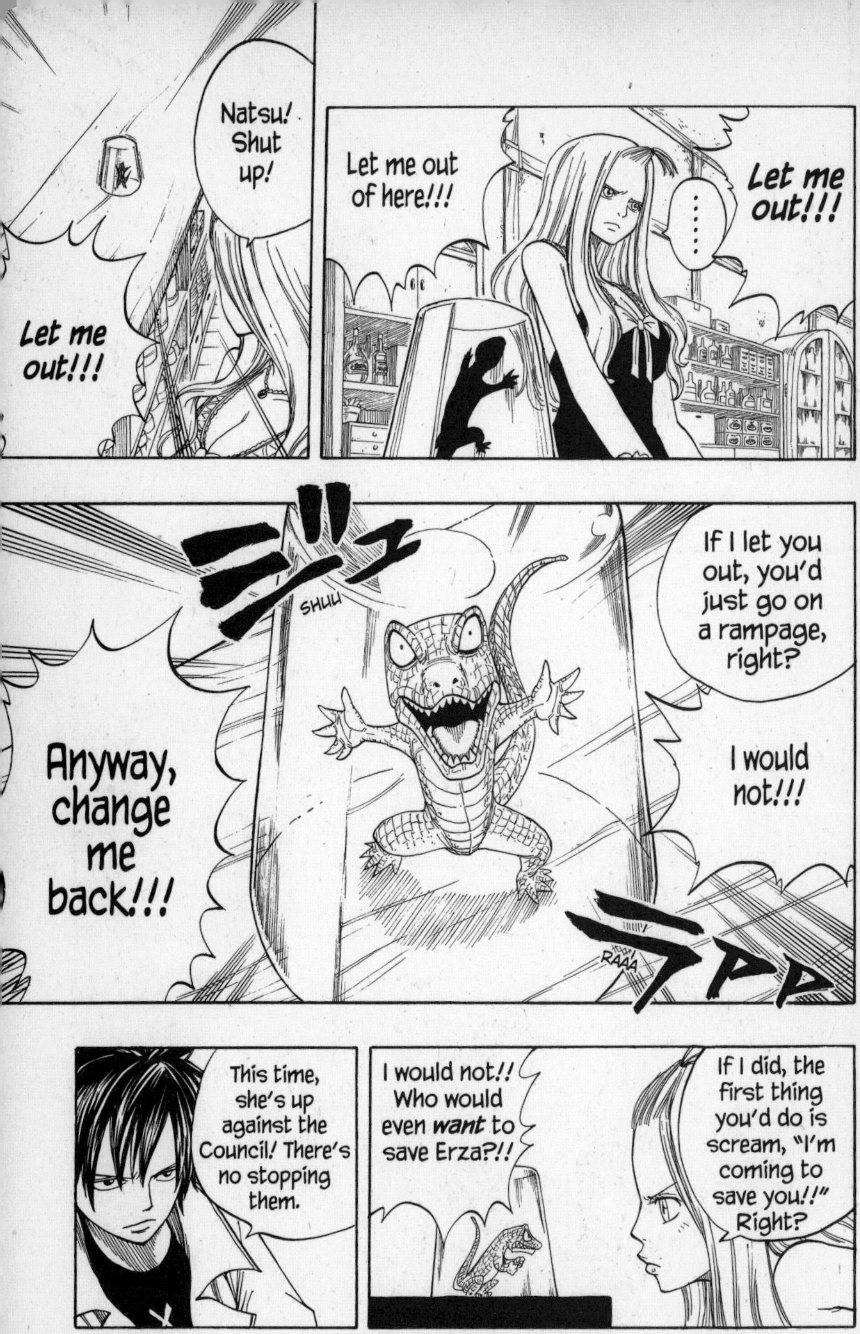
Let me out!!!
......
Let me out of here!!!
Natsu! Shut up!
Let me out!!!
If I let you out, you'd just go on a rampage, right?
I would not!!!
SHUU
RAAA
Anyway, change me back!!!
If I did, the first thing you'd do is scream, "I'm coming to save you!!" Right?
I would not!! Who would even *want* to save Erza?!!
This time, she's up against the Council! There's no stopping them.

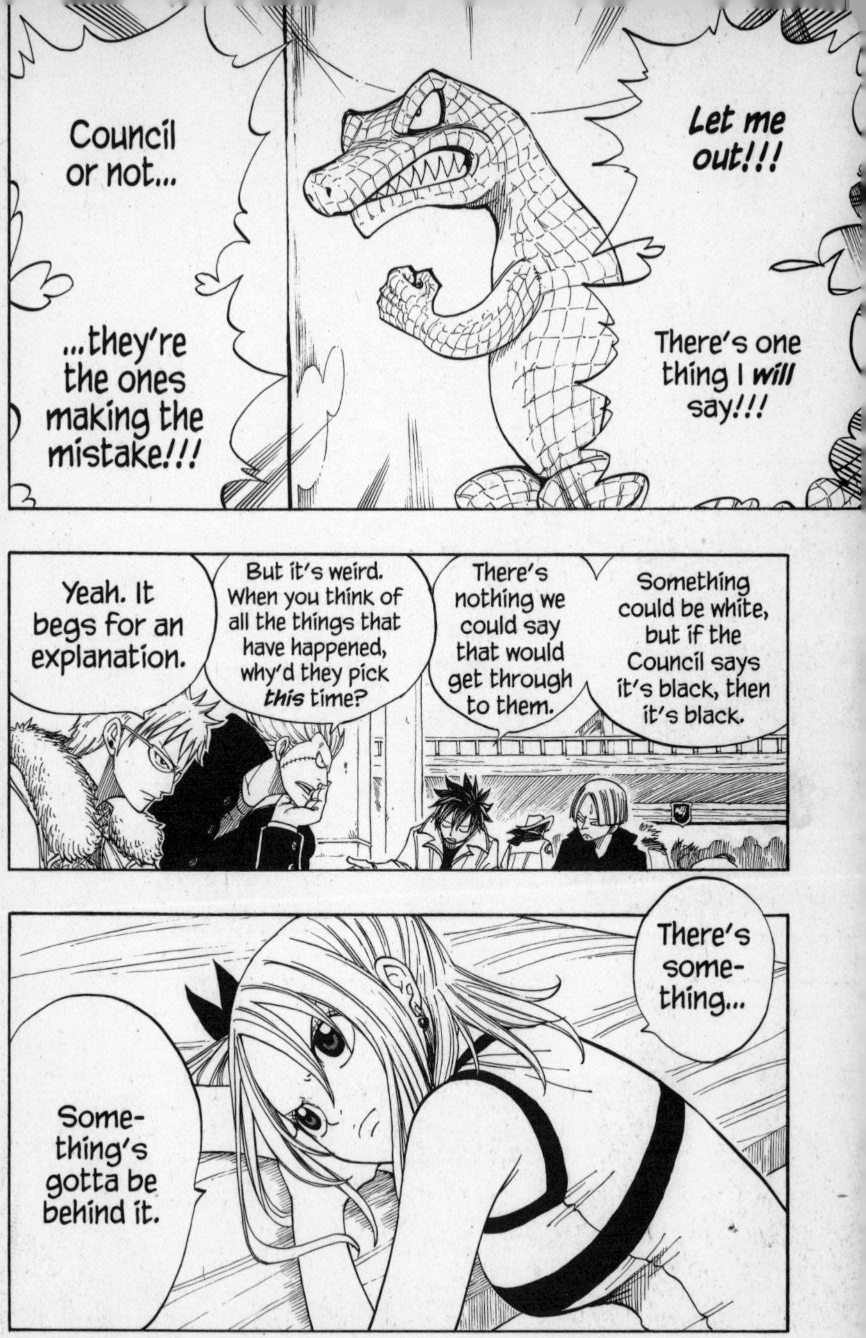
Let me out!!!
There's one thing I *will* say!!!
Council or not...
...they're the ones making the mistake!!!
Something could be white, but if the Council says it's black, then it's black.
There's nothing we could say that would get through to them.
But it's weird. When you think of all the things that have happened, why'd they pick *this* time?
Yeah. It begs for an explanation.
There's some-thing...
Some-thing's gotta be behind it.

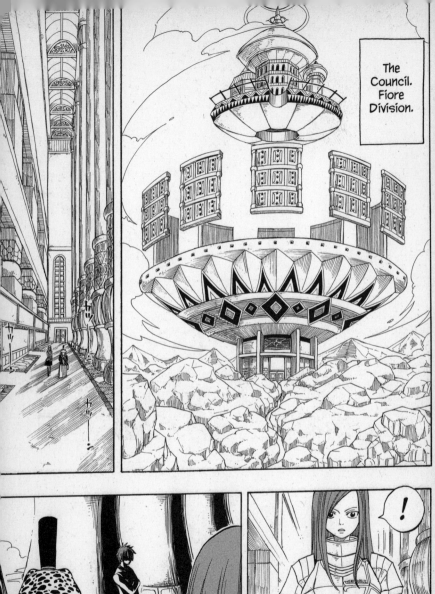

The Council.
Fiore Division.

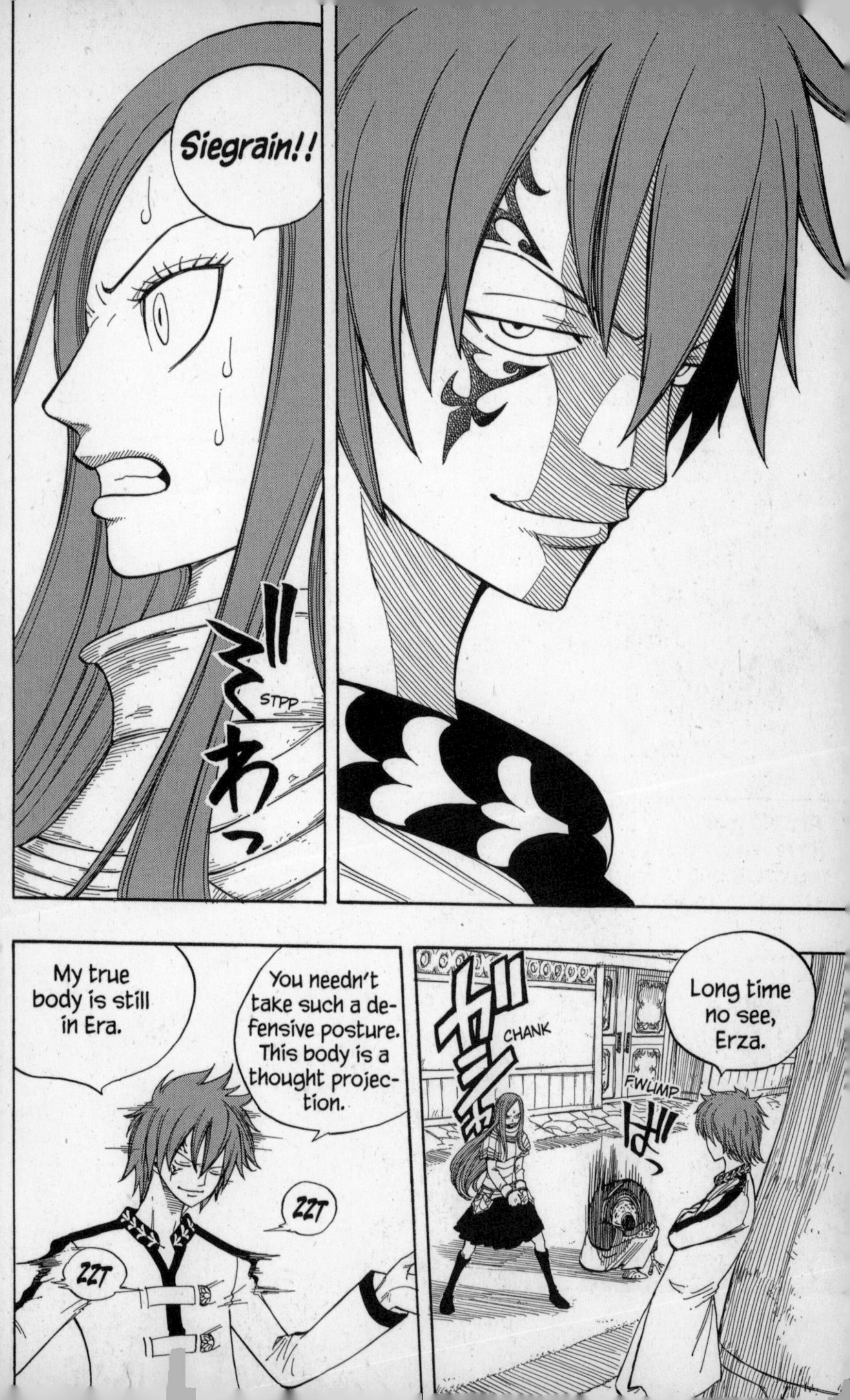
Siegrain!!
STPP
ぞわっ
CHANK
Long time no see, Erza.
FWUMP
You needn't take such a defensive posture. This body is a thought projection.
My true body is still in Era.
ZZT
ZZT

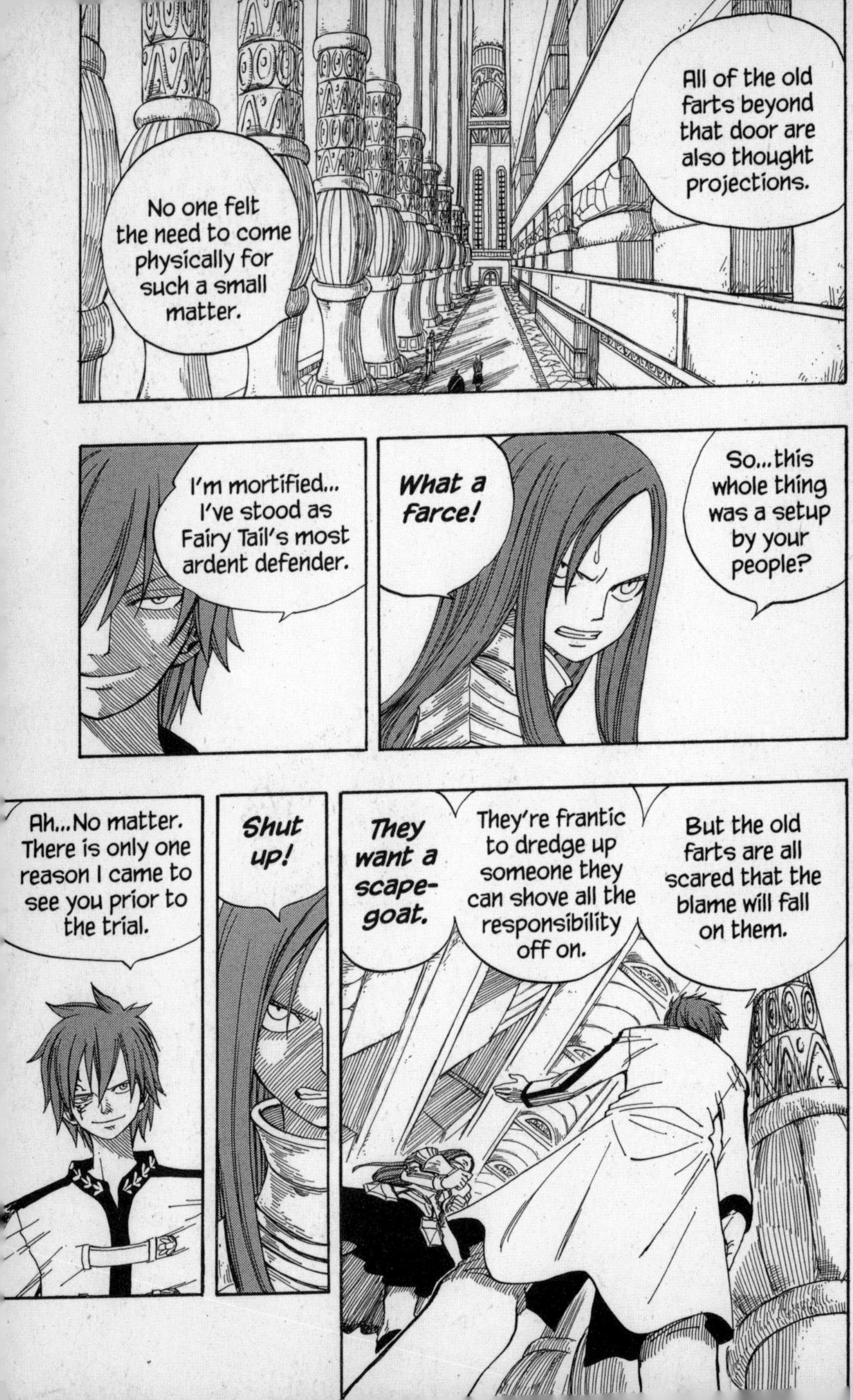
All of the old farts beyond that door are also thought projections.
No one felt the need to come physically for such a small matter.
So...this whole thing was a setup by your people?
What a farce!
I'm mortified... I've stood as Fairy Tail's most ardent defender.
But the old farts are all scared that the blame will fall on them.
They're frantic to dredge up someone they can shove all the responsibility off on.
They want a scape-goat.
Shut up!
Ah...No matter. There is only one reason I came to see you prior to the trial.

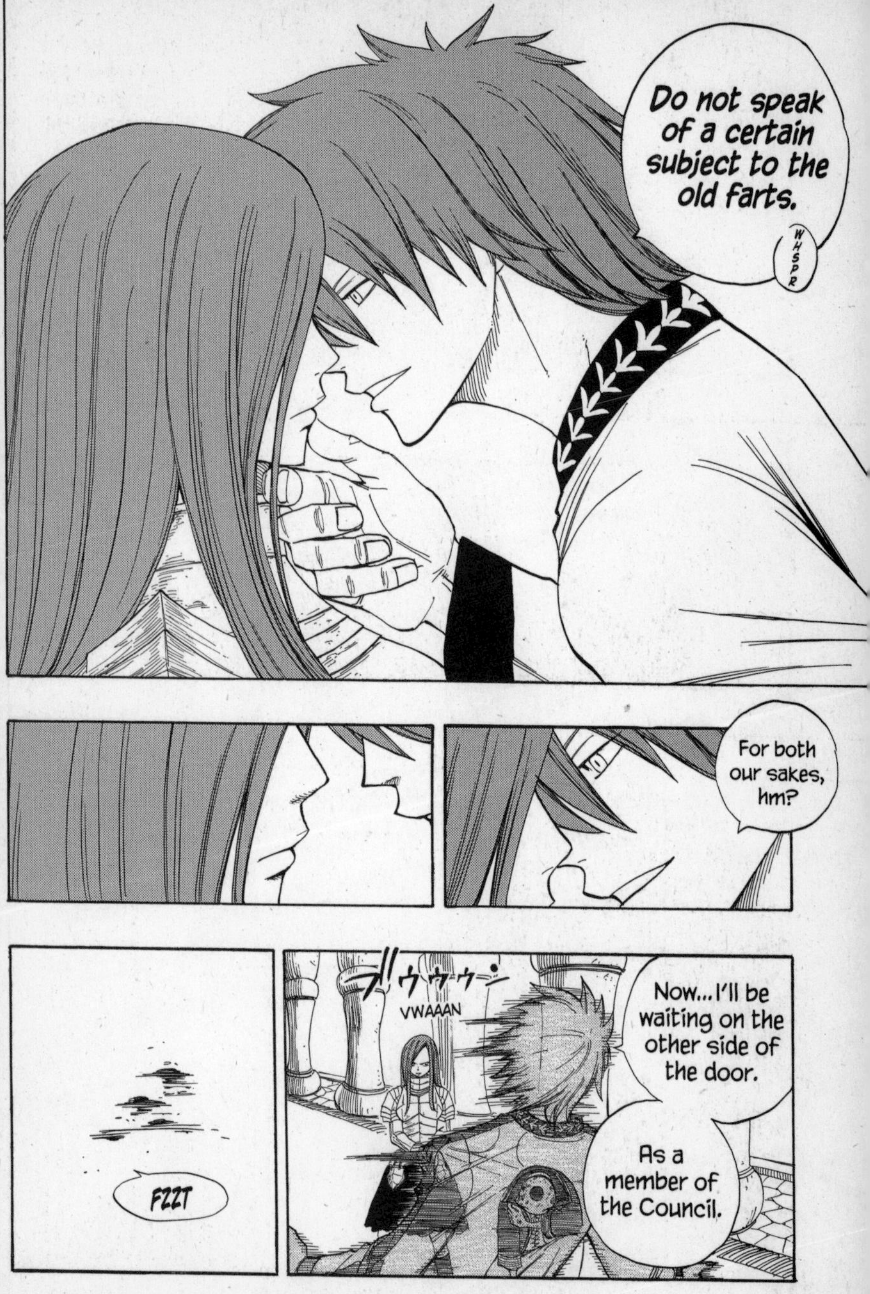
Do not speak of a certain subject to the old farts.
WHSPR
For both our sakes, hm?
VWAAAN
Now...I'll be waiting on the other side of the door.
As a member of the Council.
FZZT

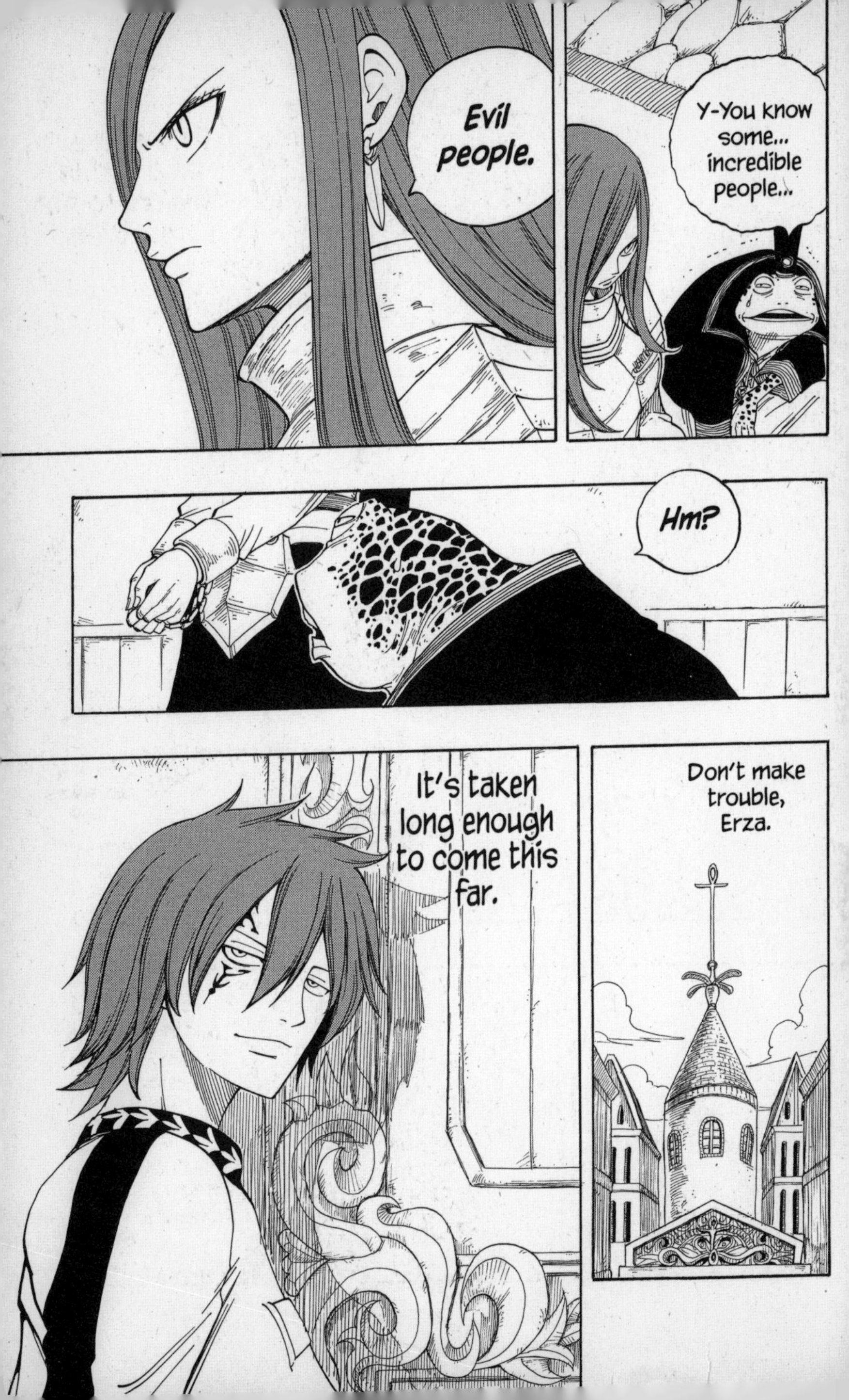

Evil people.
Y-You know some... incredible people...
Hm?
Don't make trouble, Erza.
It's taken long enough to come this far.

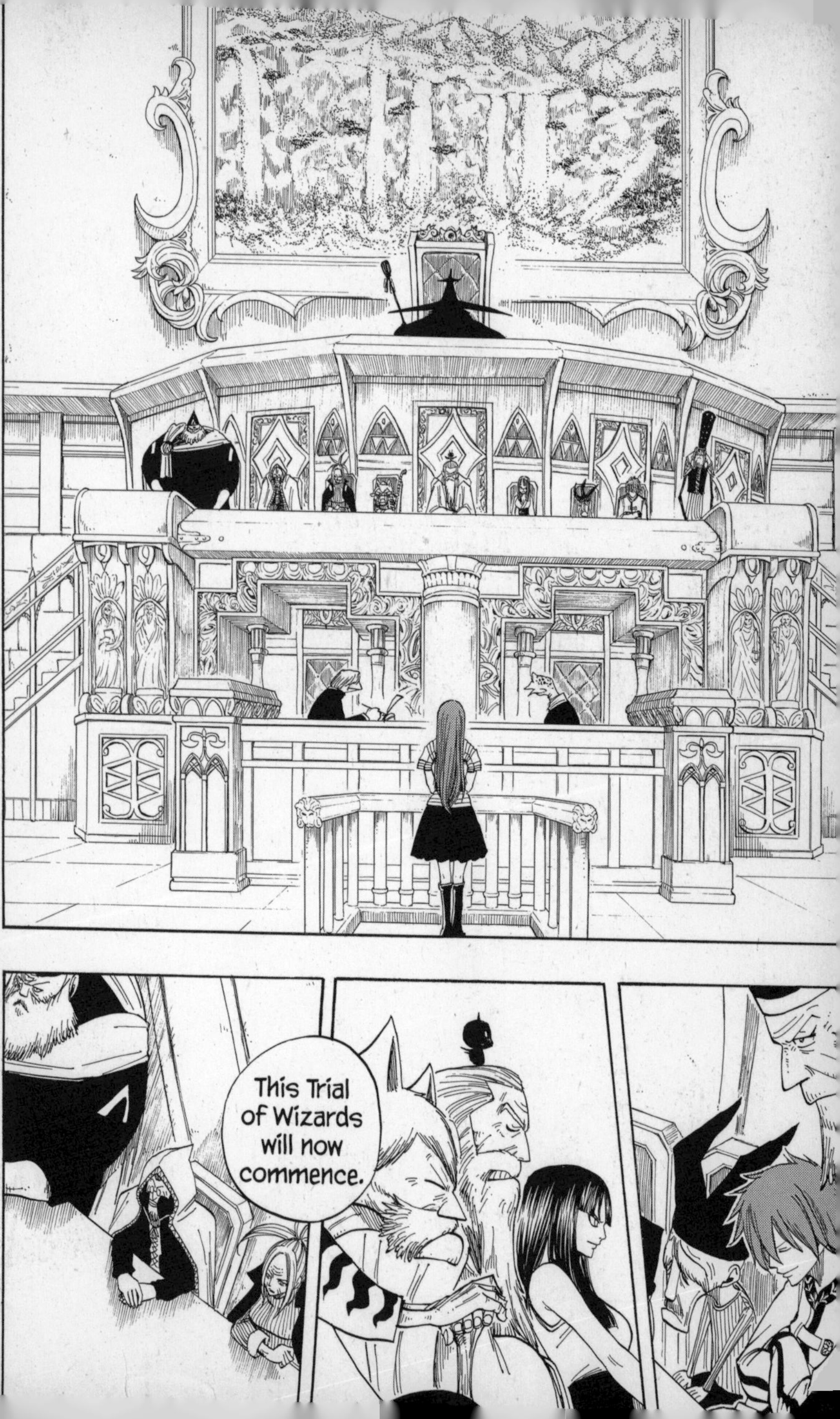
This Trial of Wizards will now commence.

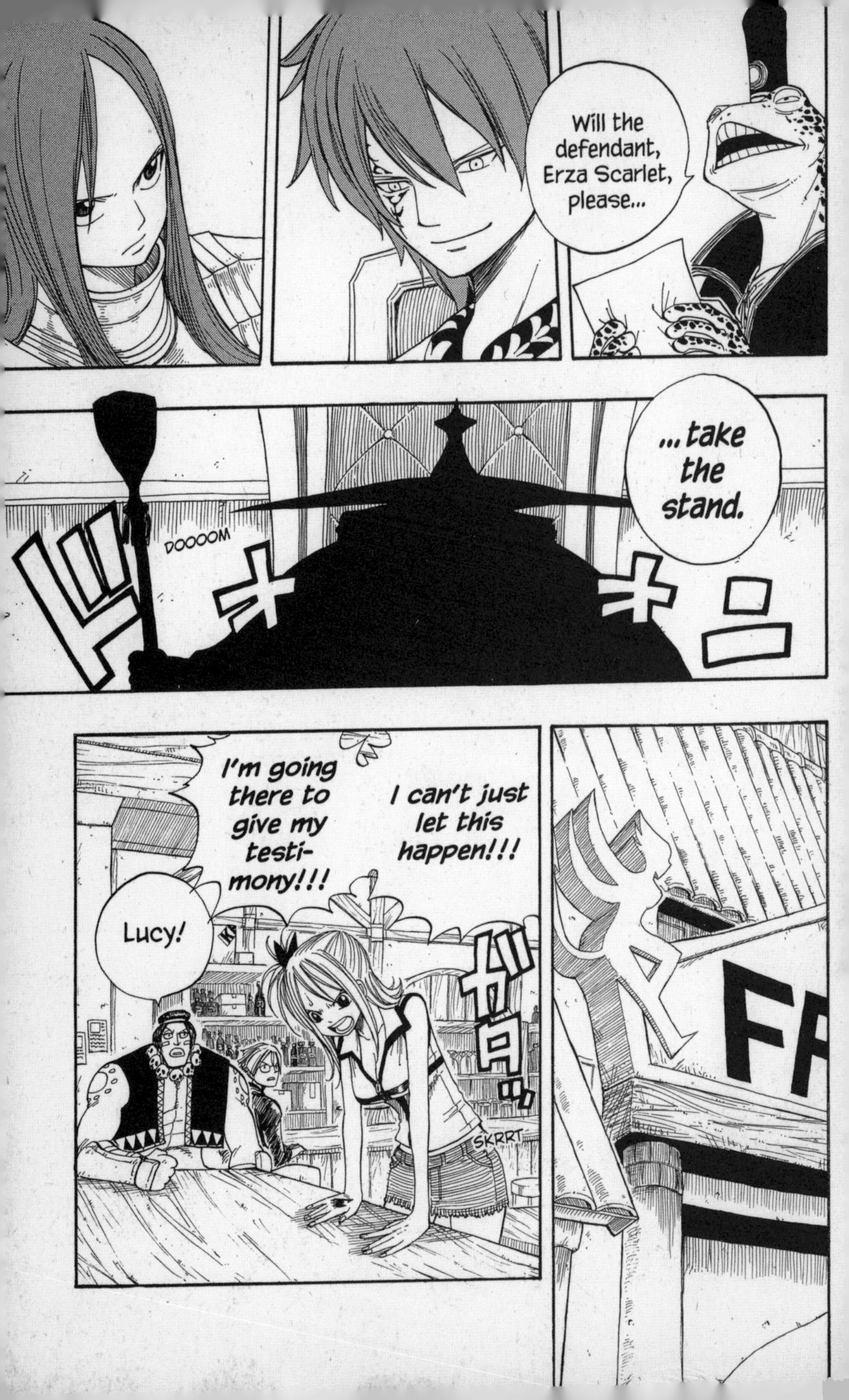
Will the defendant, Erza Scarlet, please...
...take the stand.
DOOOOM
I'm going there to give my testi-mony!!!
I can't just let this happen!!!
Lucy!
SKRRT
FA

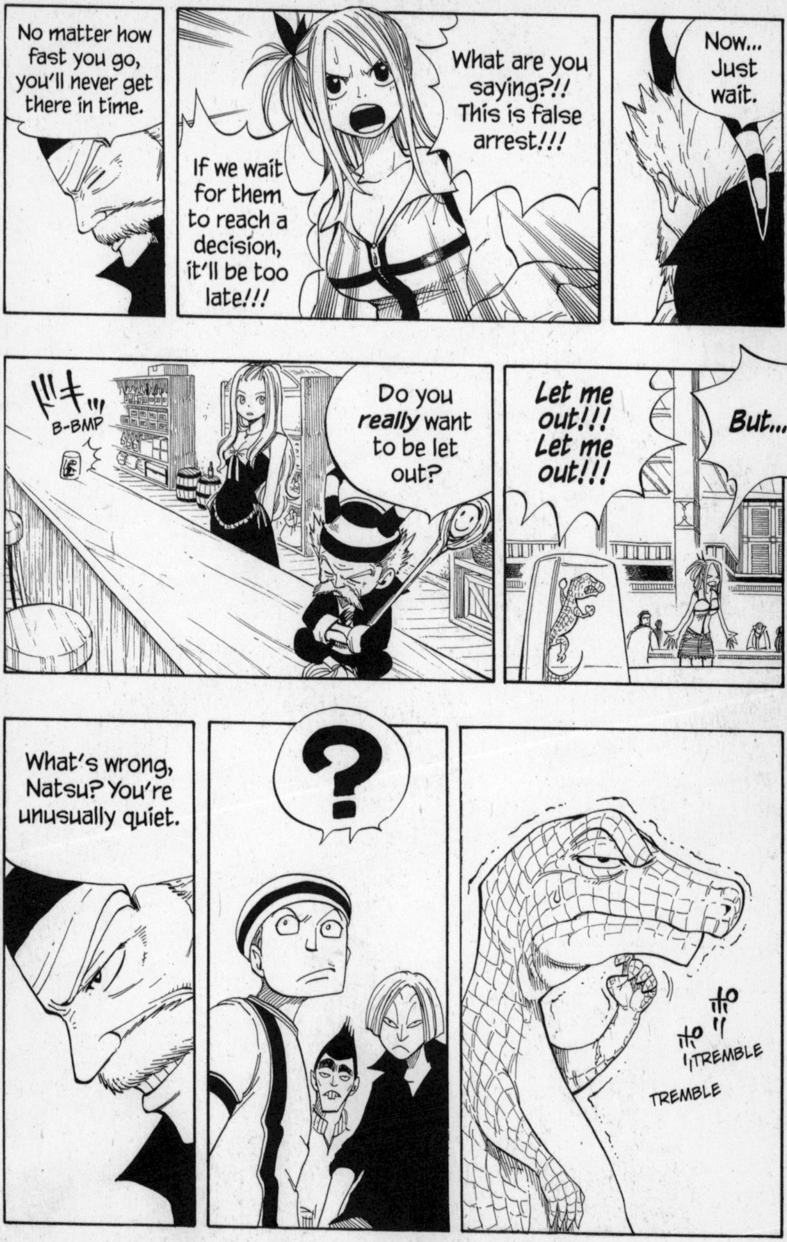

Now... Just wait.
What are you saying?!! This is false arrest!!!
If we wait for them to reach a decision, it'll be too late!!!
No matter how fast you go, you'll never get there in time.
But...
Let me out!!! Let me out!!!
Do you *really* want to be let out?
ドキッ
B-BMP
TREMBLE
TREMBLE
?
What's wrong, Natsu? You're unusually quiet.

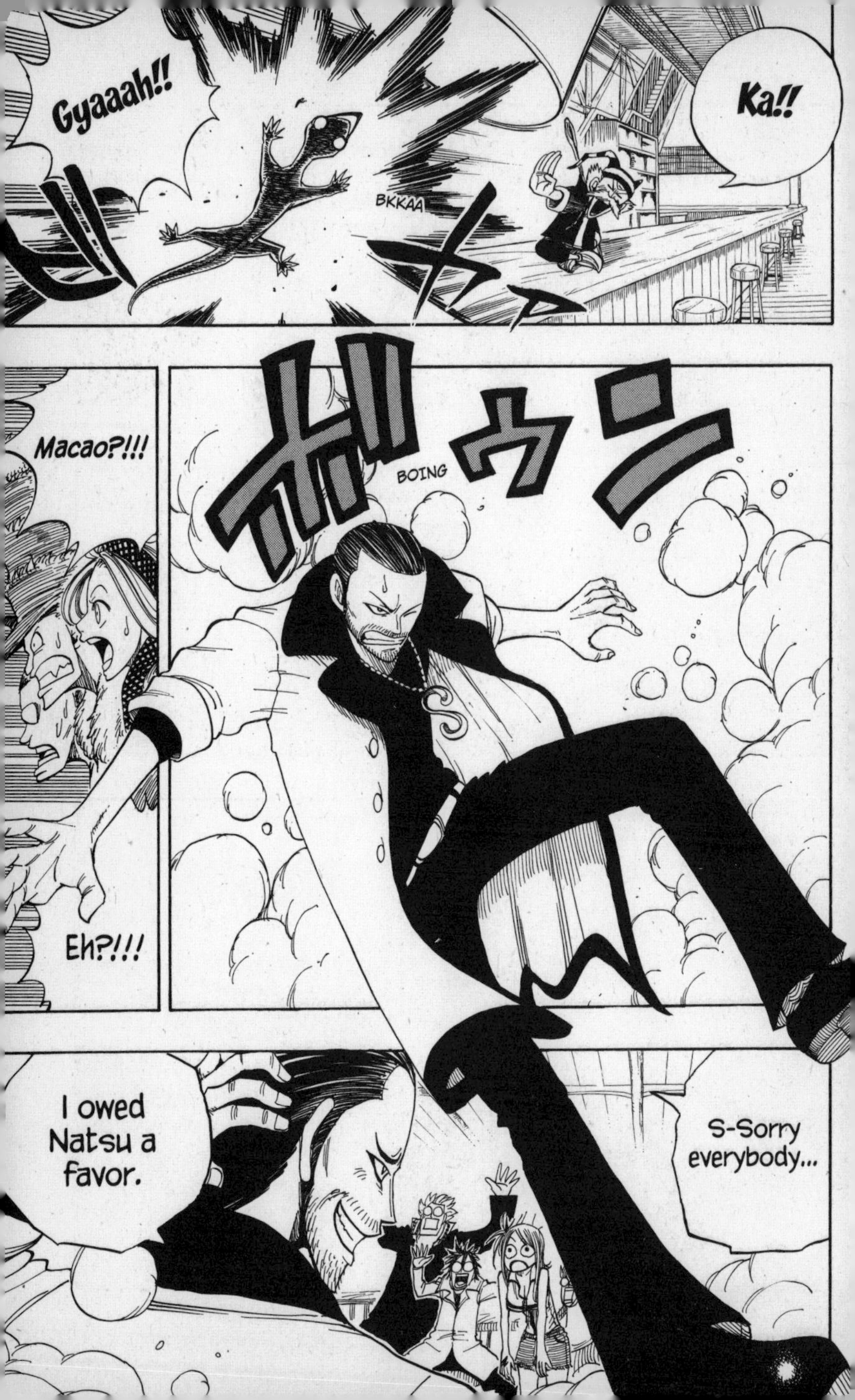
Ka!!
BKKAA
Gyaaah!!
BOING
Macao?!!!
Eh?!!!
S-Sorry everybody...
I owed Natsu a favor.

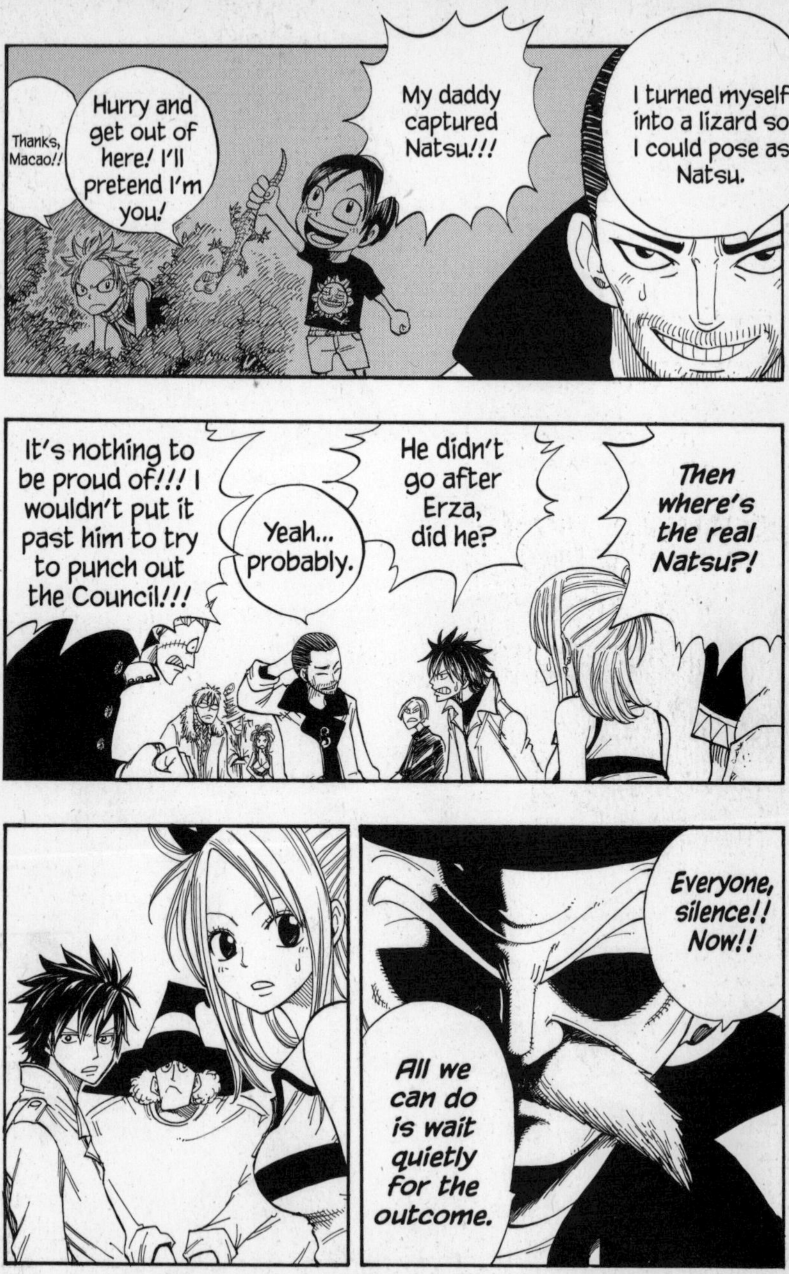
I turned myself into a lizard so I could pose as Natsu.
My daddy captured Natsu!!!
Hurry and get out of here! I'll pretend I'm you!
Thanks, Macao!!
Then where's the real Natsu?!
He didn't go after Erza, did he?
Yeah... probably.
It's nothing to be proud of!!! I wouldn't put it past him to try to punch out the Council!!!
Everyone, silence!! Now!!
All we can do is wait quietly for the outcome.

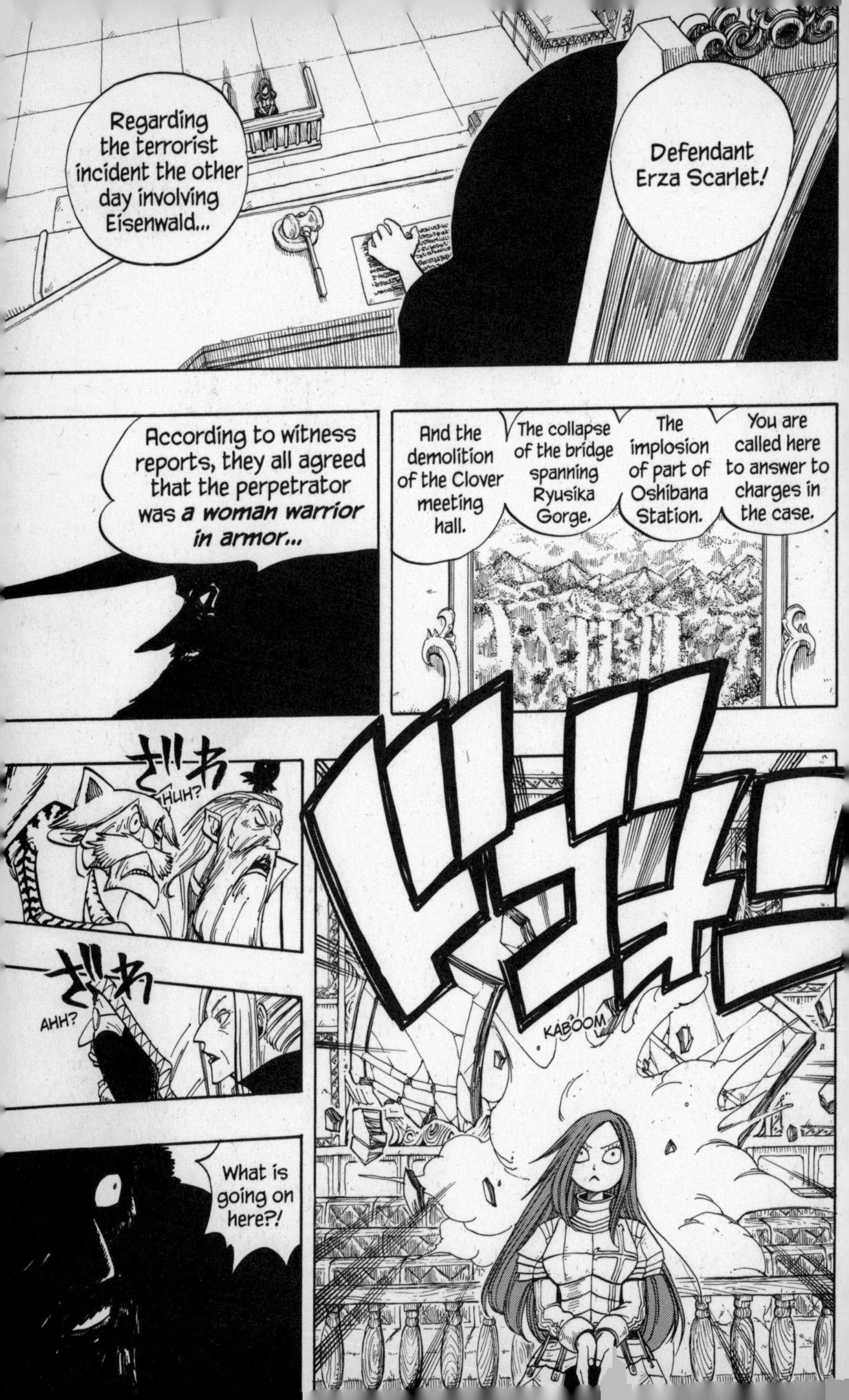
Defendant Erza Scarlet!
Regarding the terrorist incident the other day involving Eisenwald...
You are called here to answer to charges in the case.
The implosion of part of Oshibana Station.
The collapse of the bridge spanning Ryusika Gorge.
And the demolition of the Clover meeting hall.
According to witness reports, they all agreed that the perpetrator was *a woman warrior in armor...*
KABOOM
HUH?
AHH?
What is going on here?!

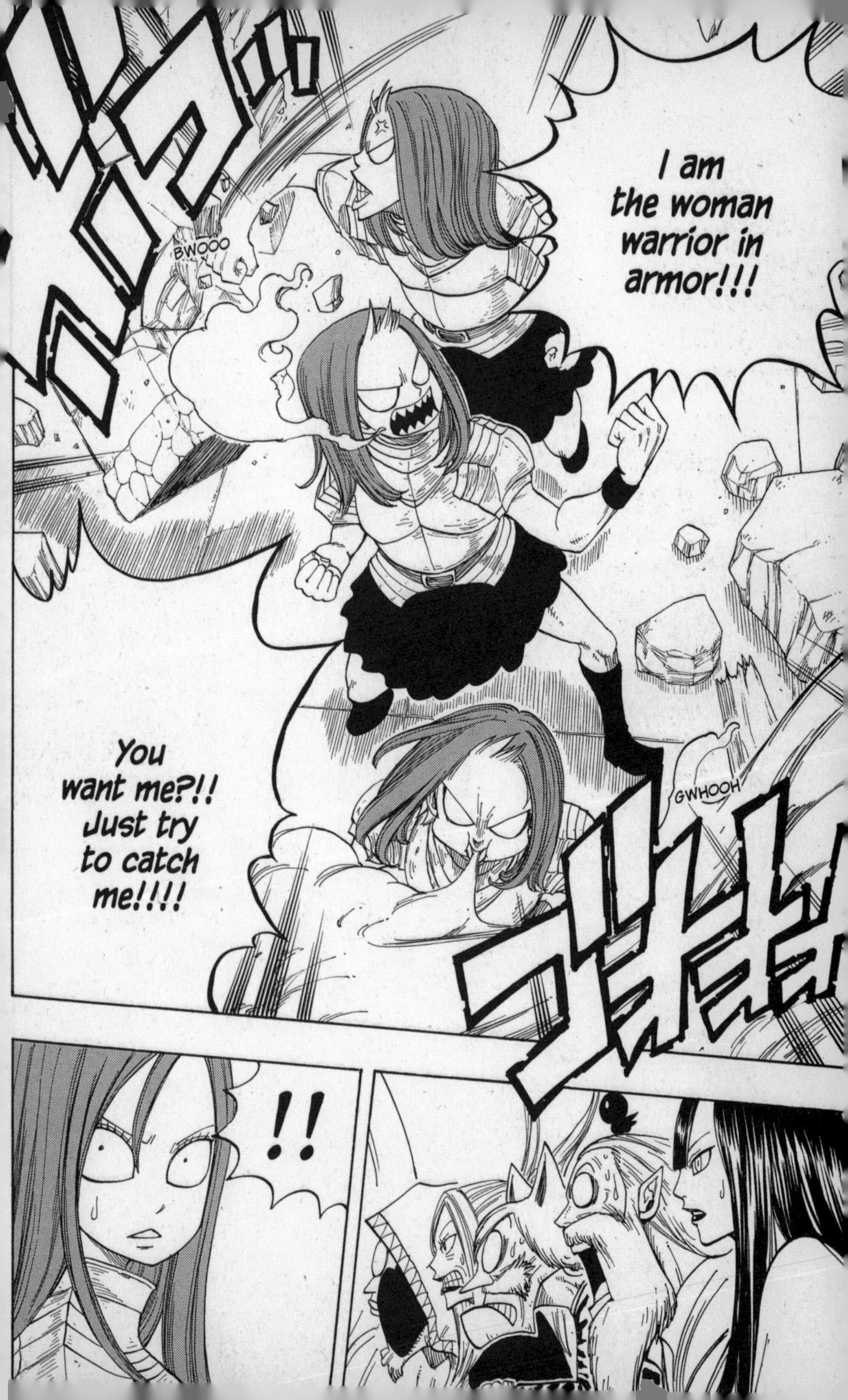
BWOOO
I am the woman warrior in armor!!!
You want me?!! Just try to catch me!!!!
GWHOOH
!!

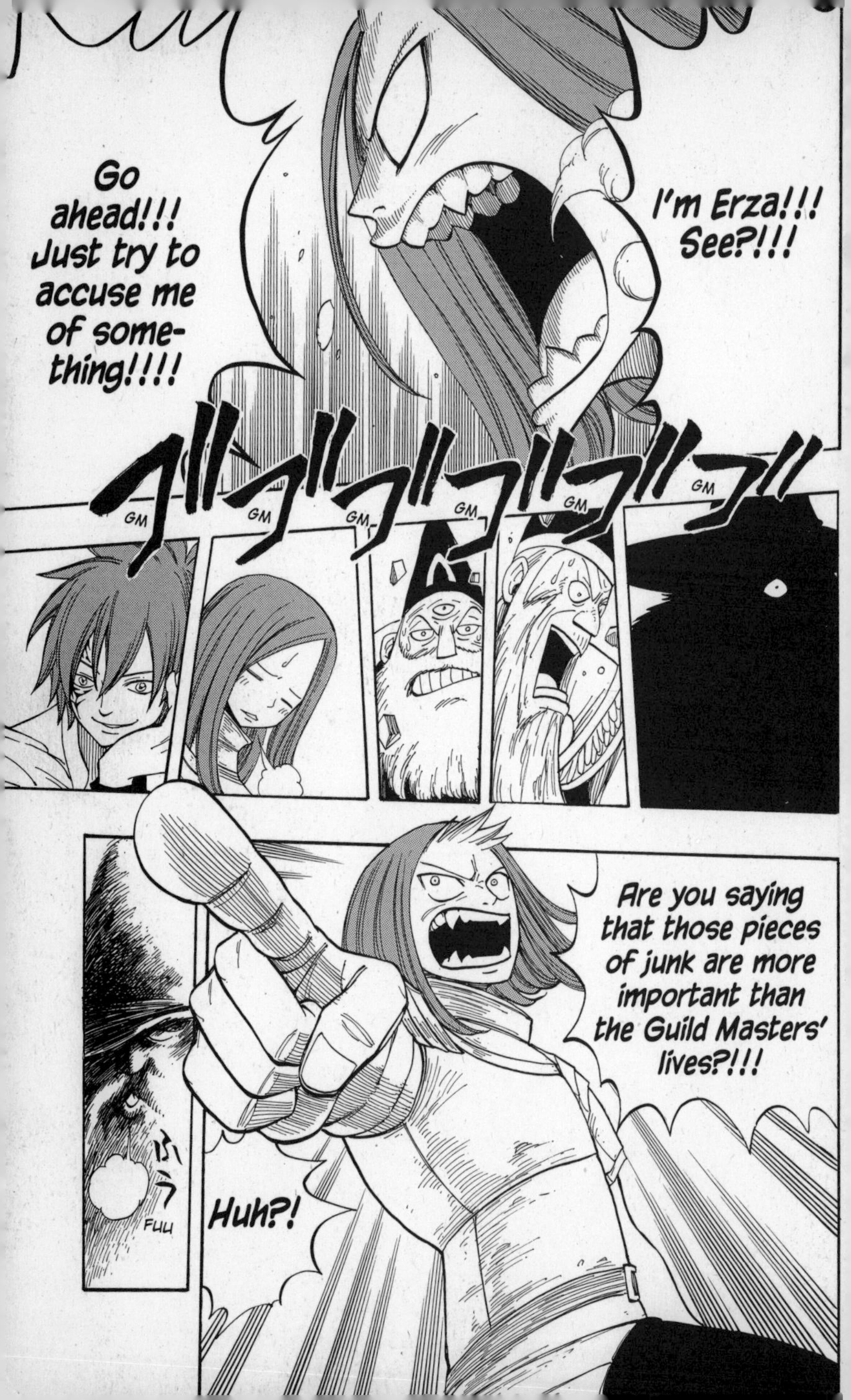

I'm Erza!!! See?!!!
Go ahead!!! Just try to accuse me of some-thing!!!!
GM
GM
GM
GM
GM
GM
Are you saying that those pieces of junk are more important than the Guild Masters' lives?!!!
Huh?!
FUU

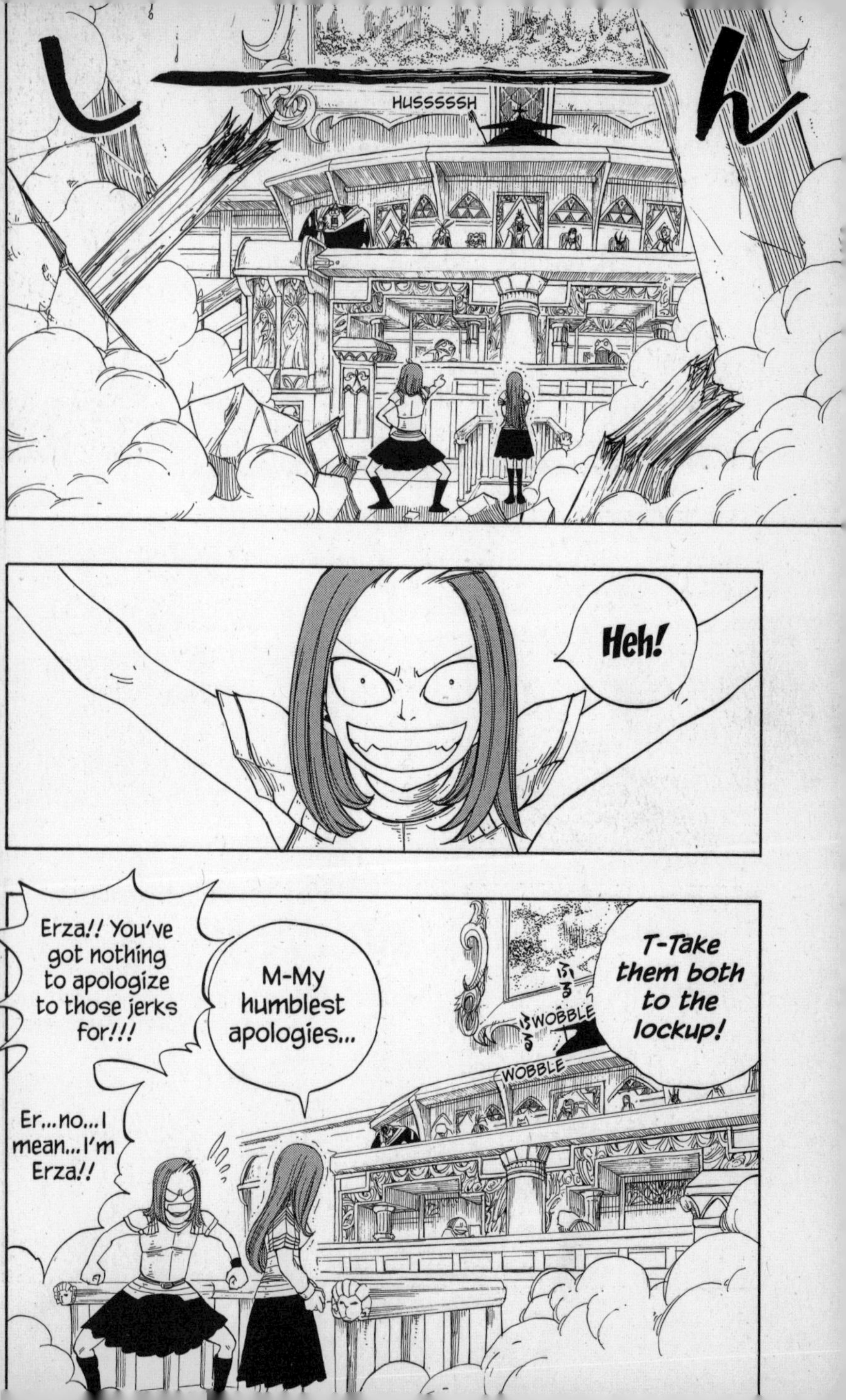

しーん
HUSSSSSH
Heh!
T-Take them both to the lockup!
ふる ふる
WOBBLE
WOBBLE
M-My humblest apologies...
Erza!! You've got nothing to apologize to those jerks for!!!
Er...no...I mean...I'm Erza!!

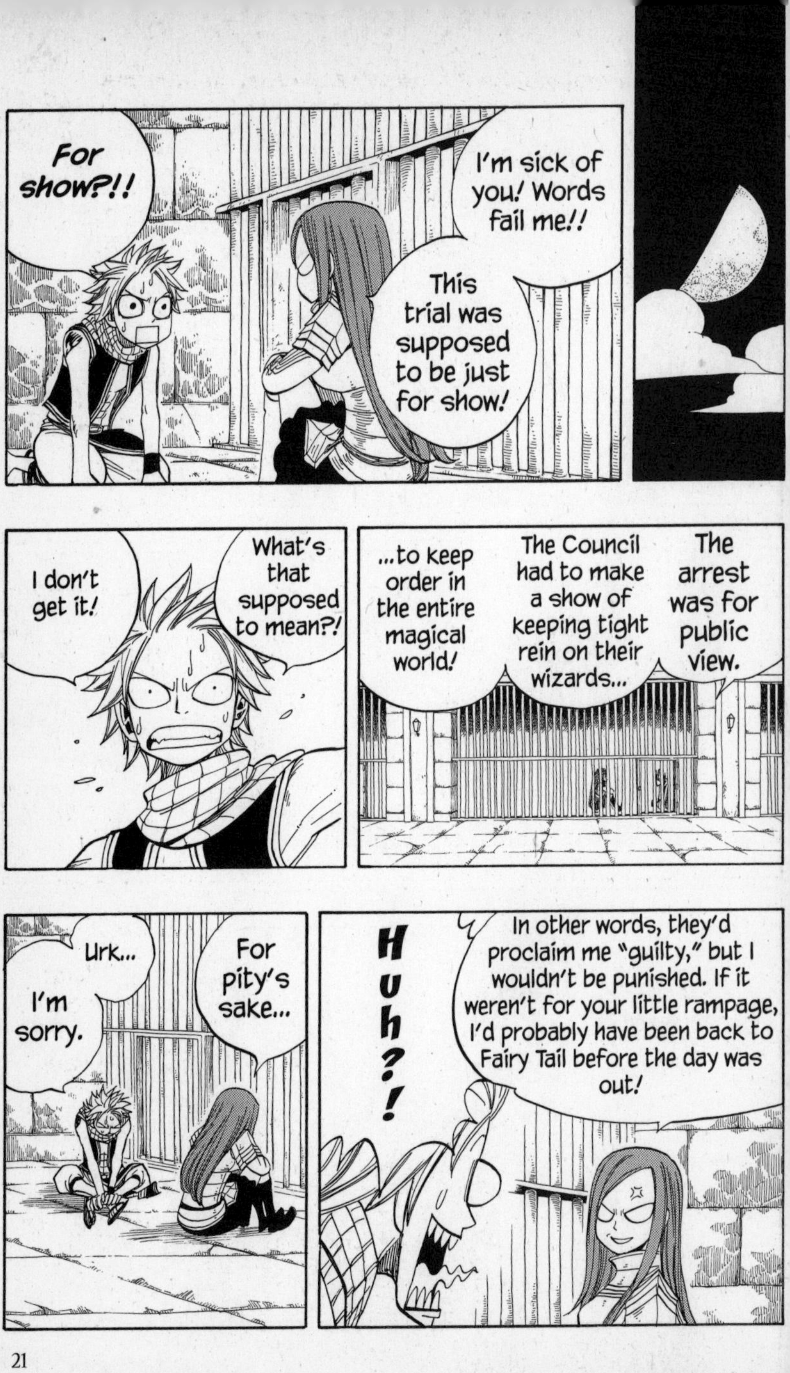
I'm sick of you! Words fail me!!
This trial was supposed to be just for show!
For show?!!
The arrest was for public view.
The Council had to make a show of keeping tight rein on their wizards...
...to keep order in the entire magical world!
What's that supposed to mean?!
I don't get it!
In other words, they'd proclaim me "guilty," but I wouldn't be punished. If it weren't for your little rampage, I'd probably have been back to Fairy Tail before the day was out!
Huh?!
For pity's sake...
Urk... I'm sorry.

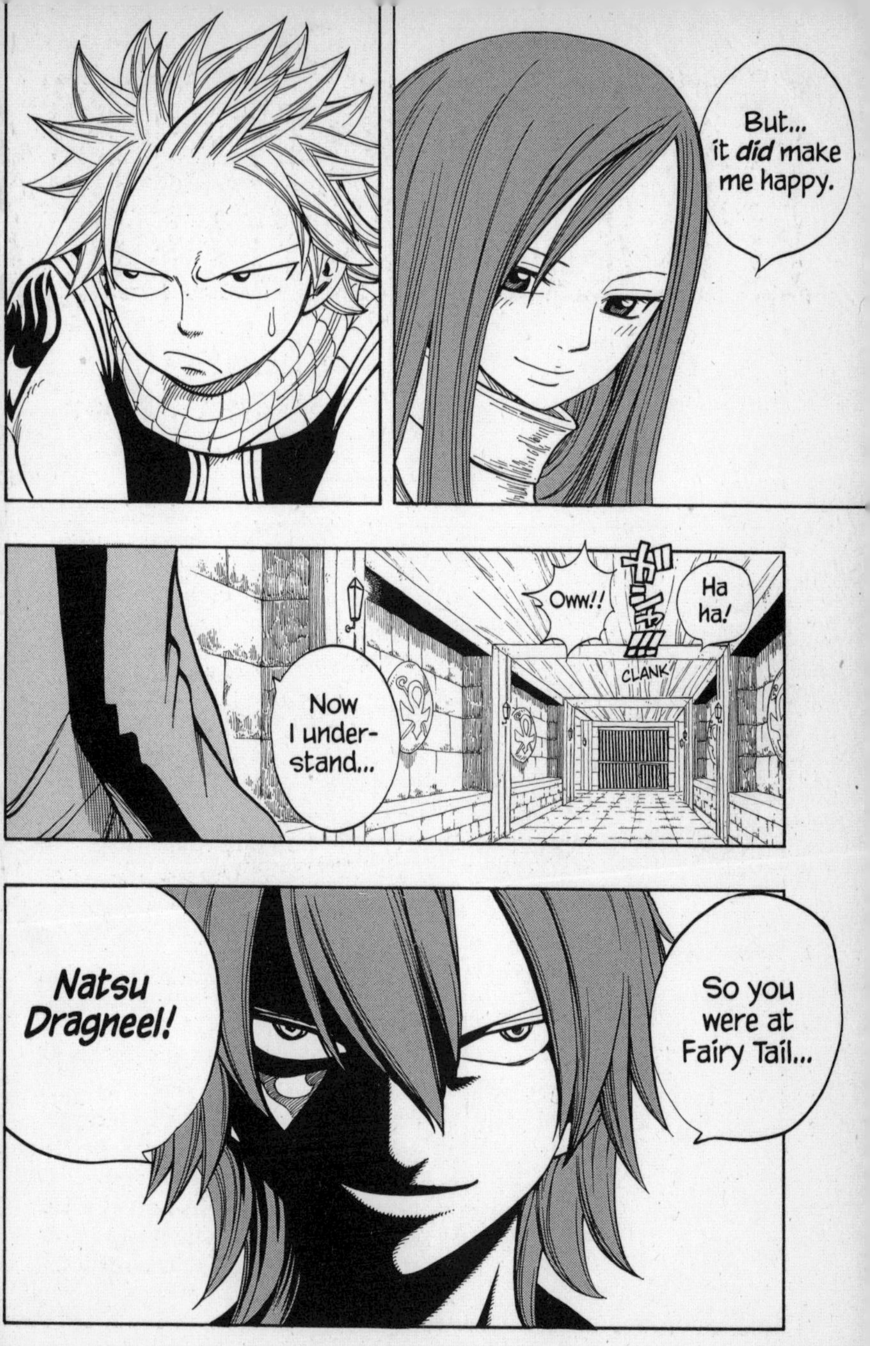
But... it *did* make me happy.
Ha ha!
Oww!!
CLANK
Now I understand...
So you were at Fairy Tail...
Natsu Dragneel!

Chapter 24:
Second Floor

FAIRY TAIL

Name: Happy   Age: 6 Yrs.

Magic: Aera

Likes: Fish   Dislikes: Dogs (but is fine with Plue)

Remarks

The cat (?) that is always with Natsu. He talks and can use magic, but nobody seems to question him about it. Everyone probably just figures that's just the kind of animal that he is, and lets it go at that. The story of his meeting with Natsu is a tale for another day.

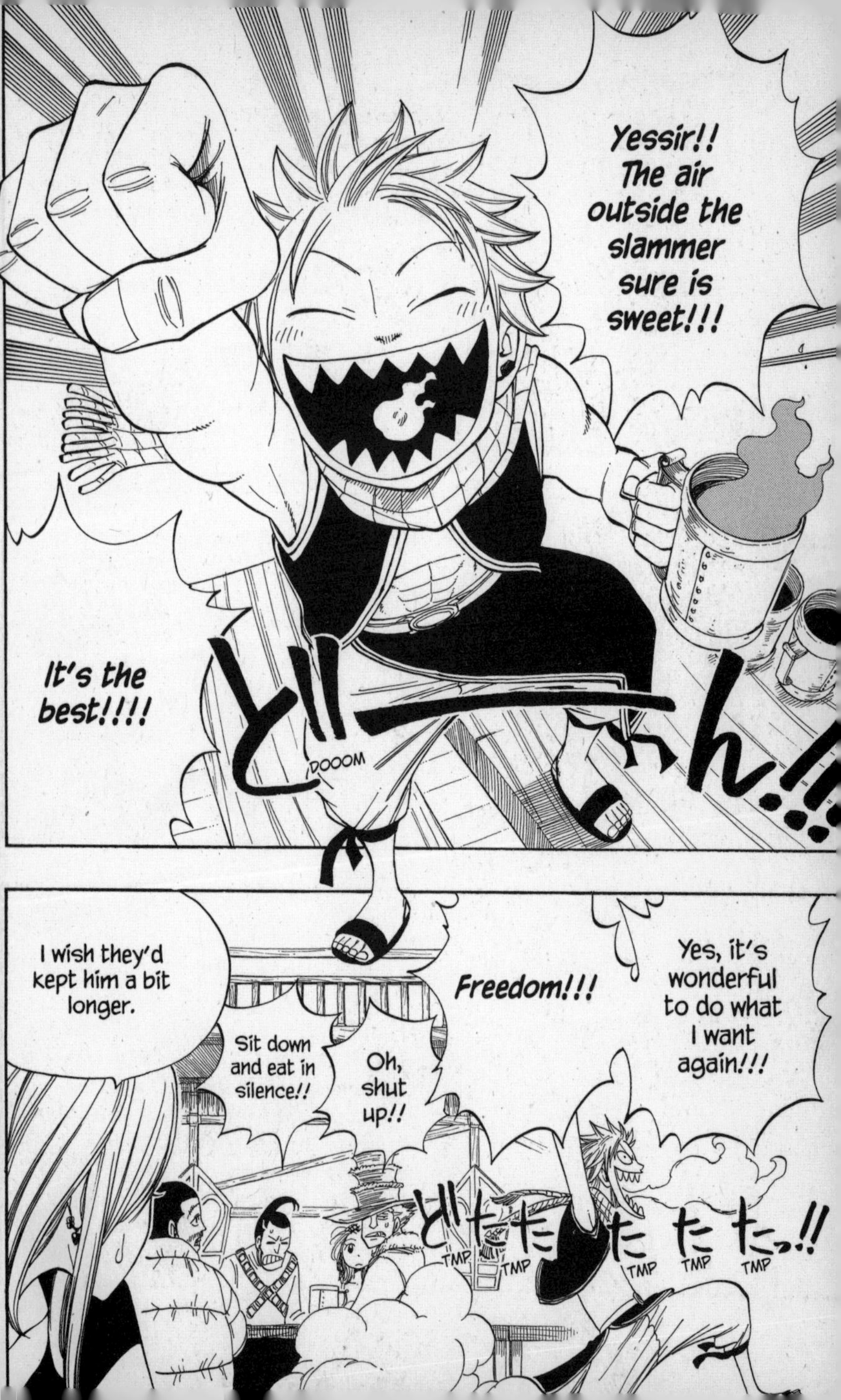

Yessir!! The air outside the slammer sure is sweet!!!
It's the best!!!!
どーん!!!
DOOOM
Yes, it's wonderful to do what I want again!!!
Freedom!!!
Oh, shut up!!
Sit down and eat in silence!!
I wish they'd kept him a bit longer.
どたたたたたっ!!
TMP TMP TMP TMP TMP

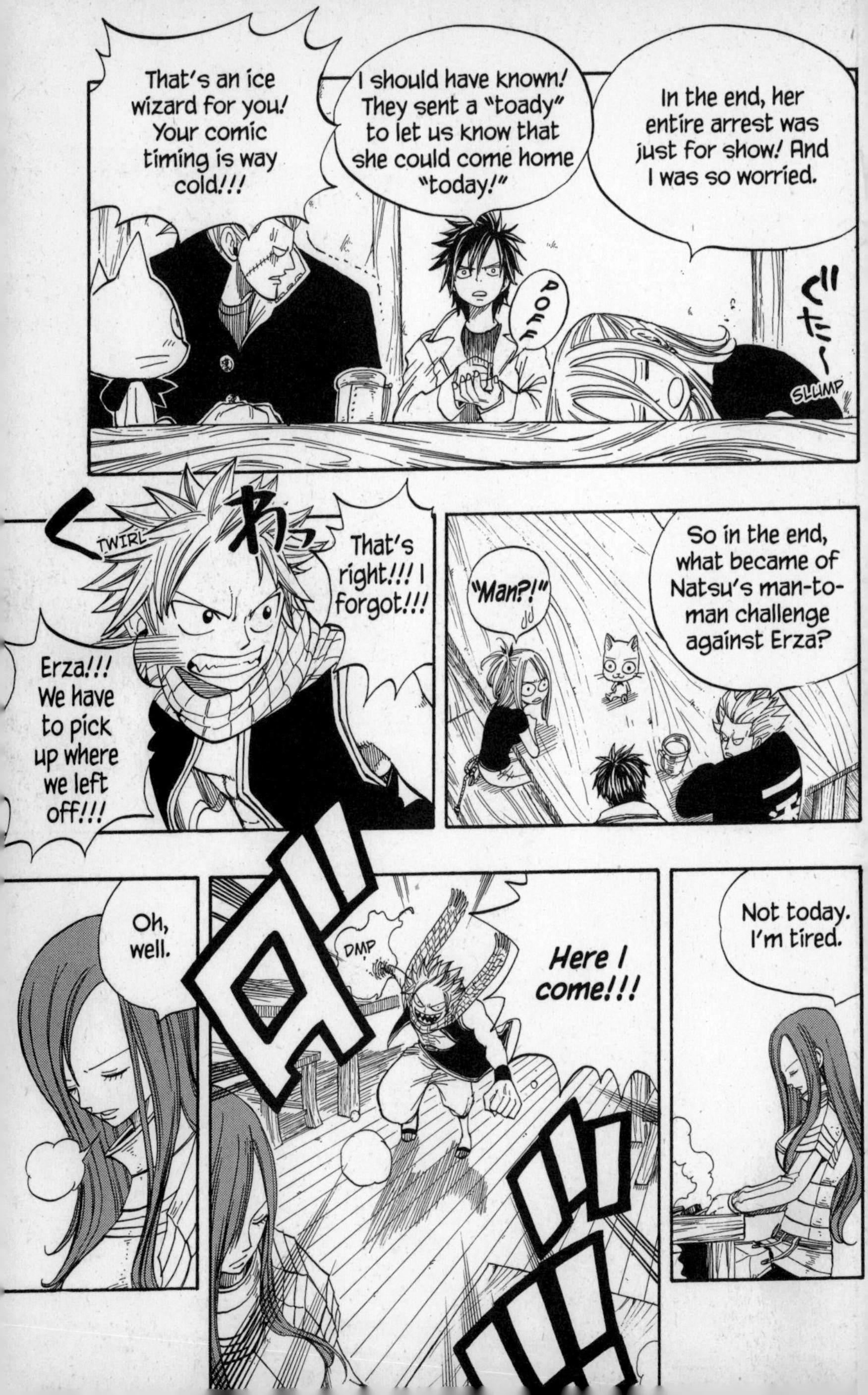
In the end, her entire arrest was just for show! And I was so worried.
SLUMP
POFF
I should have known! They sent a "toady" to let us know that she could come home "today!"
That's an ice wizard for you! Your comic timing is way cold!!!
So in the end, what became of Natsu's man-to-man challenge against Erza?
"Man?!"
That's right!!! I forgot!!!
TWIRL
Erza!!! We have to pick up where we left off!!!
Not today. I'm tired.
Here I come!!!
DMP
Oh, well.

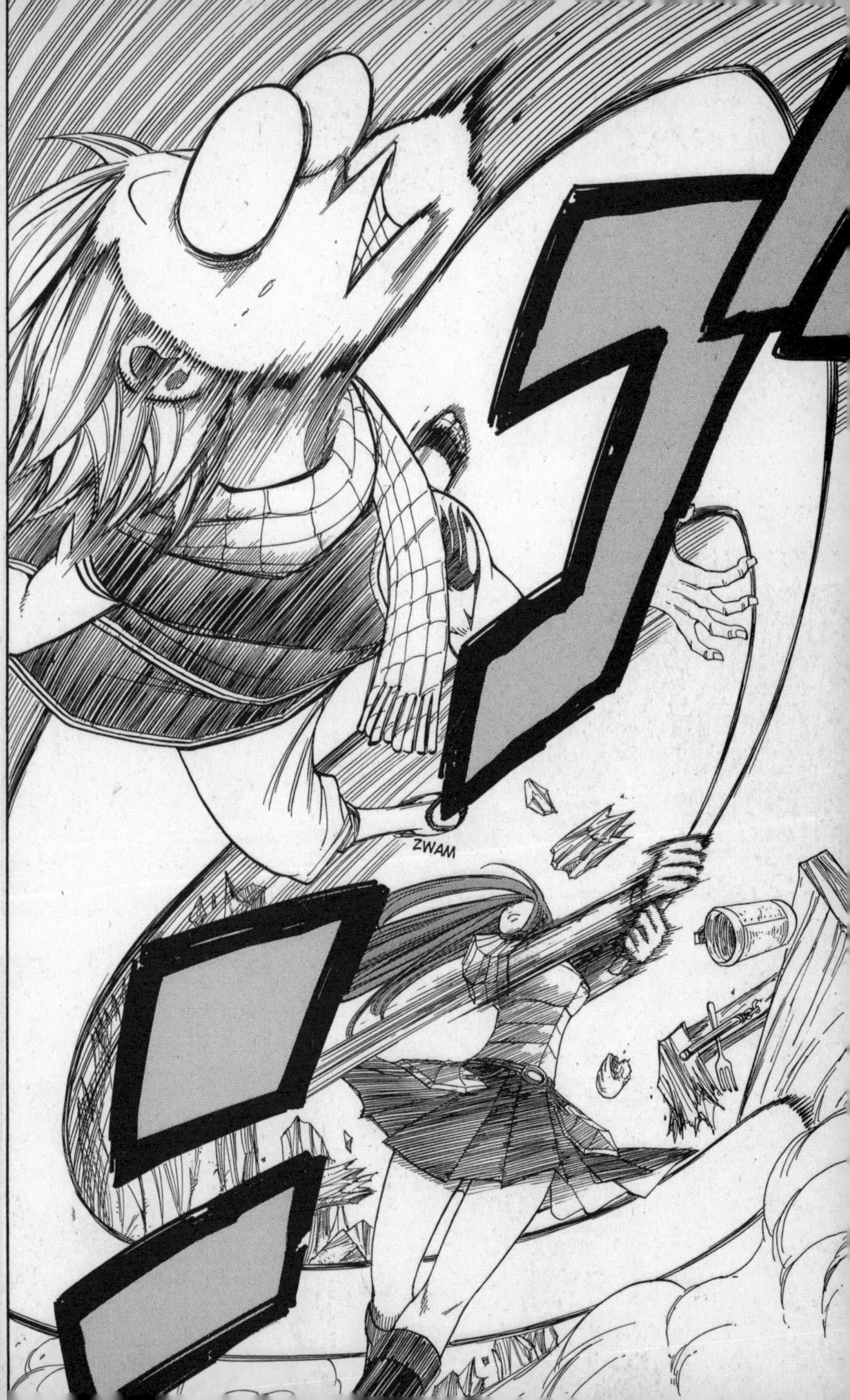
ZWAM

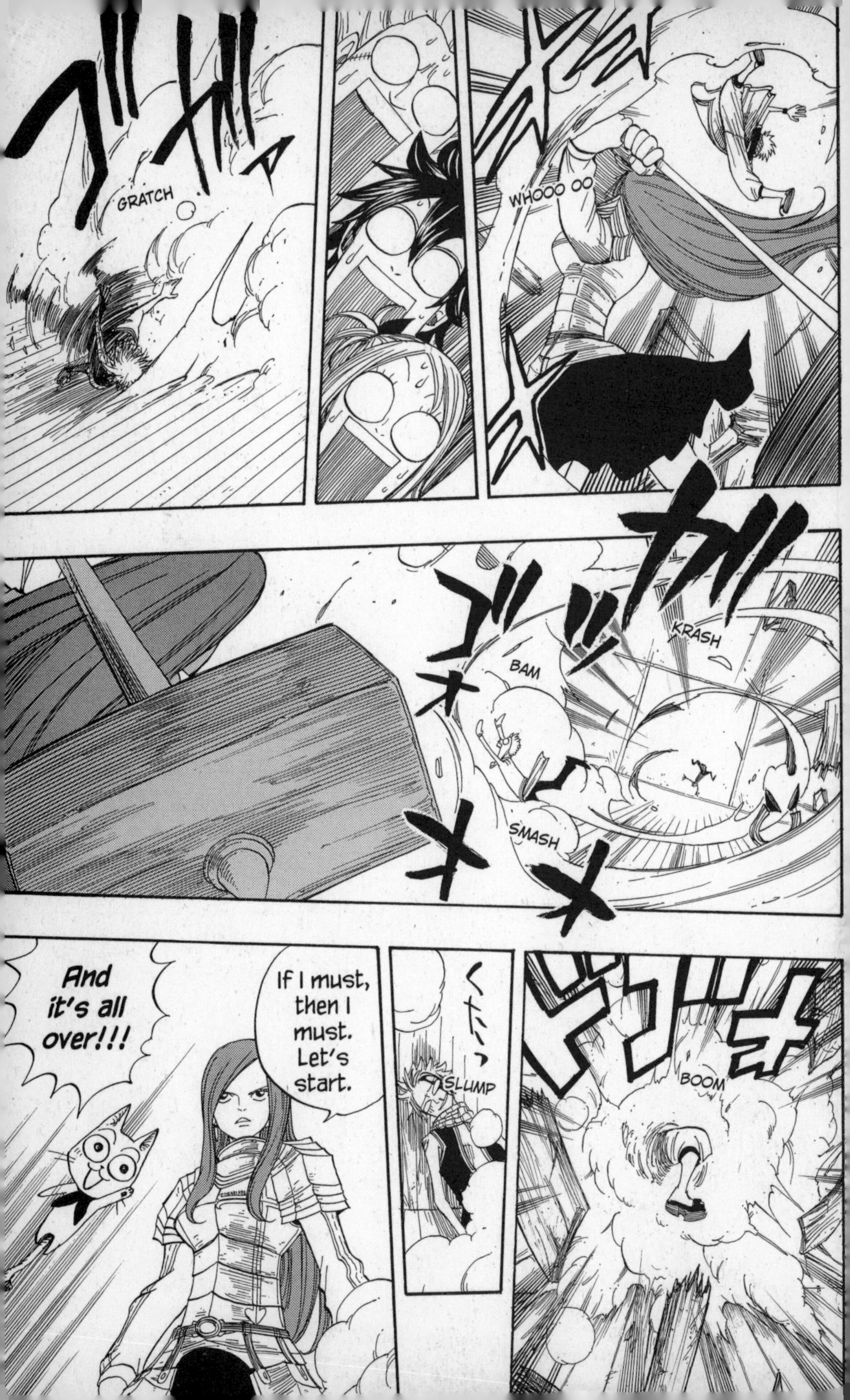
WHOOO OO
GRATCH
KRASH
BAM
SMASH
BOOM
SLUMP
If I must, then I must. Let's start.
And it's all over!!!

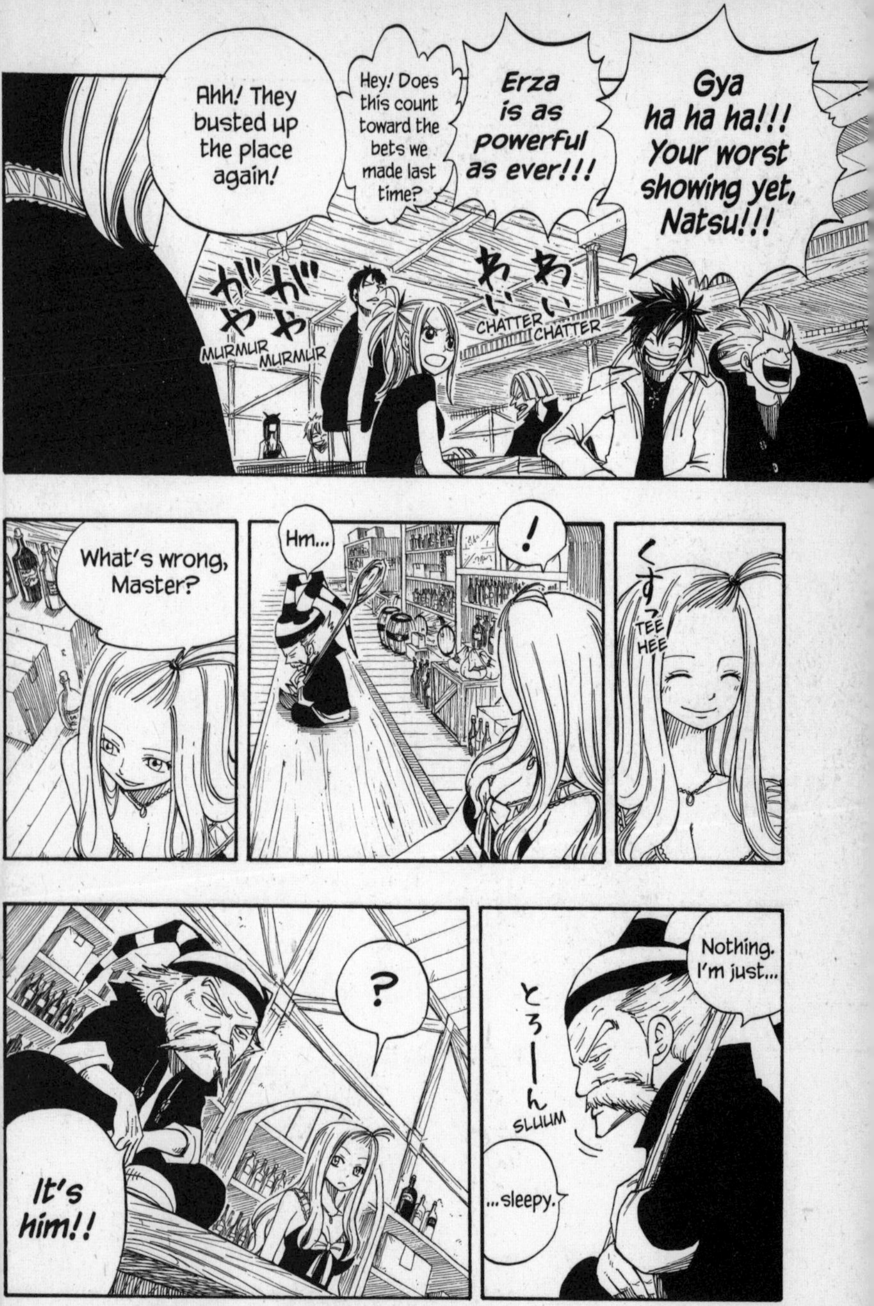
Gya ha ha ha!!! Your worst showing yet, Natsu!!!
Erza is as powerful as ever!!!
Hey! Does this count toward the bets we made last time?
Ahh! They busted up the place again!
わいわい
CHATTER CHATTER
ガヤガヤ
MURMUR MURMUR
くすっ
TEE HEE
!
Hm...
What's wrong, Master?
Nothing. I'm just...
とろーん
SLUUM
...sleepy.
?
It's him!!

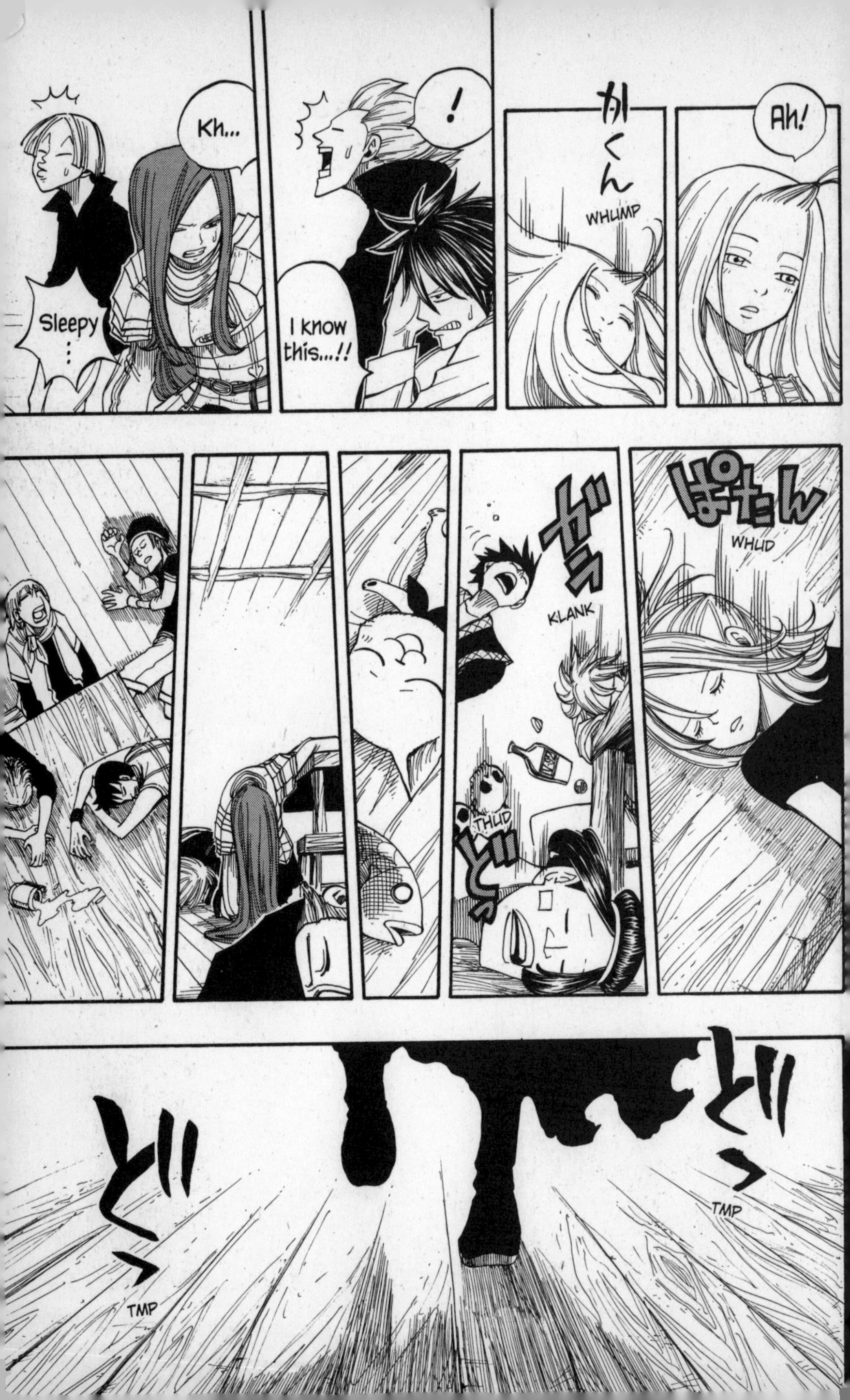
Ah!
かくん
WHUMP
!
I know this...!!
Kh...
Sleepy
...
ぱたん
WHUD
KLANK
THUD
TMP
TMP

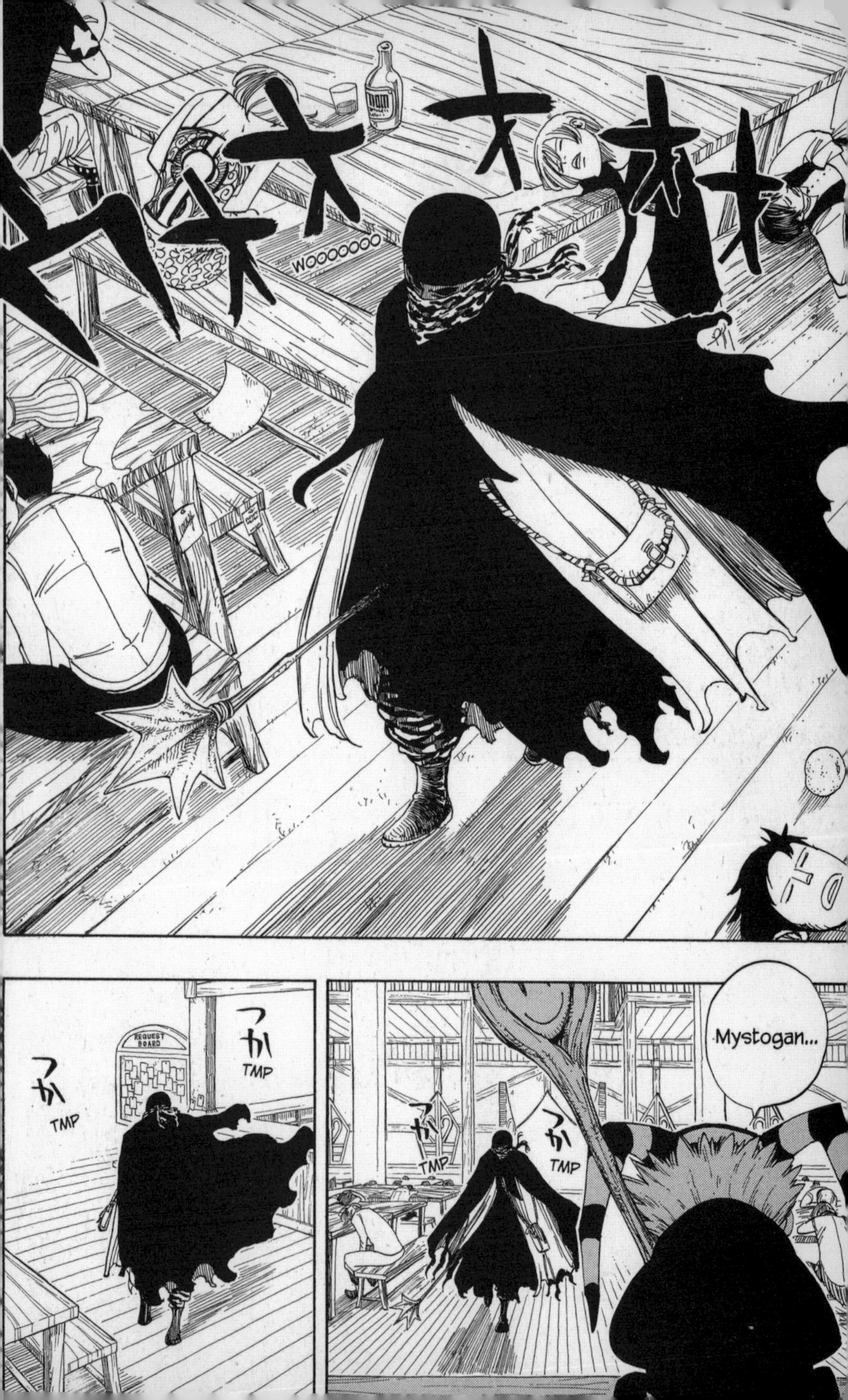
WOOOOOOO
つか
TMP
つか
TMP
Mystogan...
つか
TMP
つか
TMP

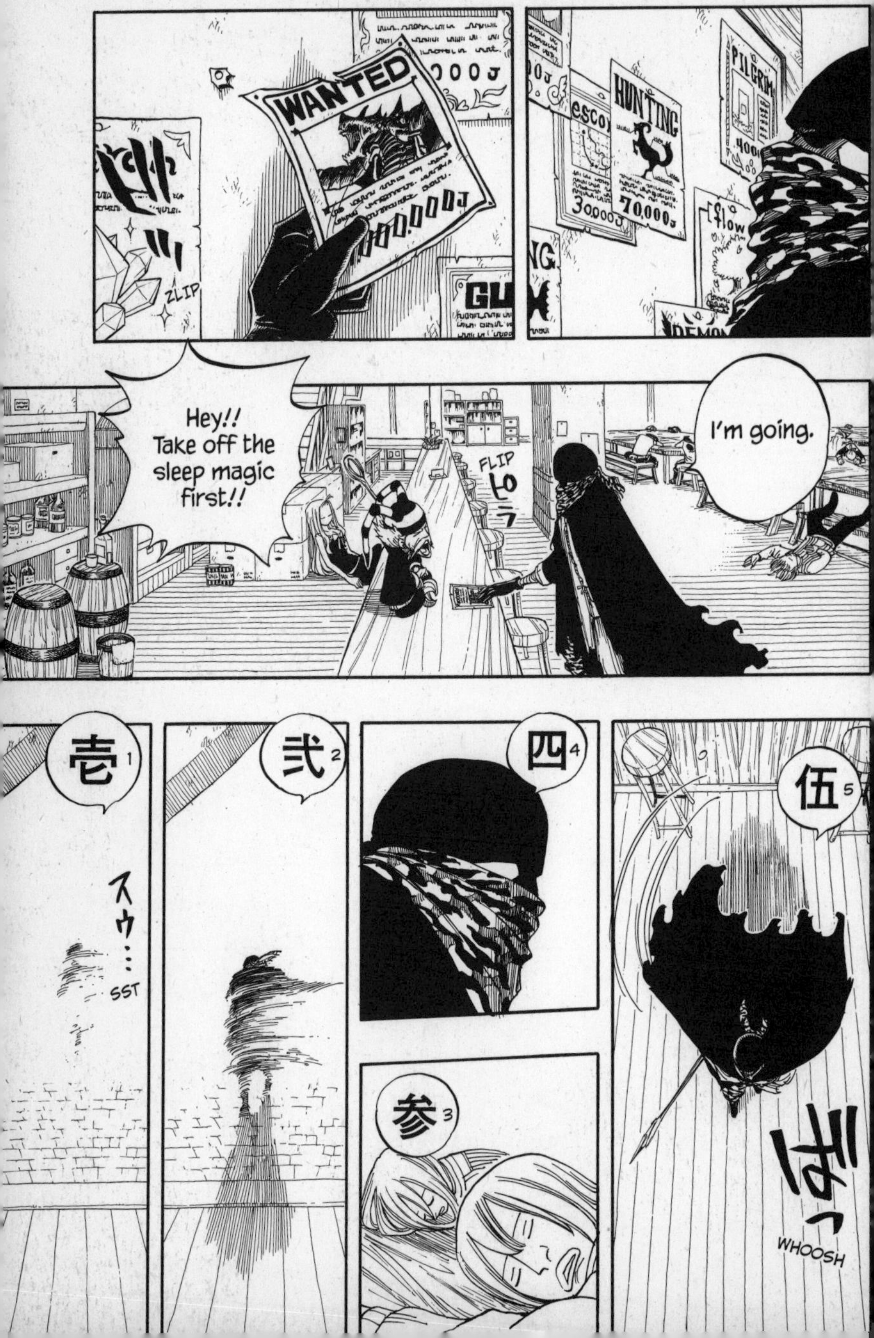

WANTED
000.000J
ZLIP
HUNTING
70,000J
30,000J
PILGRIM
flow
Hey!! Take off the sleep magic first!!
FLIP
ヒラ
I'm going.
壱1
スウ…
SST
弐2
参3
四4
伍5
ばっ
WHOOSH

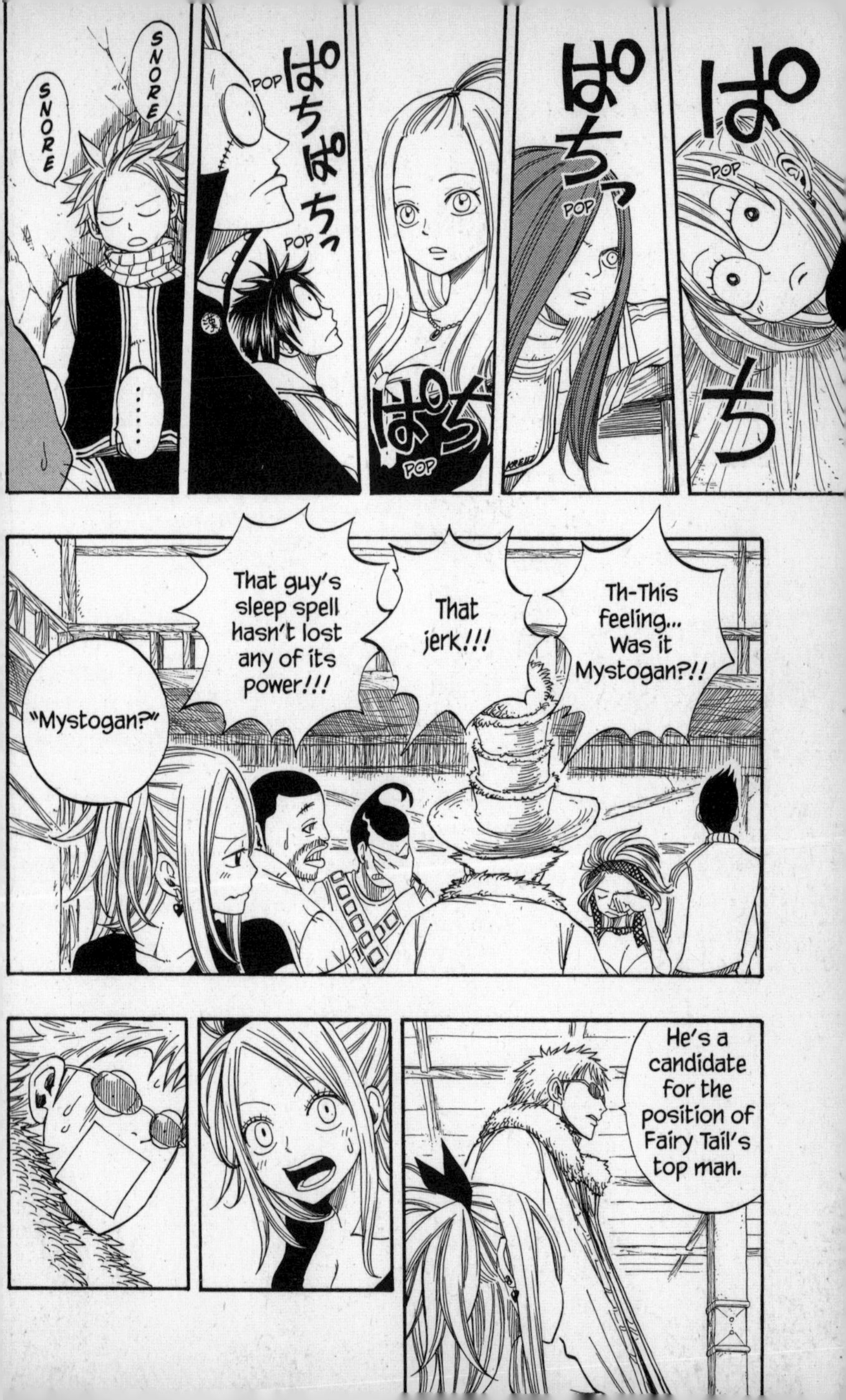
ぱち
POP
ぱちっ
POP
ぱち
POP
ぱちぱちっ
POP
POP
SNORE
SNORE
......
Th-This feeling... Was it Mystogan?!!
That jerk!!!
That guy's sleep spell hasn't lost any of its power!!!
"Mystogan?"
He's a candidate for the position of Fairy Tail's top man.

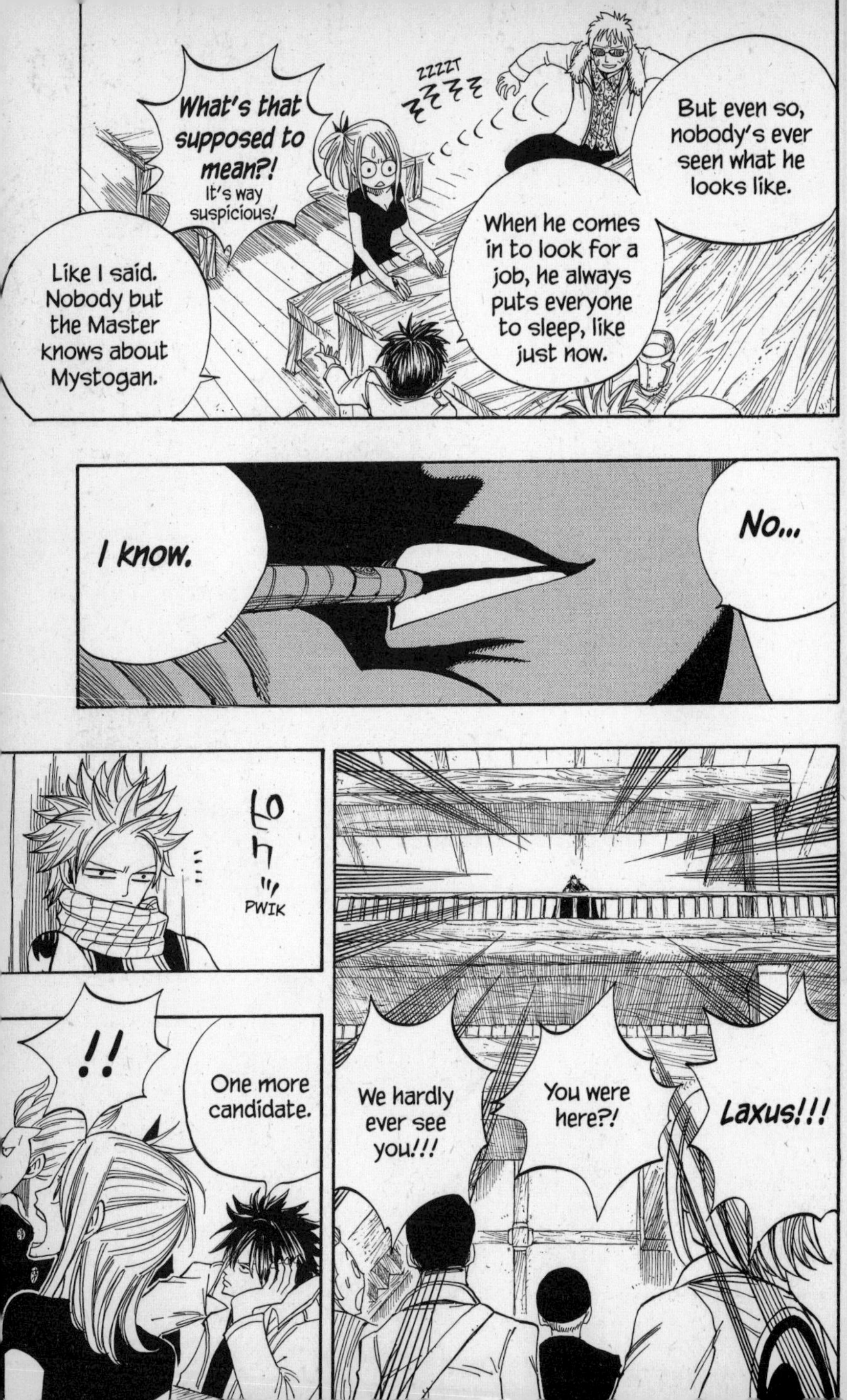
But even so, nobody's ever seen what he looks like.
ZZZZT
When he comes in to look for a job, he always puts everyone to sleep, like just now.
What's that supposed to mean?!
It's way suspicious!
Like I said. Nobody but the Master knows about Mystogan.
No...
I know.
Laxus!!!
You were here?!
We hardly ever see you!!!
PWIK
One more candidate.
!!

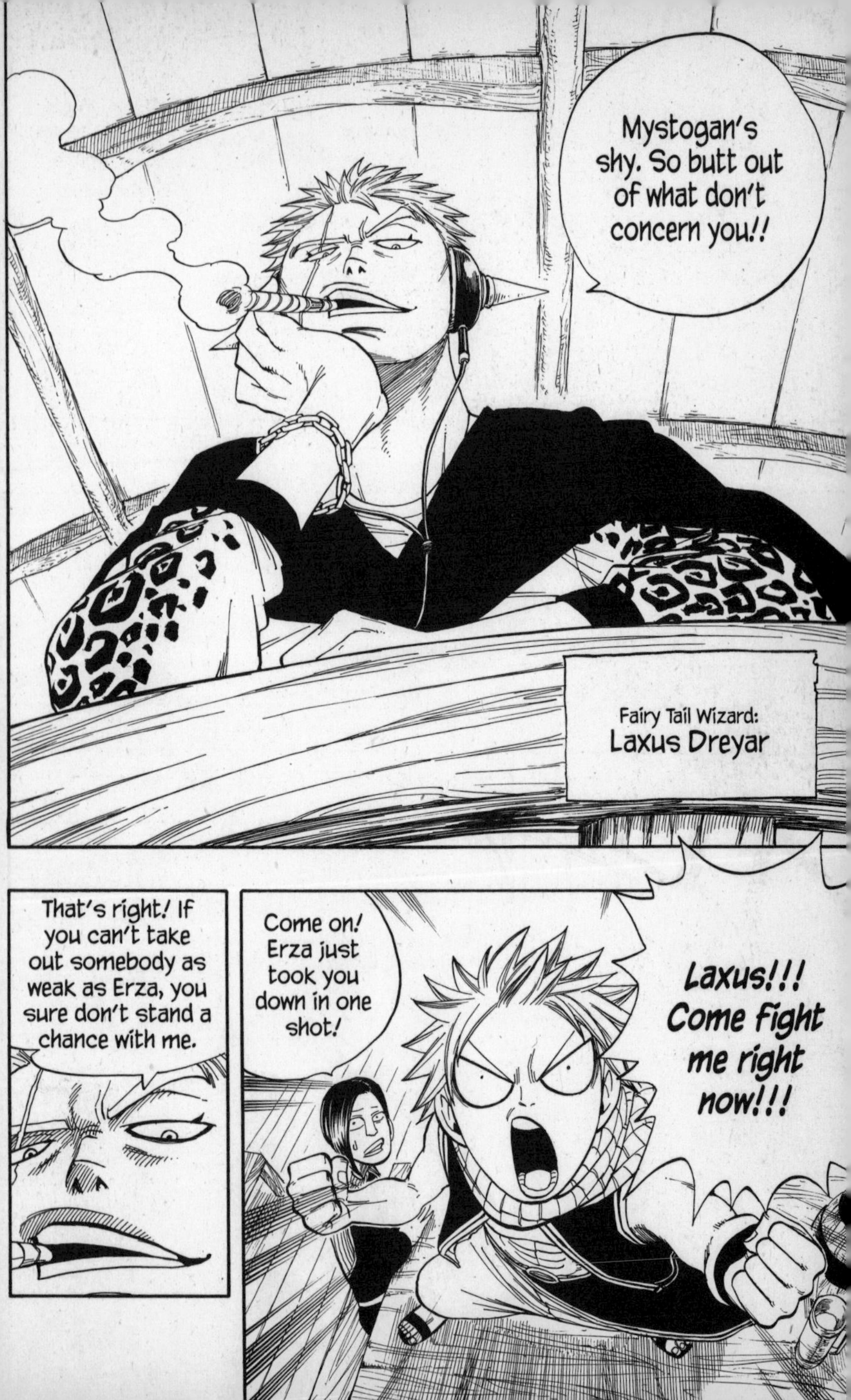
Mystogan's shy. So butt out of what don't concern you!!
Fairy Tail Wizard: Laxus Dreyar
Laxus!!! Come fight me right now!!!
Come on! Erza just took you down in one shot!
That's right! If you can't take out somebody as weak as Erza, you sure don't stand a chance with me.

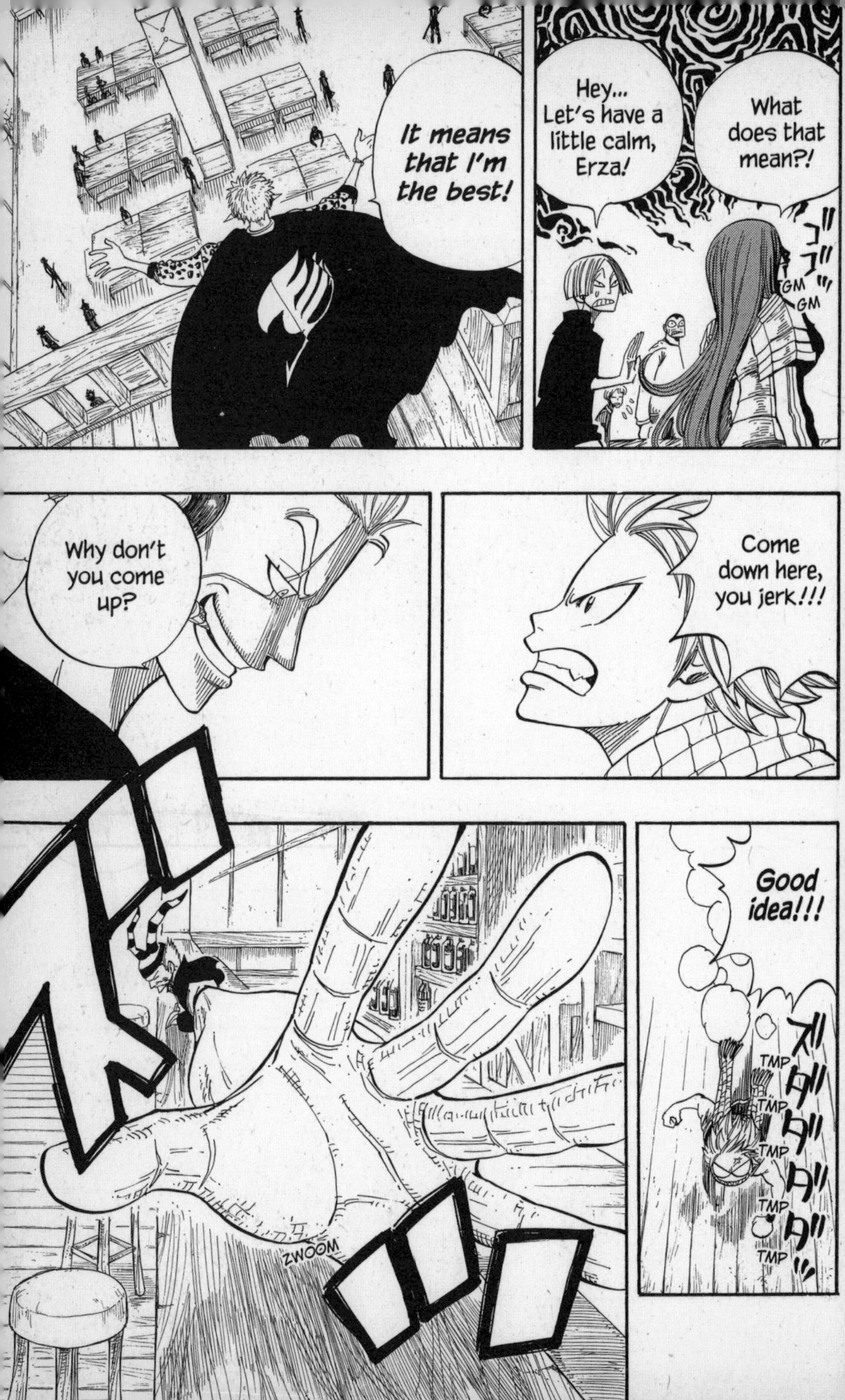
What does that mean?!
Hey... Let's have a little calm, Erza!
GM GM
It means that I'm the best!
Come down here, you jerk!!!
Why don't you come up?
Good idea!!!
TMP TMP TMP TMP TMP
ZWOOM

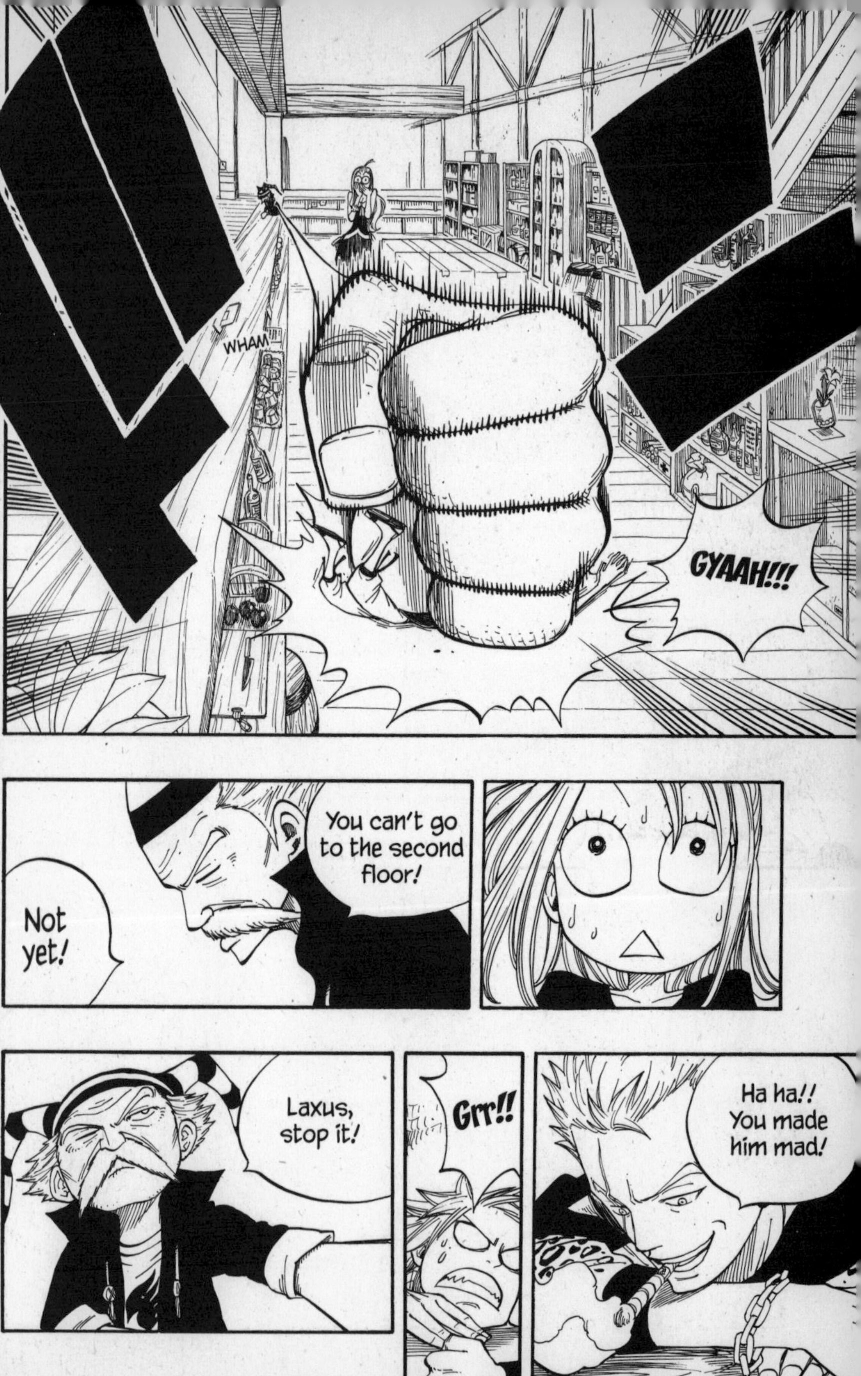
GYAAH!!!
WHAM
You can't go to the second floor!
Not yet!
Ha ha!! You made him mad!
Grr!!
Laxus, stop it!

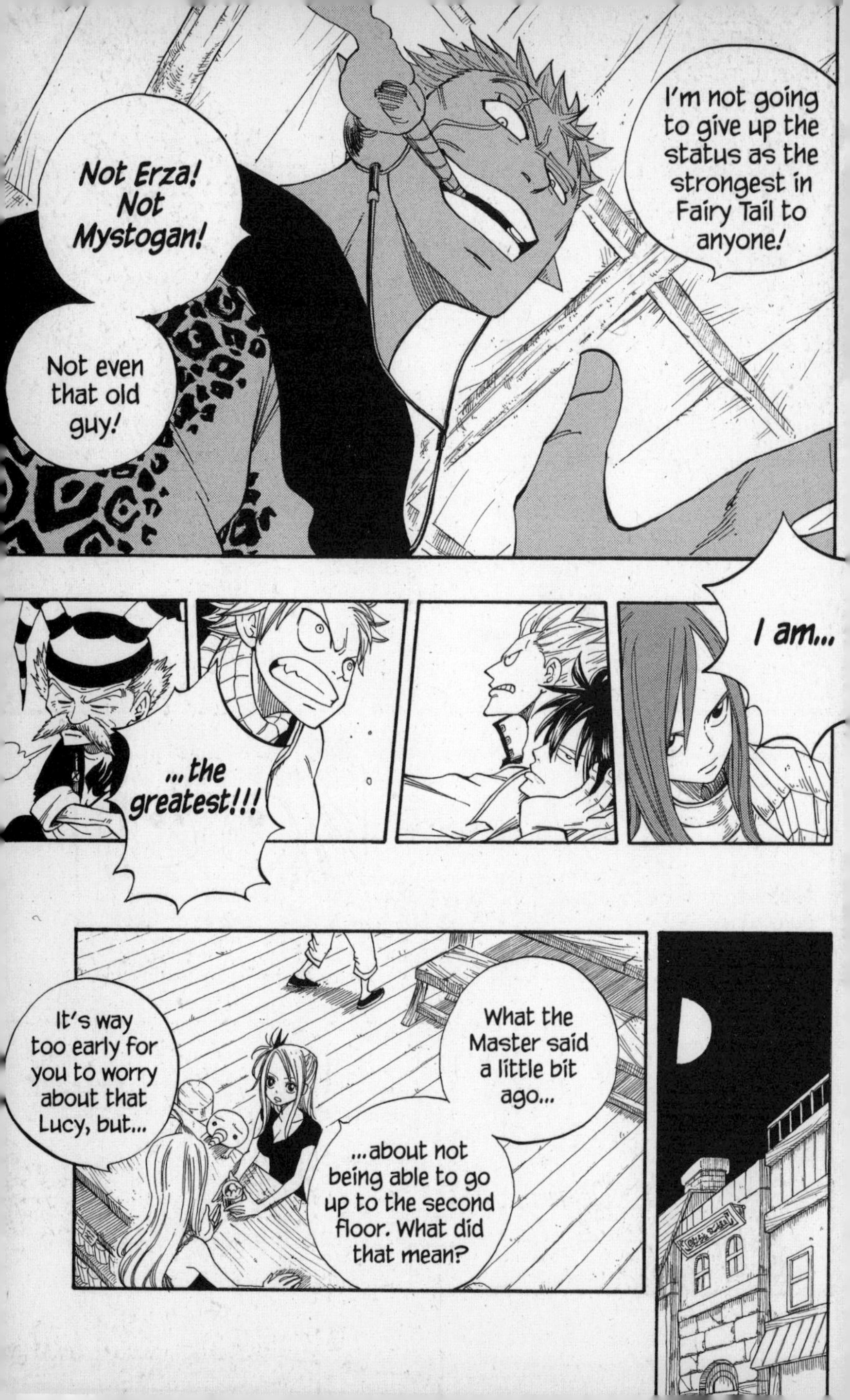
I'm not going to give up the status as the strongest in Fairy Tail to anyone!
Not Erza! Not Mystogan!
Not even that old guy!
I am...
...the greatest!!!
What the Master said a little bit ago...
...about not being able to go up to the second floor. What did that mean?
It's way too early for you to worry about that Lucy, but...

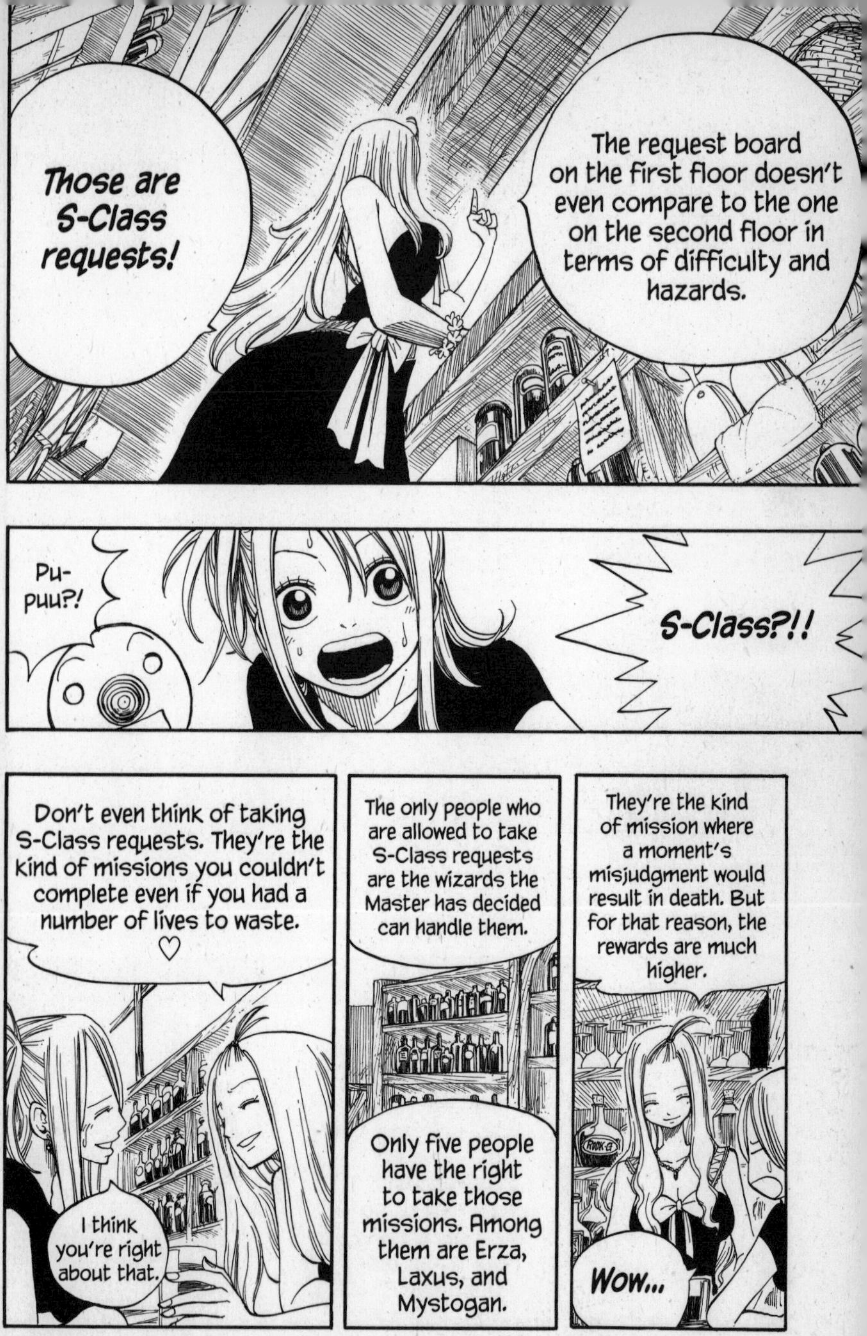
The request board on the first floor doesn't even compare to the one on the second floor in terms of difficulty and hazards.
Those are S-Class requests!
S-Class?!!
Pu-puu?!
They're the kind of mission where a moment's misjudgment would result in death. But for that reason, the rewards are much higher.
Wow...
The only people who are allowed to take S-Class requests are the wizards the Master has decided can handle them.
Only five people have the right to take those missions. Among them are Erza, Laxus, and Mystogan.
Don't even think of taking S-Class requests. They're the kind of missions you couldn't complete even if you had a number of lives to waste. ♡
I think you're right about that.

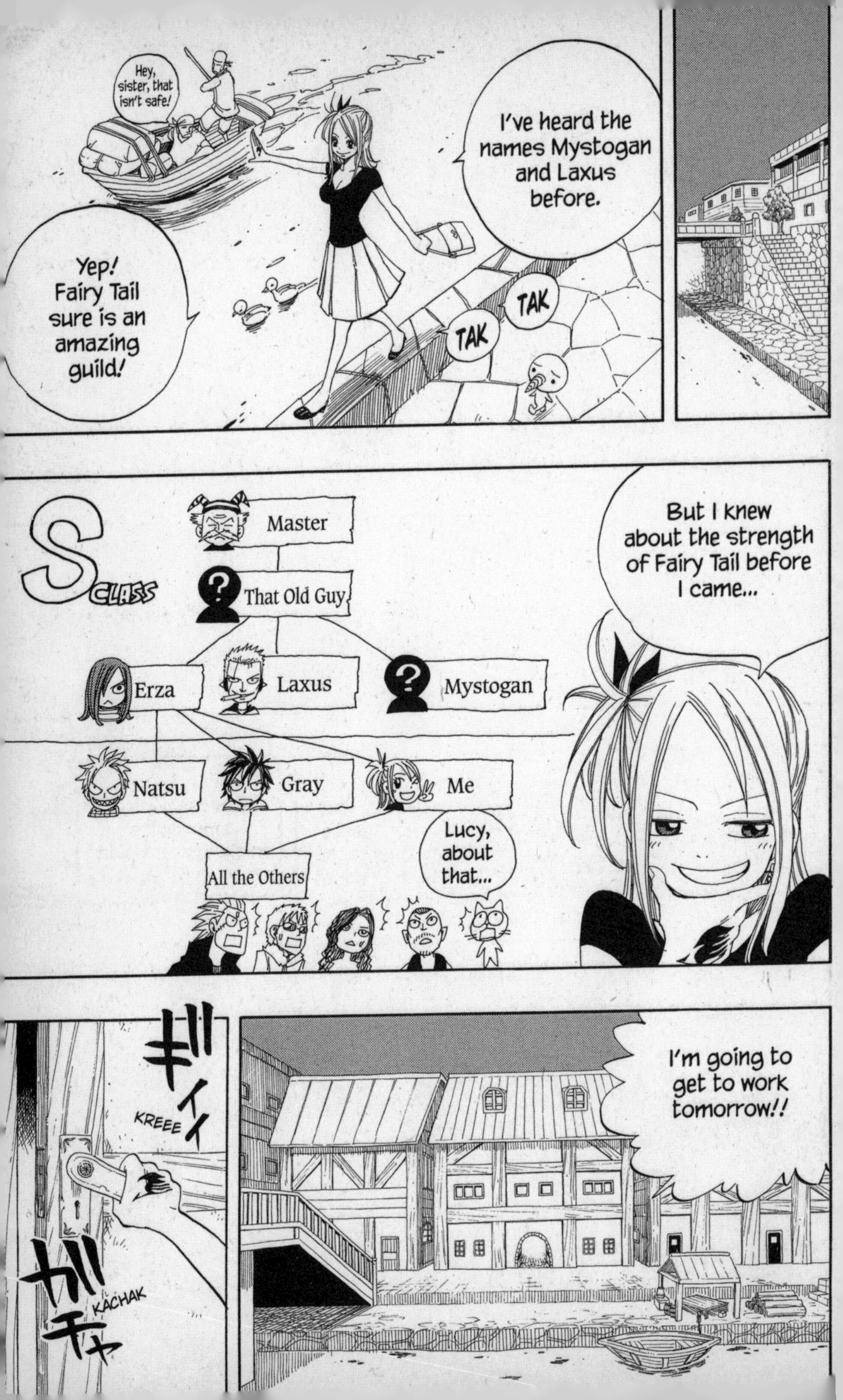
Hey, sister, that isn't safe!
I've heard the names Mystogan and Laxus before.
Yep! Fairy Tail sure is an amazing guild!
TAK
TAK
S CLASS
Master
That Old Guy
Erza
Laxus
Mystogan
Natsu
Gray
Me
All the Others
But I knew about the strength of Fairy Tail before I came...
Lucy, about that...
KREEE
KACHAK
I'm going to get to work tomorrow!!

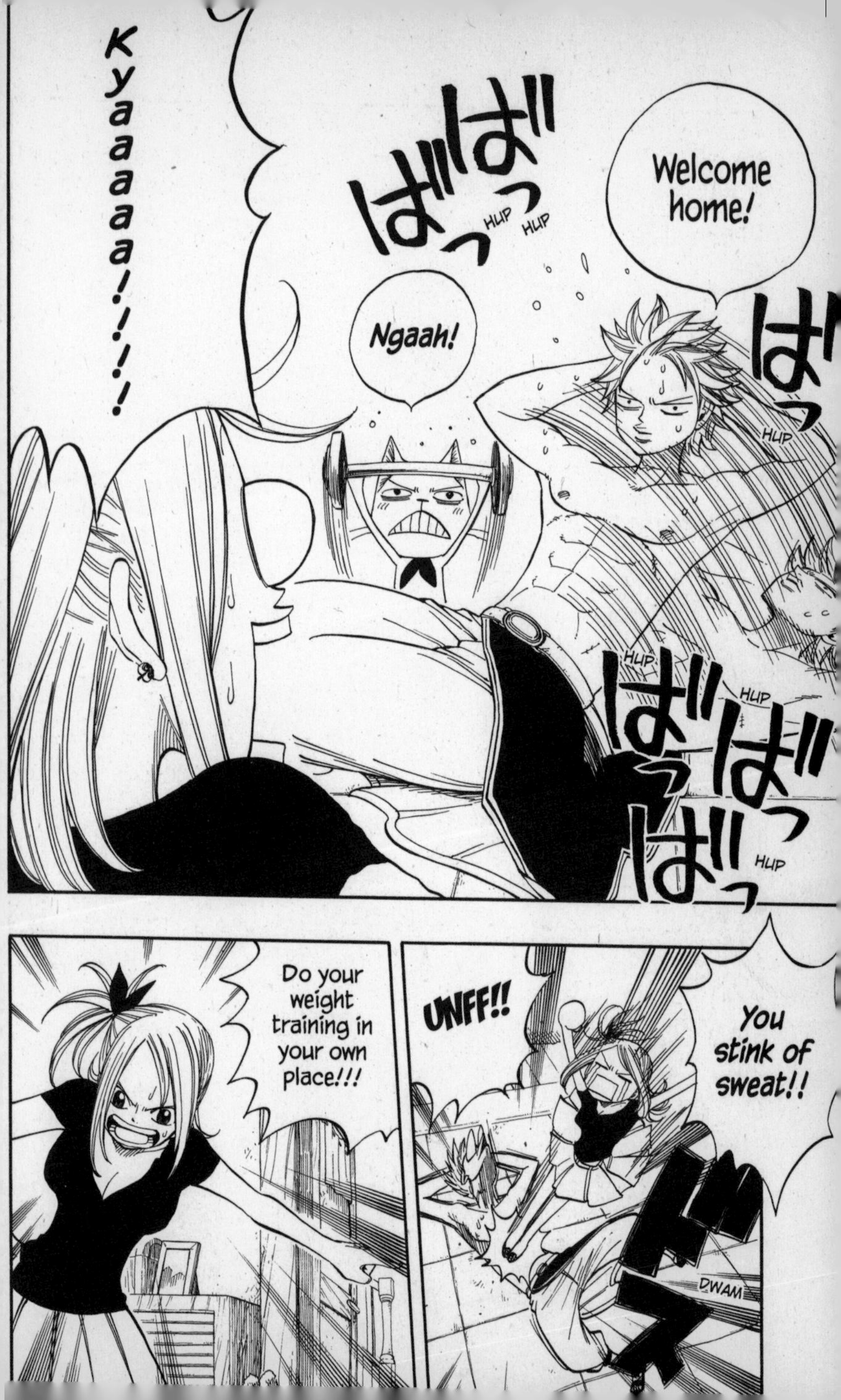
Welcome home!
ぱっ HUP
ばっばっ HUP HUP
Ngaah!
Kyaaaaaa!!!!!
ばっばっばっ HUP HUP HUP
You stink of sweat!!
UNFF!!
DWAM
Do your weight training in your own place!!!

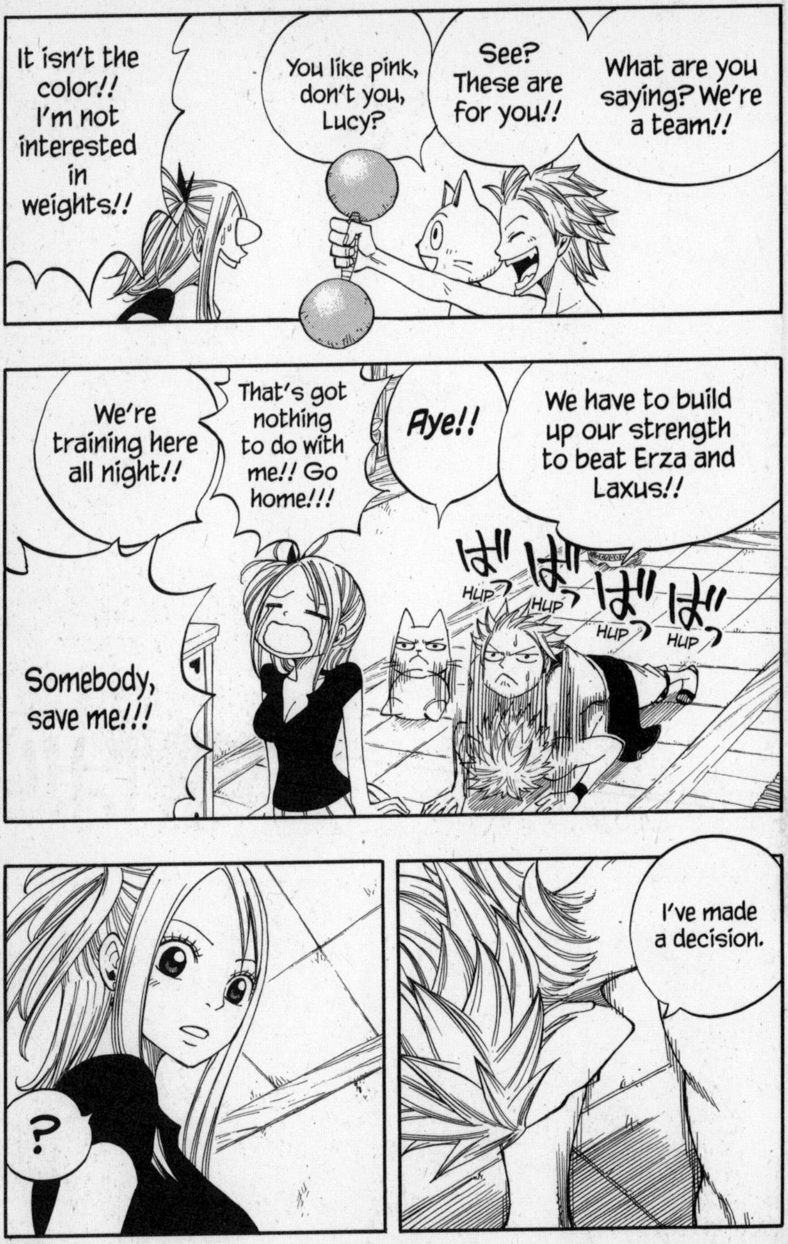

What are you saying? We're a team!!
See? These are for you!!
You like pink, don't you, Lucy?
It isn't the color!! I'm not interested in weights!!
We have to build up our strength to beat Erza and Laxus!!
Aye!!
That's got nothing to do with me!! Go home!!!
We're training here all night!!
Hup
Hup
Hup
Hup
Somebody, save me!!!
I've made a decision.
?

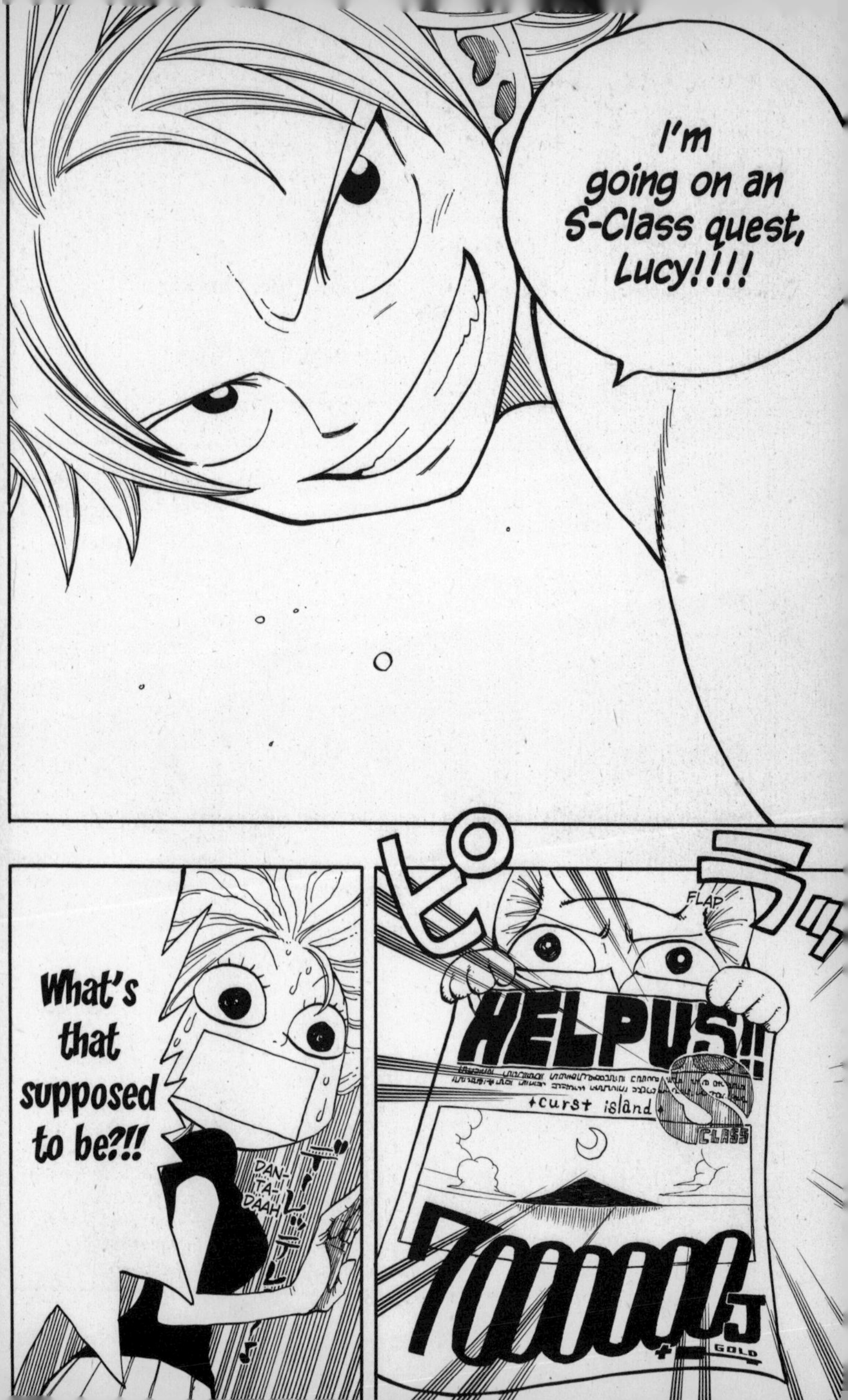
I'm going on an S-Class quest, Lucy!!!!
FLAP
HELPUS!!
curst island
CLASS
700000J
GOLD
What's that supposed to be?!!
DAN-TA-DAAH

Chapter 25: The Cursed Island

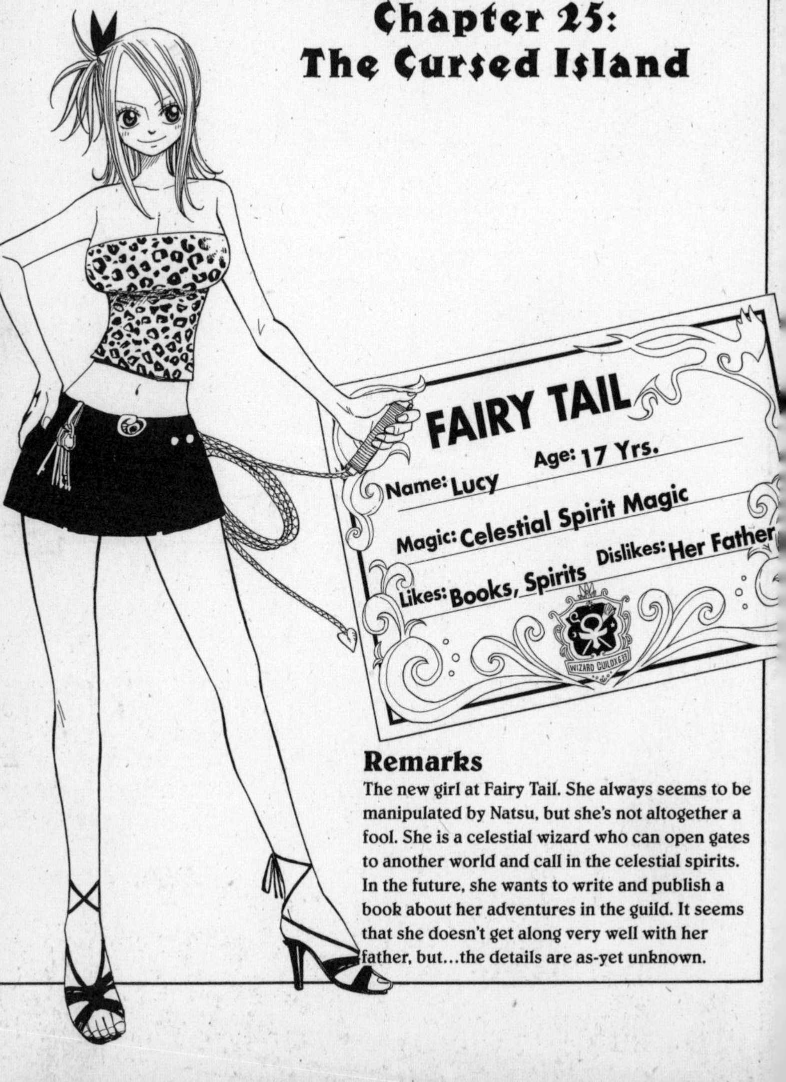
FAIRY TAIL
Age: 17 Yrs.
Name: Lucy
Magic: Celestial Spirit Magic
Dislikes: Her Father
Likes: Books, Spirits
WIZARD GUILD X633

Remarks

The new girl at Fairy Tail. She always seems to be manipulated by Natsu, but she's not altogether a fool. She is a celestial wizard who can open gates to another world and call in the celestial spirits. In the future, she wants to write and publish a book about her adventures in the guild. It seems that she doesn't get along very well with her father, but…the details are as-yet unknown.

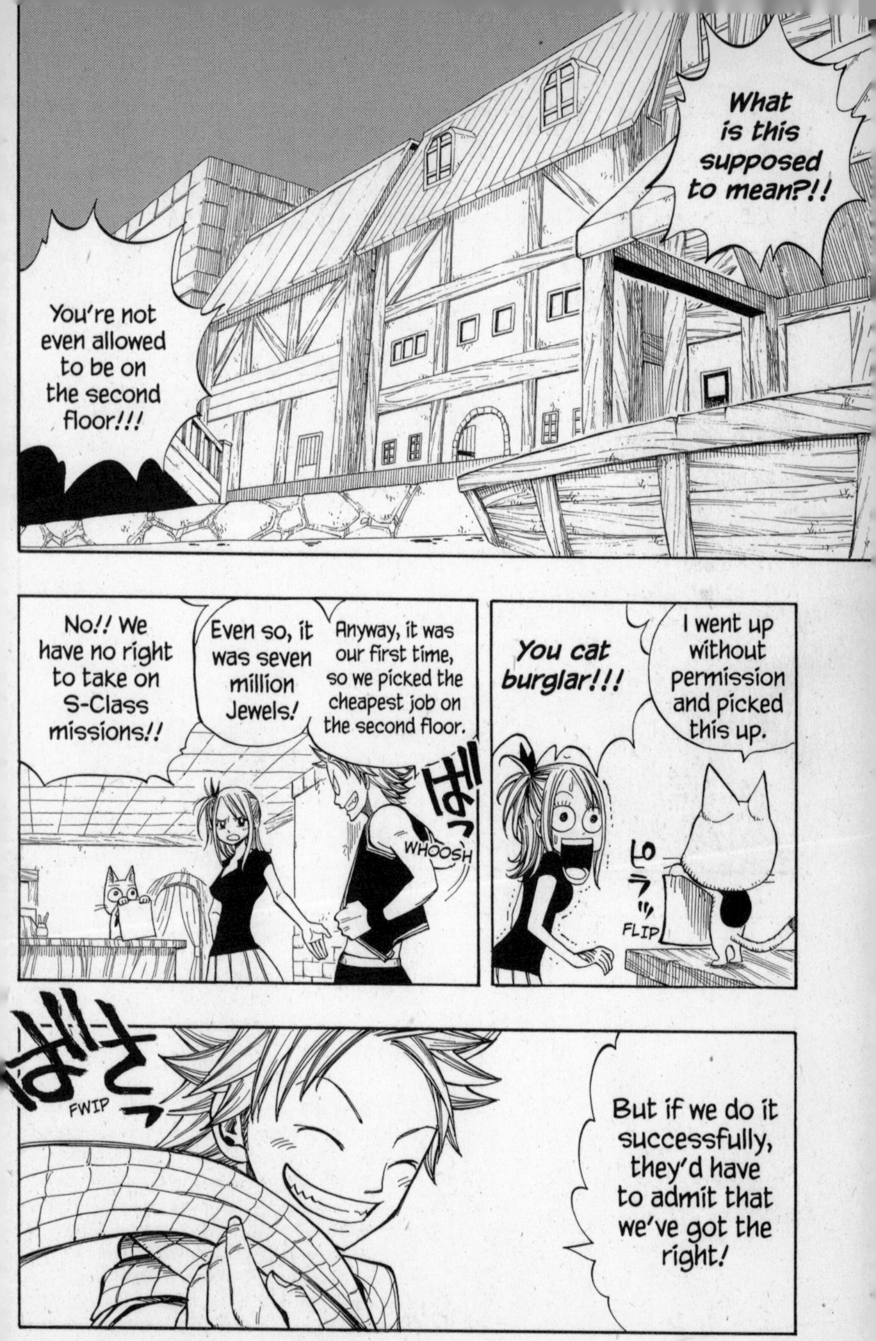
What is this supposed to mean?!!
You're not even allowed to be on the second floor!!!
I went up without permission and picked this up.
FLIP
You cat burglar!!!
Anyway, it was our first time, so we picked the cheapest job on the second floor.
Even so, it was seven million Jewels!
No!! We have no right to take on S-Class missions!!
WHOOSH
FWIP
But if we do it successfully, they'd have to admit that we've got the right!

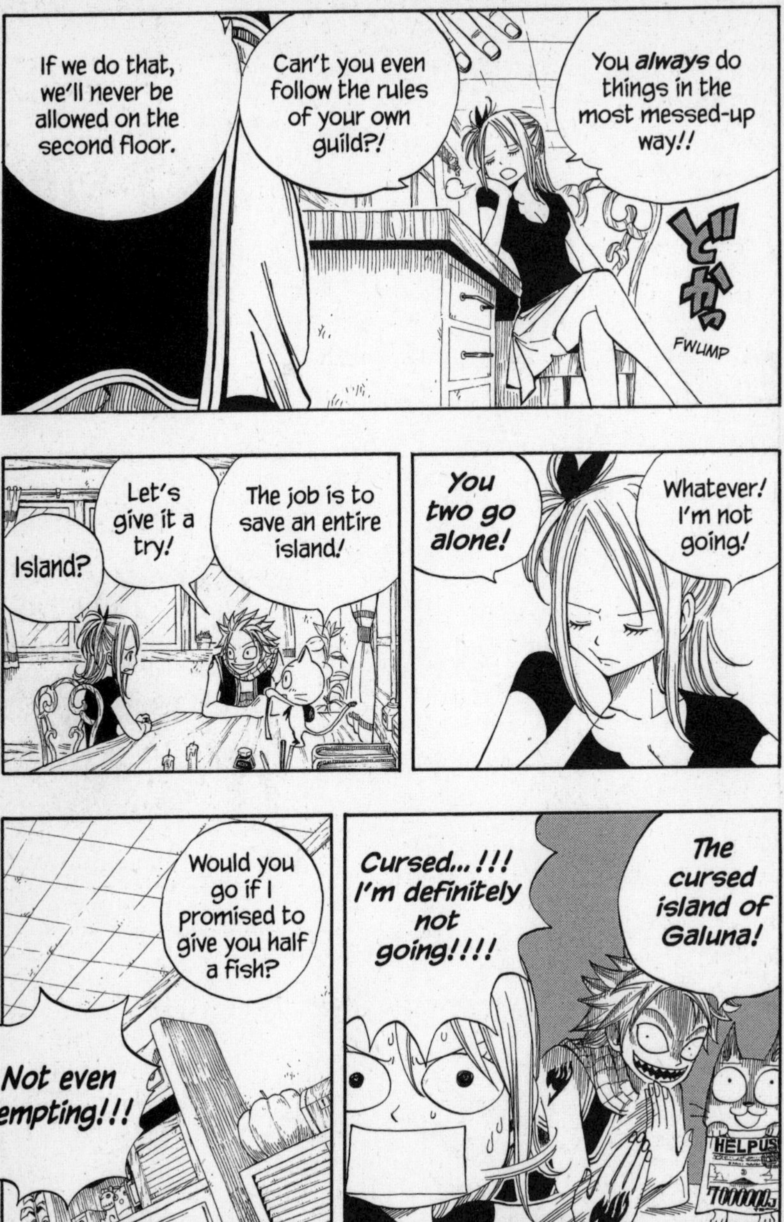
You *always* do things in the most messed-up way!!
Can't you even follow the rules of your own guild?!
If we do that, we'll never be allowed on the second floor.
どがっ
FWUMP
Whatever! I'm not going!
You two go alone!
The job is to save an entire island!
Let's give it a try!
Island?
The cursed island of Galuna!
Cursed...!!! I'm definitely not going!!!!
HELPUS
Would you go if I promised to give you half a fish?
Not even tempting!!!

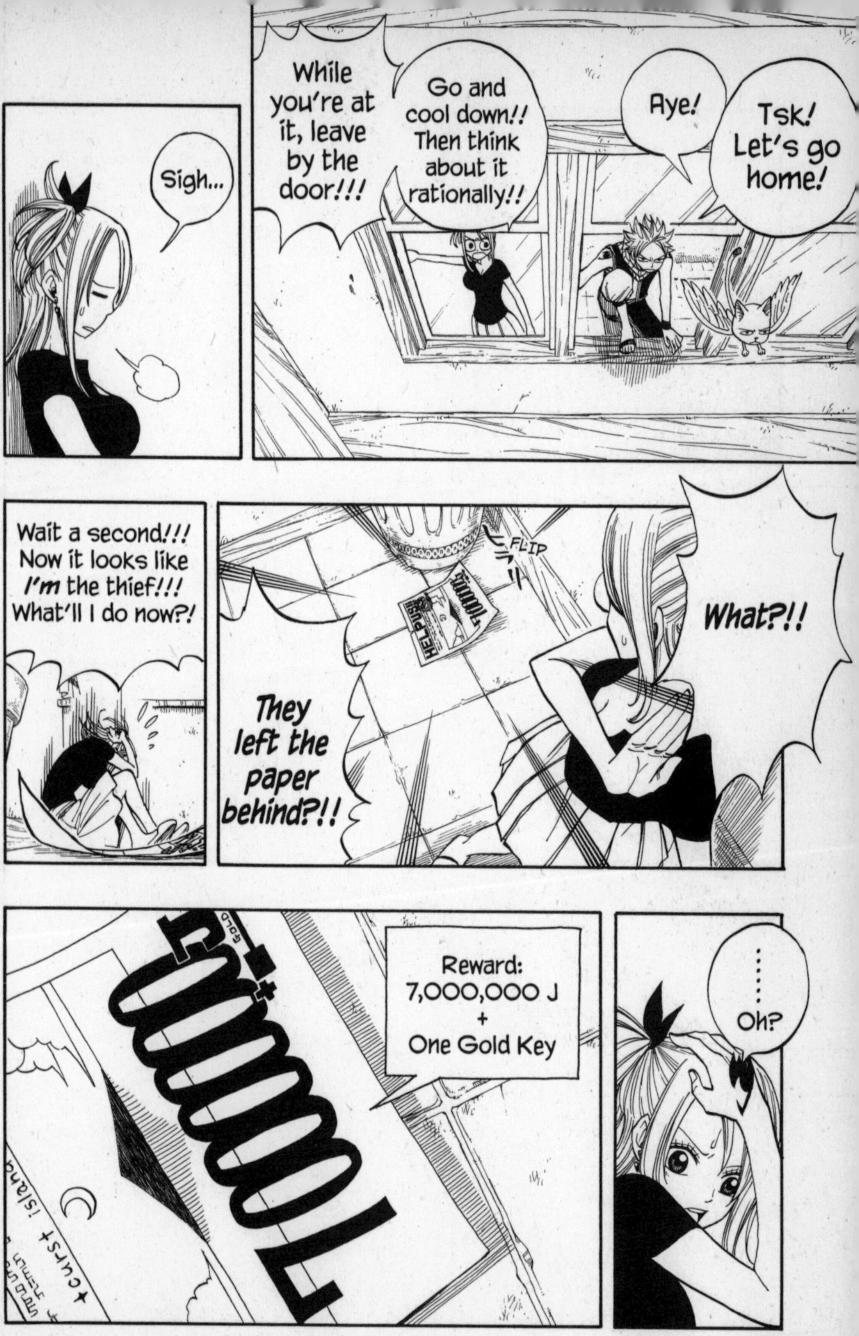
Tsk! Let's go home!
Aye!
Go and cool down!! Then think about it rationally!!
While you're at it, leave by the door!!!
Sigh...
What?!!
FLIP
They left the paper behind?!!
Wait a second!!! Now it looks like *I'm* the thief!!! What'll I do now?!
......Oh?
Reward: 7,000,000 J + One Gold Key

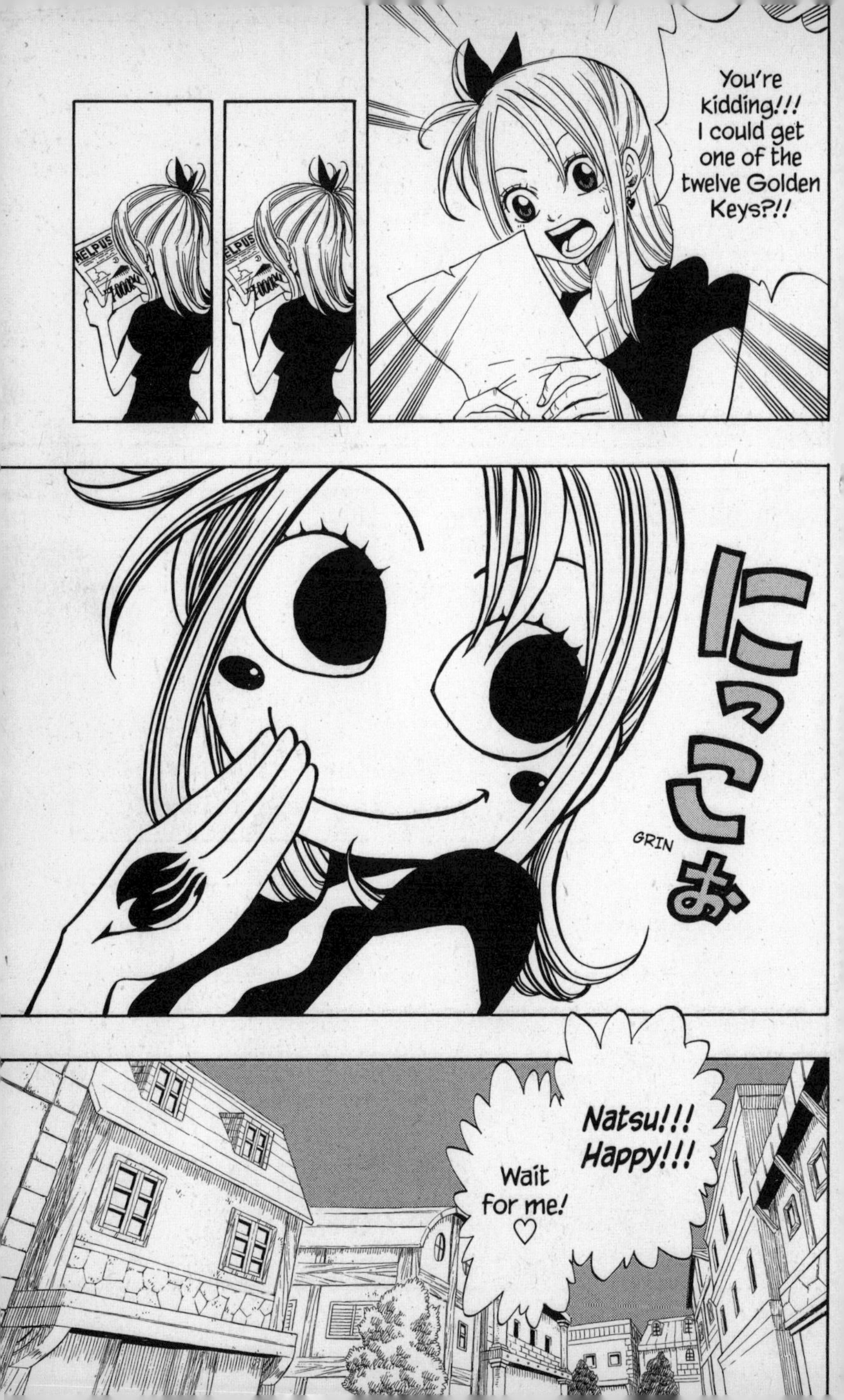
You're kidding!!! I could get one of the twelve Golden Keys?!!
にっこぉ
GRIN
Natsu!!! Happy!!!
Wait for me! ♡

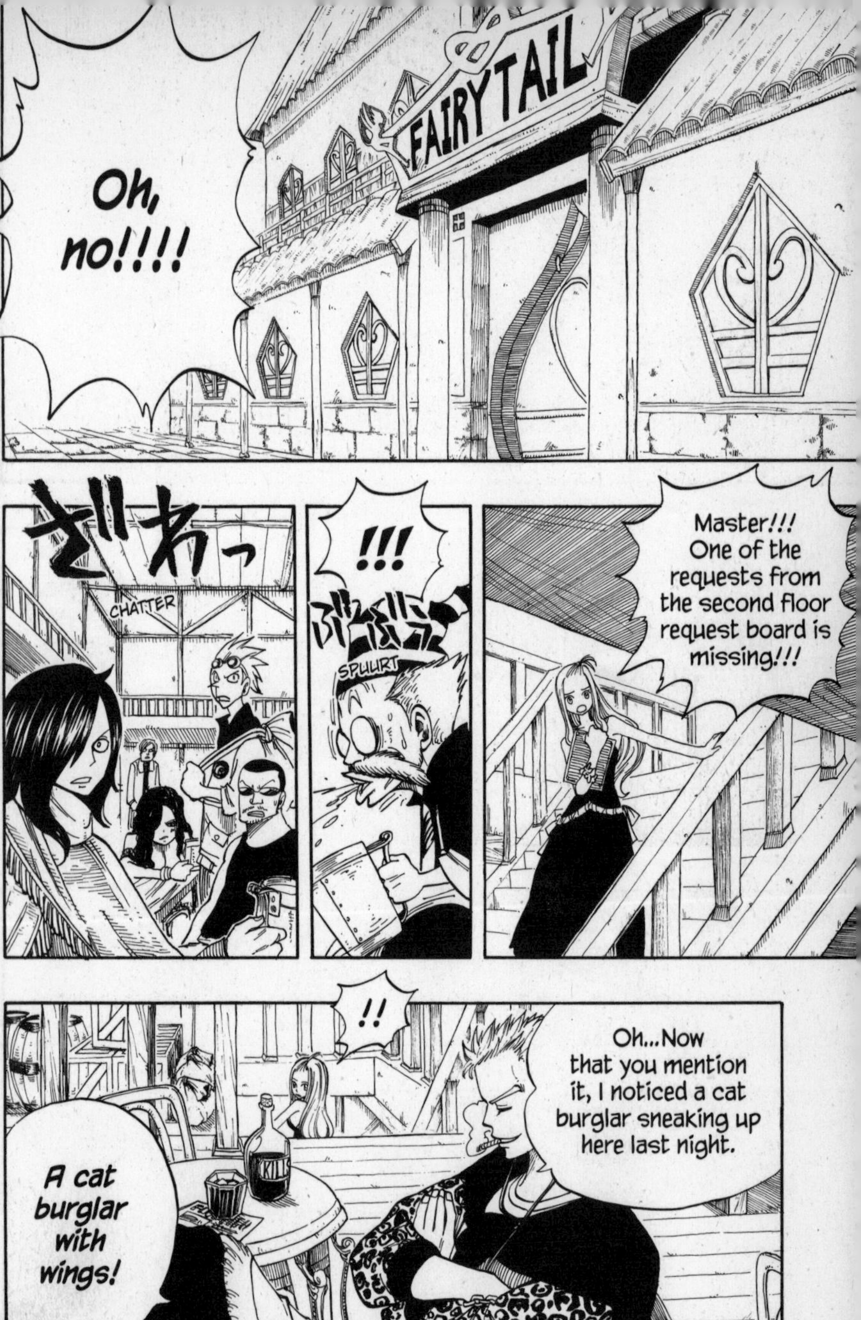
FAIRY TAIL
Oh, no!!!!
Master!!! One of the requests from the second floor request board is missing!!!
!!!
SPUURT
CHATTER
ざわっ
!!
Oh...Now that you mention it, I noticed a cat burglar sneaking up here last night.
A cat burglar with wings!

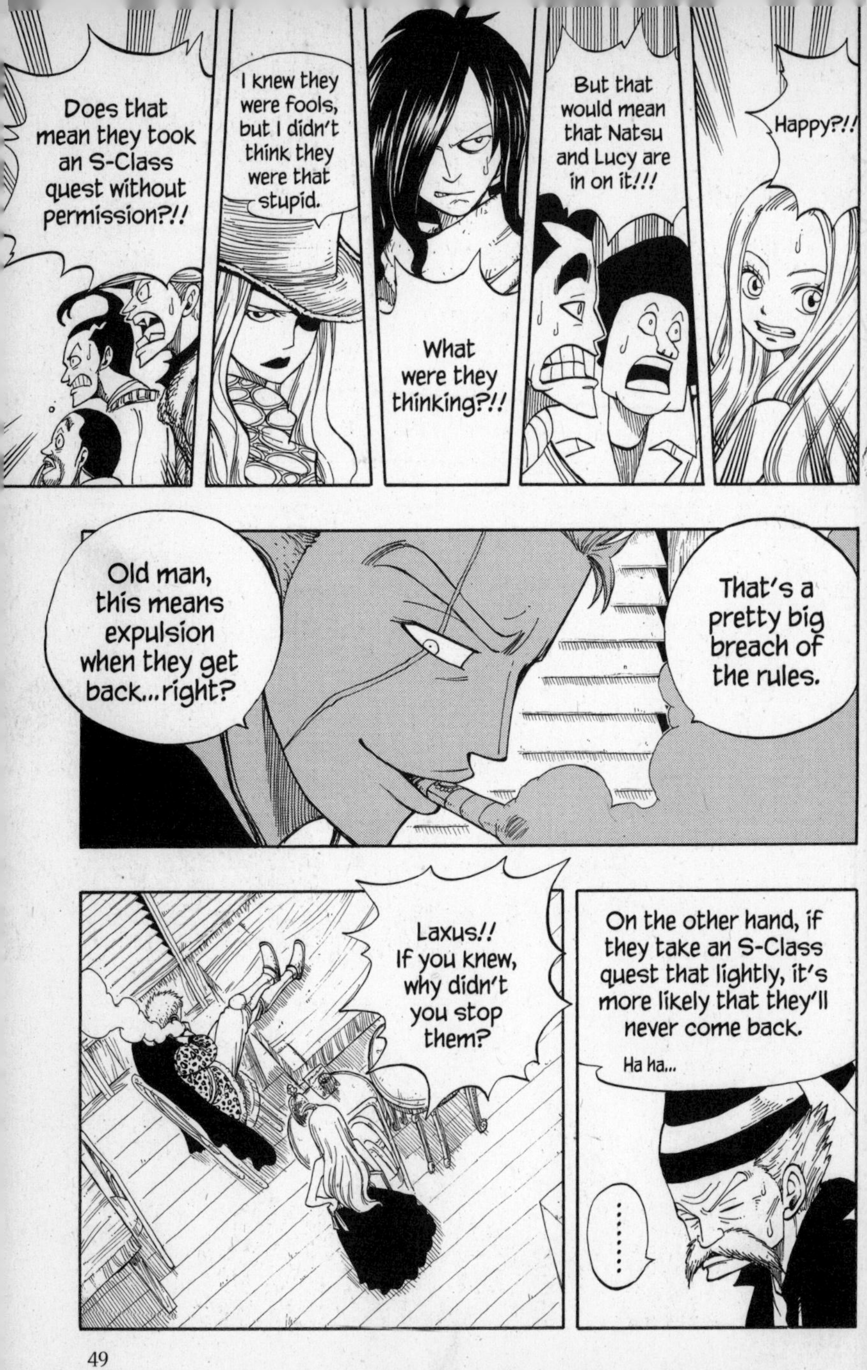

Does that mean they took an S-Class quest without permission?!!
I knew they were fools, but I didn't think they were that stupid.
What were they thinking?!!
But that would mean that Natsu and Lucy are in on it!!!
Happy?!!
Old man, this means expulsion when they get back...right?
That's a pretty big breach of the rules.
Laxus!! If you knew, why didn't you stop them?
On the other hand, if they take an S-Class quest that lightly, it's more likely that they'll never come back.
Ha ha...
....

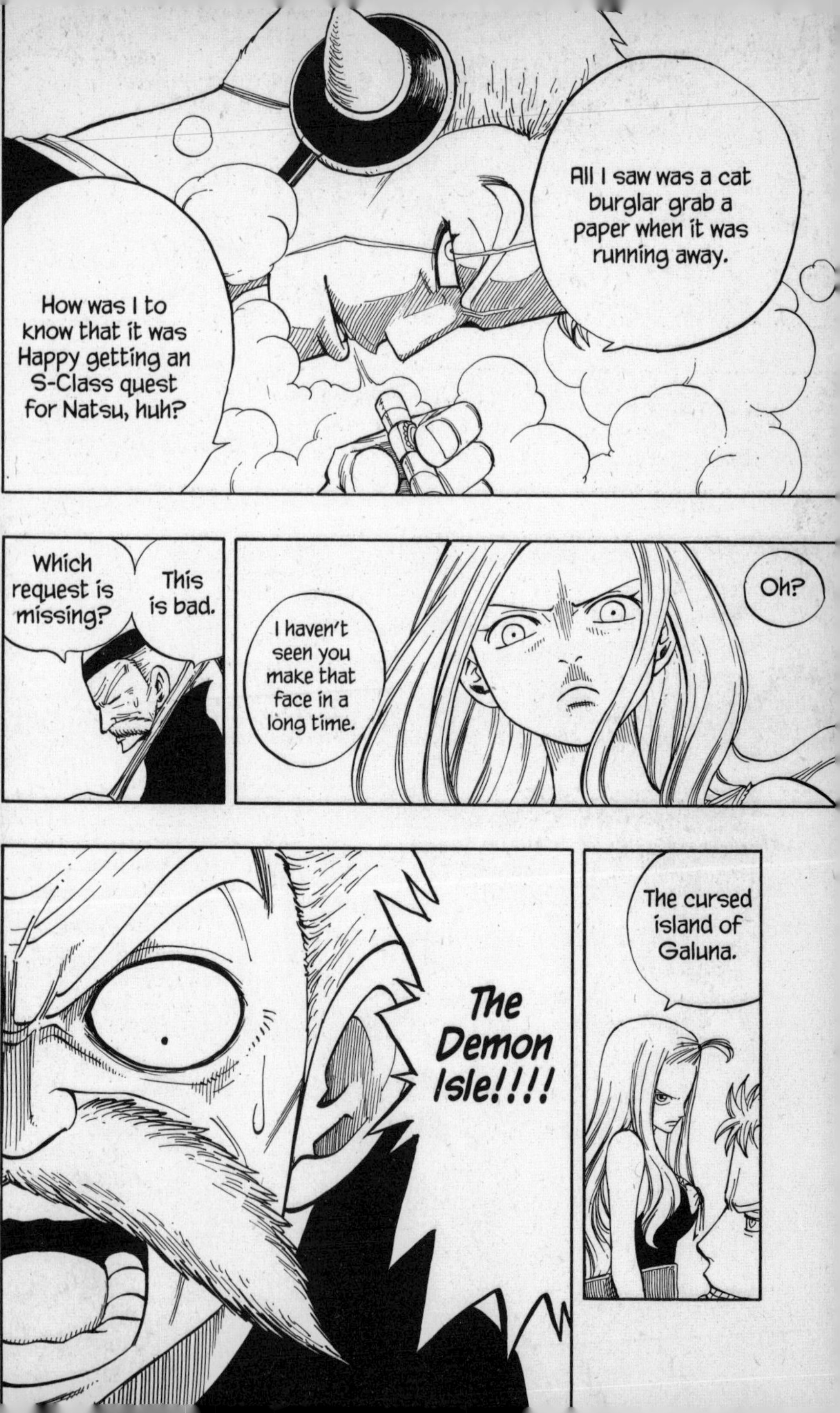
All I saw was a cat burglar grab a paper when it was running away.
How was I to know that it was Happy getting an S-Class quest for Natsu, huh?
Oh?
I haven't seen you make that face in a long time.
This is bad.
Which request is missing?
The cursed island of Galuna.
The Demon Isle!!!!

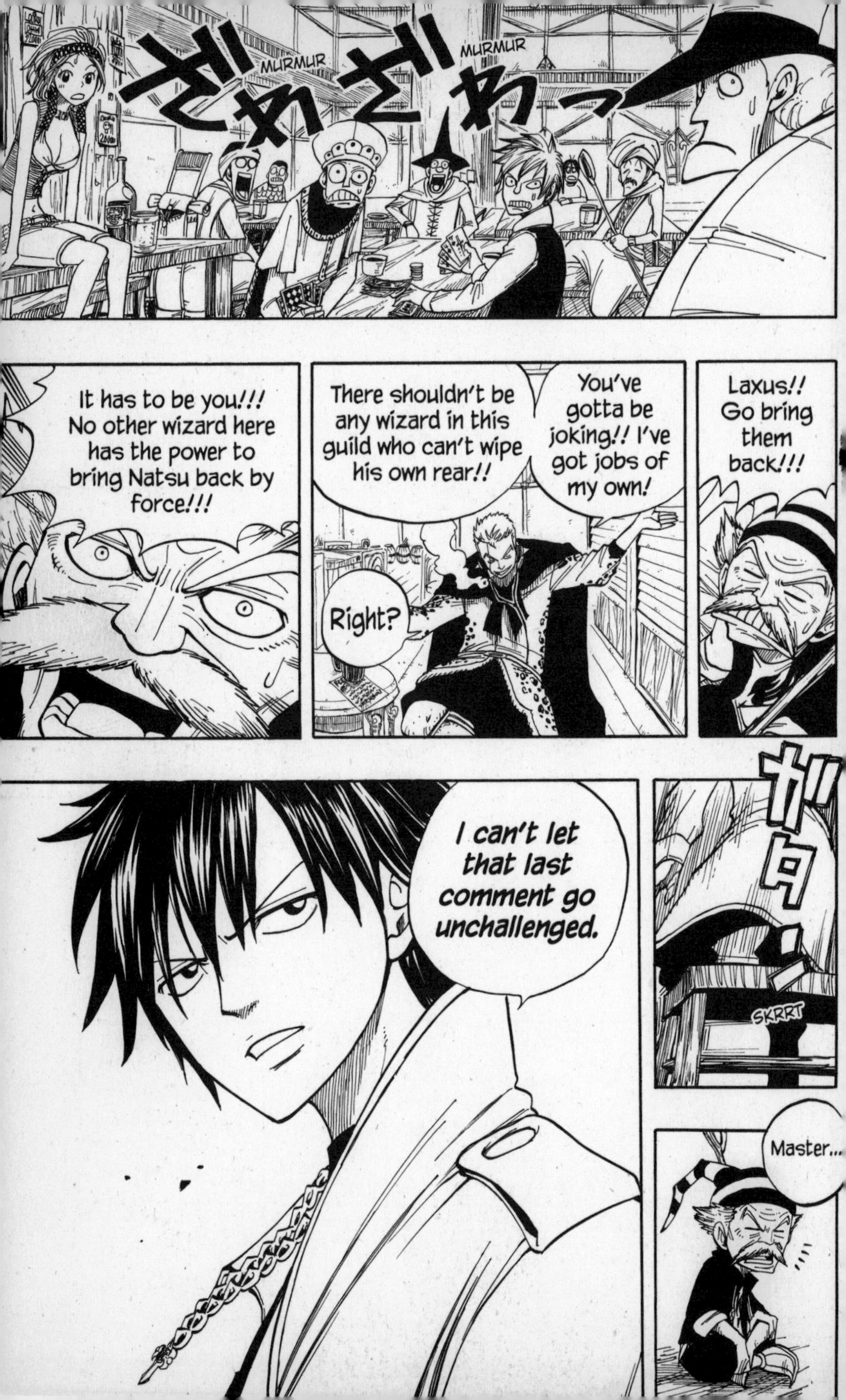
ざわざわっ
MURMUR
MURMUR
Laxus!! Go bring them back!!!
You've gotta be joking!! I've got jobs of my own!
There shouldn't be any wizard in this guild who can't wipe his own rear!!
Right?
It has to be you!!! No other wizard here has the power to bring Natsu back by force!!!
ガタッ
SKRRT
I can't let that last comment go unchallenged.
Master...

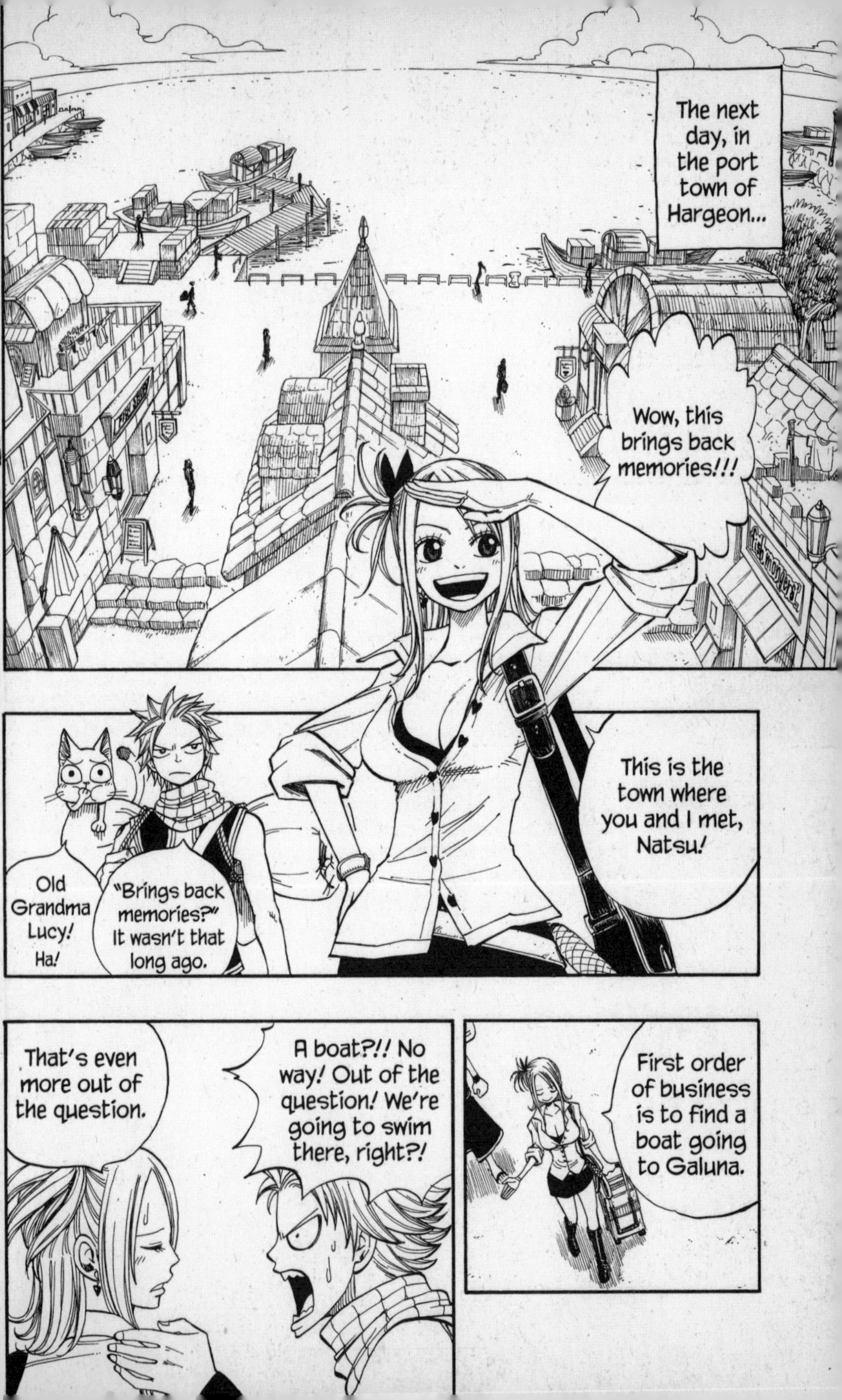
The next day, in the port town of Hargeon...
Wow, this brings back memories!!!
This is the town where you and I met, Natsu!
"Brings back memories?" It wasn't that long ago.
Old Grandma Lucy! Ha!
First order of business is to find a boat going to Galuna.
A boat?!! No way! Out of the question! We're going to swim there, right?!
That's even more out of the question.

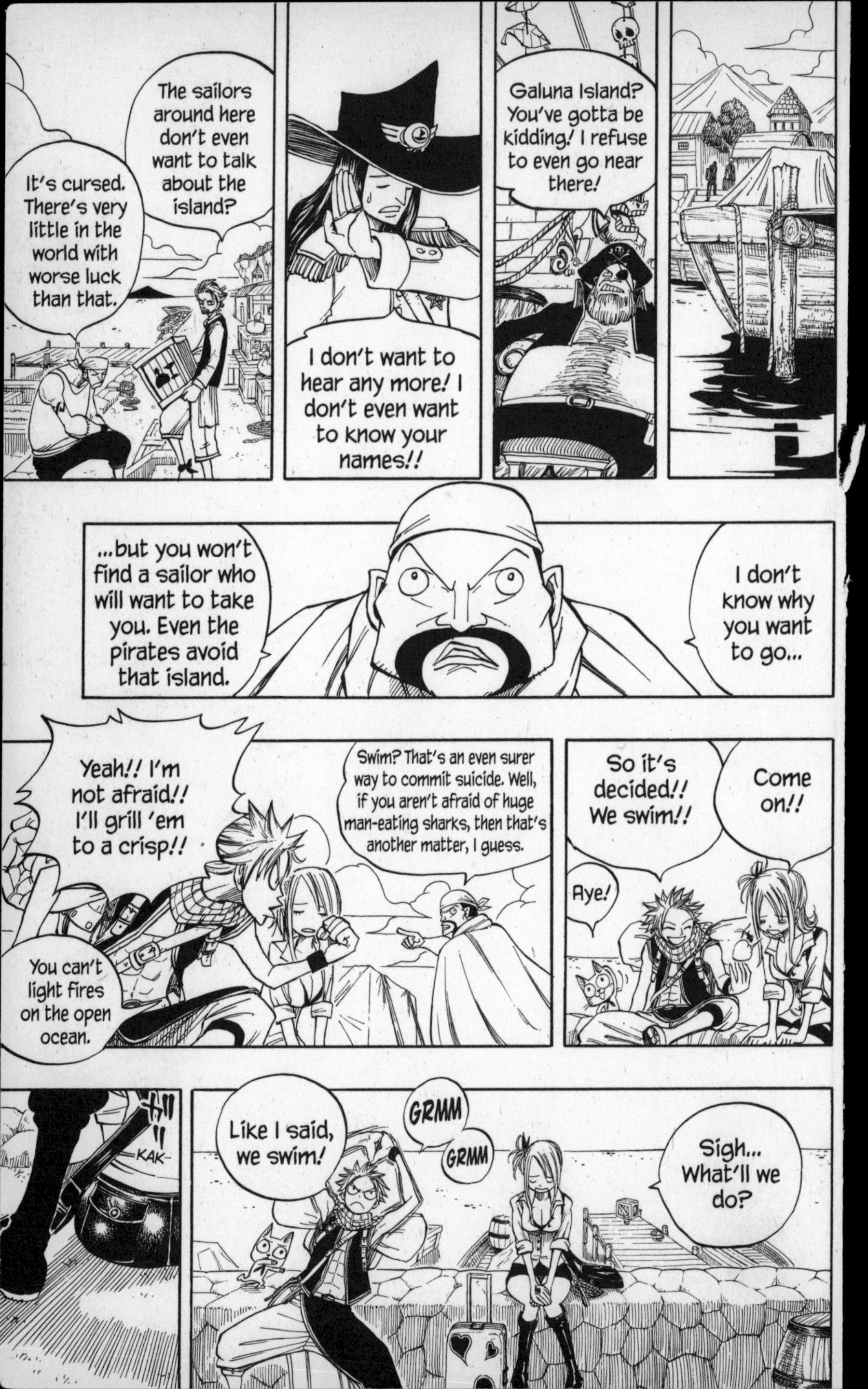
Galuna Island? You've gotta be kidding! I refuse to even go near there!
I don't want to hear any more! I don't even want to know your names!!
The sailors around here don't even want to talk about the island?
It's cursed. There's very little in the world with worse luck than that.
I don't know why you want to go...
...but you won't find a sailor who will want to take you. Even the pirates avoid that island.
Come on!!
So it's decided!! We swim!!
Aye!
Swim? That's an even surer way to commit suicide. Well, if you aren't afraid of huge man-eating sharks, then that's another matter, I guess.
Yeah!! I'm not afraid!! I'll grill 'em to a crisp!!
You can't light fires on the open ocean.
Sigh... What'll we do?
GRMM
GRMM
Like I said, we swim!
KAK

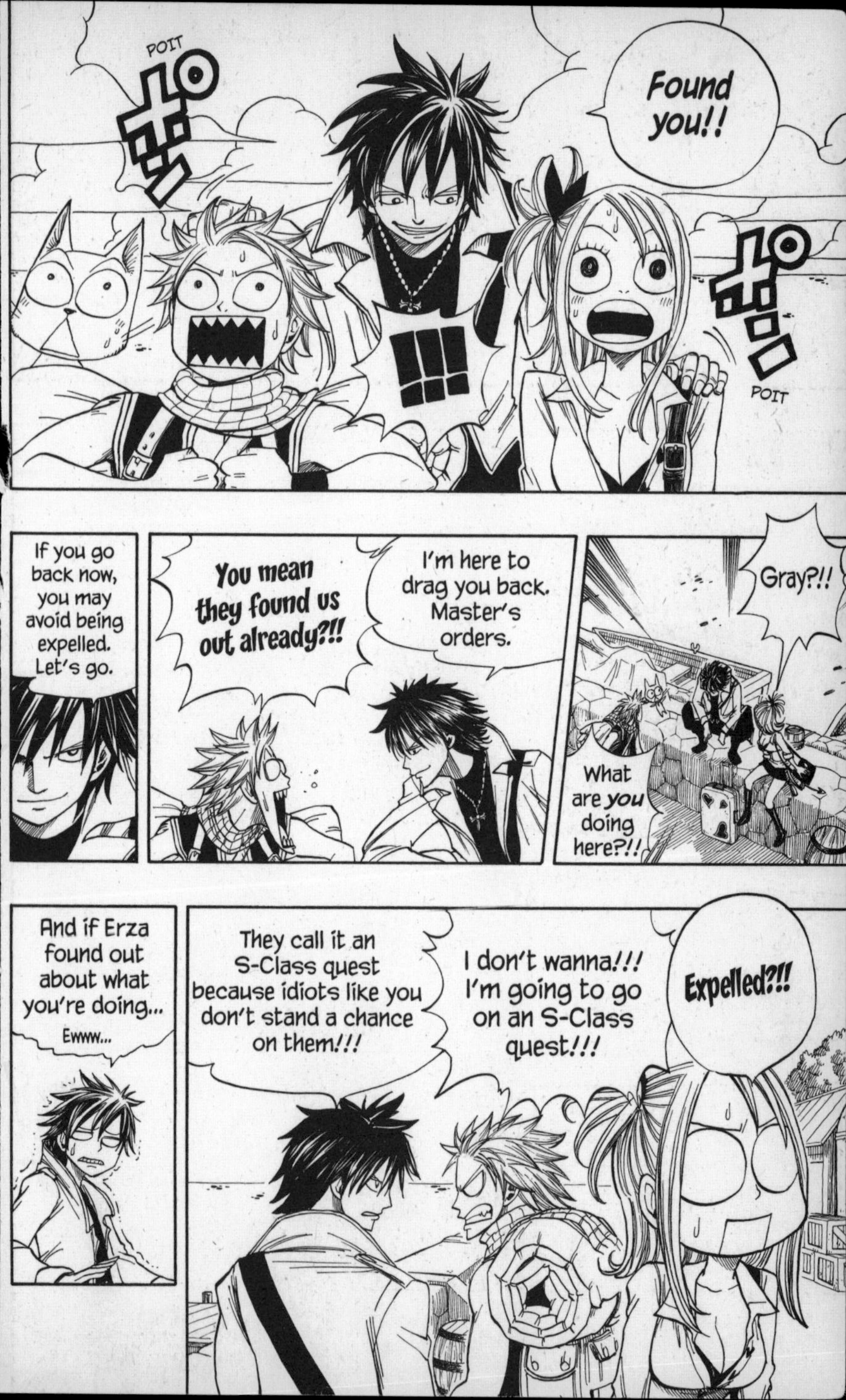
Found you!!
POIT
POIT
Gray?!!
What are *you* doing here?!!
I'm here to drag you back. Master's orders.
You mean they found us out already?!!
If you go back now, you may avoid being expelled. Let's go.
Expelled?!!
I don't wanna!!! I'm going to go on an S-Class quest!!!
They call it an S-Class quest because idiots like you don't stand a chance on them!!!
And if Erza found out about what you're doing...
Ewww...

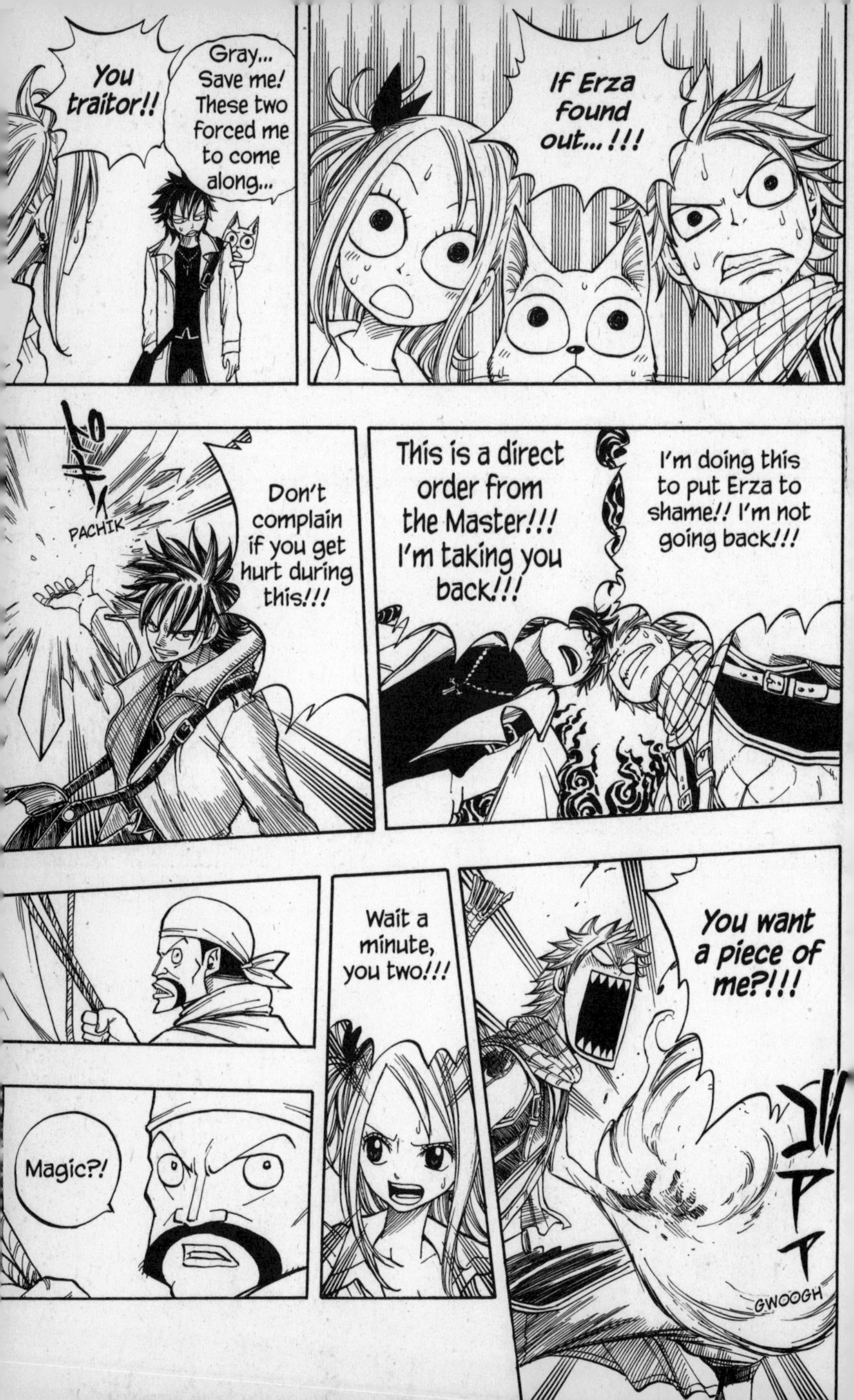
If Erza found out...!!!
Gray... Save me! These two forced me to come along...
You traitor!!
I'm doing this to put Erza to shame!! I'm not going back!!!
This is a direct order from the Master!!! I'm taking you back!!!
Don't complain if you get hurt during this!!!
PACHIK
You want a piece of me?!!!
GWOOGH
Wait a minute, you two!!!
Magic?!

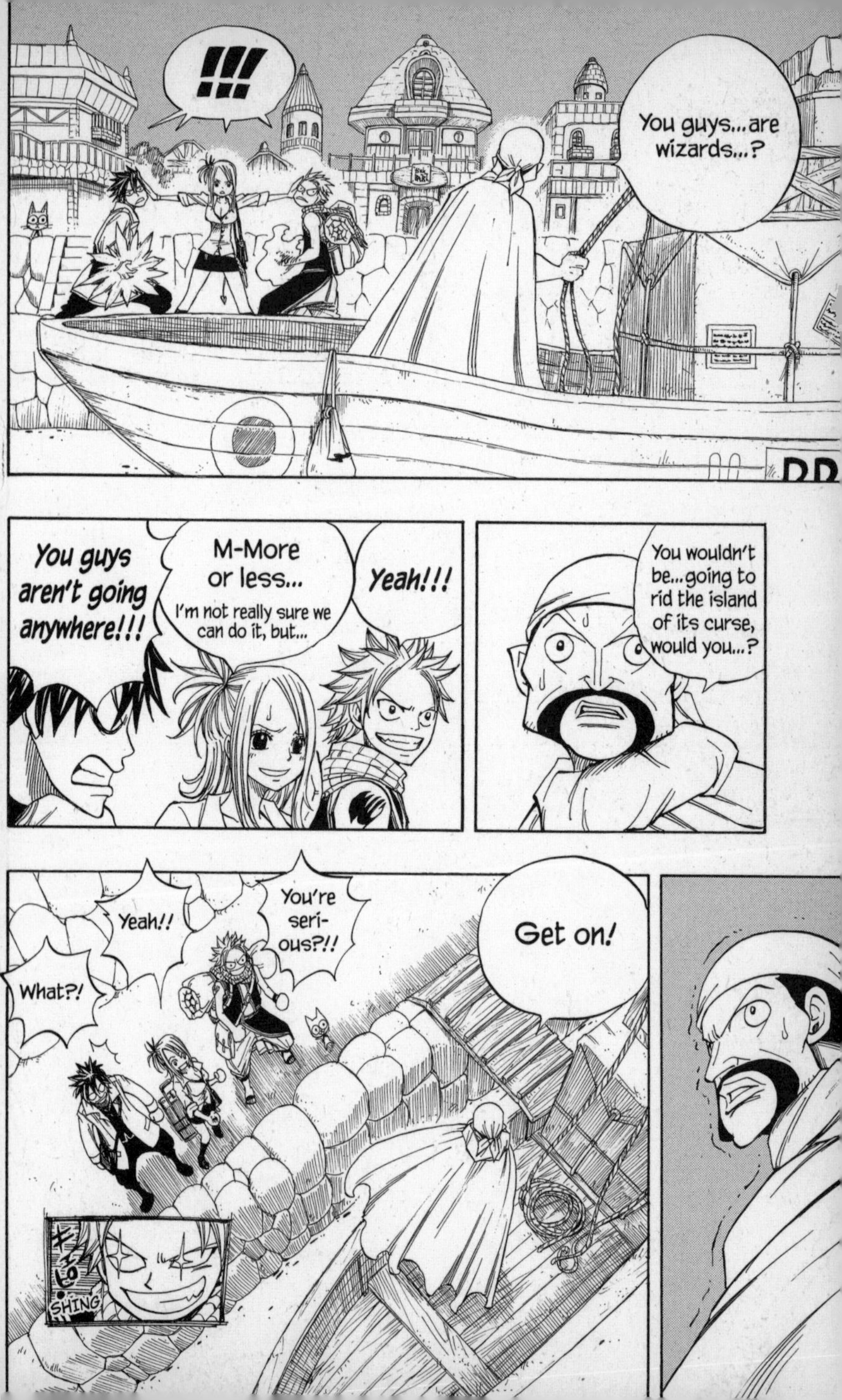
You guys...are wizards...?
!!!
You wouldn't be...going to rid the island of its curse, would you...?
Yeah!!!
M-More or less...
I'm not really sure we can do it, but...
You guys aren't going anywhere!!!
Get on!
You're seri-ous?!!
Yeah!!
What?!
SHING

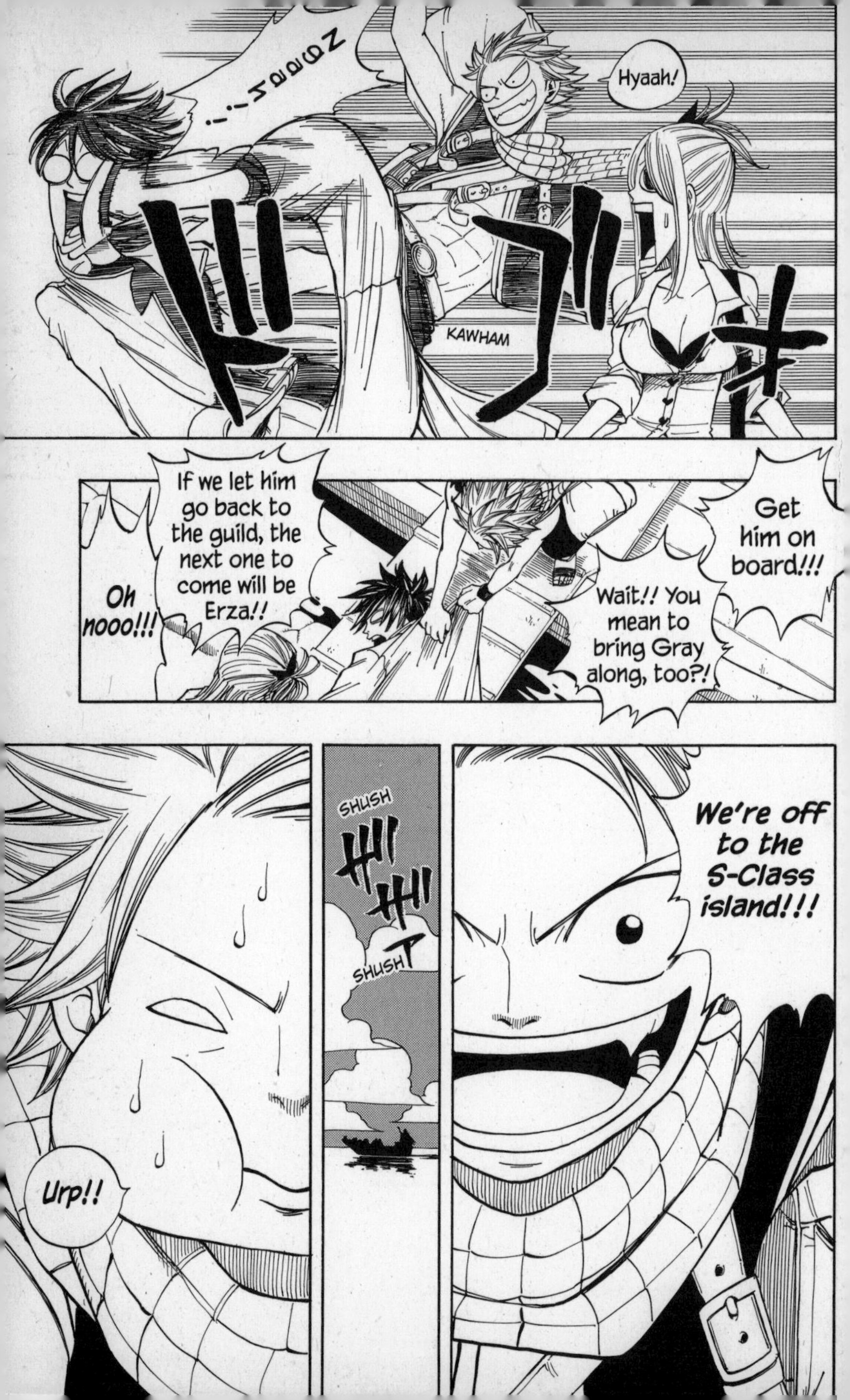

Hyaah!
KAWHAM
Get him on board!!!
Wait!! You mean to bring Gray along, too?!
If we let him go back to the guild, the next one to come will be Erza!!
Oh nooo!!!
We're off to the S-Class island!!!
SHUSH
SHUSH
Urp!!

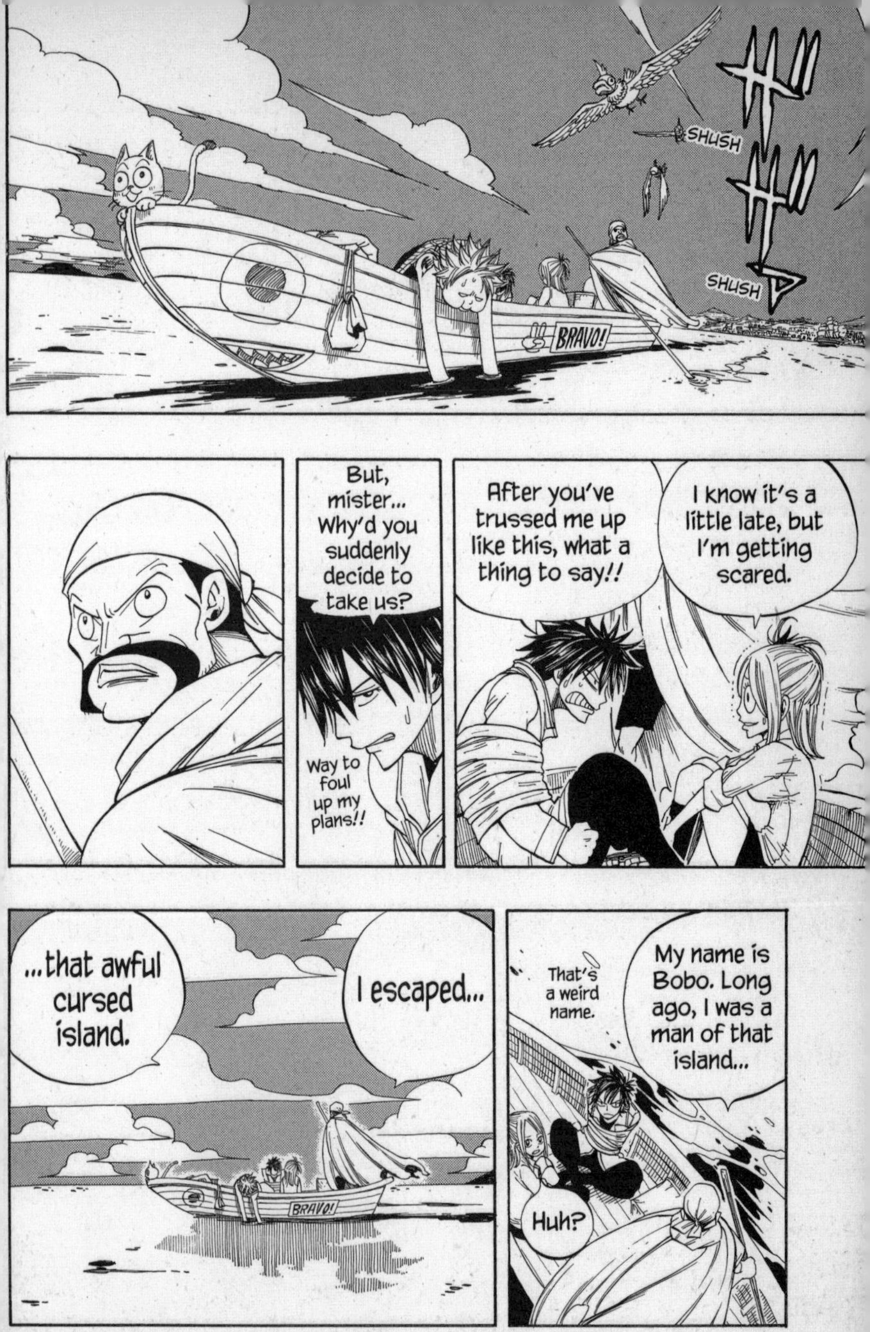
SHUSH
SHUSH
BRAVO!
I know it's a little late, but I'm getting scared.
After you've trussed me up like this, what a thing to say!!
But, mister... Why'd you suddenly decide to take us?
Way to foul up my plans!!
My name is Bobo. Long ago, I was a man of that island...
That's a weird name.
Huh?
I escaped...
...that awful cursed island.
BRAVO!

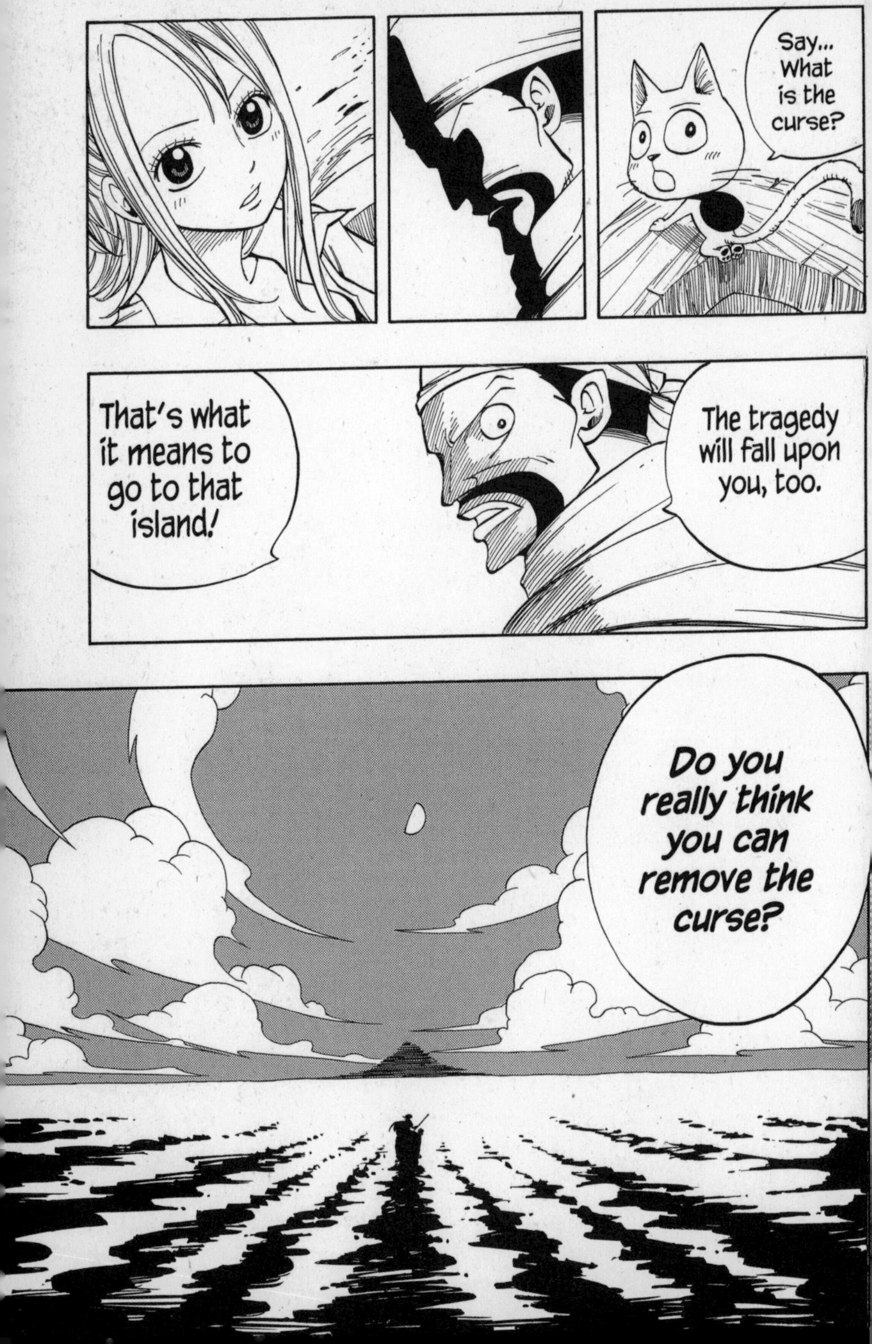
Say... What is the curse?
The tragedy will fall upon you, too.
That's what it means to go to that island!
Do you really think you can remove the curse?

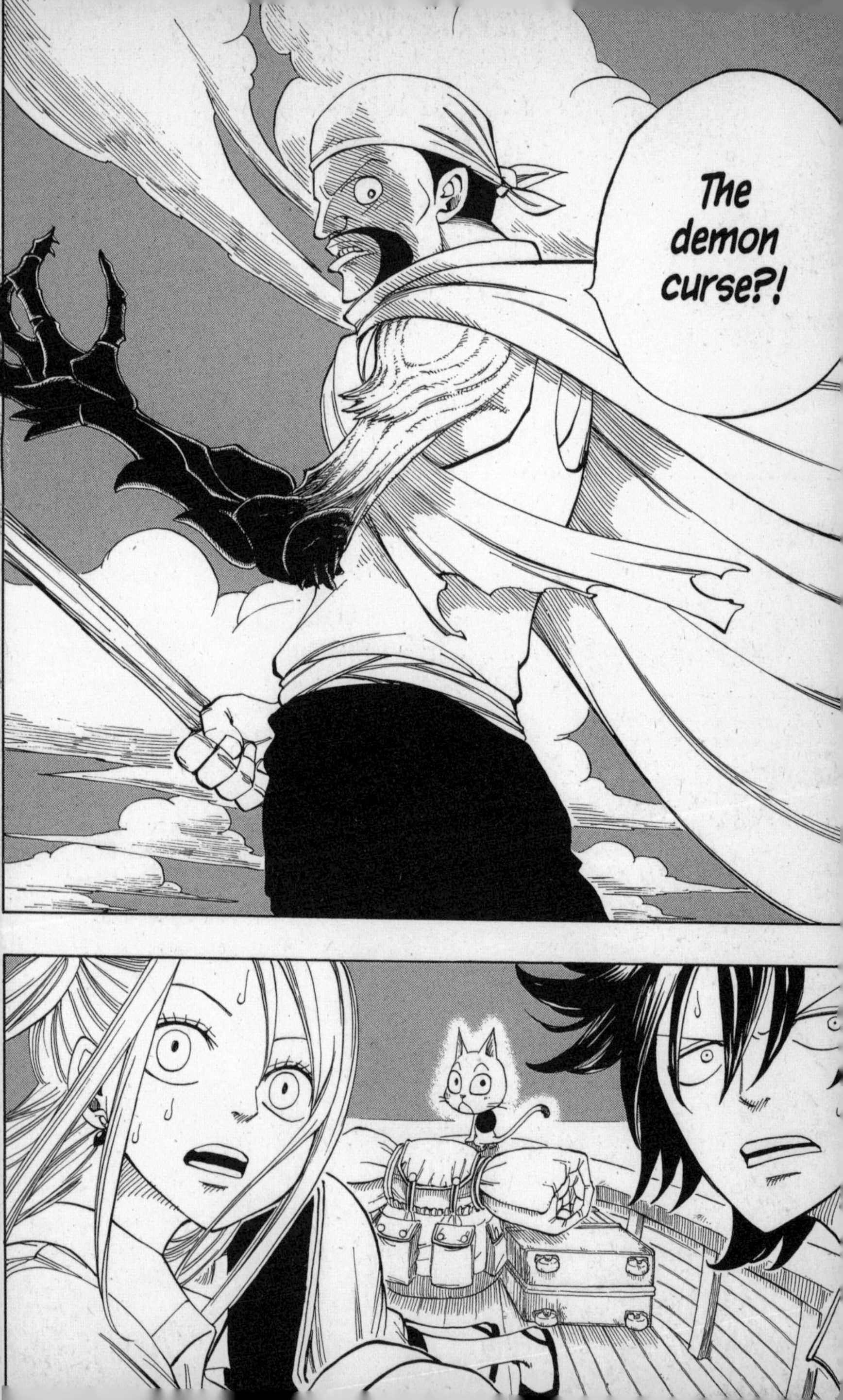
The demon curse?!

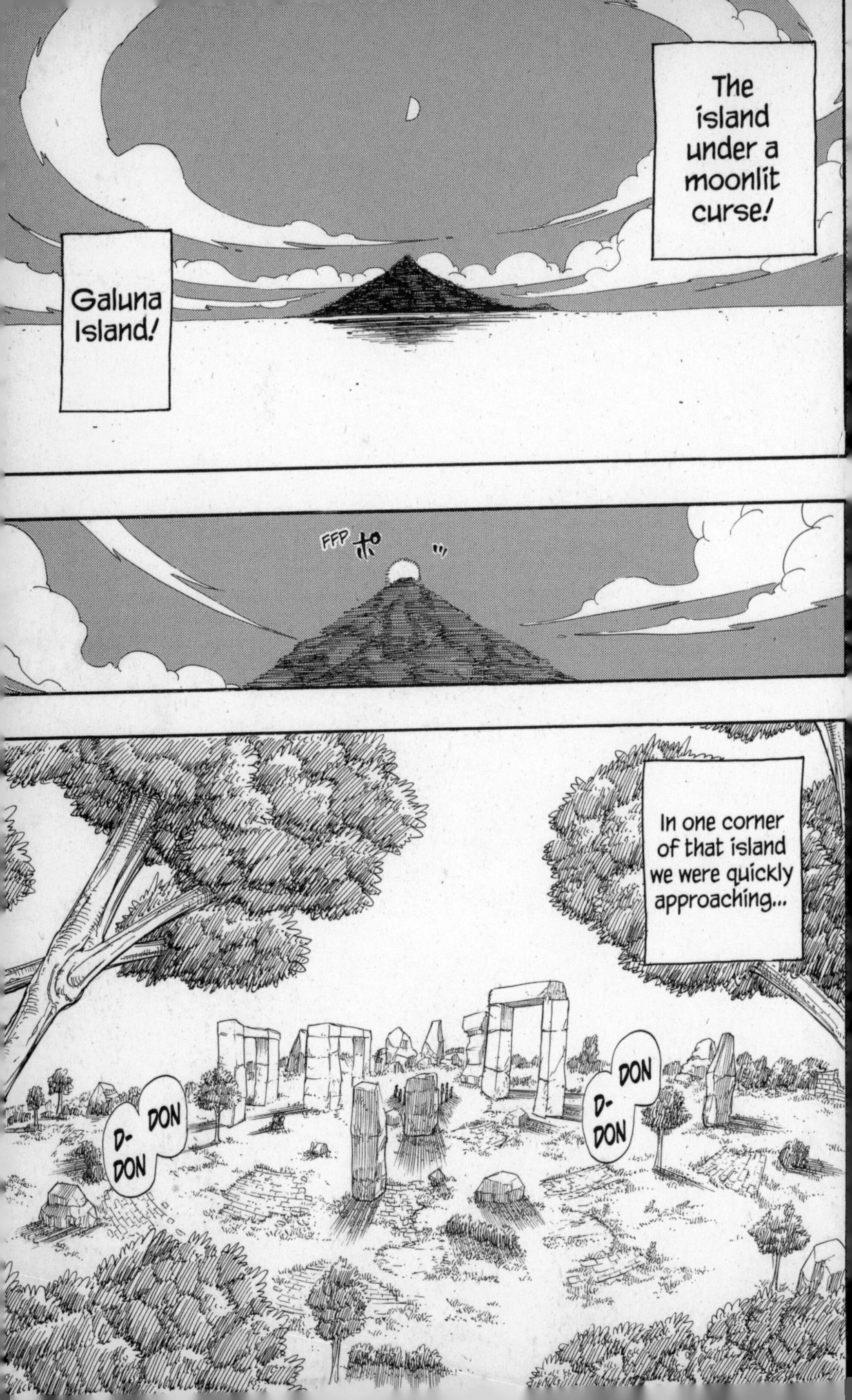
The island under a moonlit curse!
Galuna Island!
FFP
In one corner of that island we were quickly approaching...
DON D-DON
DON D-DON

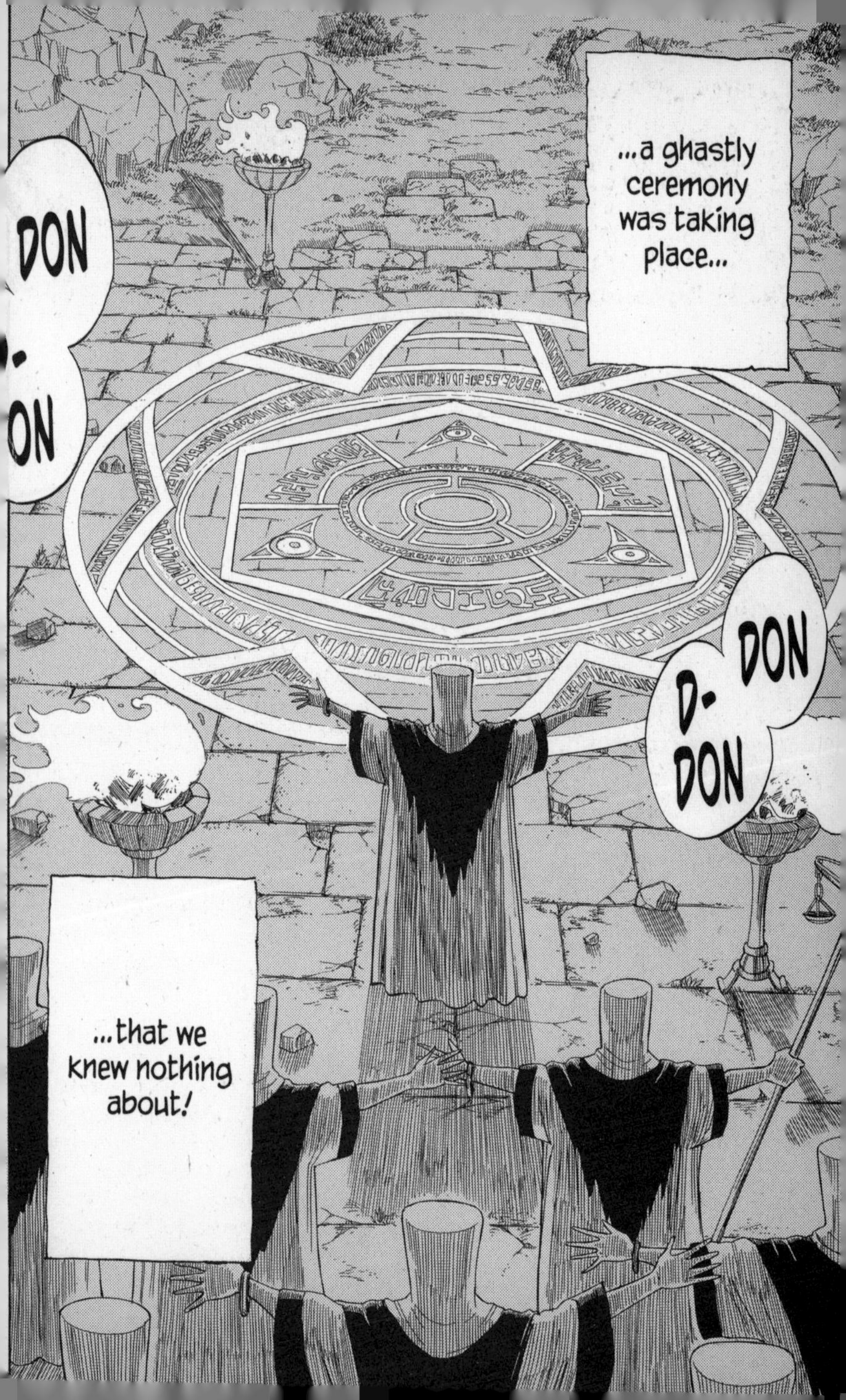

...a ghastly ceremony was taking place...
DON D-DON
DON D-DON
...that we knew nothing about!

FAIRY TAIL

Chapter 26: Is the Moon Out Tonight?

FAIRY TAIL
Name: Makarov
Age: 88 Yrs.
Magic: Giant (among many others)
Likes: Fairy Tail
Dislikes: The Council
WIZARD GUILDX639

Remarks

The Master of Fairy Tail, a guild that is known to be a gathering of problem wizards. He is thought to possess an immeasurably high level of magic and skills. He is especially skilled at giant magic, the ability to vastly increase one's size, but he also has a general knowledge of fire, ice, and wind magic as well.
He is not known to open up even to people of the guild, so there are sides of his personality that are steeped in mystery.

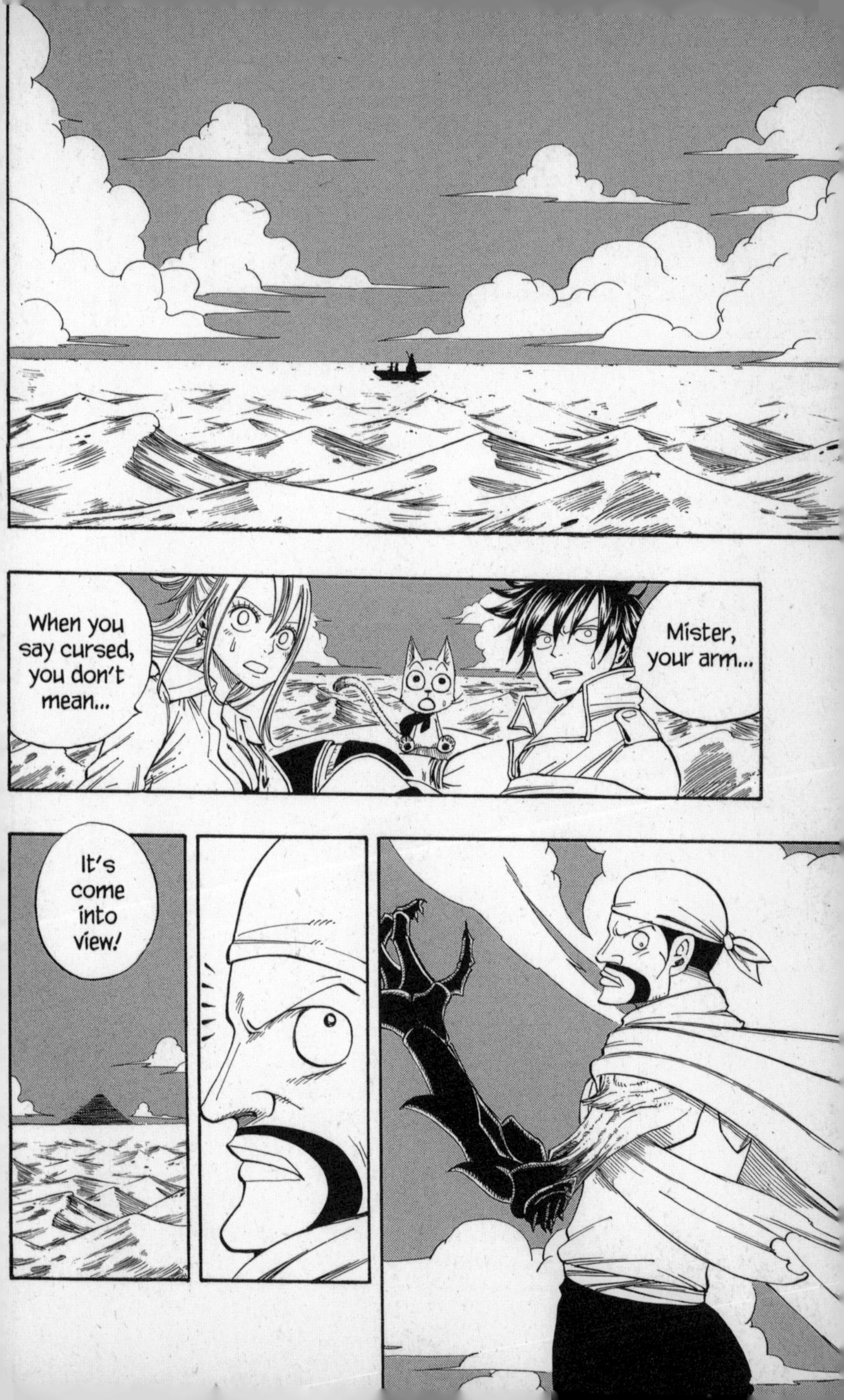
Mister, your arm...
When you say cursed, you don't mean...
It's come into view!

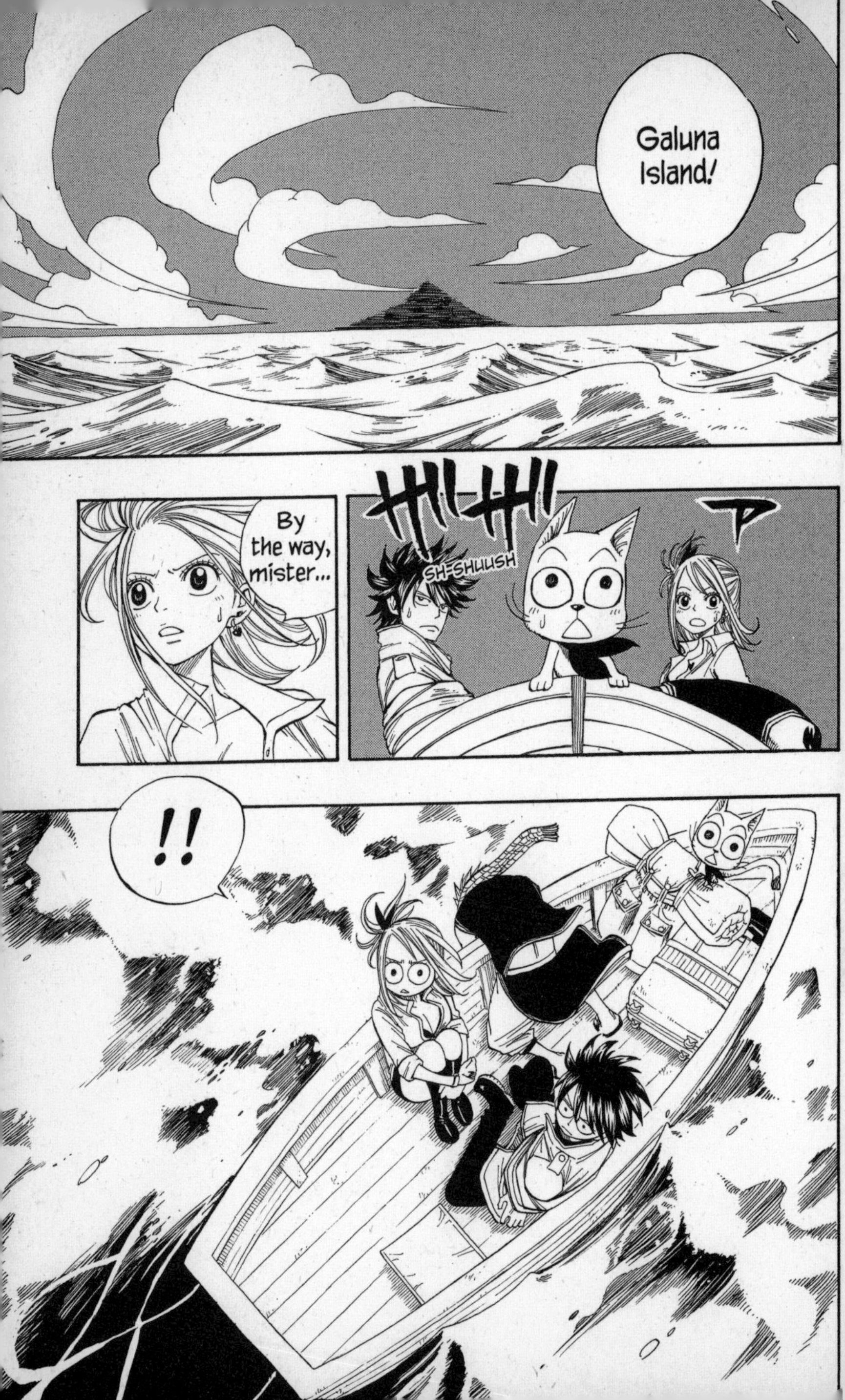
Galuna Island!
By the way, mister...
SH-SHUUSH
!!

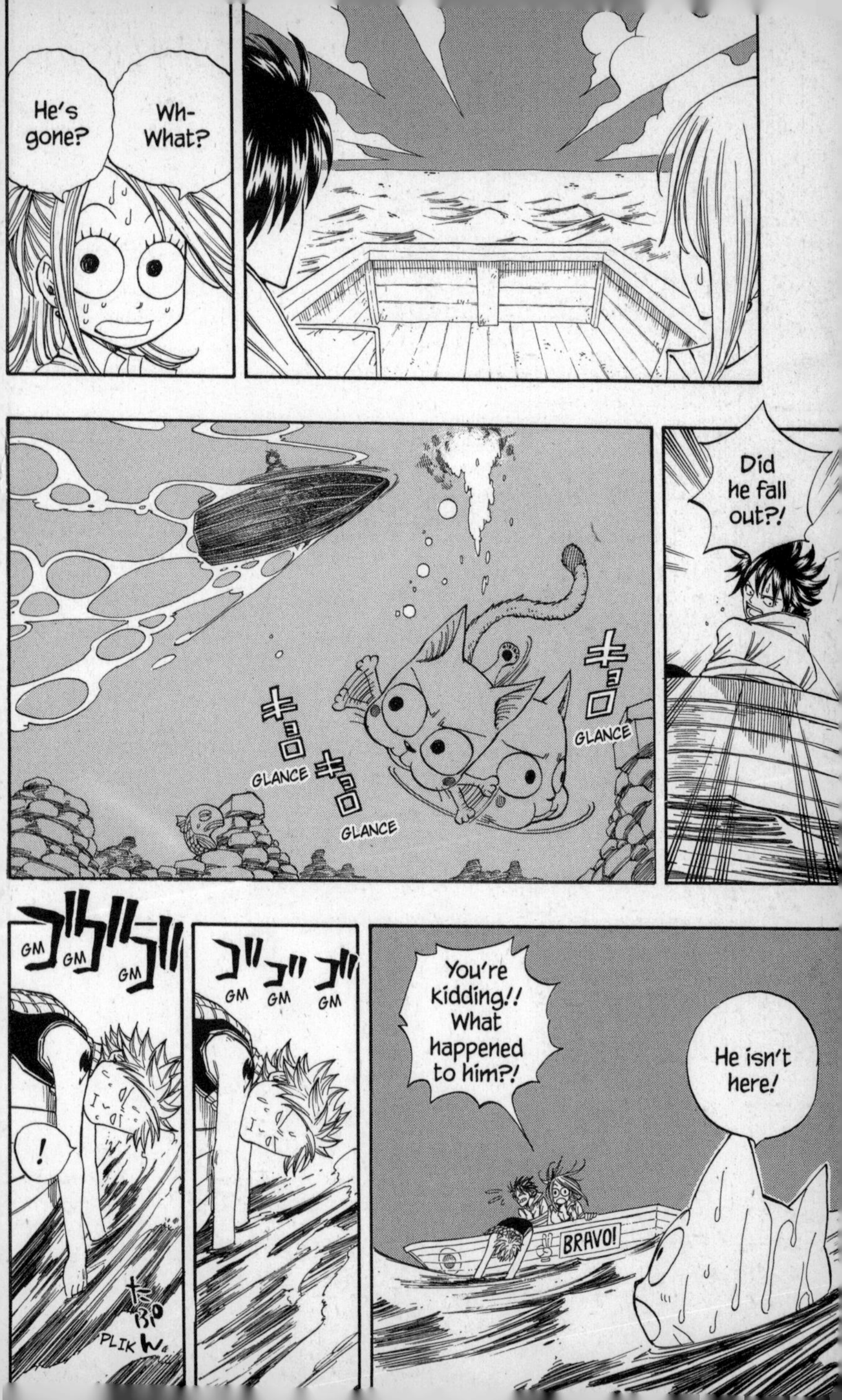
Wh- What?
He's gone?
Did he fall out?!
GLANCE
GLANCE
GLANCE
He isn't here!
You're kidding!! What happened to him?!
BRAVO!
GM
GM
GM
GM
GM
GM
!
PLIK

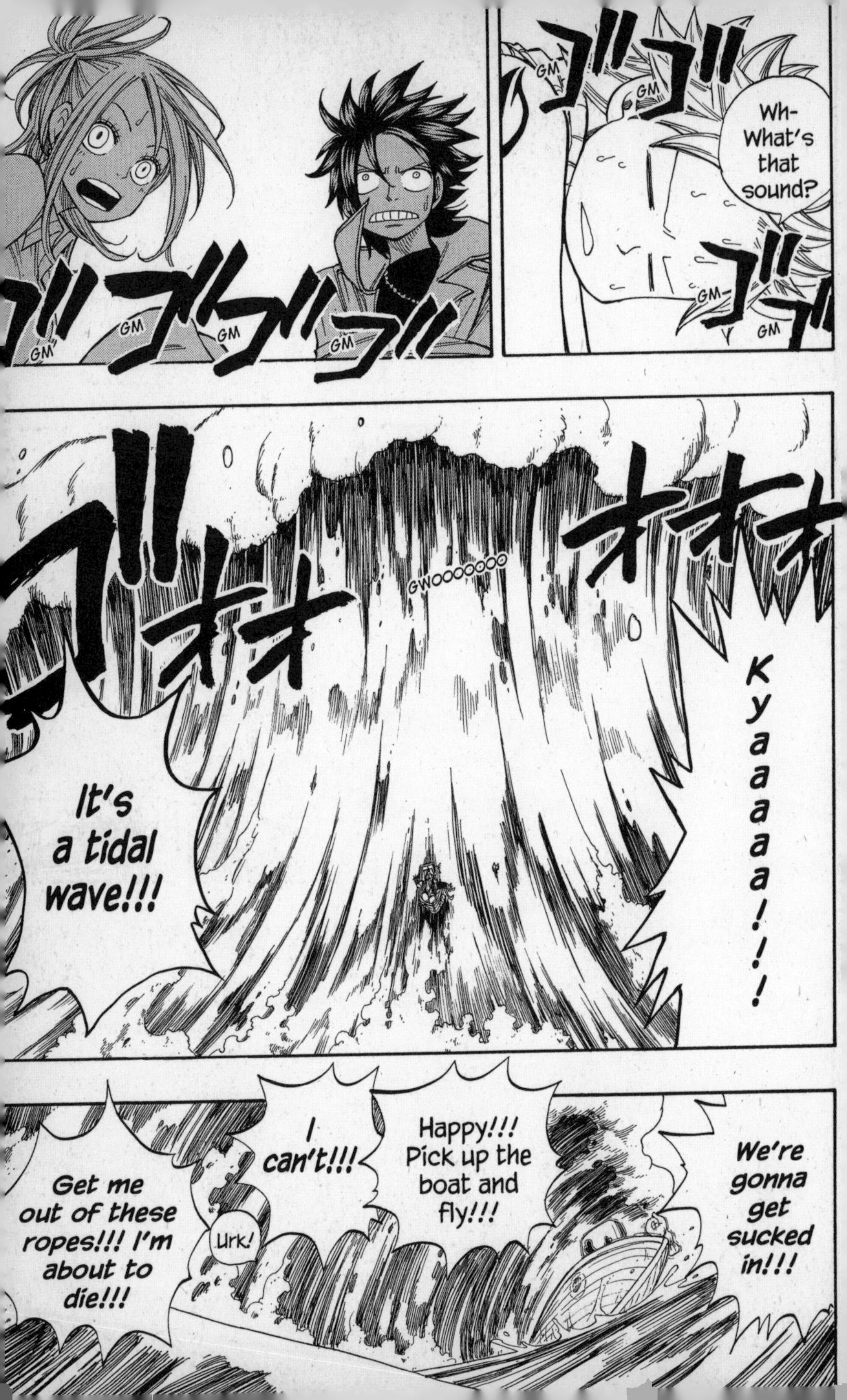

ゴゴ
GM
GM
Wh- What's that sound?
ゴゴ
GM
GM
ゴゴゴゴ
GM
GM
GM
GM
ゴオオオオオ
GWOOOOOOO
Kyaaaaaa!!!
It's a tidal wave!!!
We're gonna get sucked in!!!
Happy!!! Pick up the boat and fly!!!
I can't!!!
Urk!
Get me out of these ropes!!! I'm about to die!!!

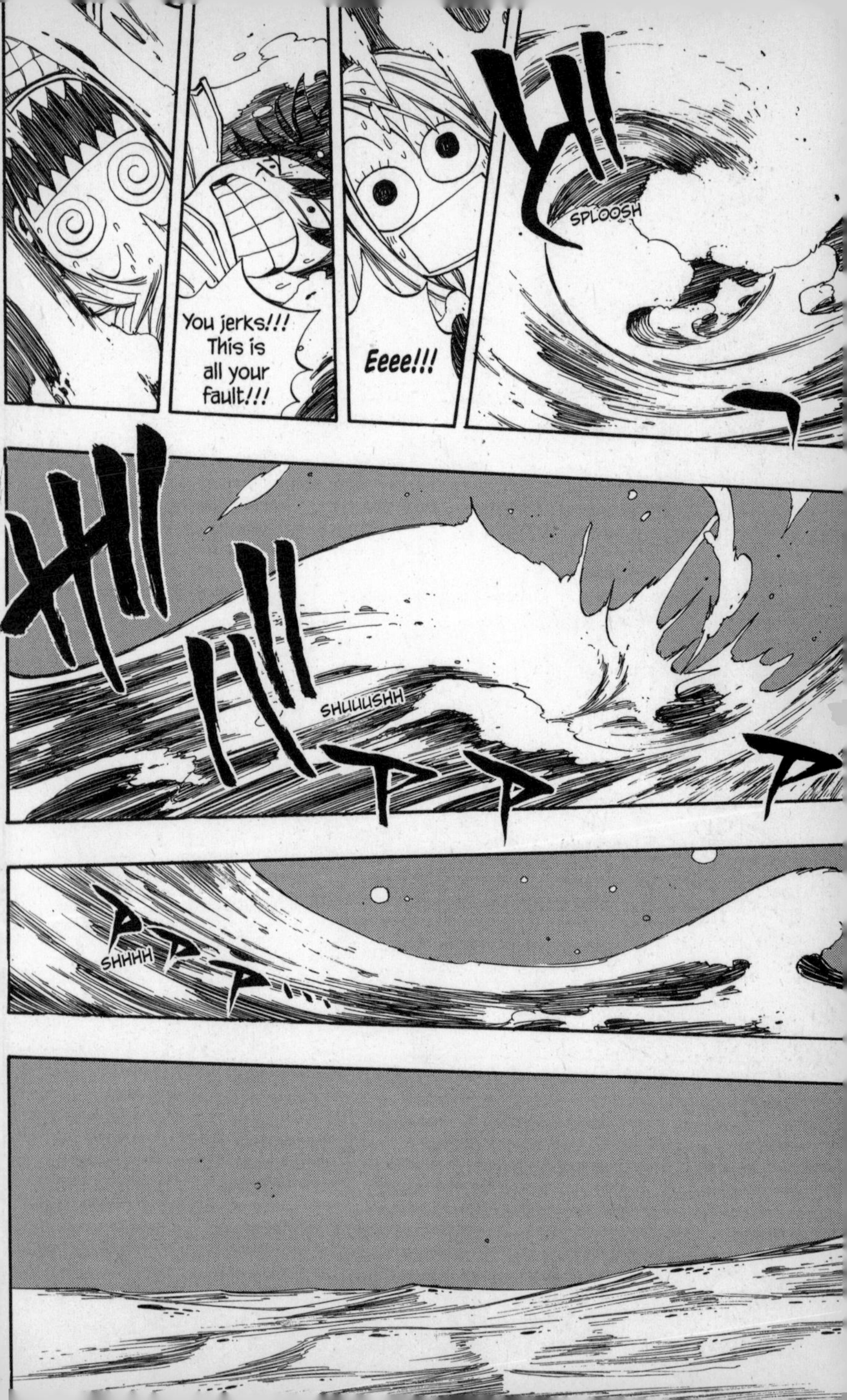
SPLOOSH
Eeee!!!
You jerks!!! This is all your fault!!!
SHUUUSHH
SHHHH

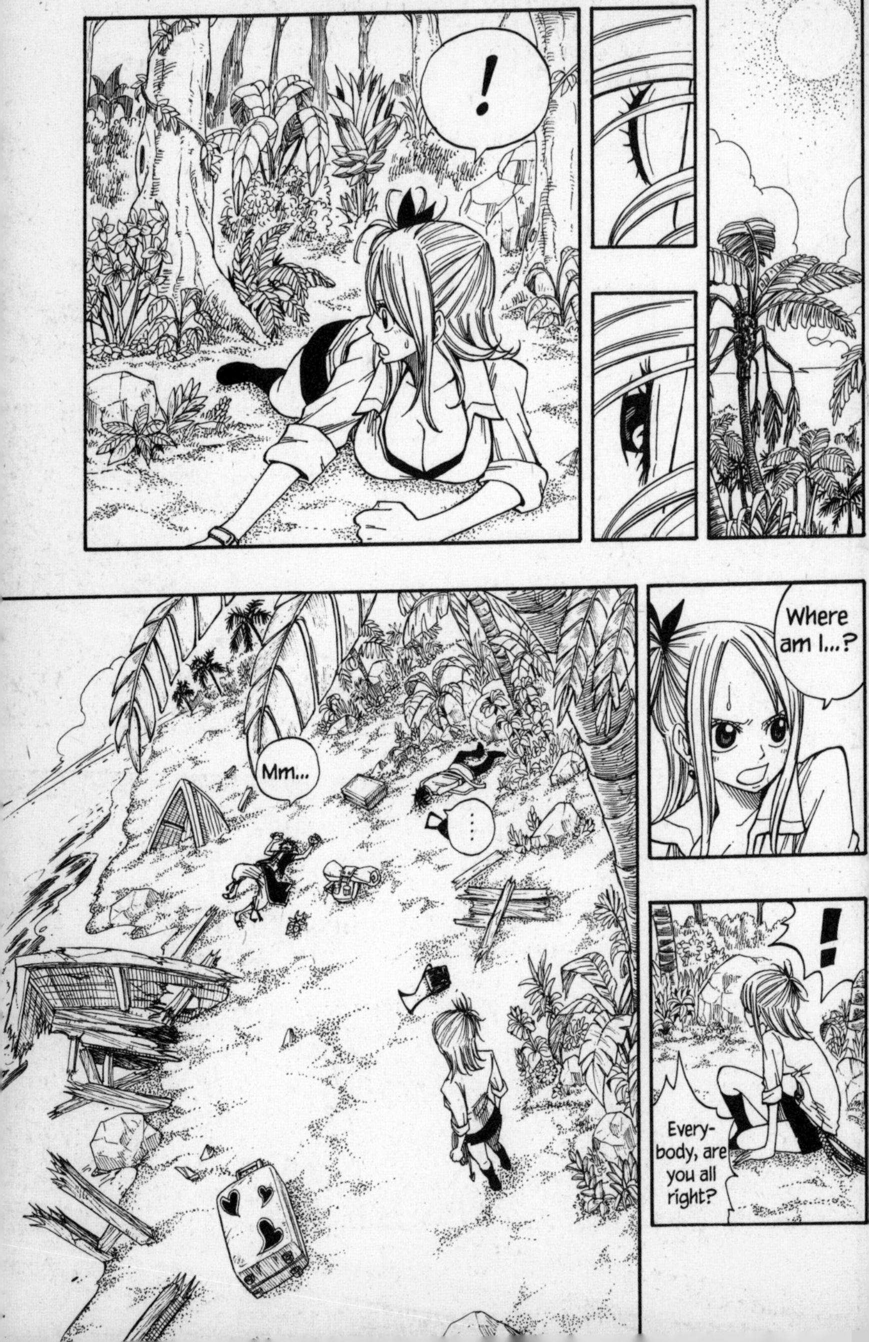
!
Where am I...?
!
Every-body, are you all right?
Mm...
......

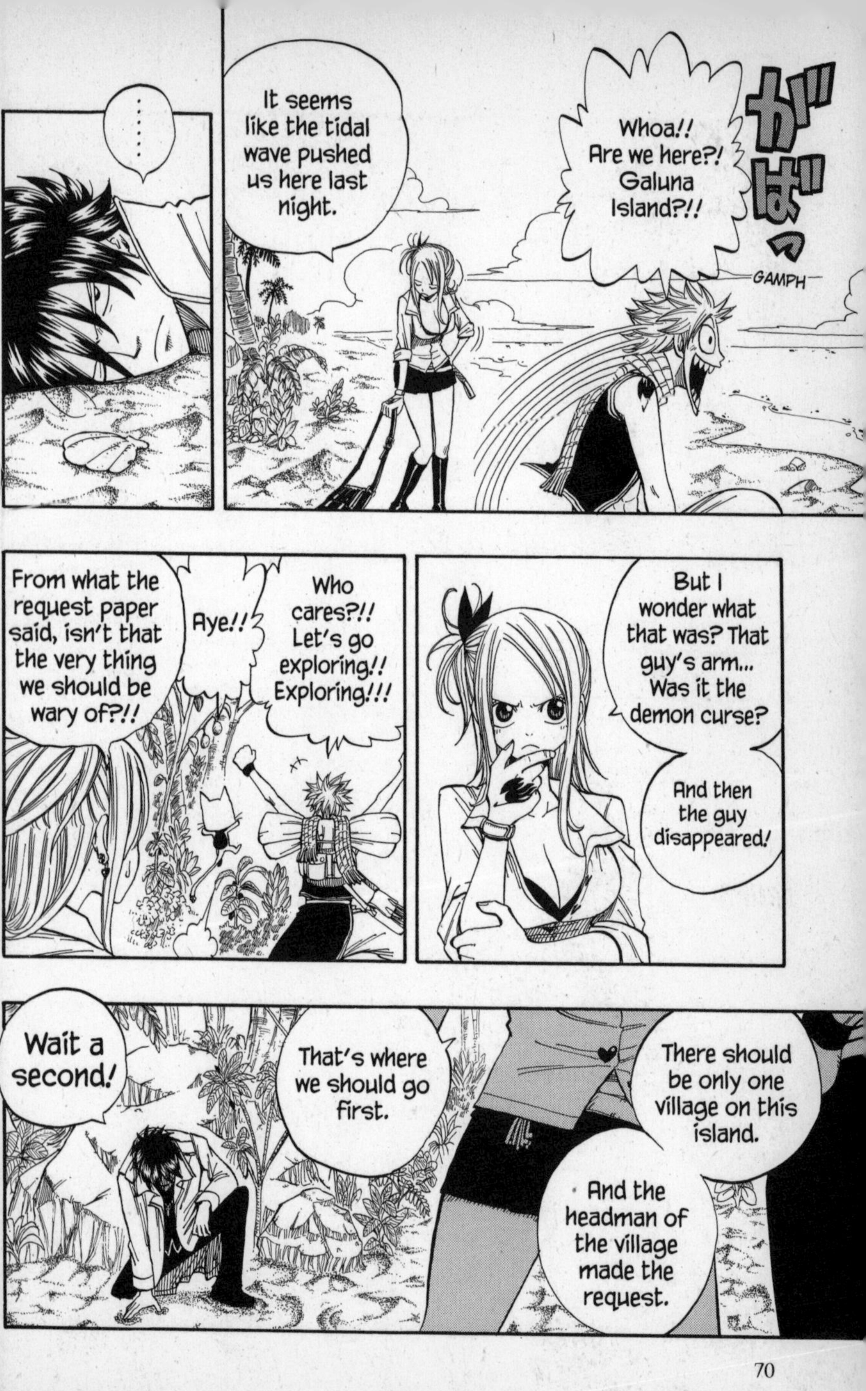

がばっ
GAMPH
Whoa!! Are we here?! Galuna Island?!!
It seems like the tidal wave pushed us here last night.
......
But I wonder what that was? That guy's arm... Was it the demon curse?
And then the guy disappeared!
Who cares?!! Let's go exploring!! Exploring!!!
Aye!!
From what the request paper said, isn't that the very thing we should be wary of?!!
There should be only one village on this island.
And the headman of the village made the request.
That's where we should go first.
Wait a second!

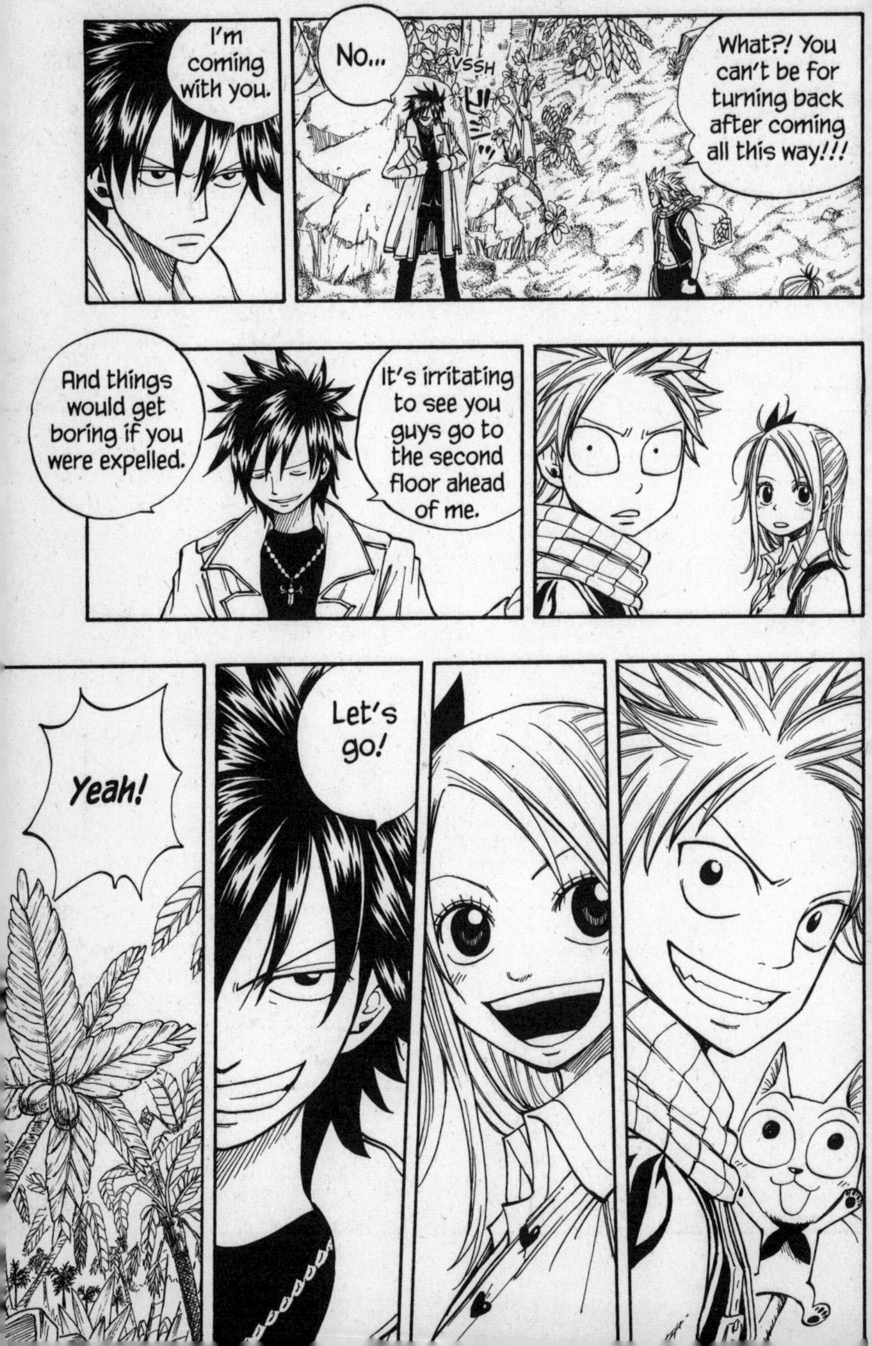
What?! You can't be for turning back after coming all this way!!!
VSSH
No...
I'm coming with you.
It's irritating to see you guys go to the second floor ahead of me.
And things would get boring if you were expelled.
Let's go!
Yeah!

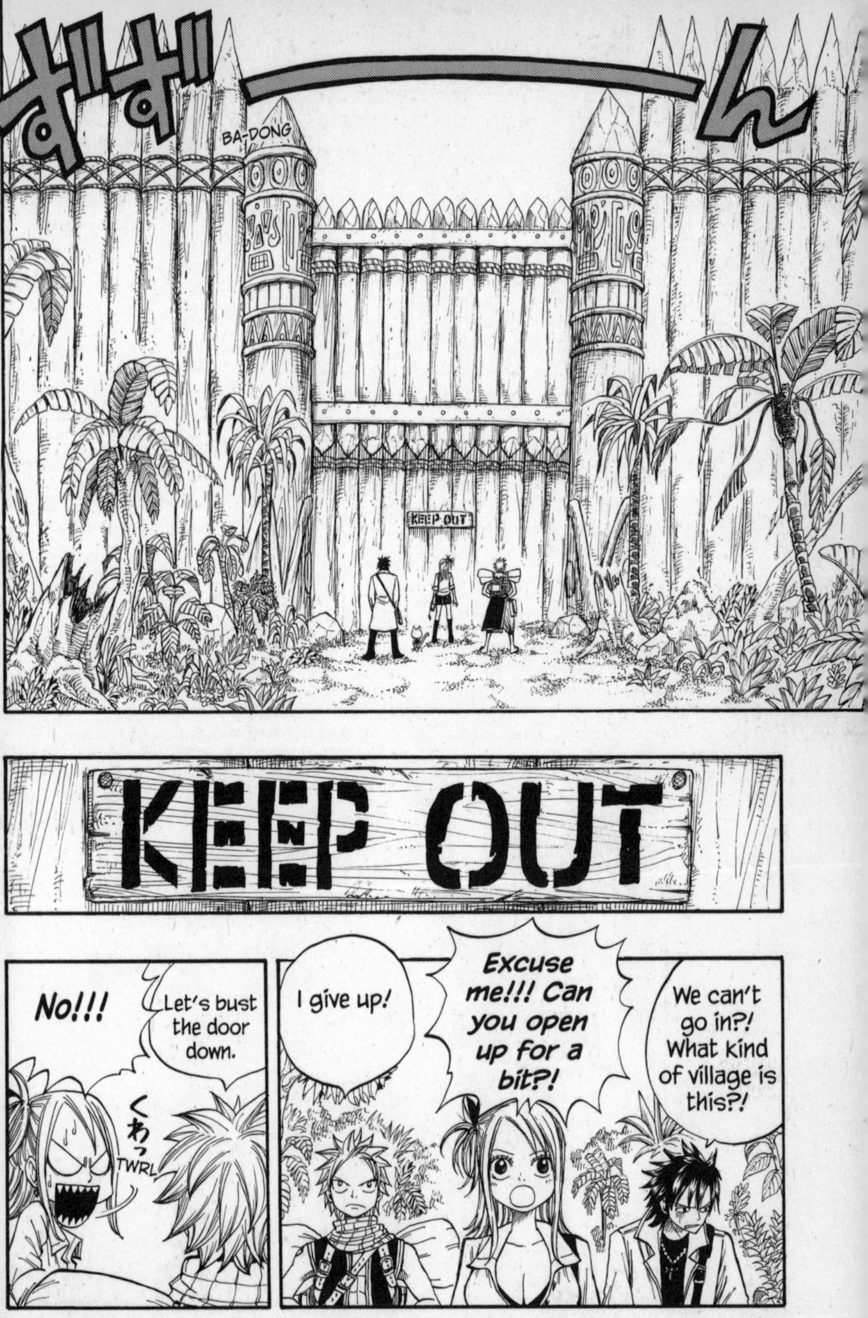

ずずーん
BA-DONG
KEEP OUT
KEEP OUT
We can't go in?! What kind of village is this?!
Excuse me!!! Can you open up for a bit?!
I give up!
Let's bust the door down.
No!!!
くわっ
TWRL

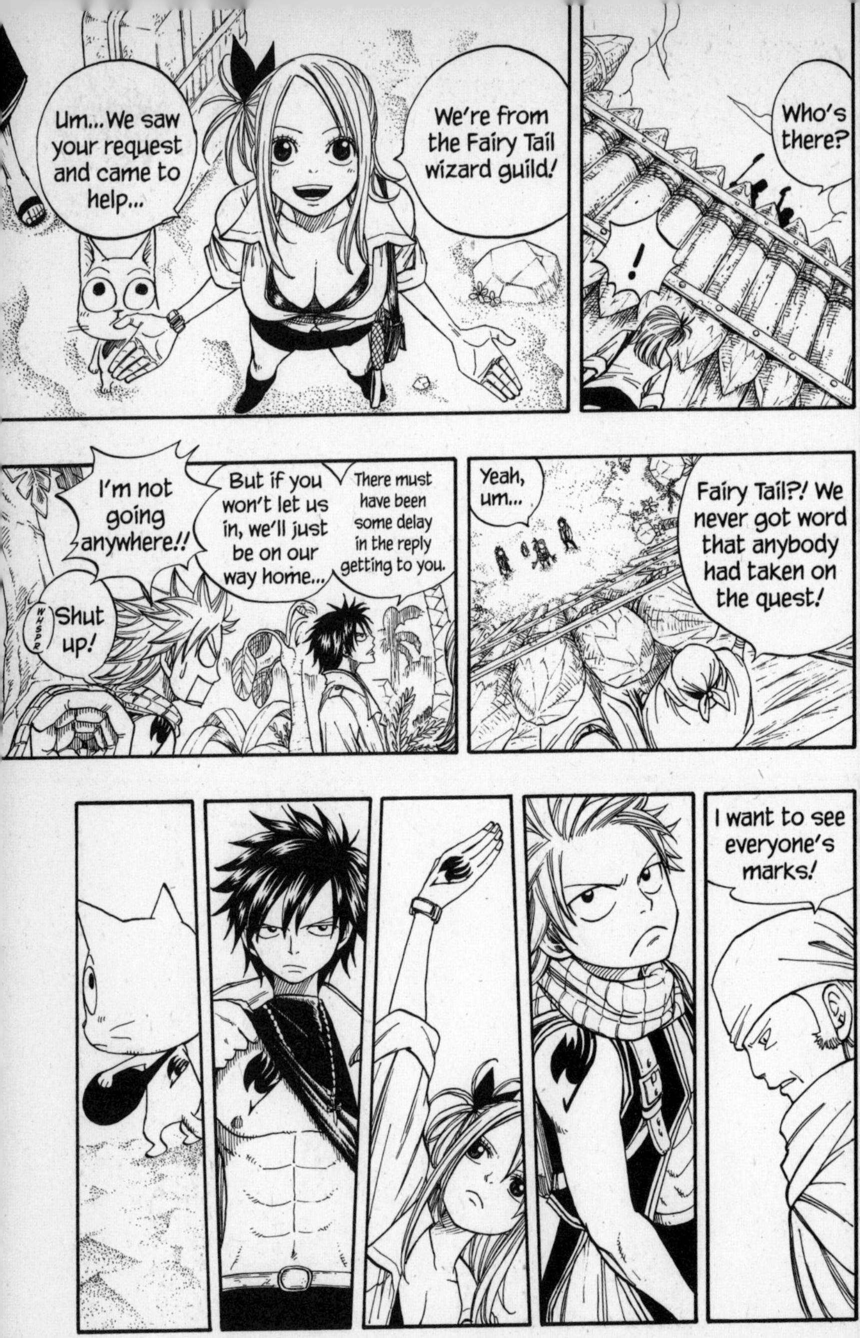
Who's there?
!
We're from the Fairy Tail wizard guild!
Um...We saw your request and came to help...
Fairy Tail?! We never got word that anybody had taken on the quest!
Yeah, um...
There must have been some delay in the reply getting to you.
But if you won't let us in, we'll just be on our way home...
I'm not going anywhere!!
WHSPR
Shut up!
I want to see everyone's marks!

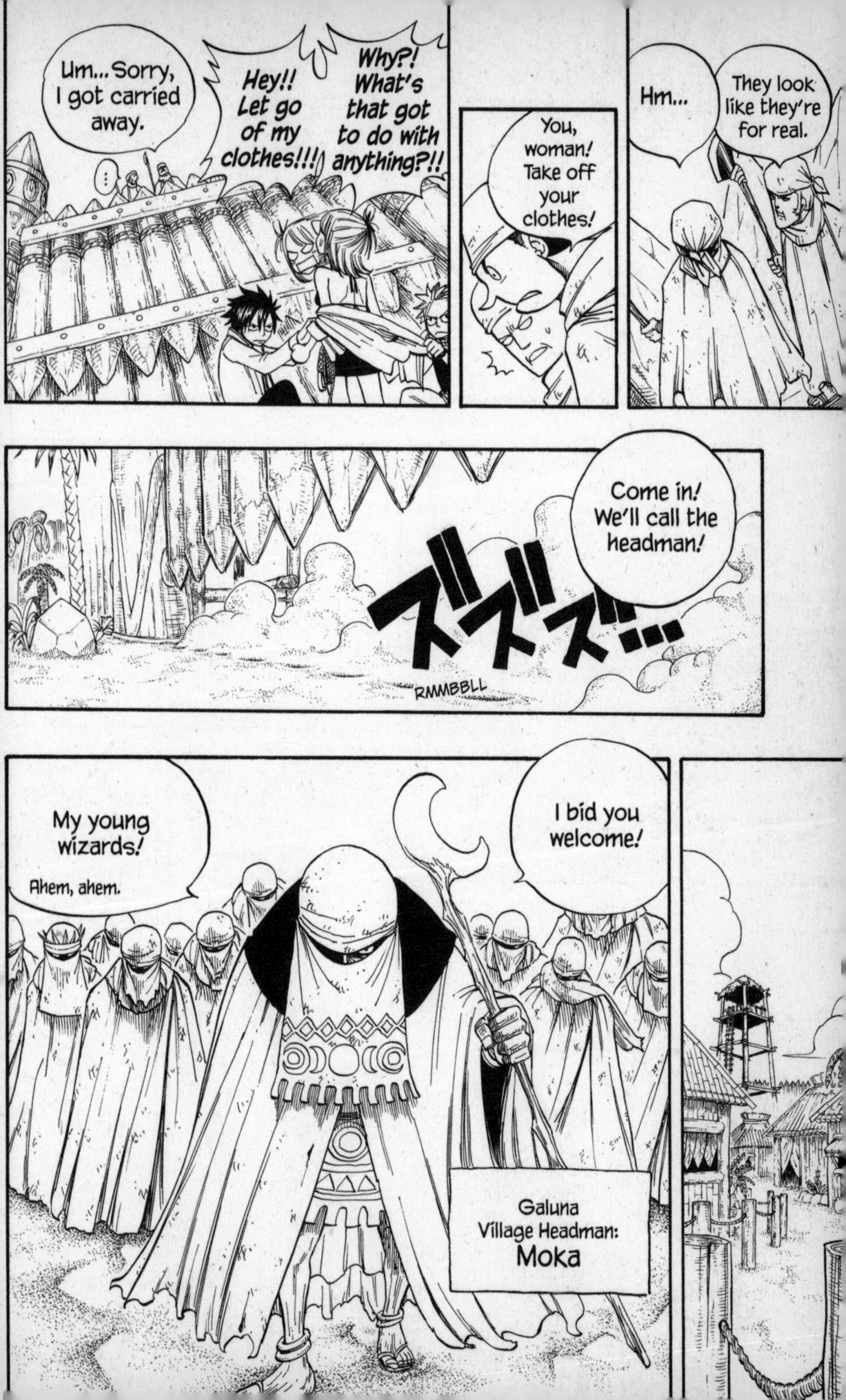
They look like they're for real.
Hm...
You, woman! Take off your clothes!
Why?! What's that got to do with anything?!!
Hey!! Let go of my clothes!!!
...
Um... Sorry, I got carried away.
Come in! We'll call the headman!
ズズズ...
RMMBBLL
I bid you welcome!
My young wizards!
Ahem, ahem.
Galuna Village Headman: Moka

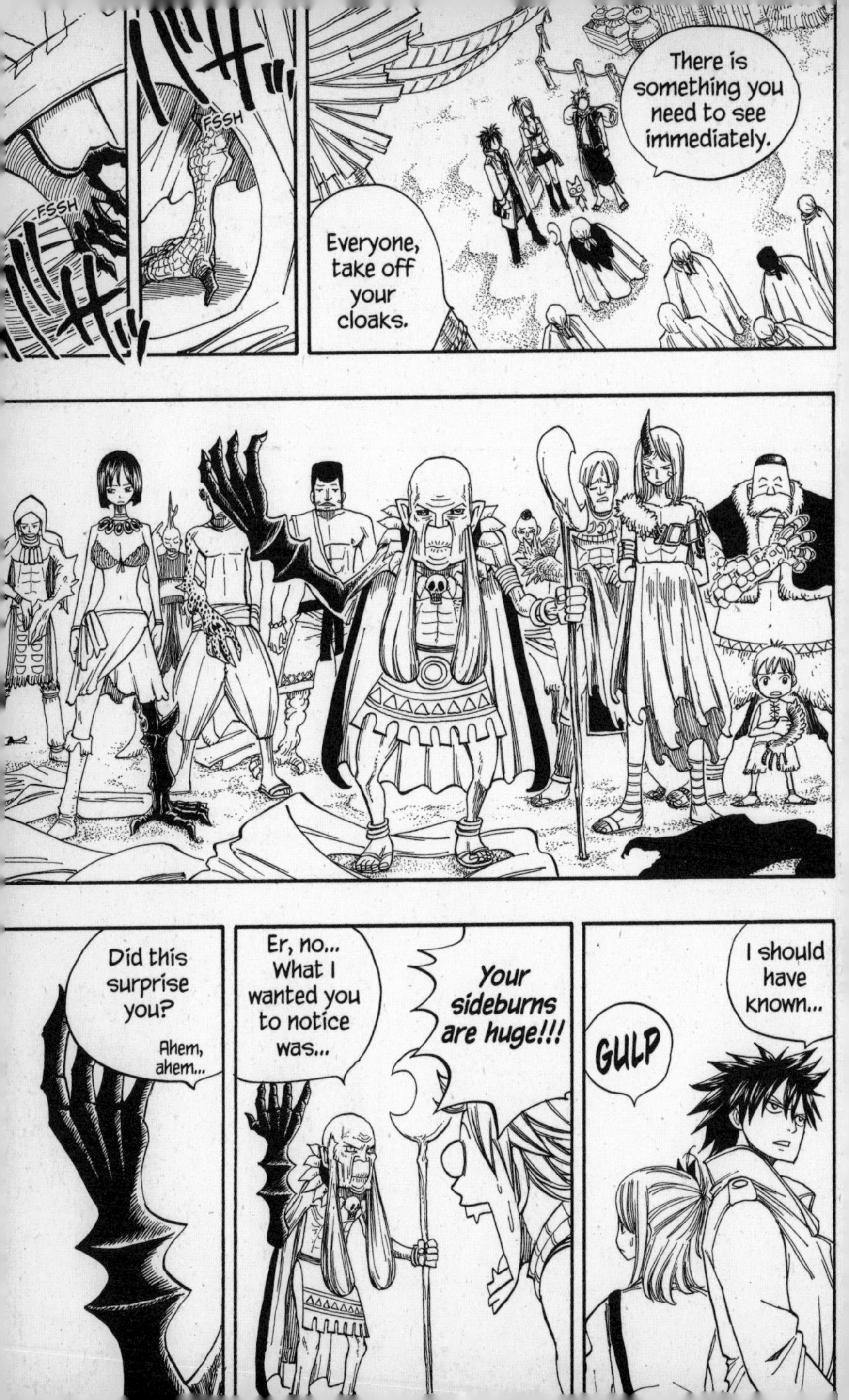

FSSH
FSSH
There is something you need to see immediately.
Everyone, take off your cloaks.
Did this surprise you?
Ahem, ahem...
Er, no... What I wanted you to notice was...
Your sideburns are huge!!!
GULP
I should have known...

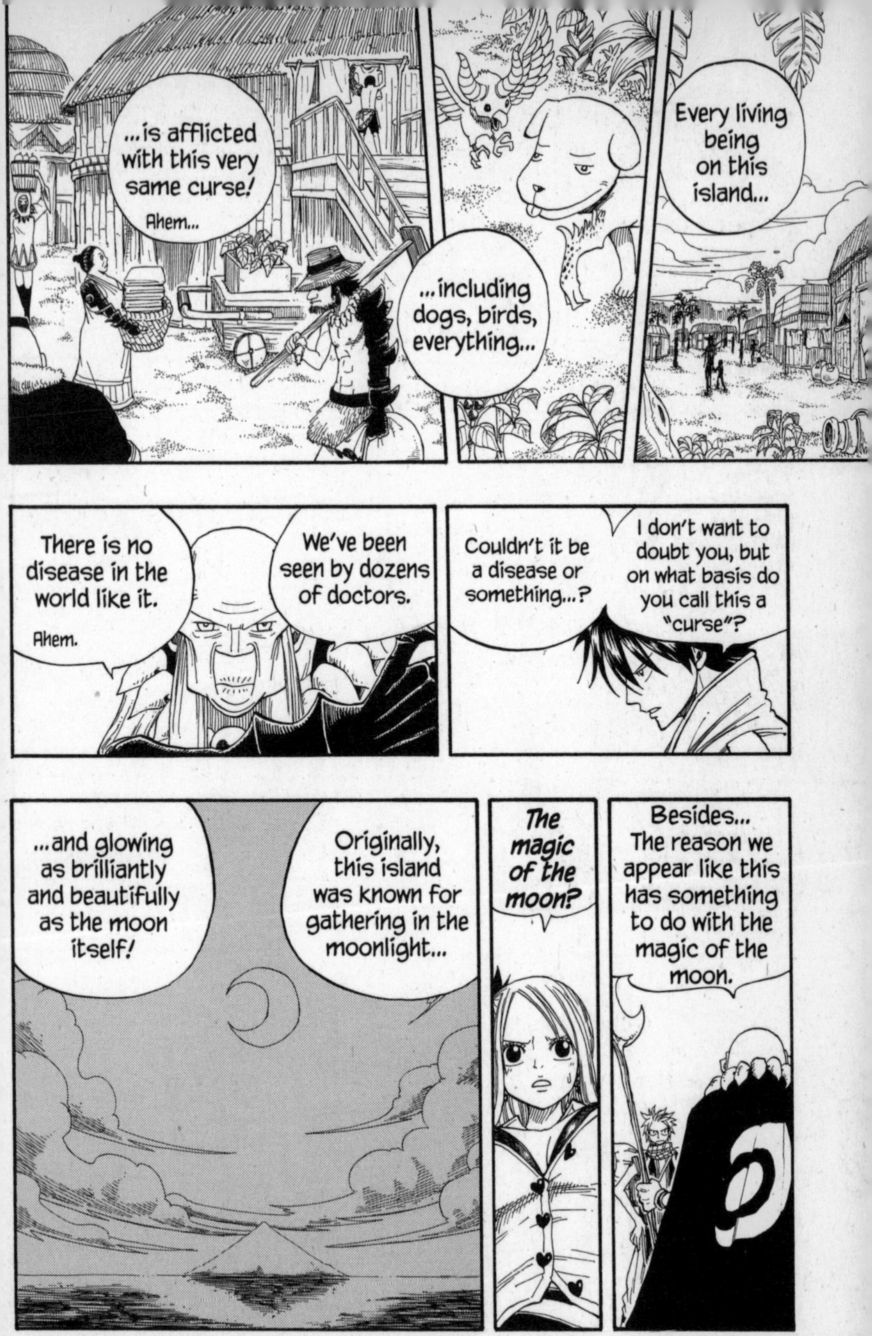
Every living being on this island...
...including dogs, birds, everything...
...is afflicted with this very same curse!
Ahem...
I don't want to doubt you, but on what basis do you call this a "curse"?
Couldn't it be a disease or something...?
We've been seen by dozens of doctors.
There is no disease in the world like it.
Ahem.
Besides... The reason we appear like this has something to do with the magic of the moon.
The magic of the moon?
Originally, this island was known for gathering in the moonlight...
...and glowing as brilliantly and beautifully as the moon itself!

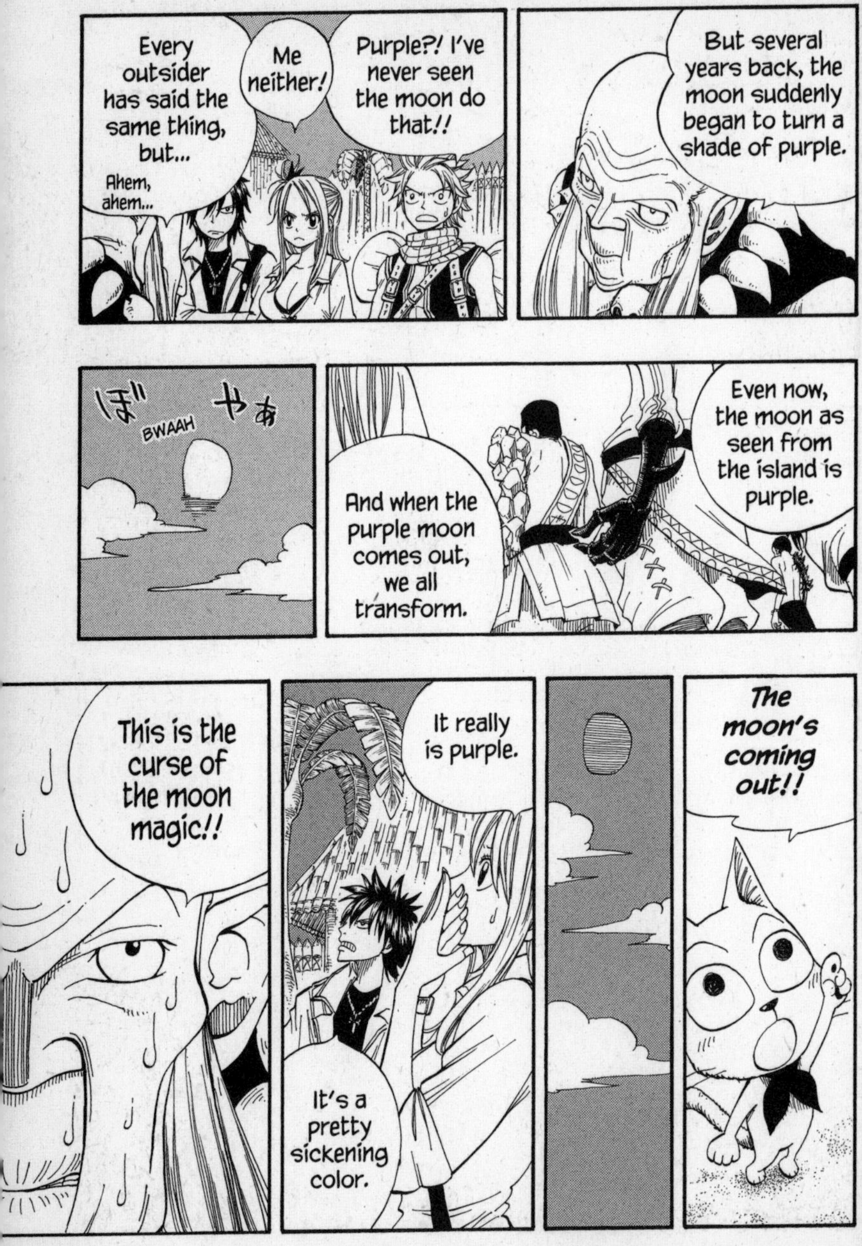

But several years back, the moon suddenly began to turn a shade of purple.
Purple?! I've never seen the moon do that!!
Me neither!
Every outsider has said the same thing, but...
Ahem, ahem...
Even now, the moon as seen from the island is purple.
And when the purple moon comes out, we all transform.
ぼやぁ
BWAAH
The moon's coming out!!
It really is purple.
It's a pretty sickening color.
This is the curse of the moon magic!!

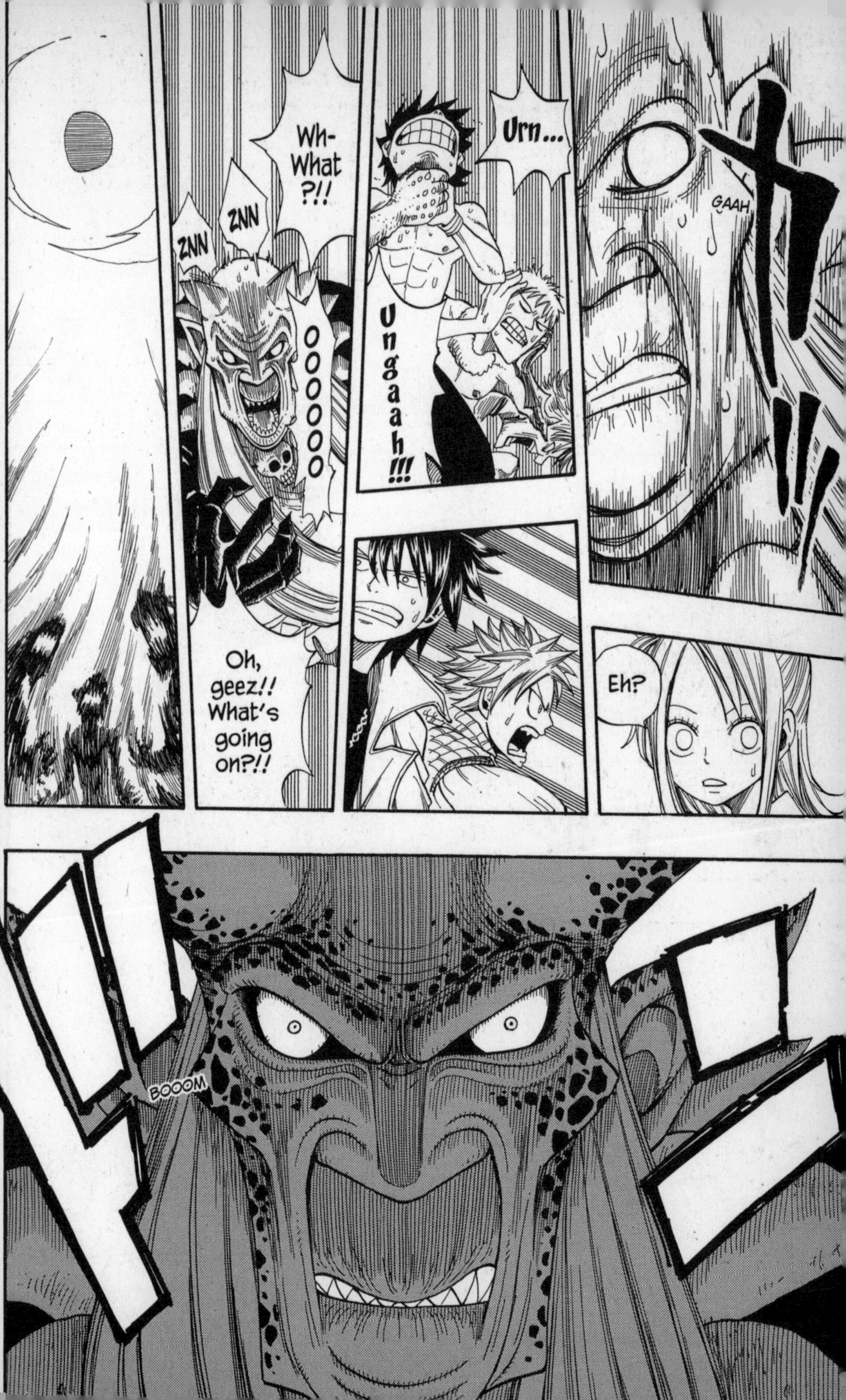
GAAH
Urn...
Ungaah!!!
Wh-What?!!
ZNN
ZNN
OOOOOOO
Eh?
Oh, geez!! What's going on?!!
BOOOM

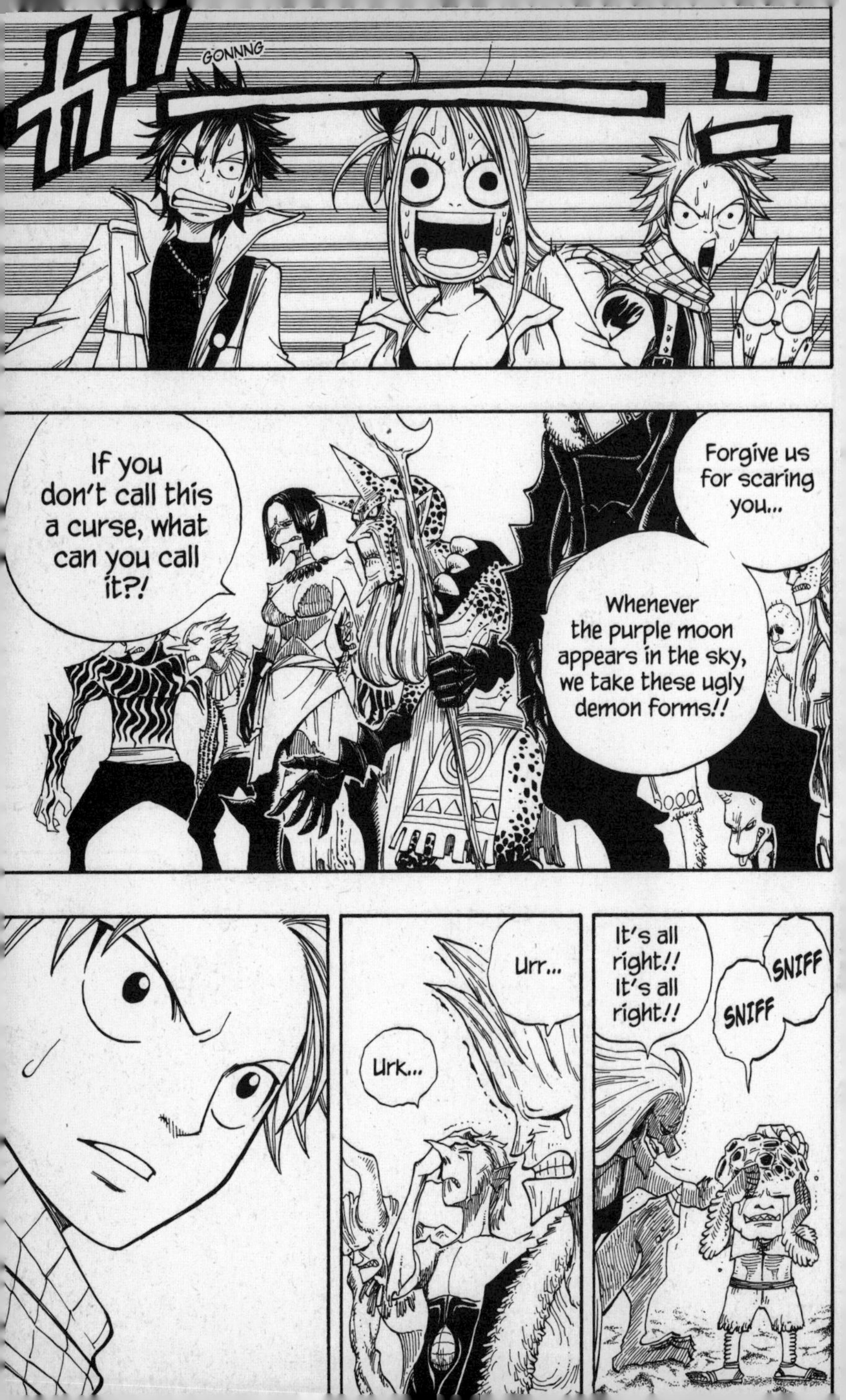
GONNNG
Forgive us for scaring you...
Whenever the purple moon appears in the sky, we take these ugly demon forms!!
If you don't call this a curse, what can you call it?!
SNIFF
SNIFF
It's all right!! It's all right!!
Urr...
Urk...

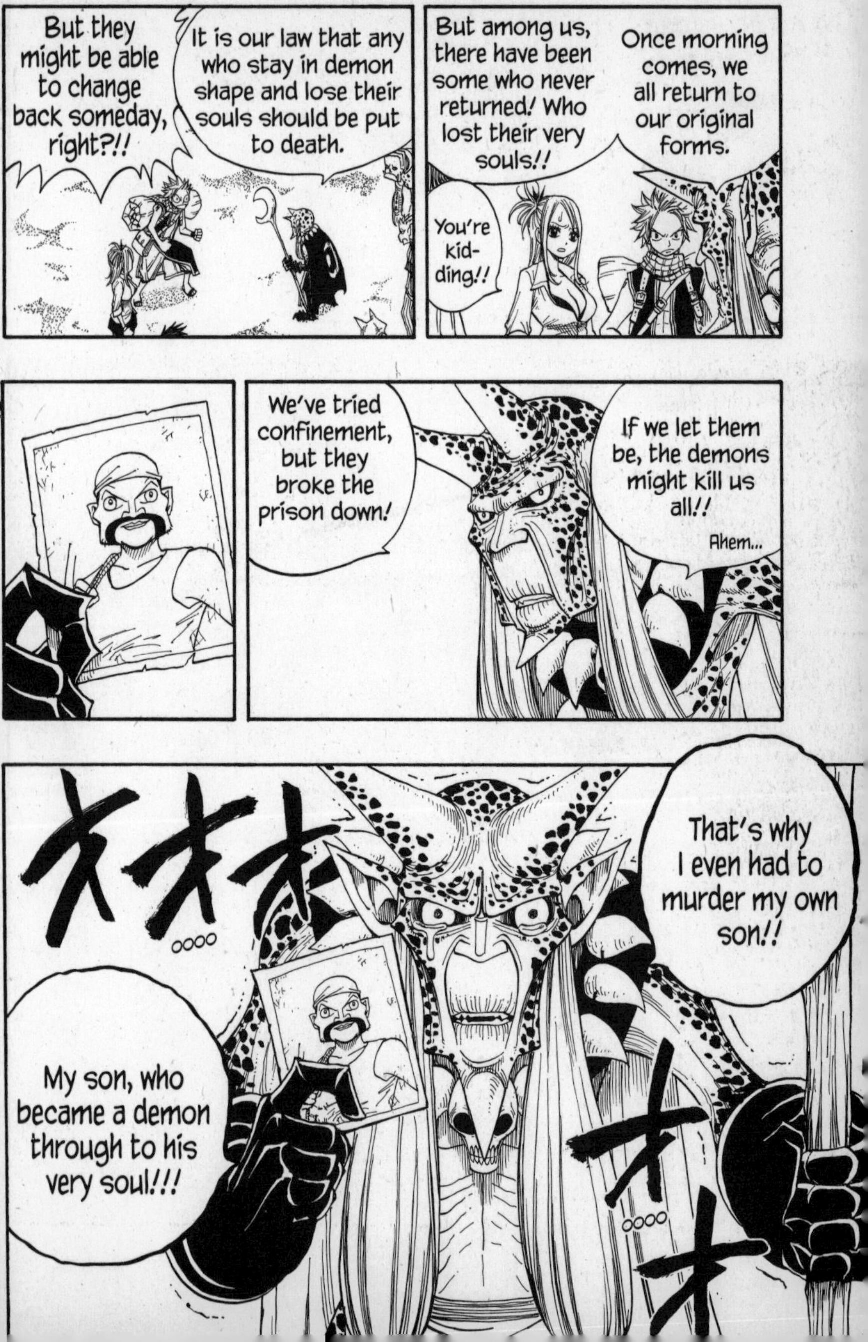
Once morning comes, we all return to our original forms.
But among us, there have been some who never returned! Who lost their very souls!!
You're kidding!!
It is our law that any who stay in demon shape and lose their souls should be put to death.
But they might be able to change back someday, right?!!
If we let them be, the demons might kill us all!!
Ahem...
We've tried confinement, but they broke the prison down!
That's why I even had to murder my own son!!
oooo
My son, who became a demon through to his very soul!!!
oooo

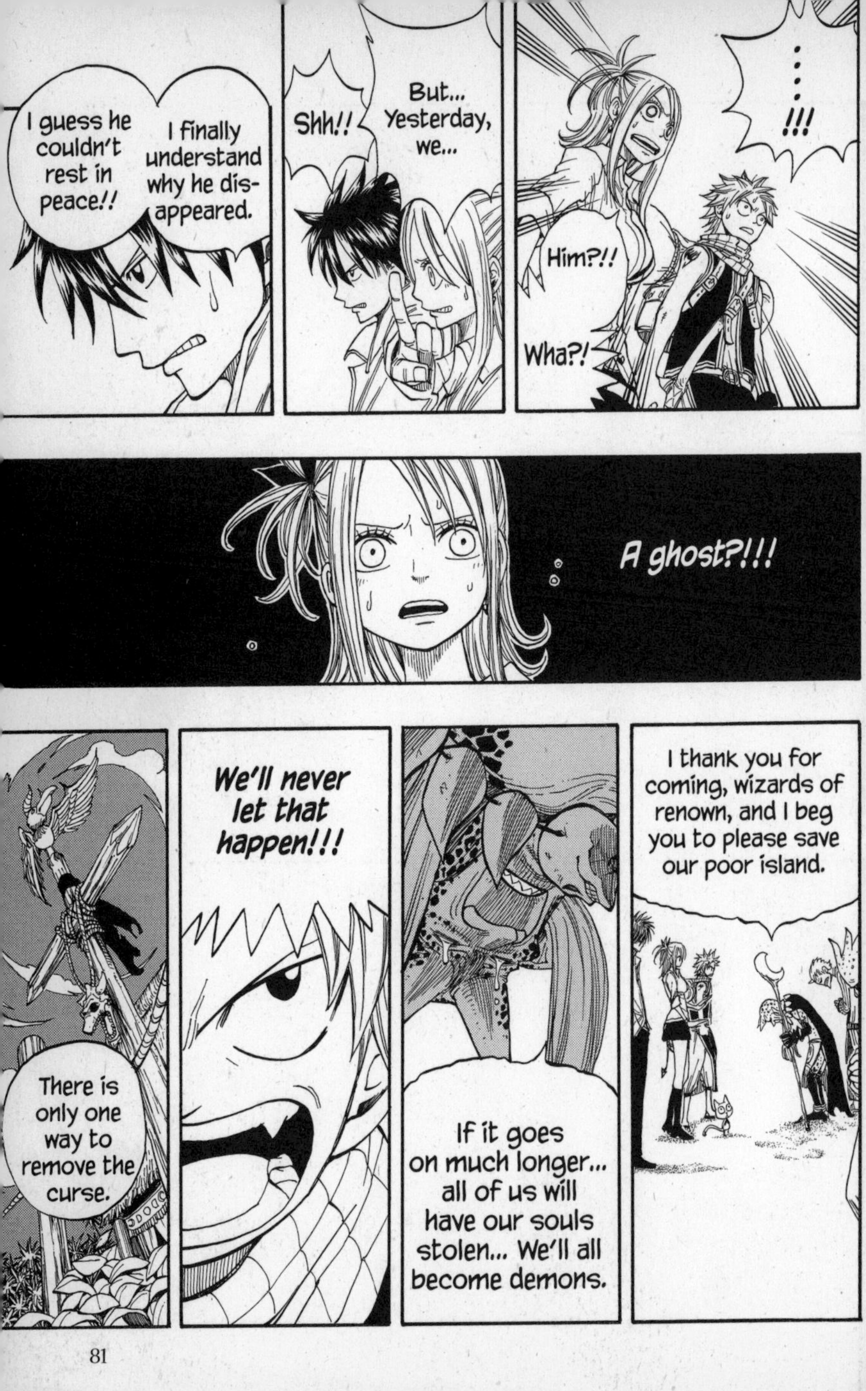

...
!!!
Him?!!
Wha?!
But... Yesterday, we...
Shh!!
I finally understand why he disappeared.
I guess he couldn't rest in peace!!
A ghost?!!!
I thank you for coming, wizards of renown, and I beg you to please save our poor island.
If it goes on much longer... all of us will have our souls stolen... We'll all become demons.
We'll never let that happen!!!
There is only one way to remove the curse.

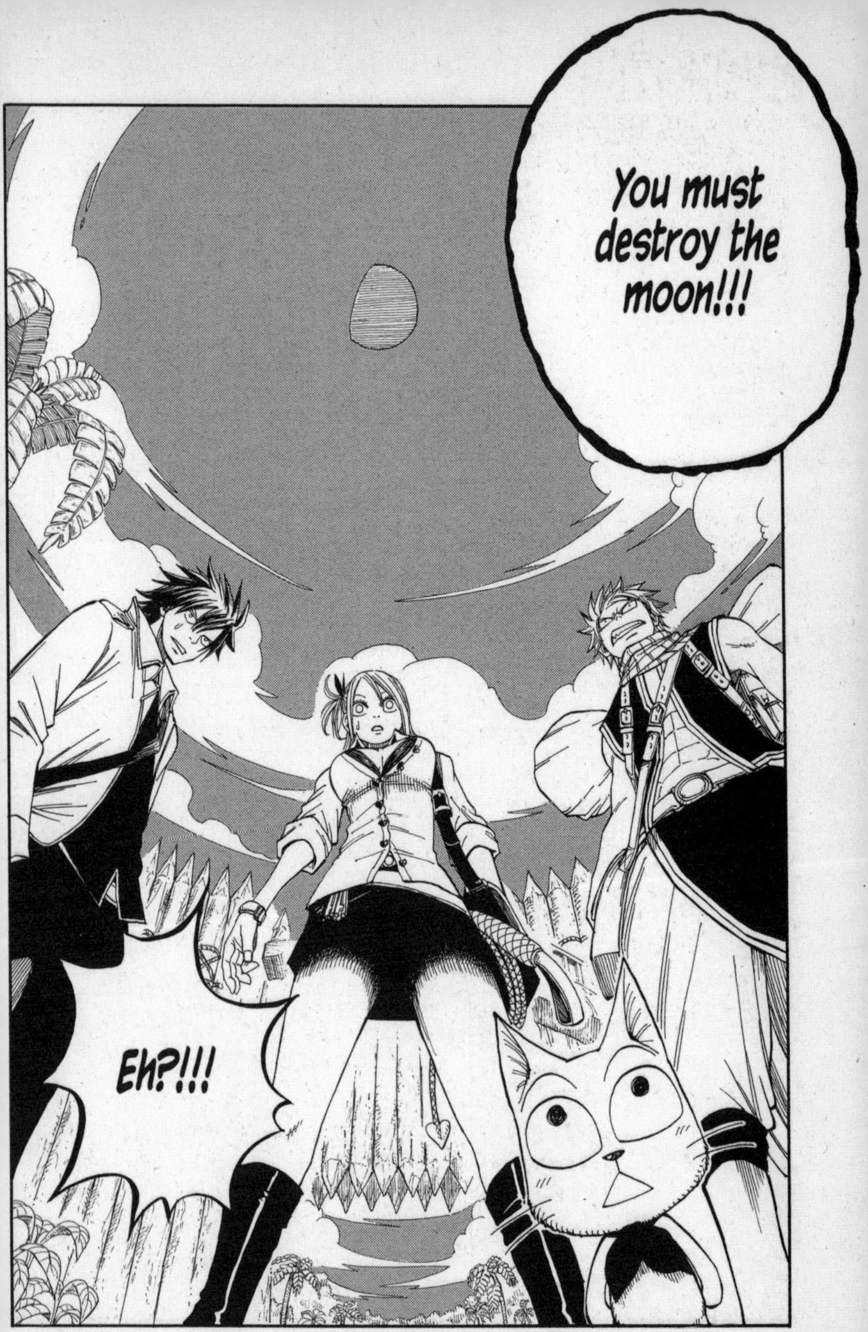
You must destroy the moon!!!
Eh?!!!

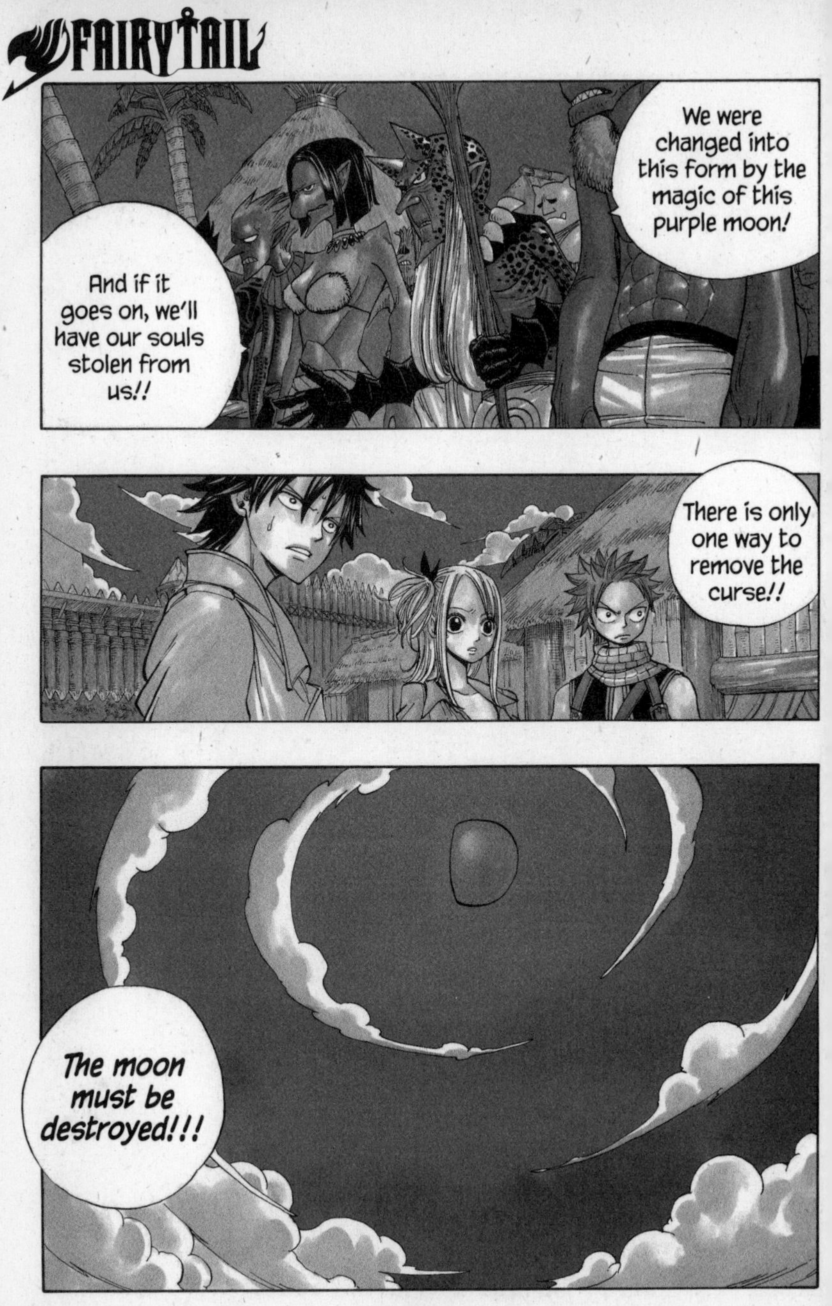
We were changed into this form by the magic of this purple moon!
And if it goes on, we'll have our souls stolen from us!!
There is only one way to remove the curse!!
The moon must be destroyed!!!

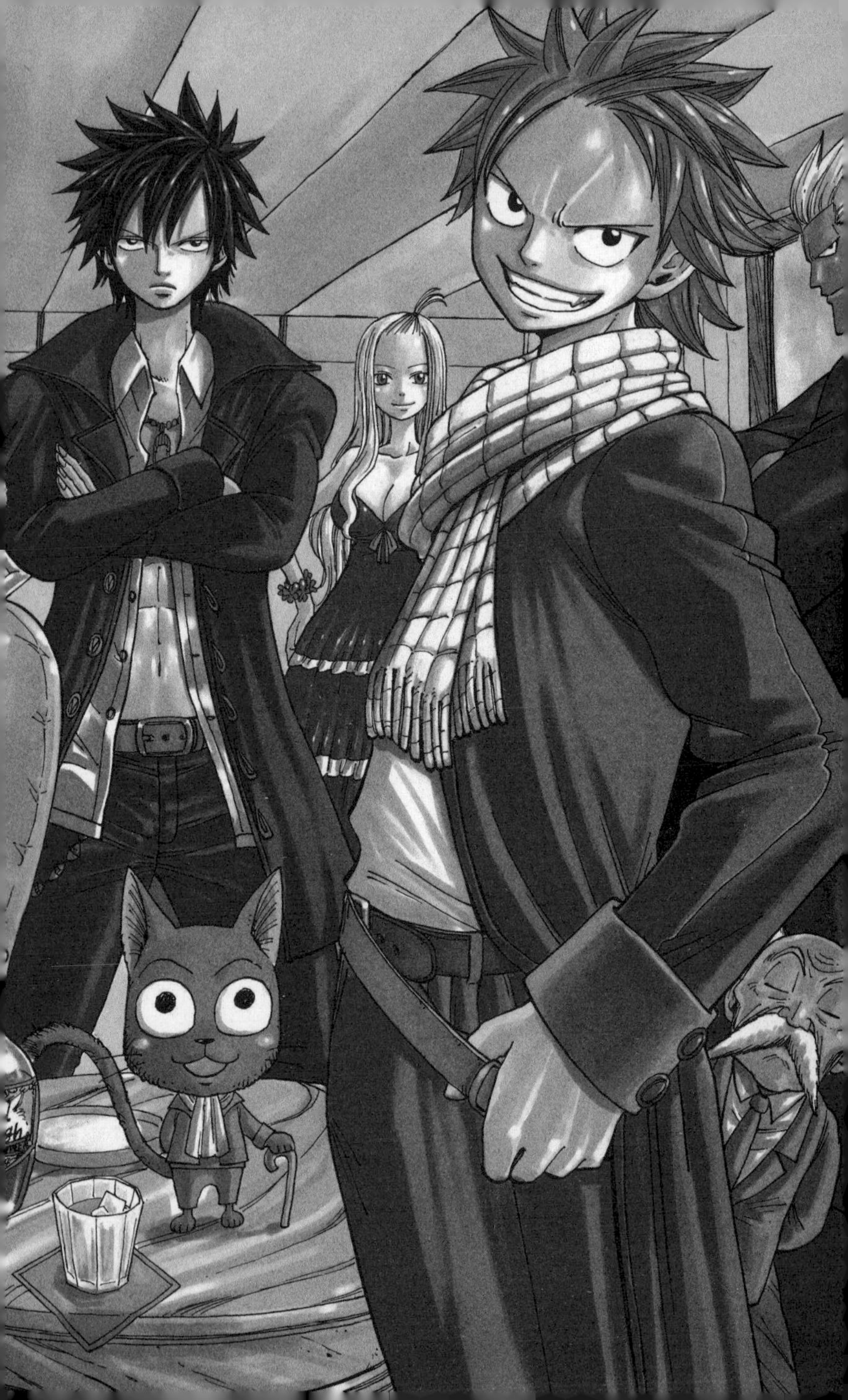

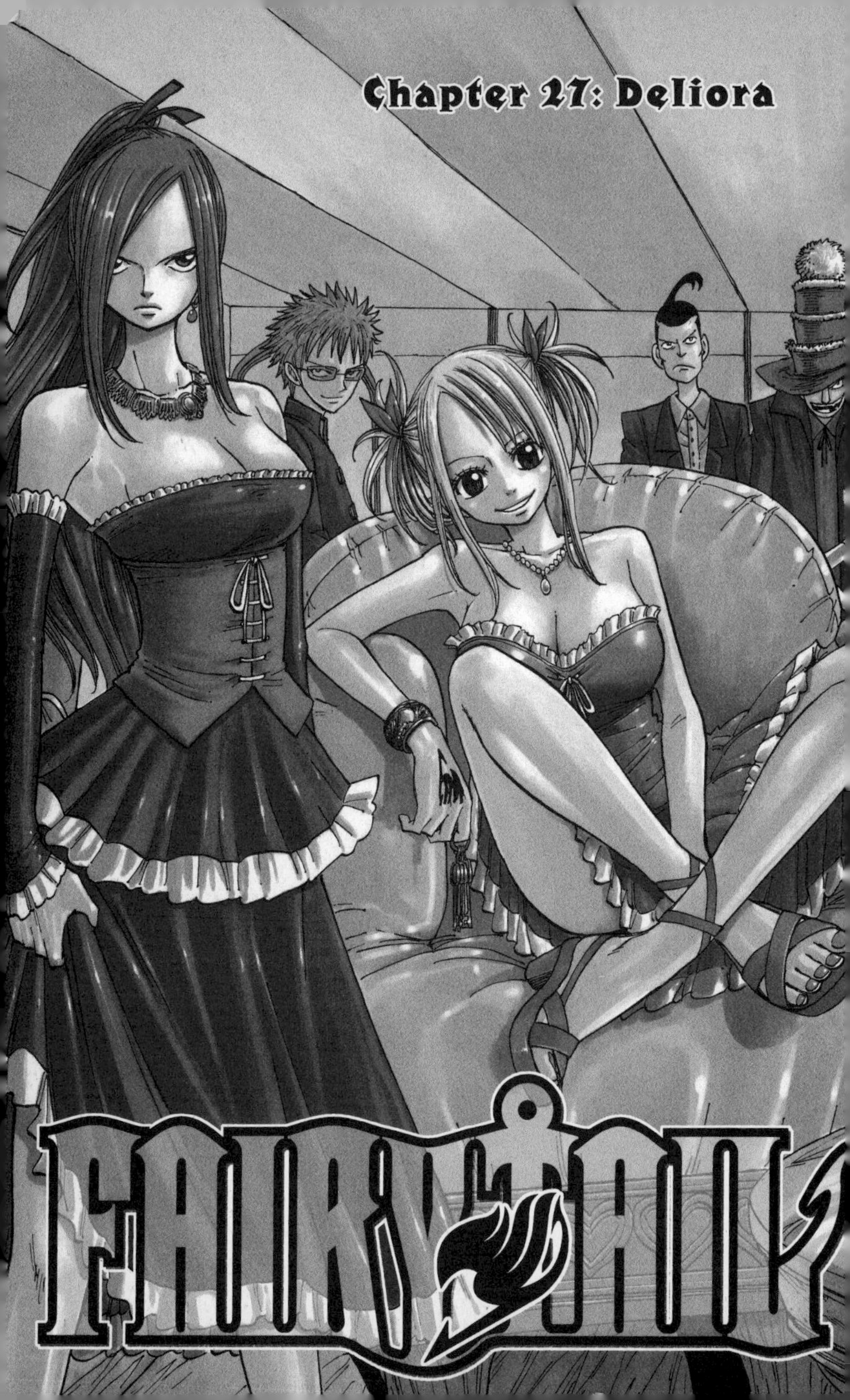

Chapter 27: Deliora
FAIRY TAIL

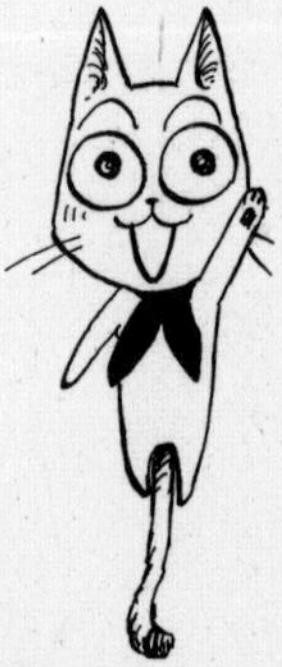

FAIRY TAIL

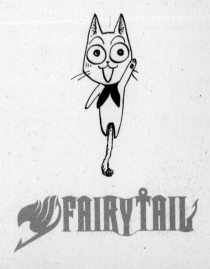

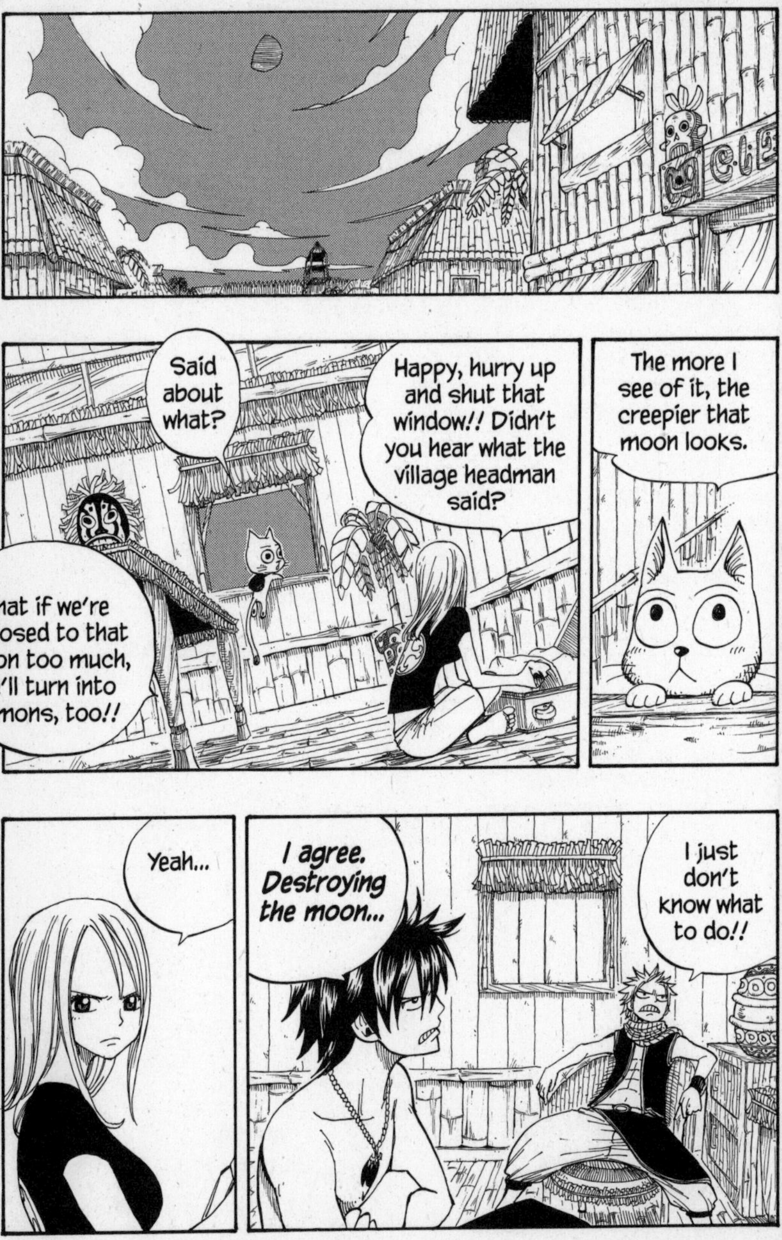
The more I see of it, the creepier that moon looks.
Happy, hurry up and shut that window!! Didn't you hear what the village headman said?
Said about what?
That if we're exposed to that moon too much, we'll turn into demons, too!!
I just don't know what to do!!
I agree. Destroying the moon...
Yeah...

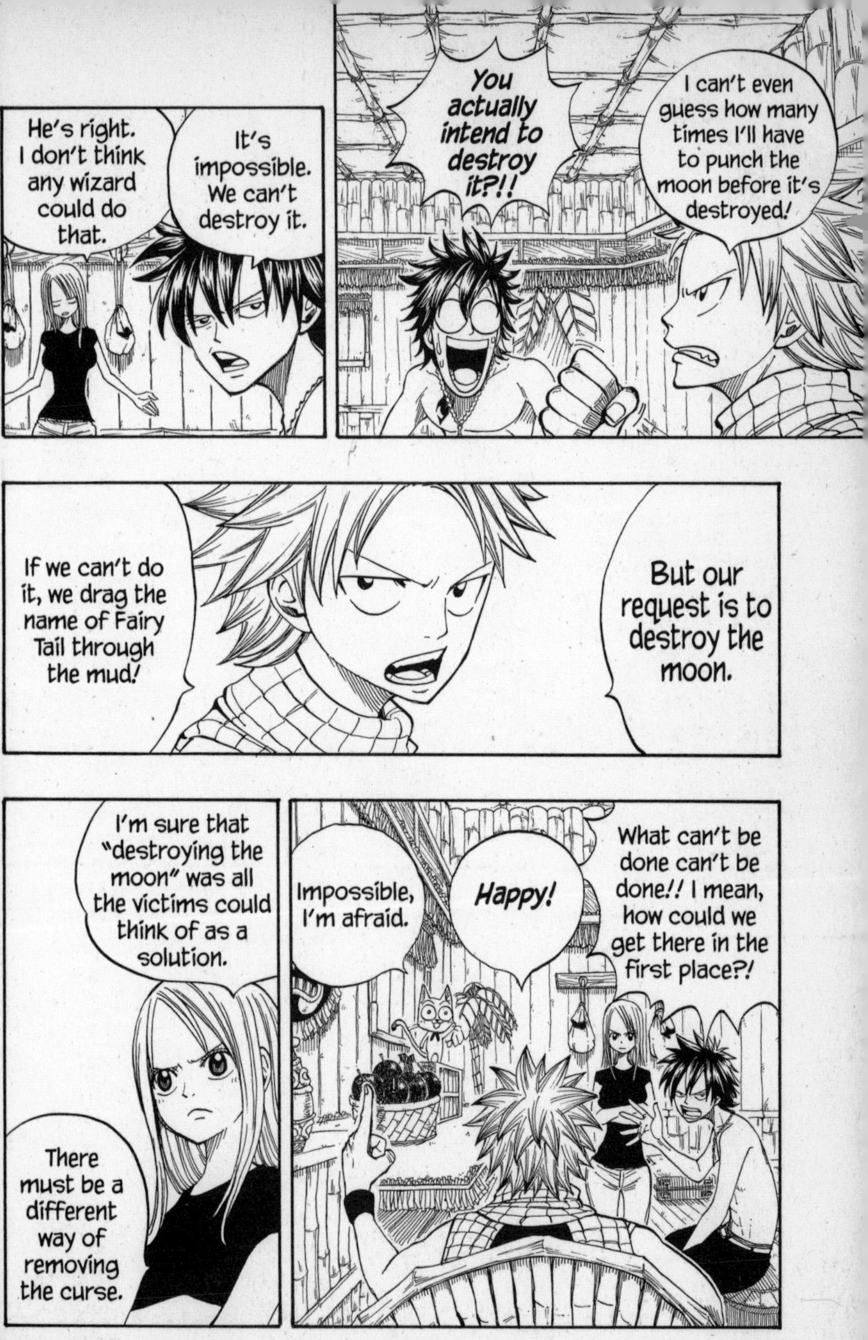

I can't even guess how many times I'll have to punch the moon before it's destroyed!
You actually intend to destroy it?!!
It's impossible. We can't destroy it.
He's right. I don't think any wizard could do that.
But our request is to destroy the moon.
If we can't do it, we drag the name of Fairy Tail through the mud!
What can't be done can't be done!! I mean, how could we get there in the first place?!
Happy!
Impossible, I'm afraid.
I'm sure that "destroying the moon" was all the victims could think of as a solution.
There must be a different way of removing the curse.

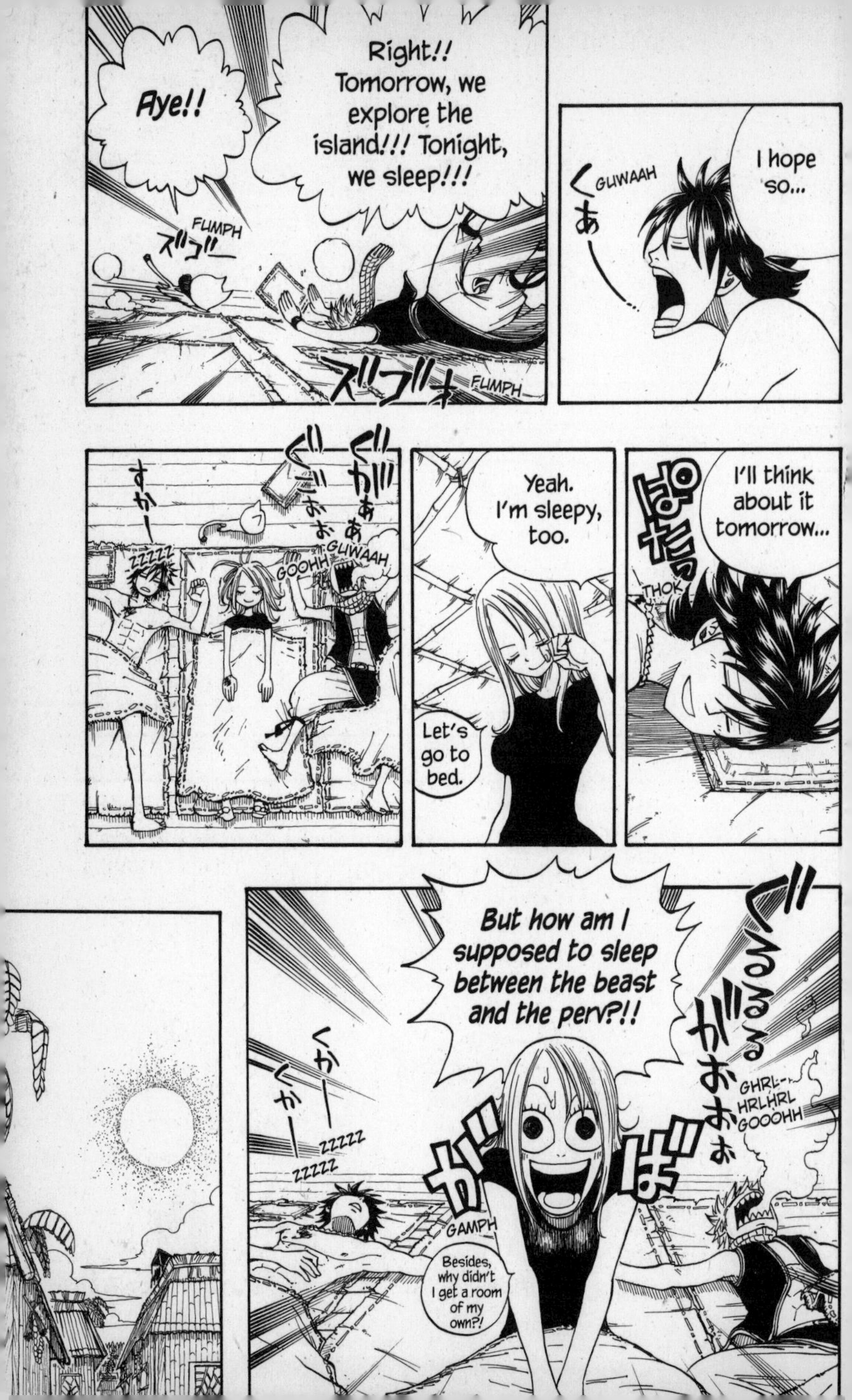
I hope so...
くあー
GUWAAH
Right!! Tomorrow, we explore the island!!! Tonight, we sleep!!!
Aye!!
ズゴー
FUMPH
ズゴオ
FUMPH
I'll think about it tomorrow...
ぽてっ
THOK
Yeah. I'm sleepy, too.
Let's go to bed.
ぐがあああ
GUWAAH
ぐごおお
GOOHH
すかー
zzzzz
But how am I supposed to sleep between the beast and the perv?!!
ぐるるるがおおぉ
GHRL-HRLHRL GOOOHH
くかー
くかー
zzzzz
zzzzz
がばっ
GAMPH
Besides, why didn't I get a room of my own?!

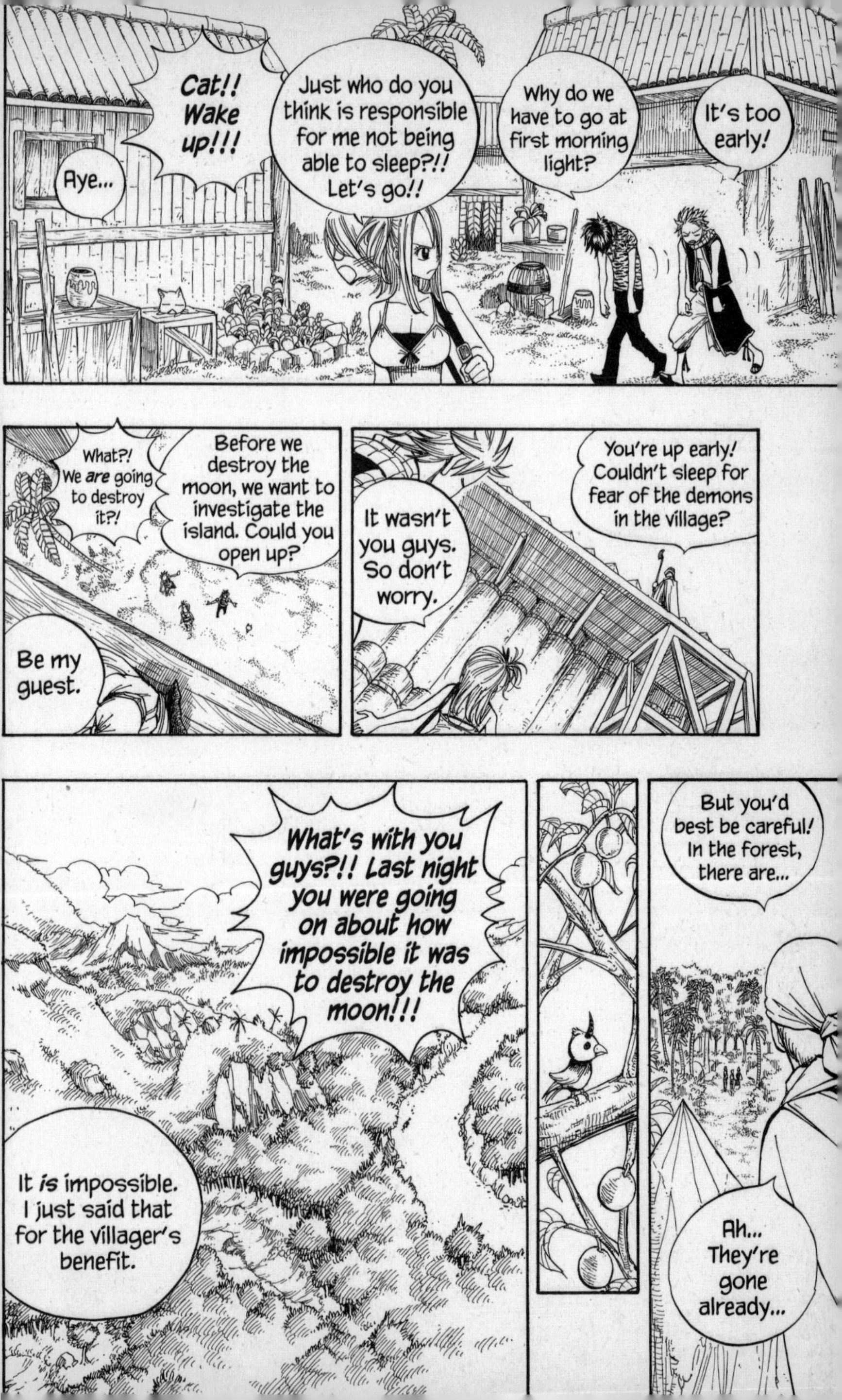
It's too early!
Why do we have to go at first morning light?
Just who do you think is responsible for me not being able to sleep?!! Let's go!!
Cat!! Wake up!!!
Aye...
You're up early! Couldn't sleep for fear of the demons in the village?
It wasn't you guys. So don't worry.
Before we destroy the moon, we want to investigate the island. Could you open up?
What?! We *are* going to destroy it?!
Be my guest.
But you'd best be careful! In the forest, there are...
Ah... They're gone already...
What's with you guys?!! Last night you were going on about how impossible it was to destroy the moon!!!
It *is* impossible. I just said that for the villager's benefit.

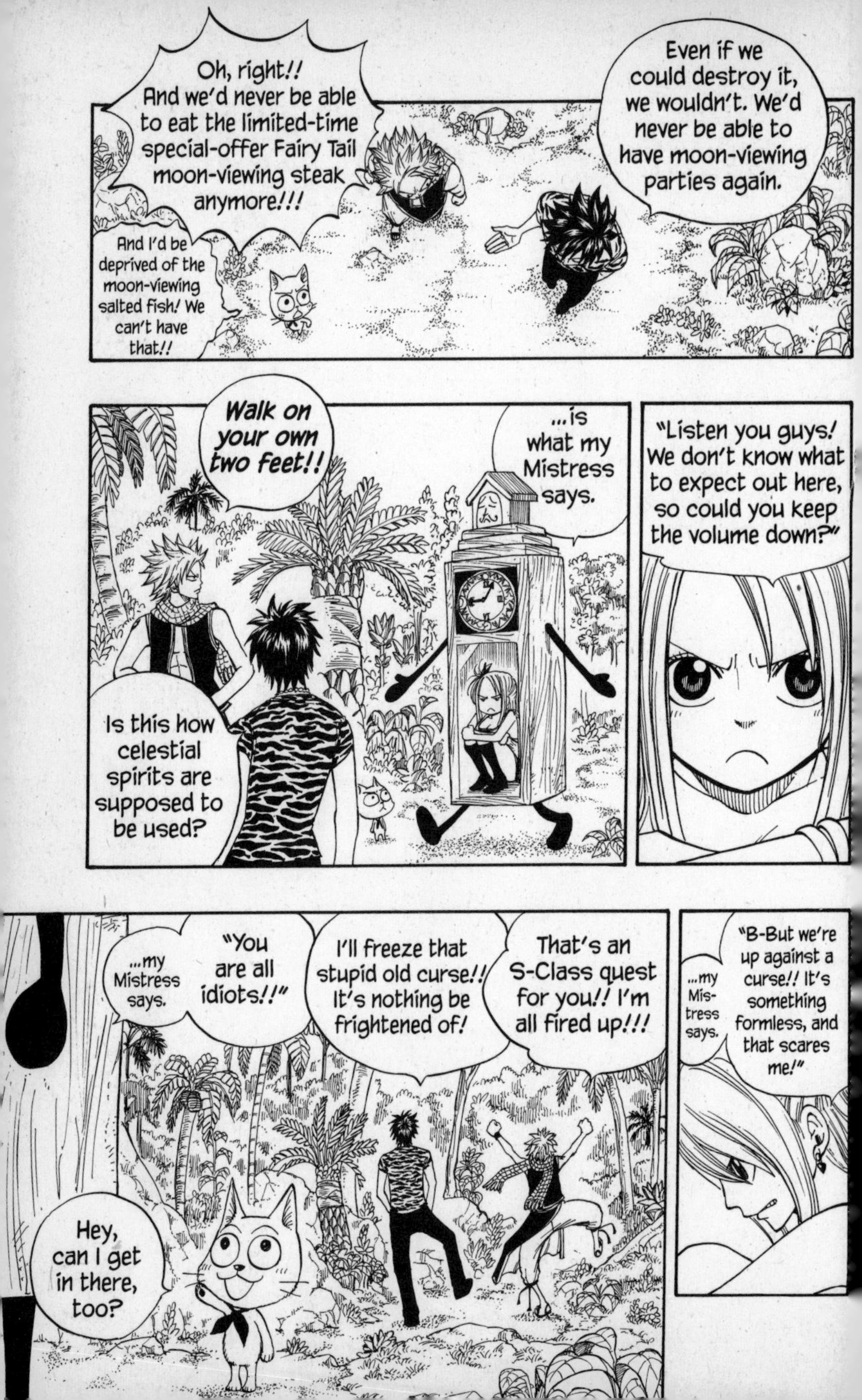

Even if we could destroy it, we wouldn't. We'd never be able to have moon-viewing parties again.
Oh, right!! And we'd never be able to eat the limited-time special-offer Fairy Tail moon-viewing steak anymore!!!
And I'd be deprived of the moon-viewing salted fish! We can't have that!!
"Listen you guys! We don't know what to expect out here, so could you keep the volume down?"
...is what my Mistress says.
Walk on your own two feet!!
Is this how celestial spirits are supposed to be used?
"B-But we're up against a curse!! It's something formless, and that scares me!"
...my Mistress says.
That's an S-Class quest for you!! I'm all fired up!!!
I'll freeze that stupid old curse!! It's nothing be frightened of!
"You are all idiots!!"
...my Mistress says.
Hey, can I get in there, too?

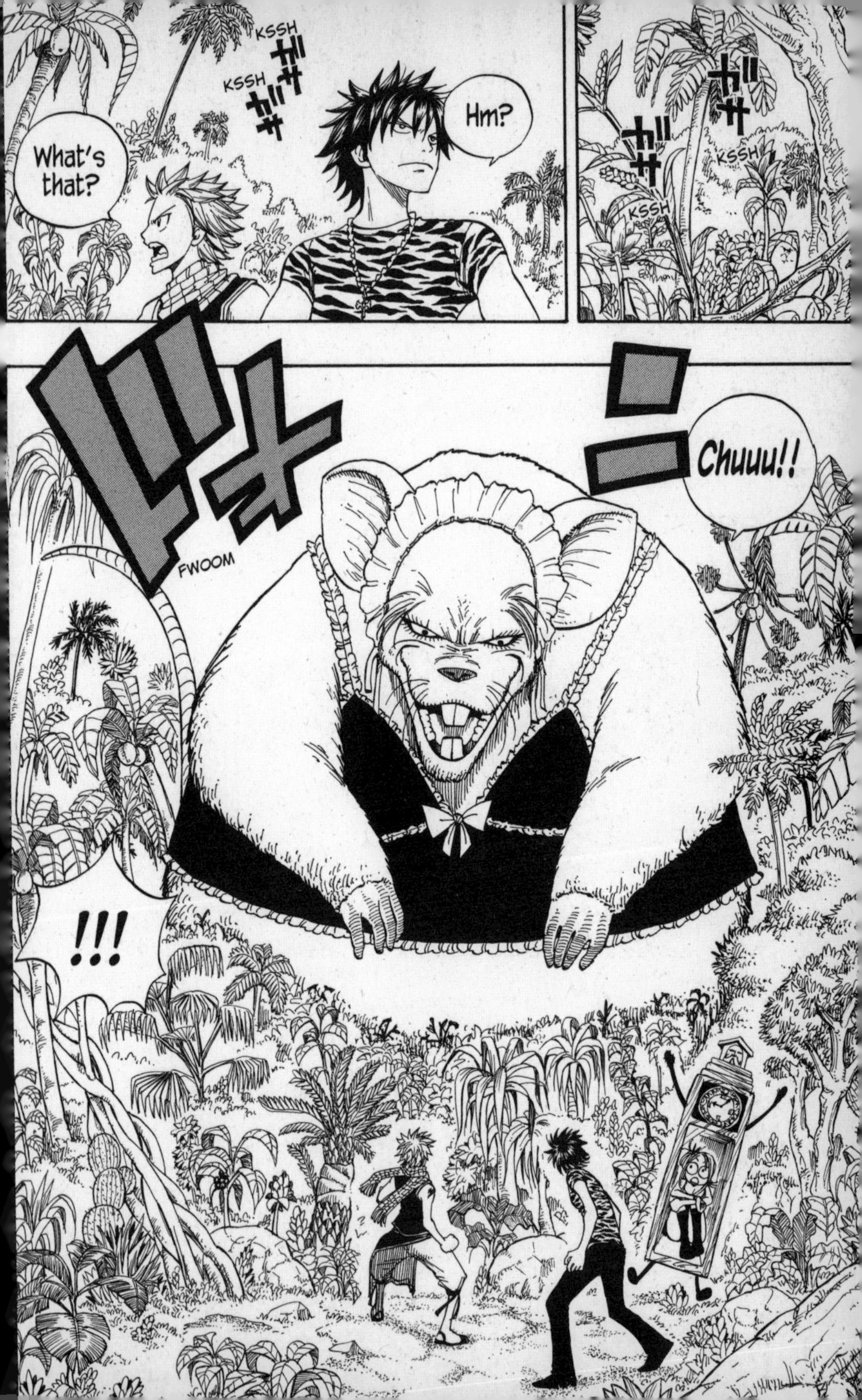

ガサ
ガサ
KSSH
KSSH
ガサ
ガサ
KSSH
KSSH
Hm?
What's that?
Chuuu!!
ドォン
FWOOM
!!!

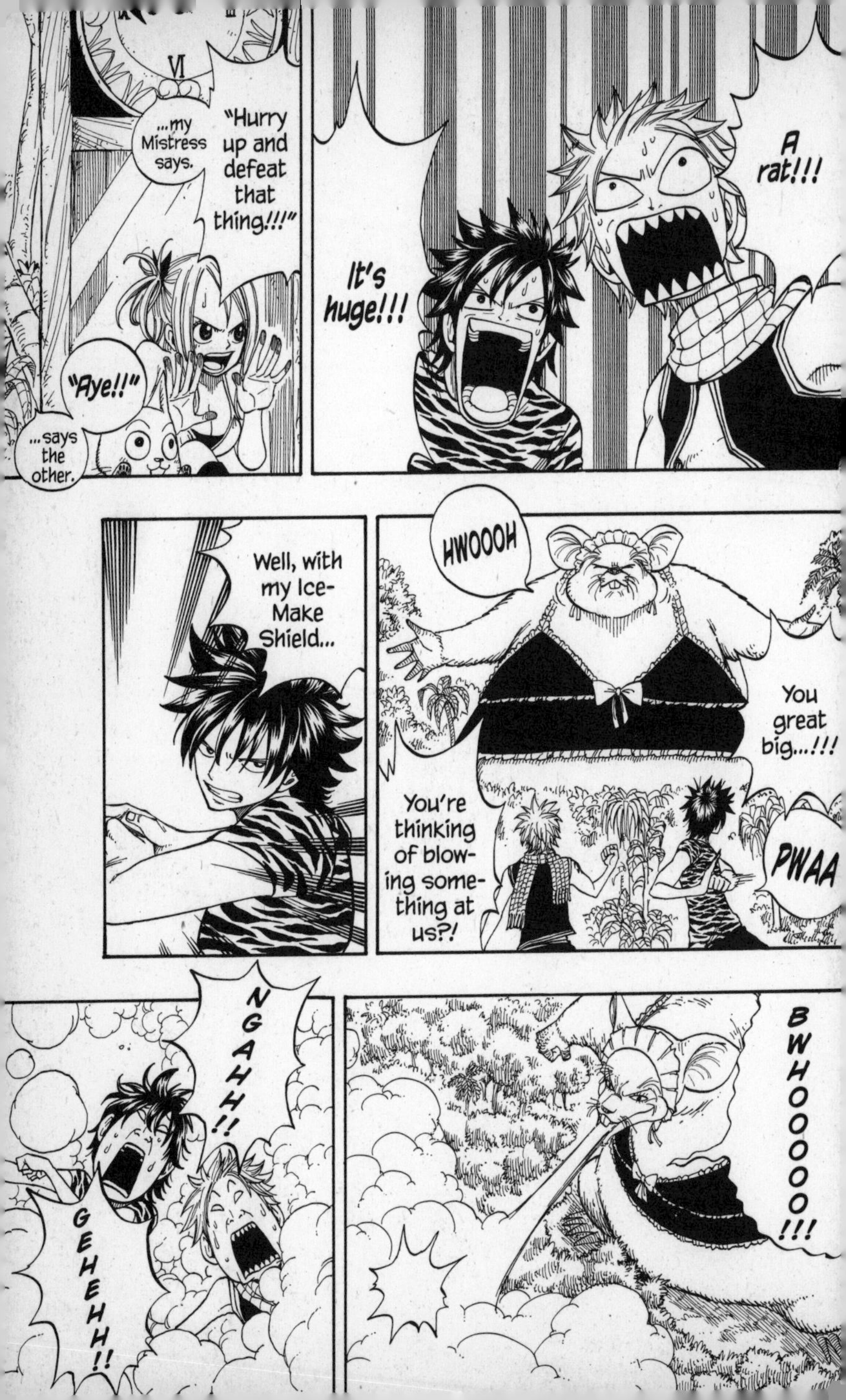
A rat!!!
It's huge!!!
"Hurry up and defeat that thing!!!"
...my Mistress says.
"Aye!!"
...says the other.
HWOOOH
You great big...!!!
You're thinking of blowing something at us?!
PWAA
Well, with my Ice-Make Shield...
BWHOOOOOOO!!!
NGAHH!!
GEHEHH!!

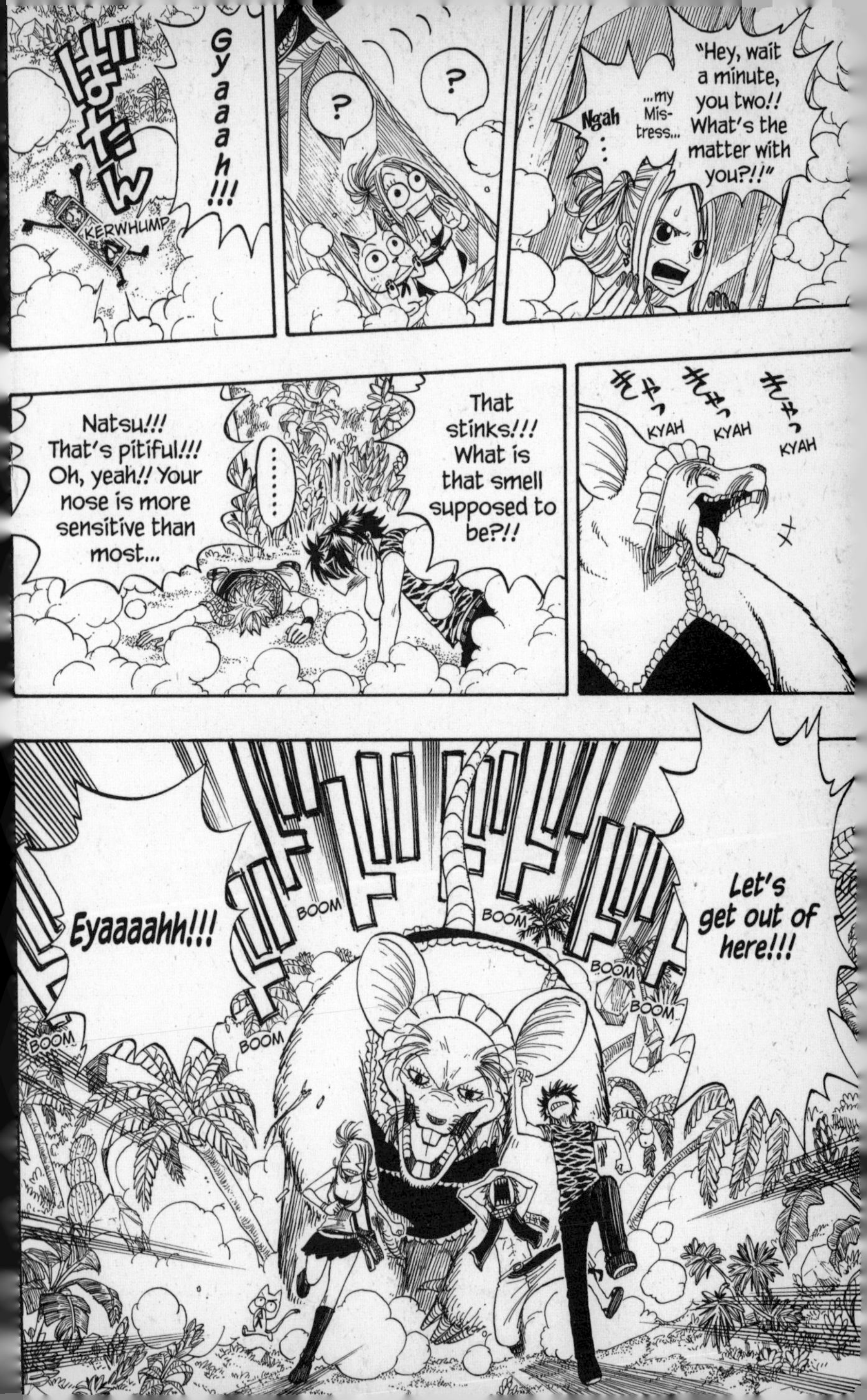
"Hey, wait a minute, you two!! What's the matter with you?!!"
...my Mistress...
Ngah...
?
?
Gyaaaah!!!
KERWHUMP
きゃっ KYAH
きゃっ KYAH
きゃっ KYAH
That stinks!!! What is that smell supposed to be?!!
......
Natsu!!! That's pitiful!!! Oh, yeah!! Your nose is more sensitive than most...
Let's get out of here!!!
BOOM
BOOM
BOOM
BOOM
Eyaaaaahh!!!
BOOM
BOOM

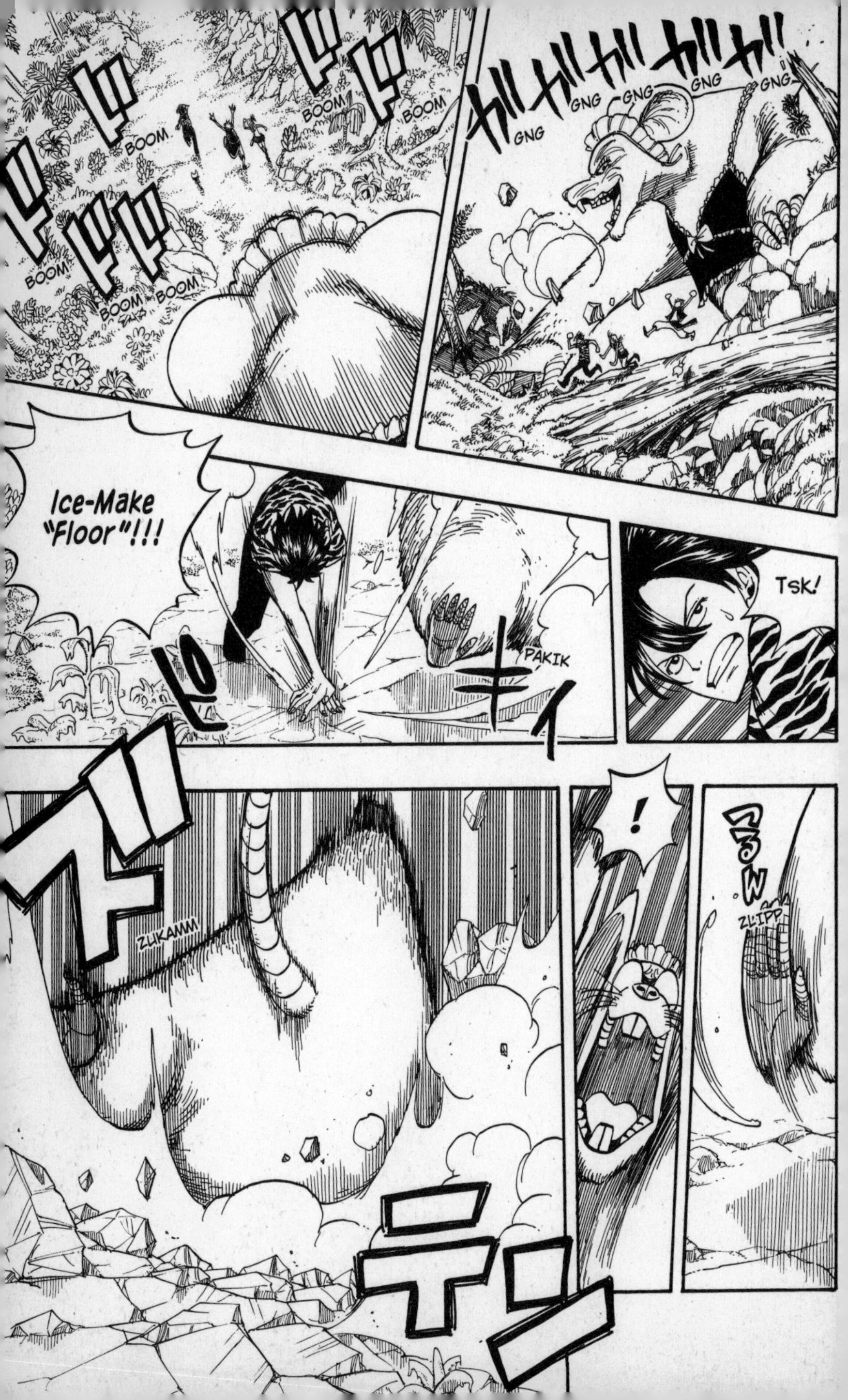
GNG GNG GNG GNG GNG
BOOM BOOM BOOM BOOM BOOM BOOM
Tsk!
Ice-Make "Floor"!!!
PAKIK
ZLIPP
!
ZUKAMM

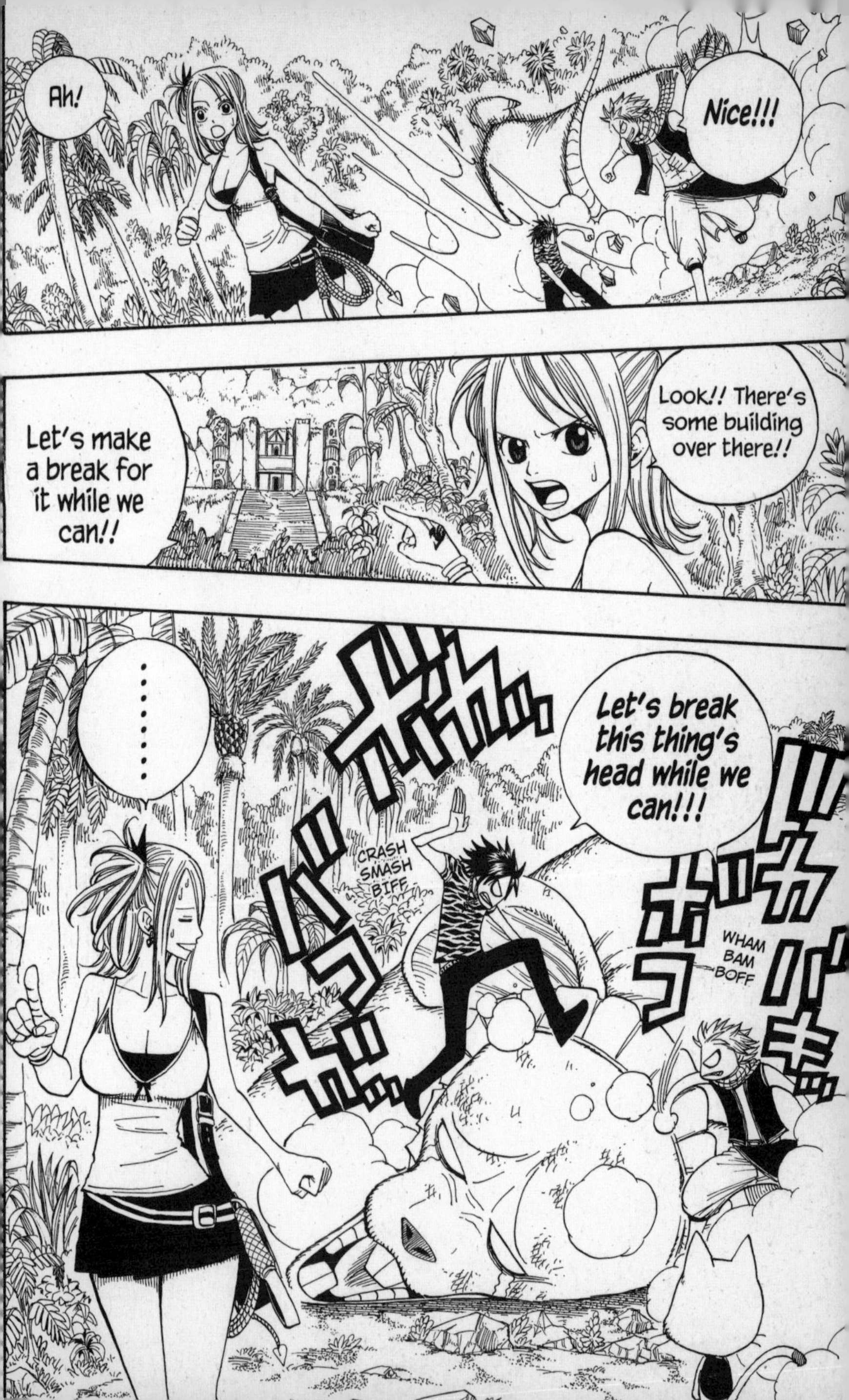

Nice!!!
Ah!
Look!! There's some building over there!!
Let's make a break for it while we can!!
Let's break this thing's head while we can!!!
WHAM BAM BOFF
CRASH SMASH BIFF
......

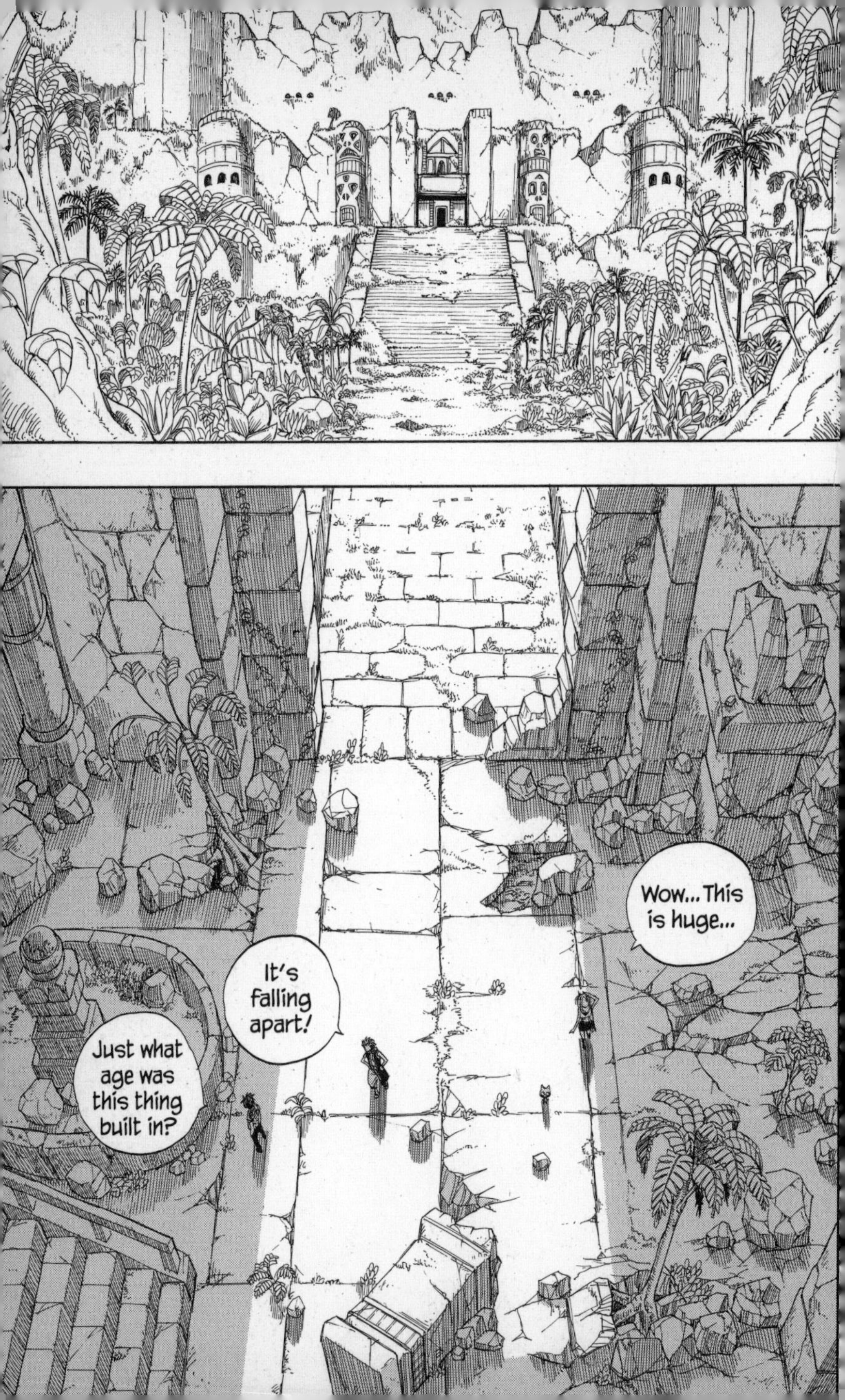
Wow... This is huge...
It's falling apart!
Just what age was this thing built in?

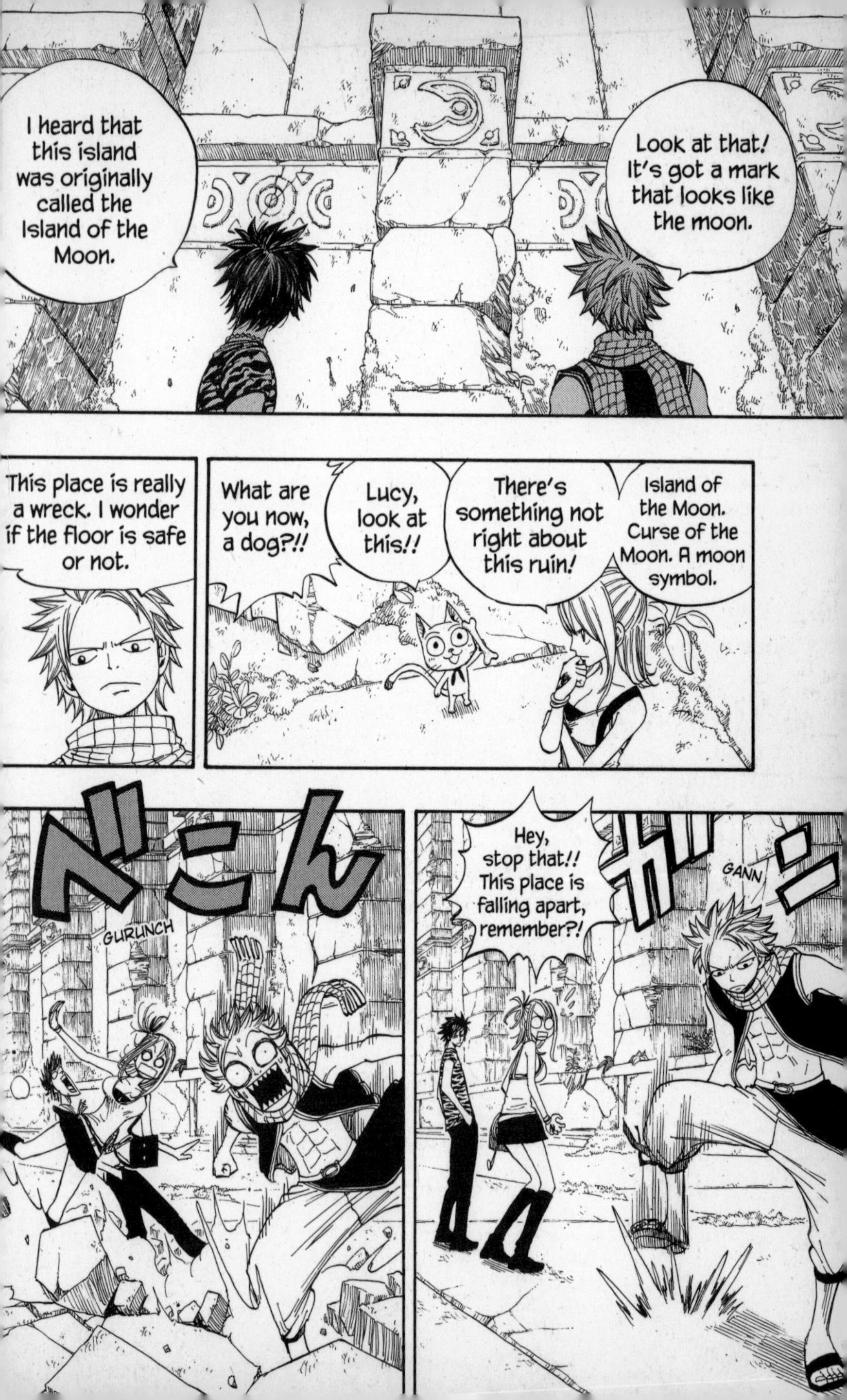

Look at that! It's got a mark that looks like the moon.
I heard that this island was originally called the Island of the Moon.
Island of the Moon. Curse of the Moon. A moon symbol.
There's something not right about this ruin!
Lucy, look at this!!
What are you now, a dog?!!
This place is really a wreck. I wonder if the floor is safe or not.
GANN
Hey, stop that!! This place is falling apart, remember?!
GURUNCH

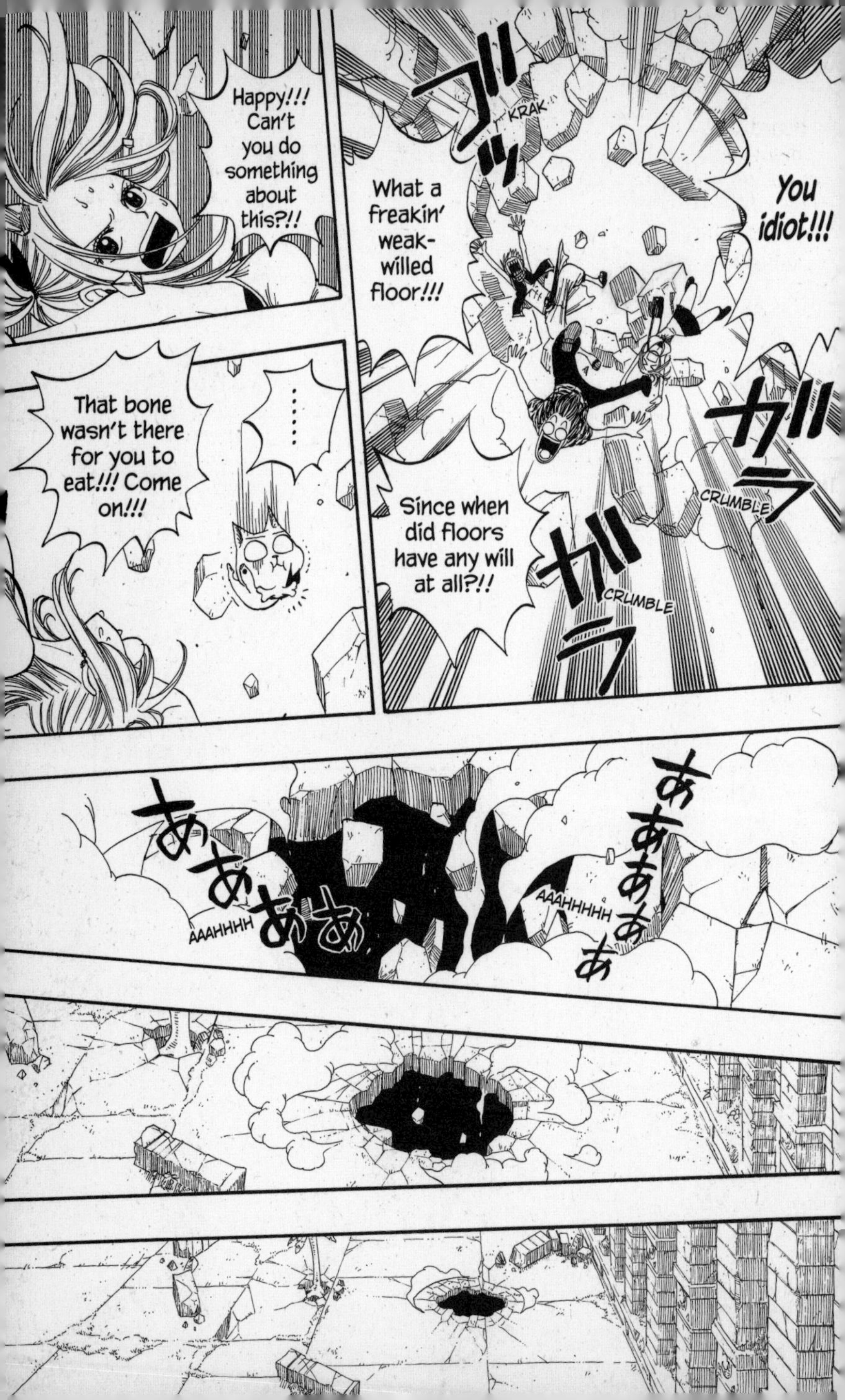
You idiot!!!
KRAK
What a freakin' weak-willed floor!!!
Since when did floors have any will at all?!!
CRUMBLE
CRUMBLE
Happy!!! Can't you do something about this?!!
......
That bone wasn't there for you to eat!!! Come on!!!
AAAHHHHHH
AAAHHHH

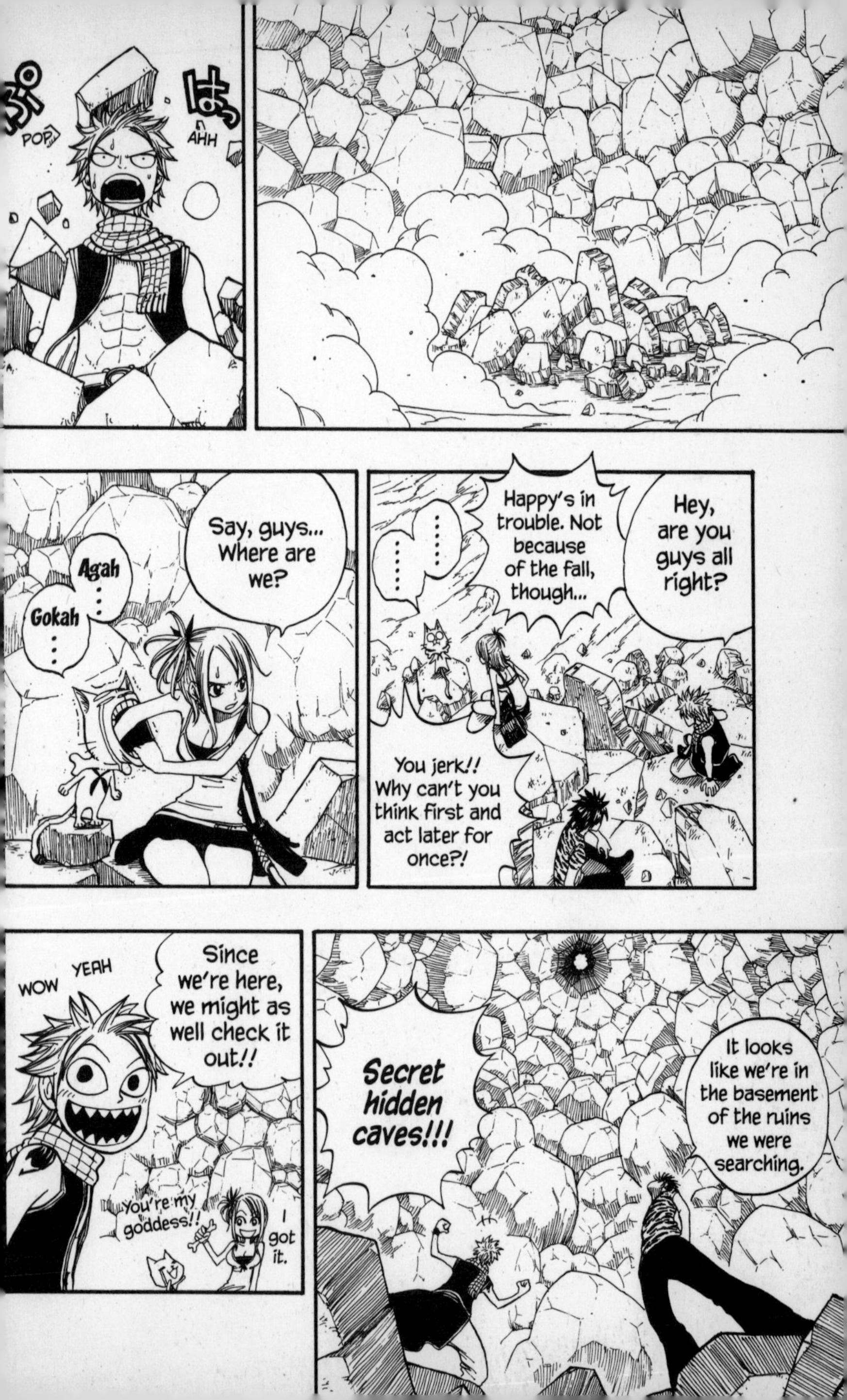
はっ
AHH
ぷ
POP
Hey, are you guys all right?
Happy's in trouble. Not because of the fall, though...
......
......
You jerk!! Why can't you think first and act later for once?!
Say, guys... Where are we?
Agah...
Gokah...
It looks like we're in the basement of the ruins we were searching.
Secret hidden caves!!!
Since we're here, we might as well check it out!!
YEAH
WOW
I got it.
You're my goddess!!

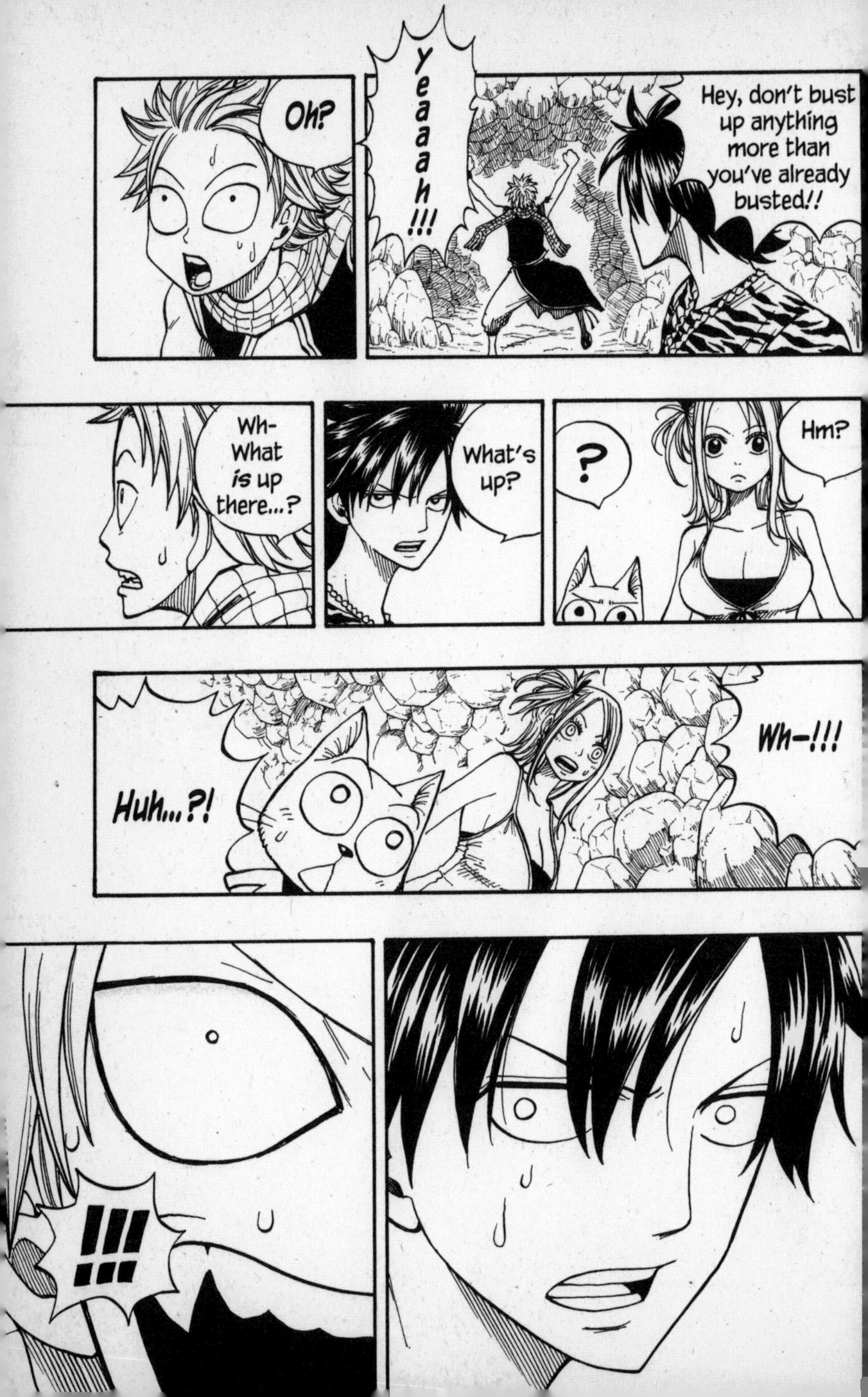
Oh?
Yeaaaah!!!
Hey, don't bust up anything more than you've already busted!!
Wh- What is up there...?
What's up?
?
Hm?
Huh...?!
Wh-!!!
!!!

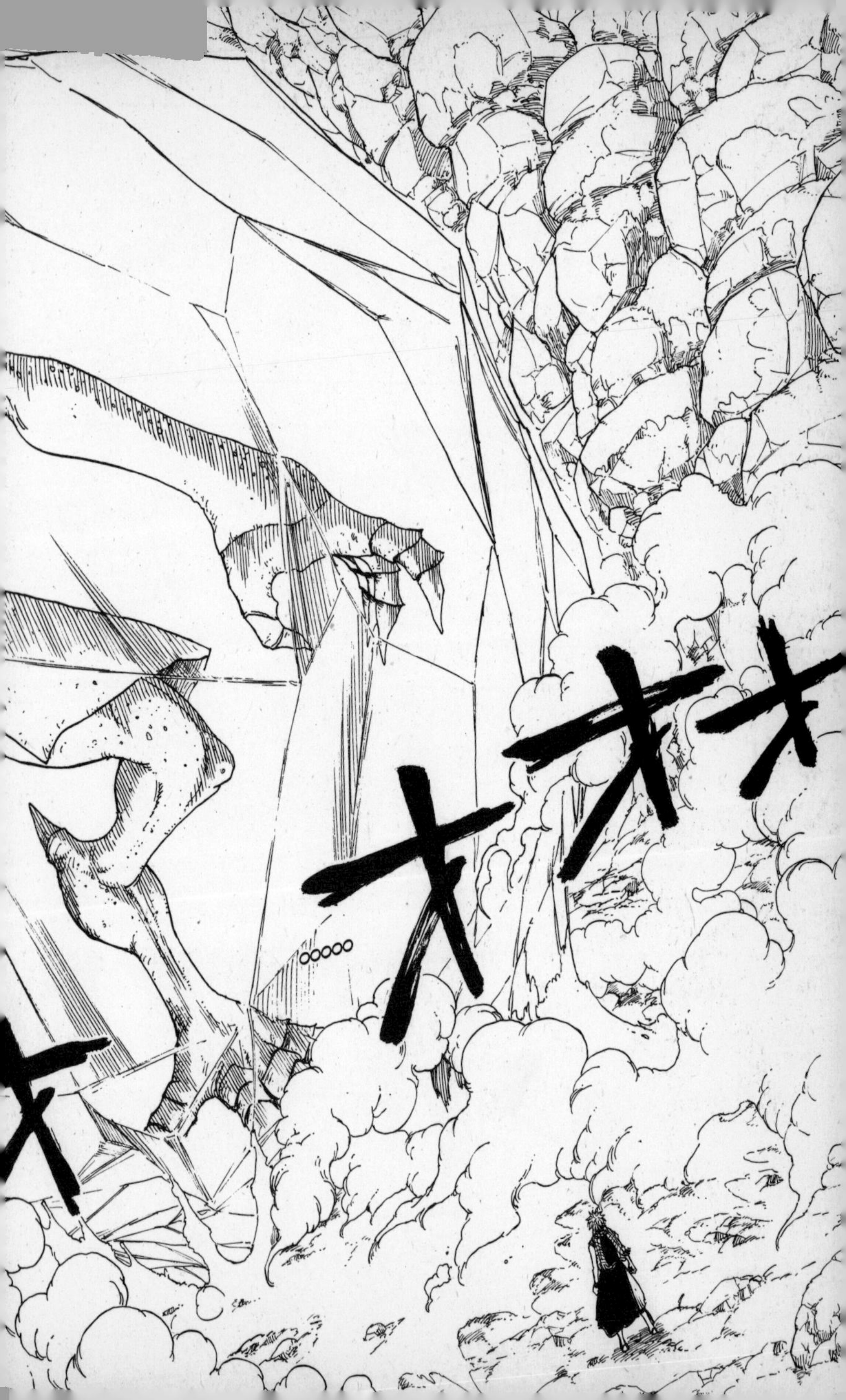
OOOOO

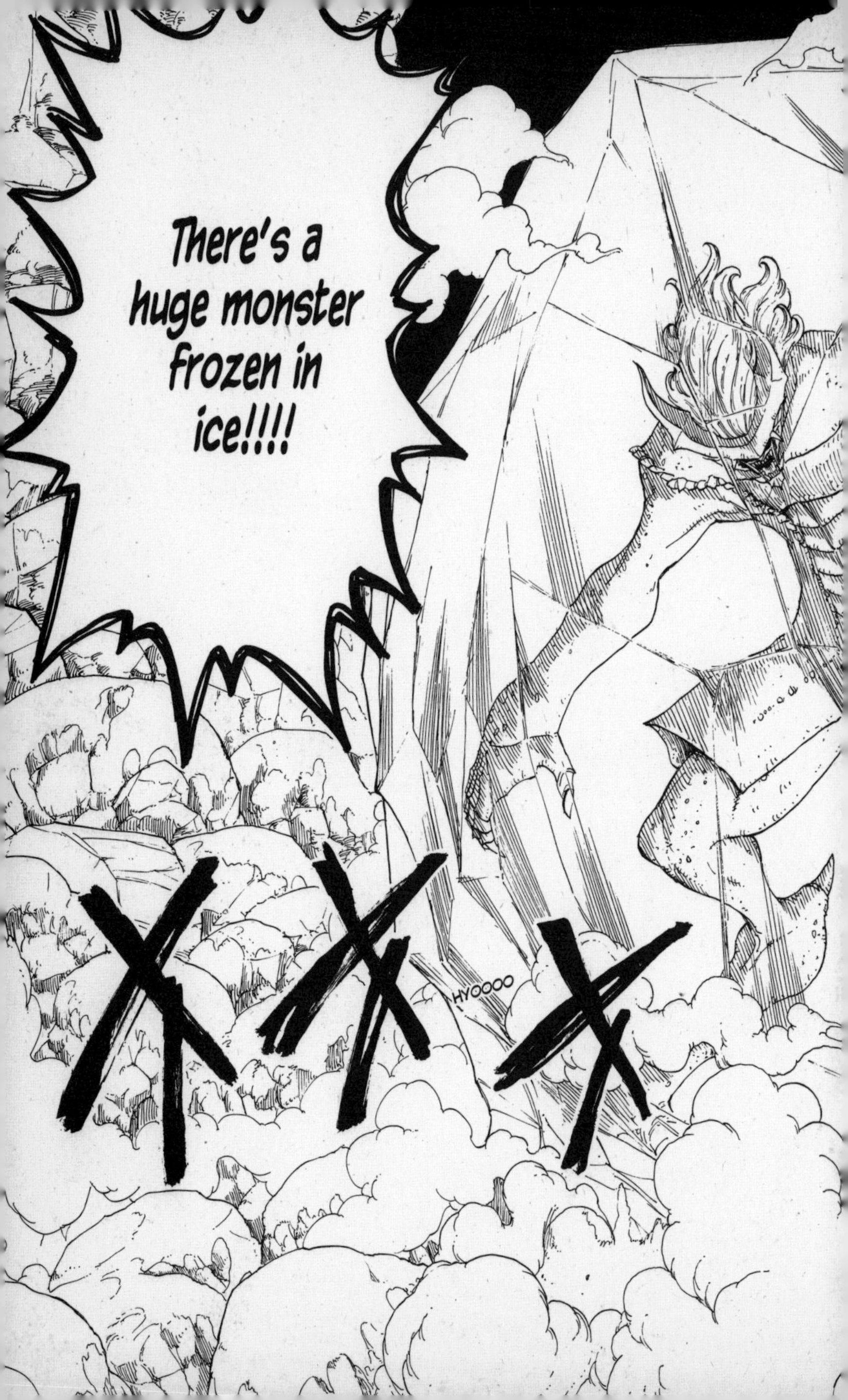
There's a huge monster frozen in ice!!!!
HYOOOO

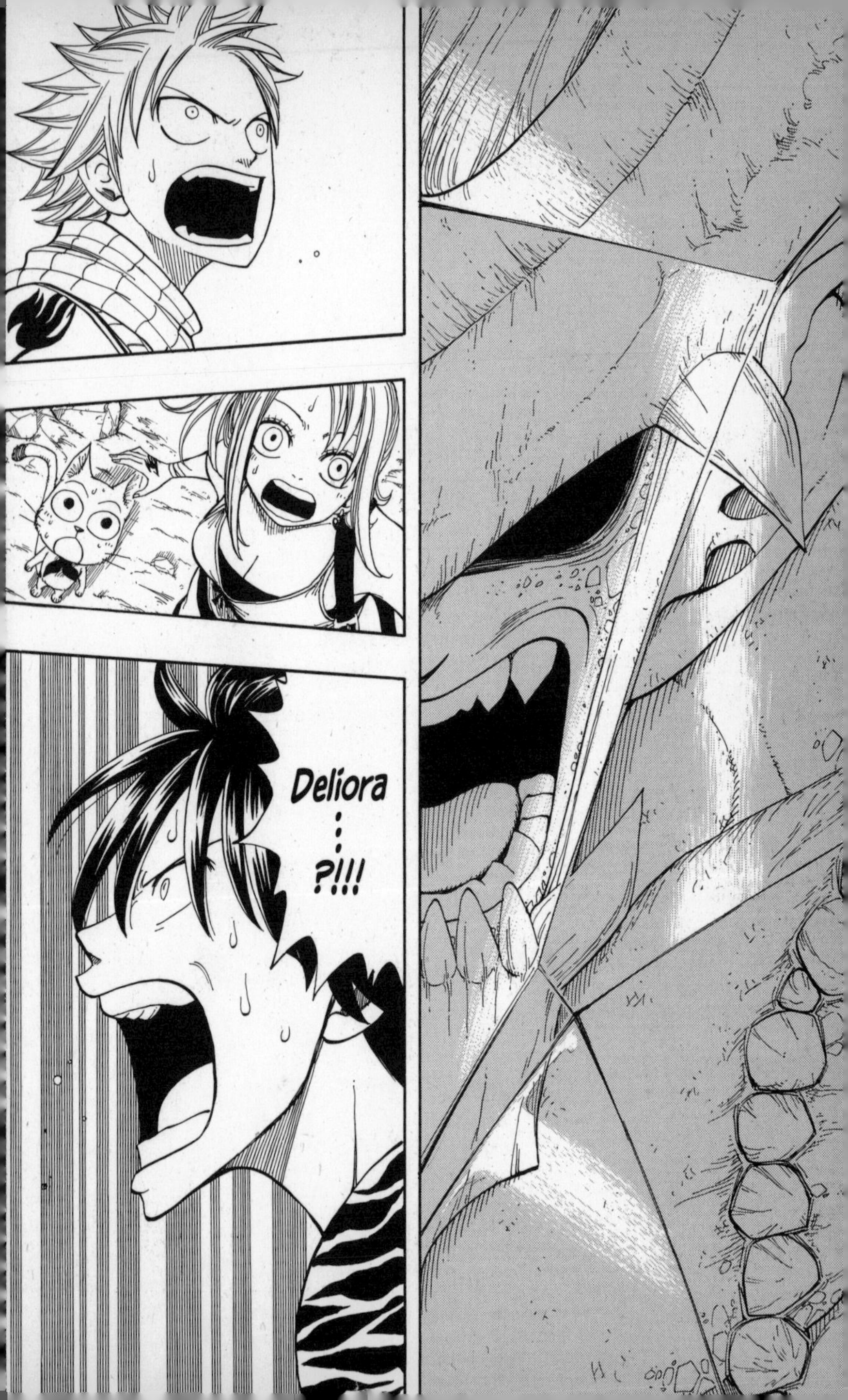
Deliora
...?!!!

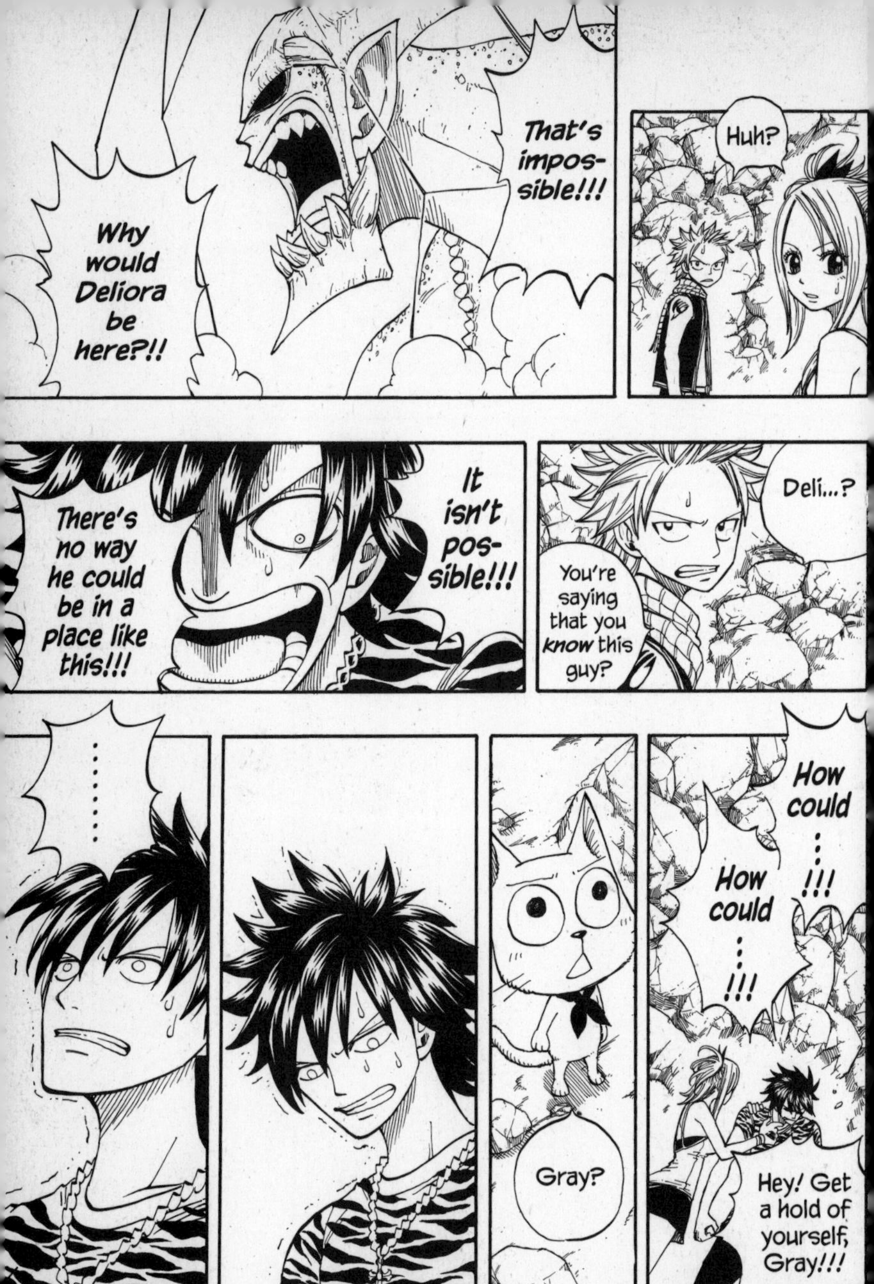

Huh?
That's impossible!!!
Why would Deliora be here?!!
Deli...?
You're saying that you *know* this guy?
It isn't possible!!!
There's no way he could be in a place like this!!!
How could...!!!
How could...!!!
Hey! Get a hold of yourself, Gray!!!
Gray?
......

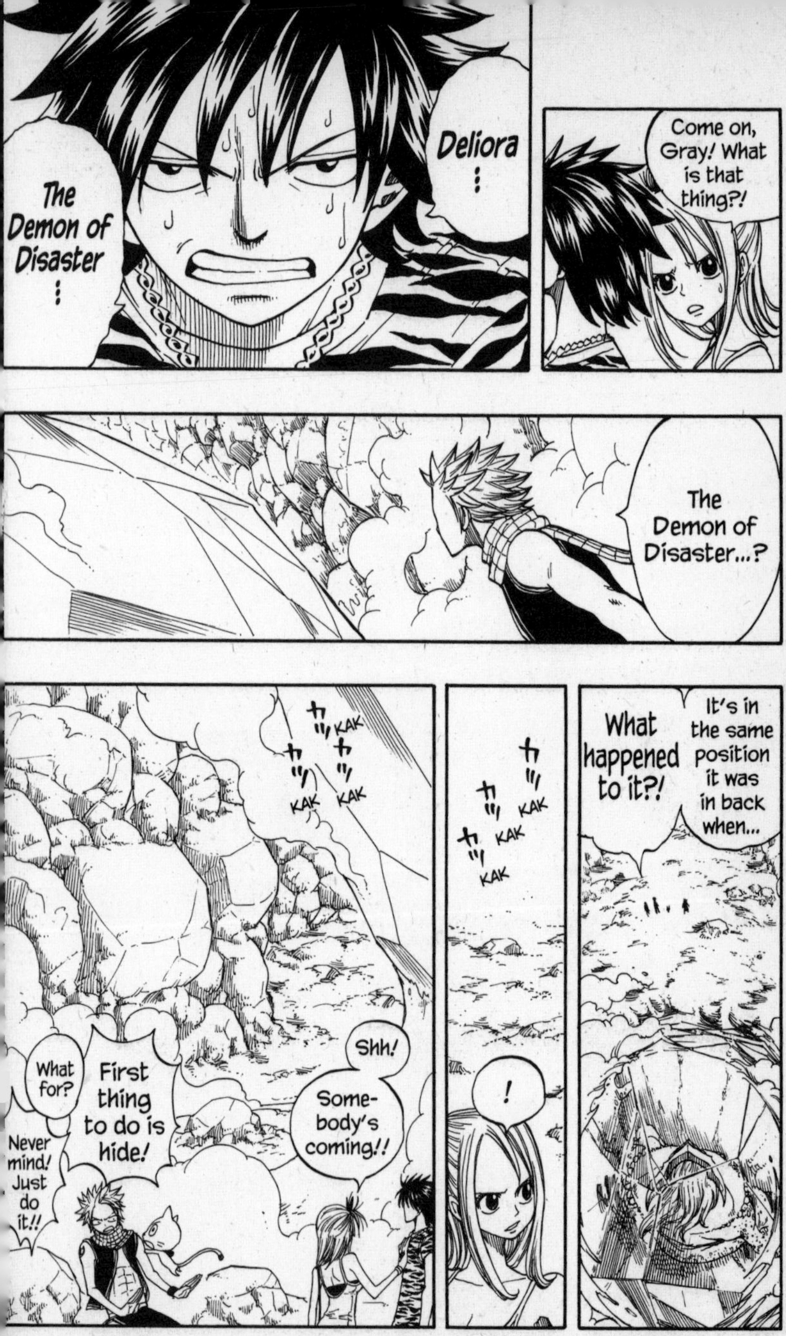

Deliora
...
The Demon of Disaster
...
Come on, Gray! What is that thing?!
The Demon of Disaster...?
It's in the same position it was in back when...
What happened to it?!
KAK KAK KAK
!
KAK KAK KAK KAK
Shh! Somebody's coming!!
First thing to do is hide!
What for?
Never mind! Just do it!!

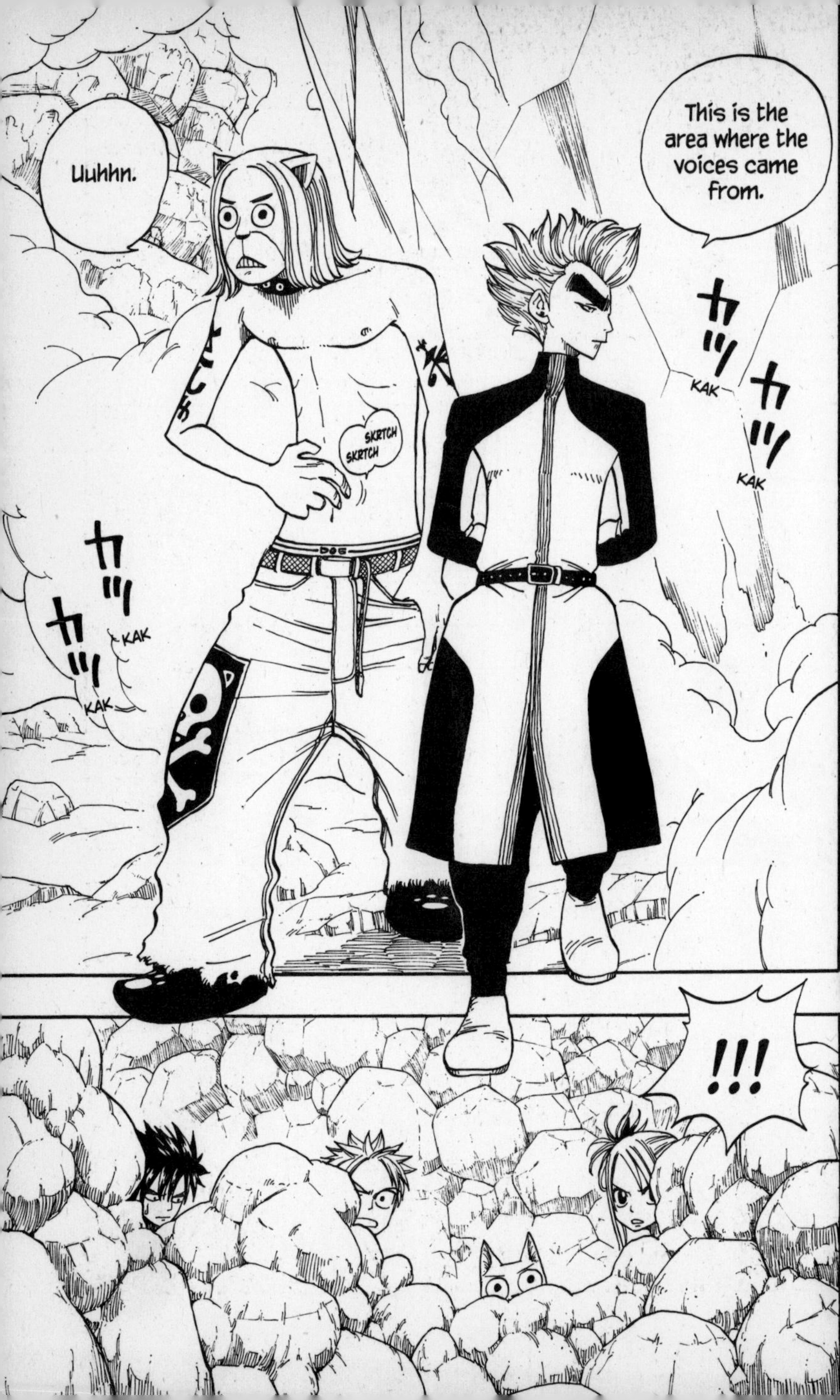
This is the area where the voices came from.
カッ
KAK
カッ
KAK
Uuhhn.
SKRTCH SKRTCH
カッ
KAK
カッ
KAK
!!!

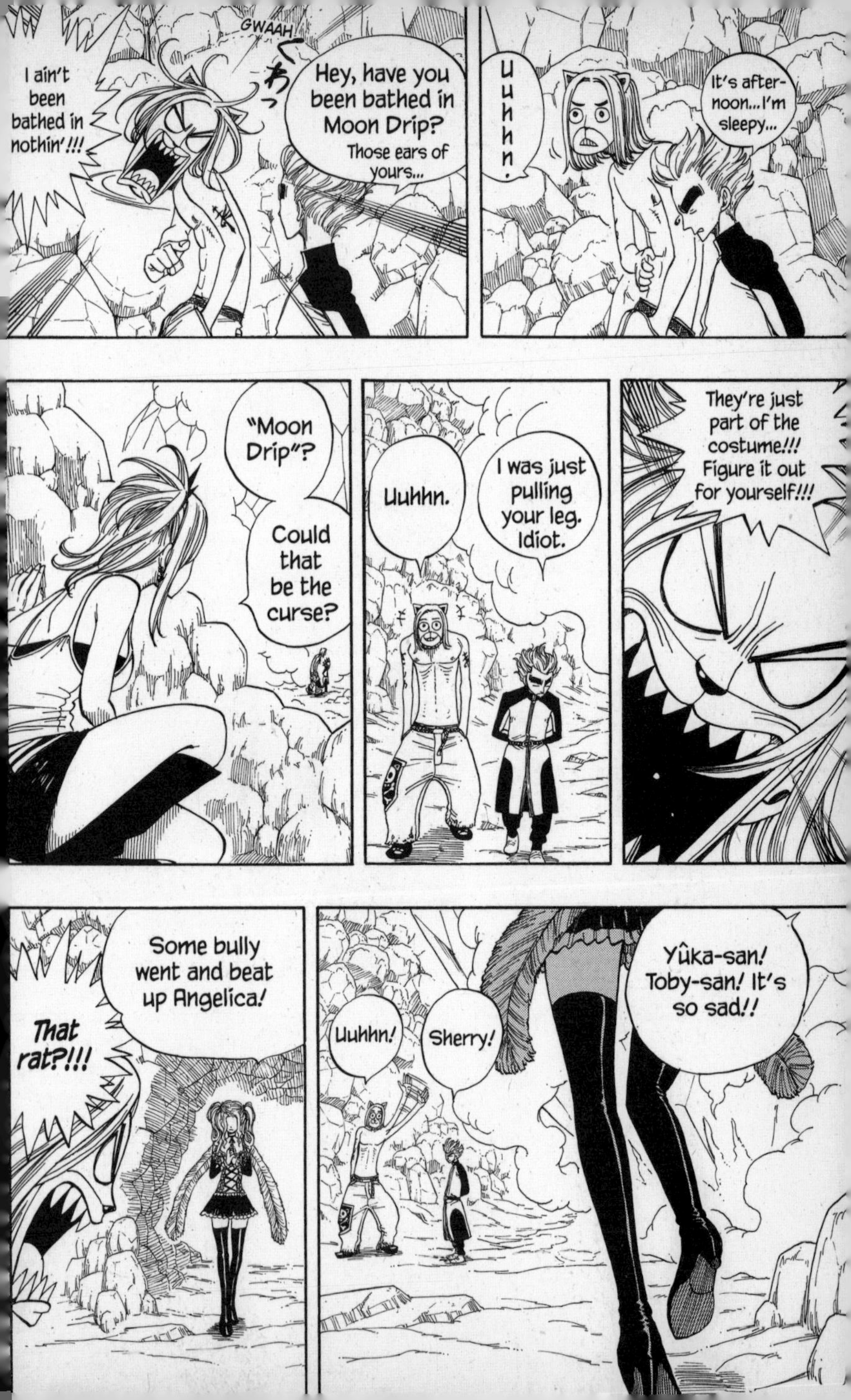
It's after-noon...I'm sleepy...
Uuhhhn.
Hey, have you been bathed in Moon Drip?
Those ears of yours...
GWAAH
I ain't been bathed in nothin'!!!
They're just part of the costume!!! Figure it out for yourself!!!
I was just pulling your leg. Idiot.
Uuhhn.
"Moon Drip"?
Could that be the curse?
Yûka-san! Toby-san! It's so sad!!
Sherry!
Uuhhn!
Some bully went and beat up Angelica!
That rat?!!!

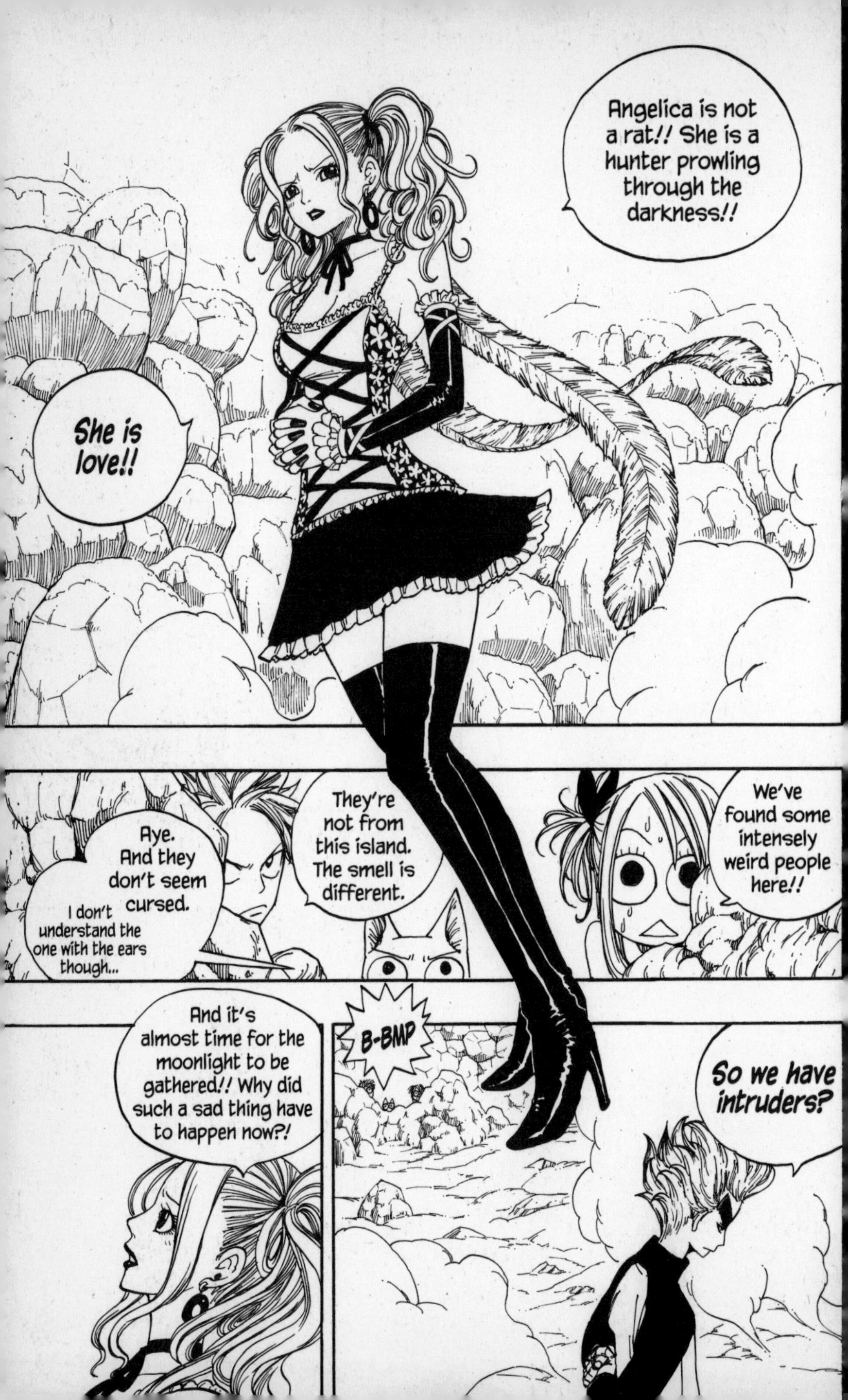
Angelica is not a rat!! She is a hunter prowling through the darkness!!
She is love!!
We've found some intensely weird people here!!
They're not from this island. The smell is different.
Aye. And they don't seem cursed.
I don't understand the one with the ears though...
So we have intruders?
B-BMP
And it's almost time for the moonlight to be gathered!! Why did such a sad thing have to happen now?!

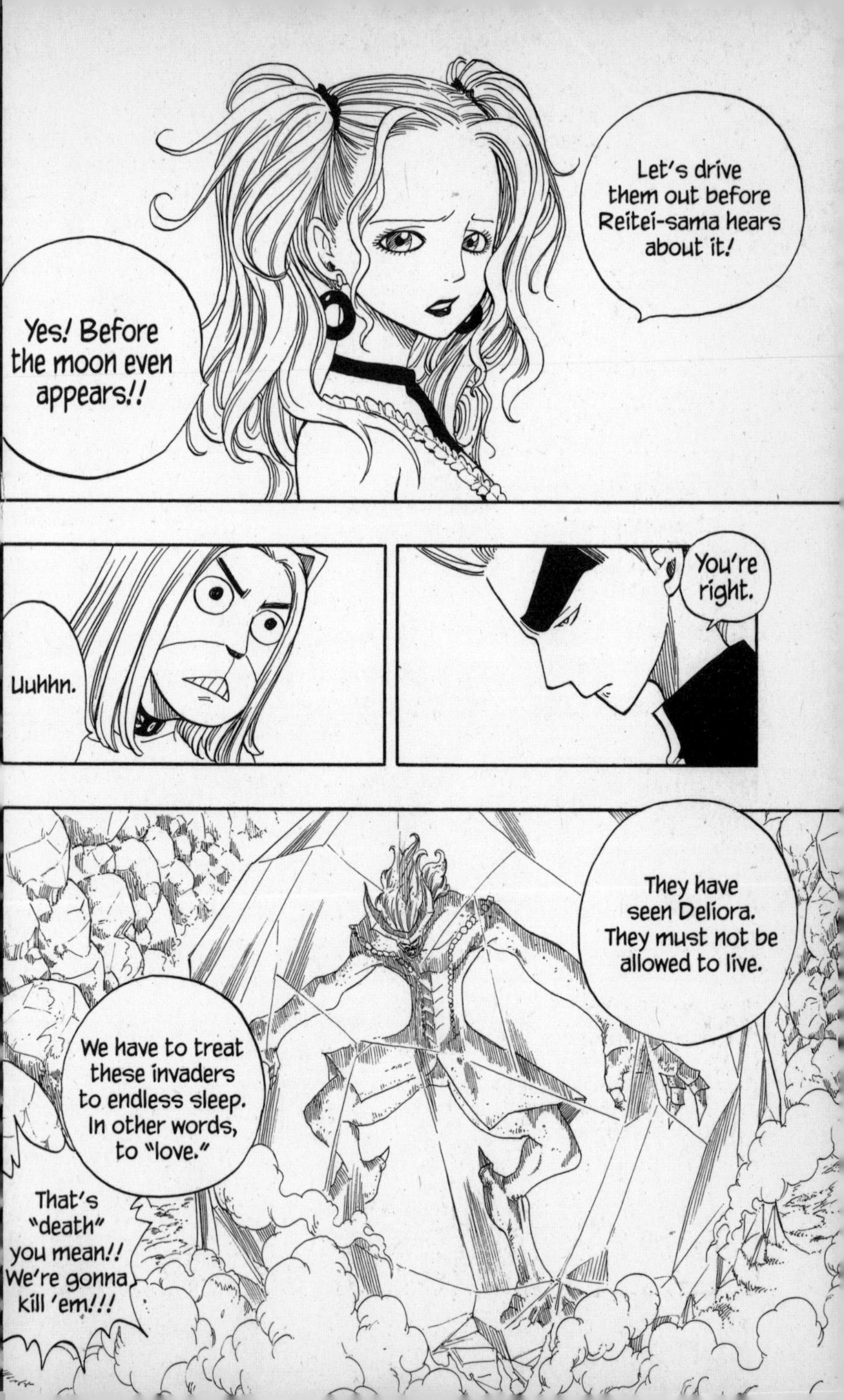
Let's drive them out before Reitei-sama hears about it!
Yes! Before the moon even appears!!
You're right.
Uuhhn.
They have seen Deliora. They must not be allowed to live.
We have to treat these invaders to endless sleep. In other words, to "love."
That's "death" you mean!! We're gonna kill 'em!!!

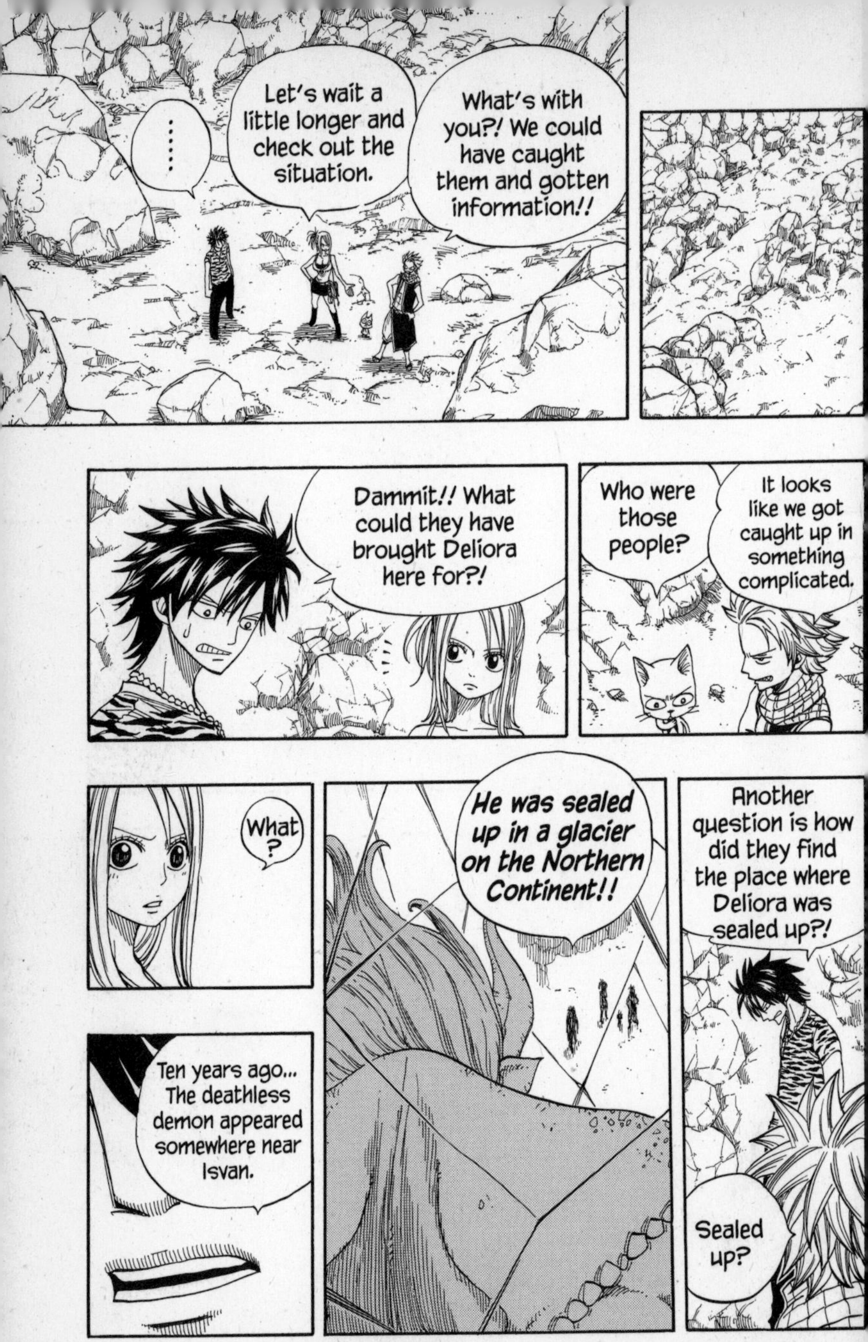

What's with you?! We could have caught them and gotten information!!
Let's wait a little longer and check out the situation.
......
It looks like we got caught up in something complicated.
Who were those people?
Dammit!! What could they have brought Deliora here for?!
Another question is how did they find the place where Deliora was sealed up?!
Sealed up?
He was sealed up in a glacier on the Northern Continent!!
What?
Ten years ago... The deathless demon appeared somewhere near Isvan.

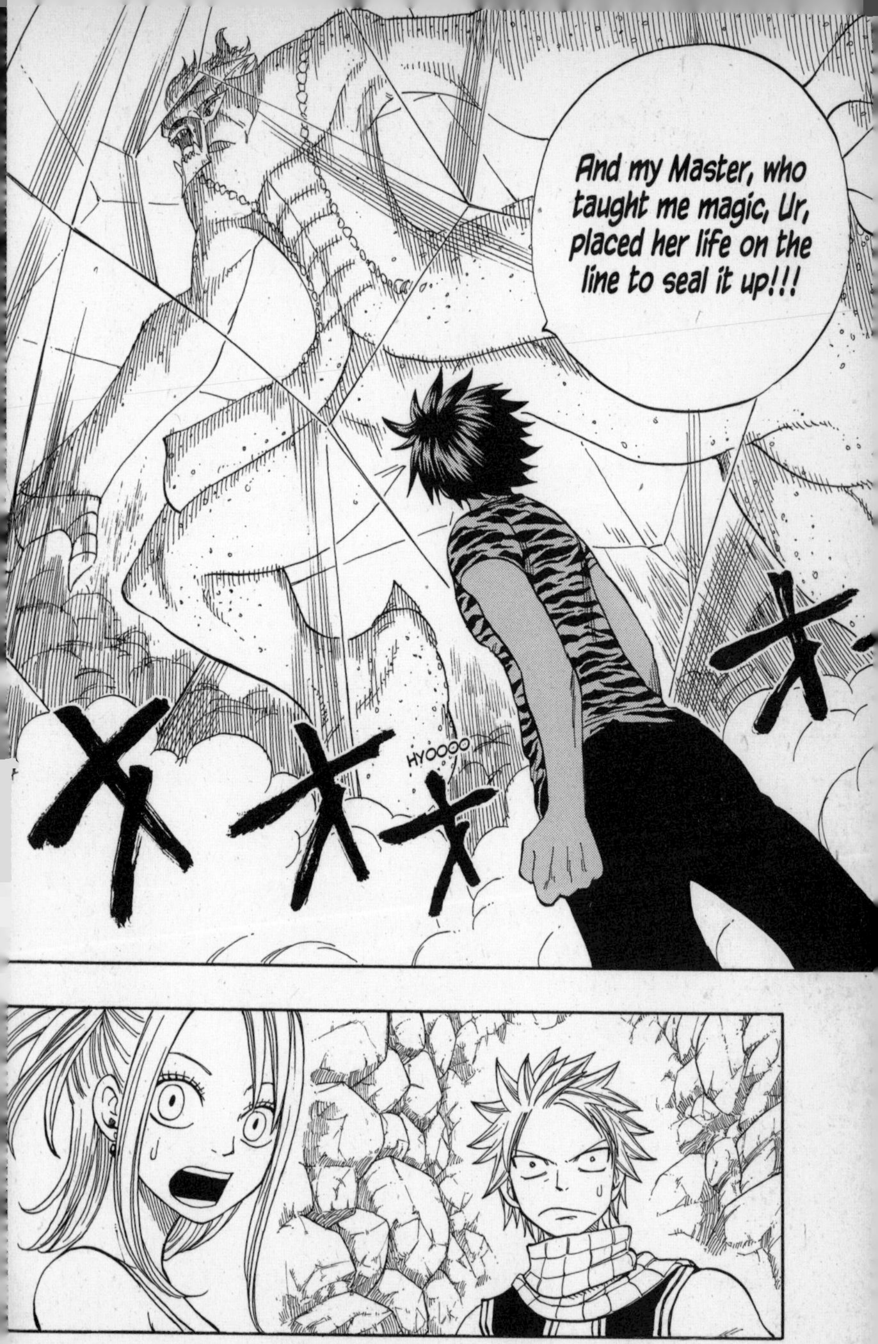
And my Master, who taught me magic, Ur, placed her life on the line to seal it up!!!
HYOOOO

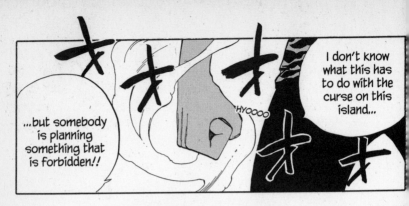

I don't know what this has to do with the curse on this island...

...but somebody is planning something that is forbidden!!

Who is he...?

Reitei...

If this Reitei is planning to disgrace the name of Ur, I won't let that happen!!!!

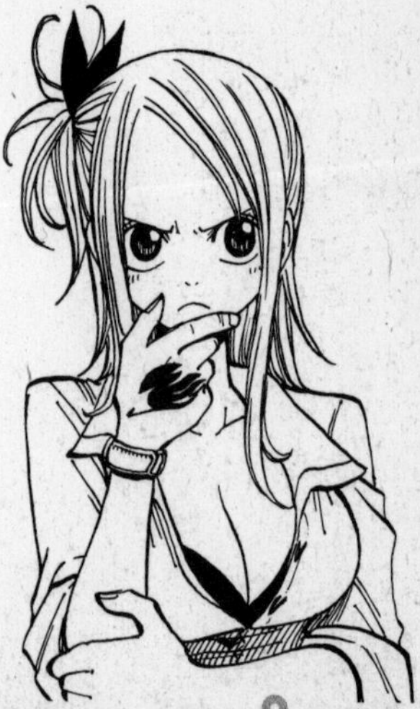

FAIRY TAIL

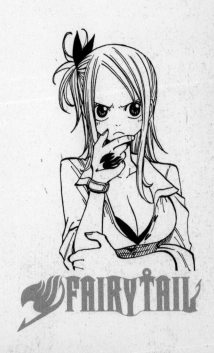

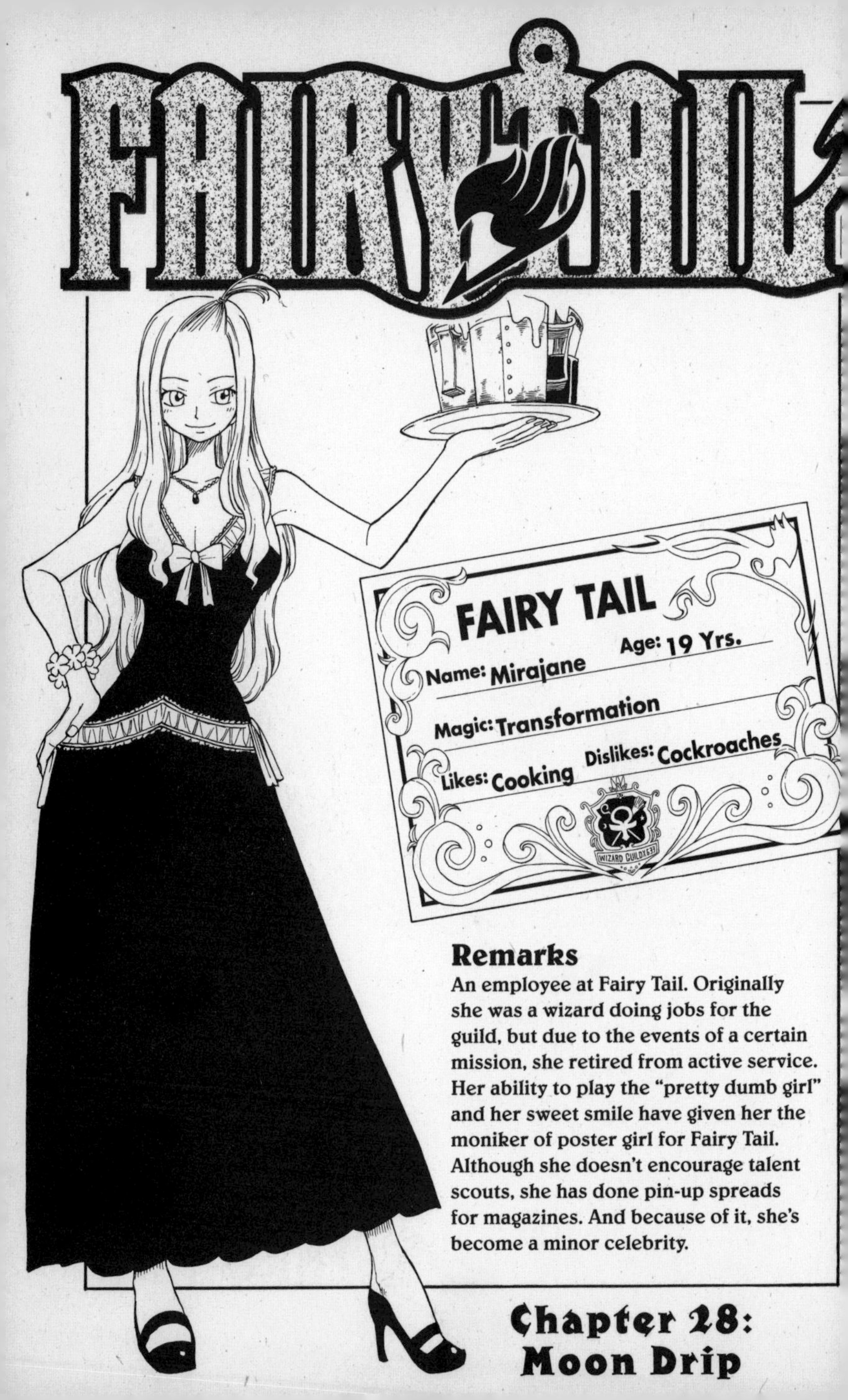
FAIRY TAIL
Name: Mirajane
Age: 19 Yrs.
Magic: Transformation
Likes: Cooking
Dislikes: Cockroaches
WIZARD GUILDX633

Remarks

An employee at Fairy Tail. Originally she was a wizard doing jobs for the guild, but due to the events of a certain mission, she retired from active service. Her ability to play the "pretty dumb girl" and her sweet smile have given her the moniker of poster girl for Fairy Tail. Although she doesn't encourage talent scouts, she has done pin-up spreads for magazines. And because of it, she's become a minor celebrity.

Chapter 28: Moon Drip

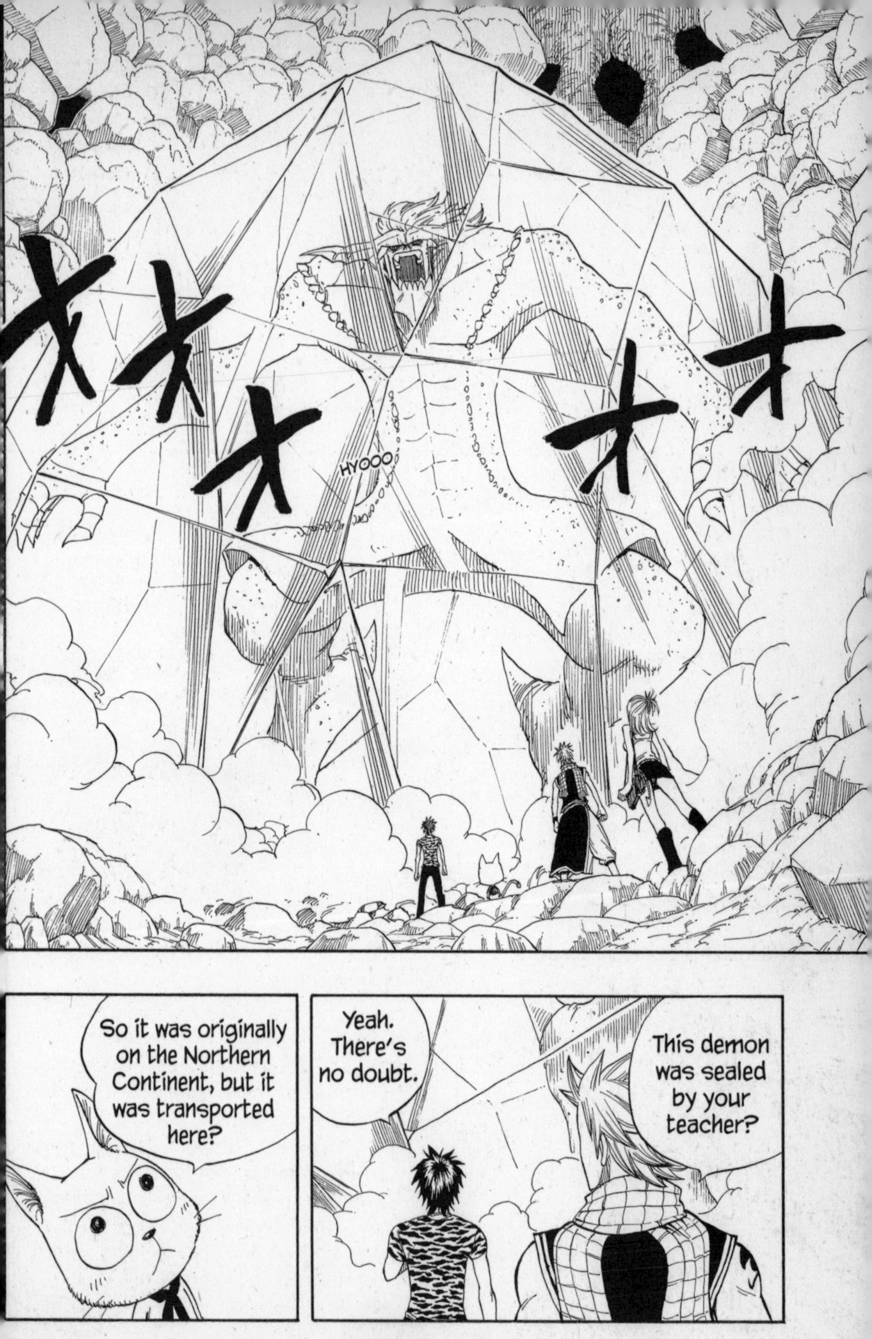
HYOOO
This demon was sealed by your teacher?
Yeah. There's no doubt.
So it was originally on the Northern Continent, but it was transported here?

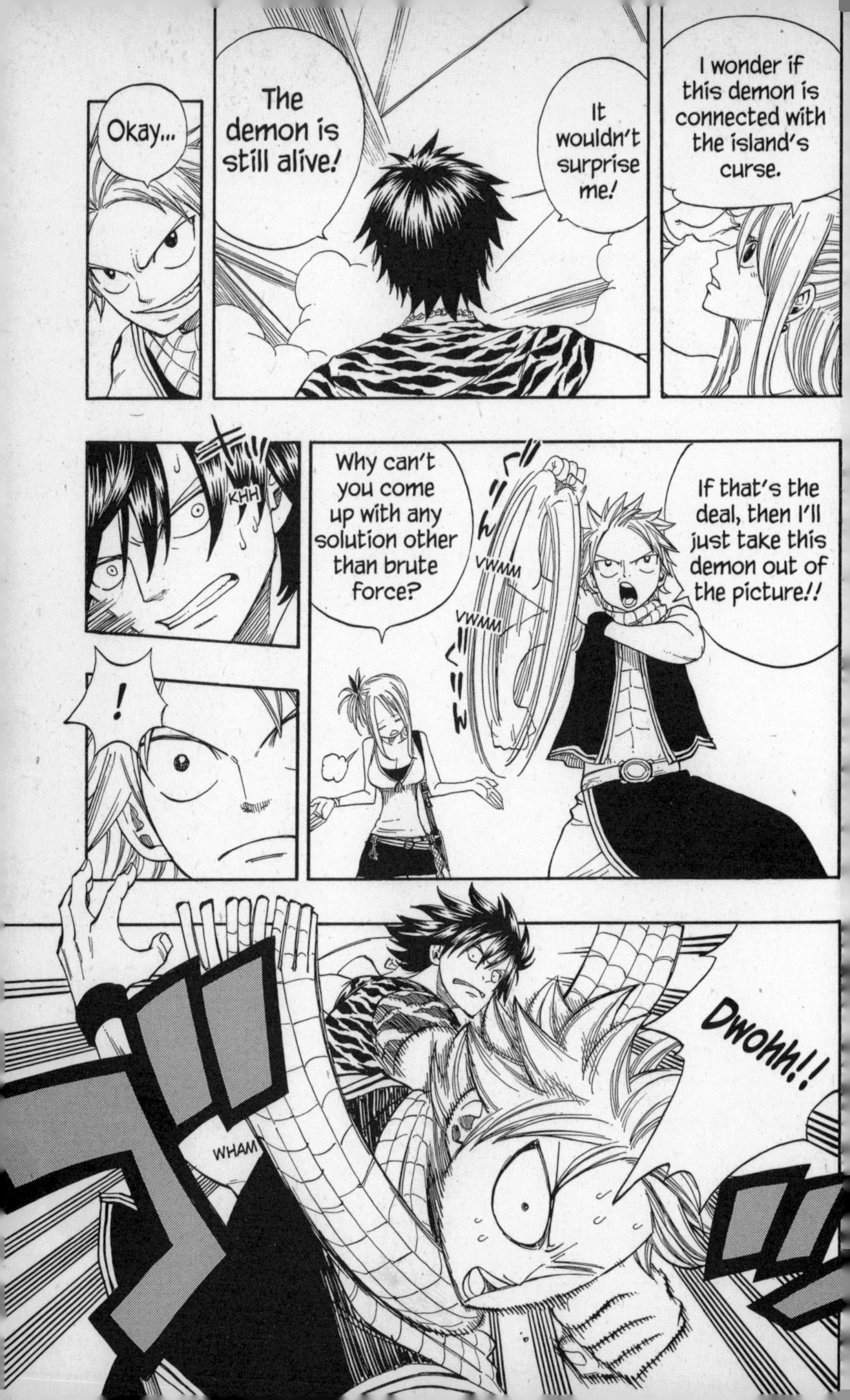
Okay...
The demon is still alive!
It wouldn't surprise me!
I wonder if this demon is connected with the island's curse.
KHH
Why can't you come up with any solution other than brute force?
VWMM
VWMM
If that's the deal, then I'll just take this demon out of the picture!!
!
Dwohh!!
WHAM

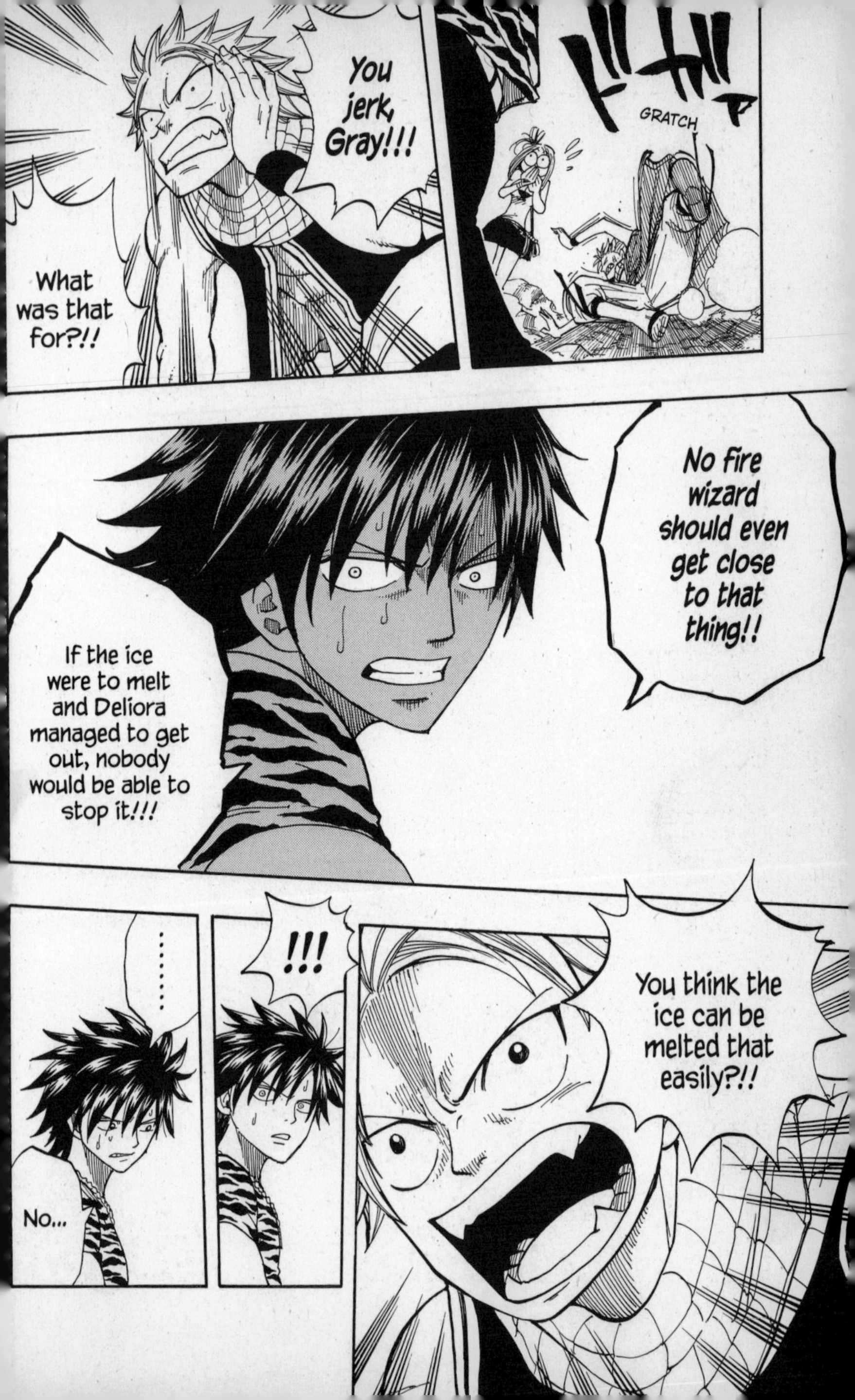
GRATCH
You jerk, Gray!!!
What was that for?!!
No fire wizard should even get close to that thing!!
If the ice were to melt and Deliora managed to get out, nobody would be able to stop it!!!
You think the ice can be melted that easily?!!
!!!
......
No...

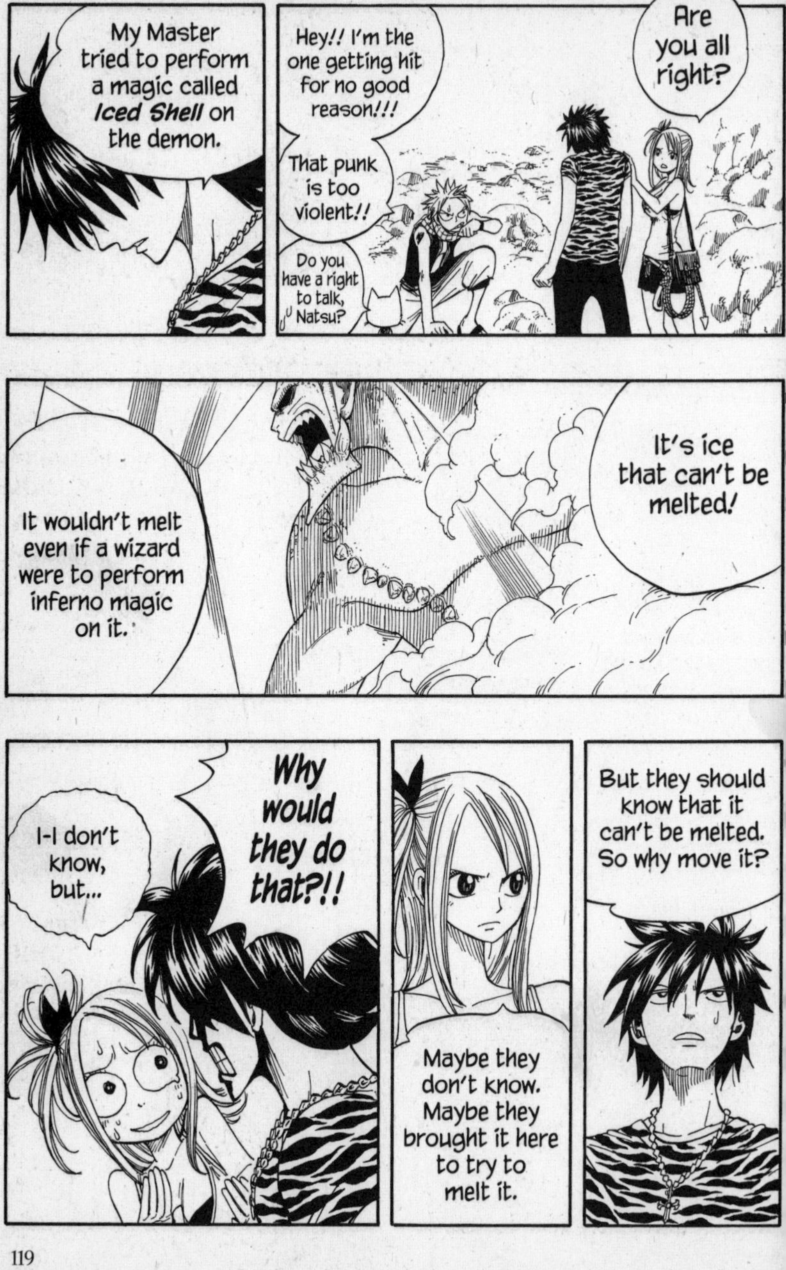

Are you all right?
Hey!! I'm the one getting hit for no good reason!!!
That punk is too violent!!
Do you have a right to talk, Natsu?
My Master tried to perform a magic called *Iced Shell* on the demon.
It's ice that can't be melted!
It wouldn't melt even if a wizard were to perform inferno magic on it.
But they should know that it can't be melted. So why move it?
Maybe they don't know. Maybe they brought it here to try to melt it.
Why would they do that?!!
I-I don't know, but...

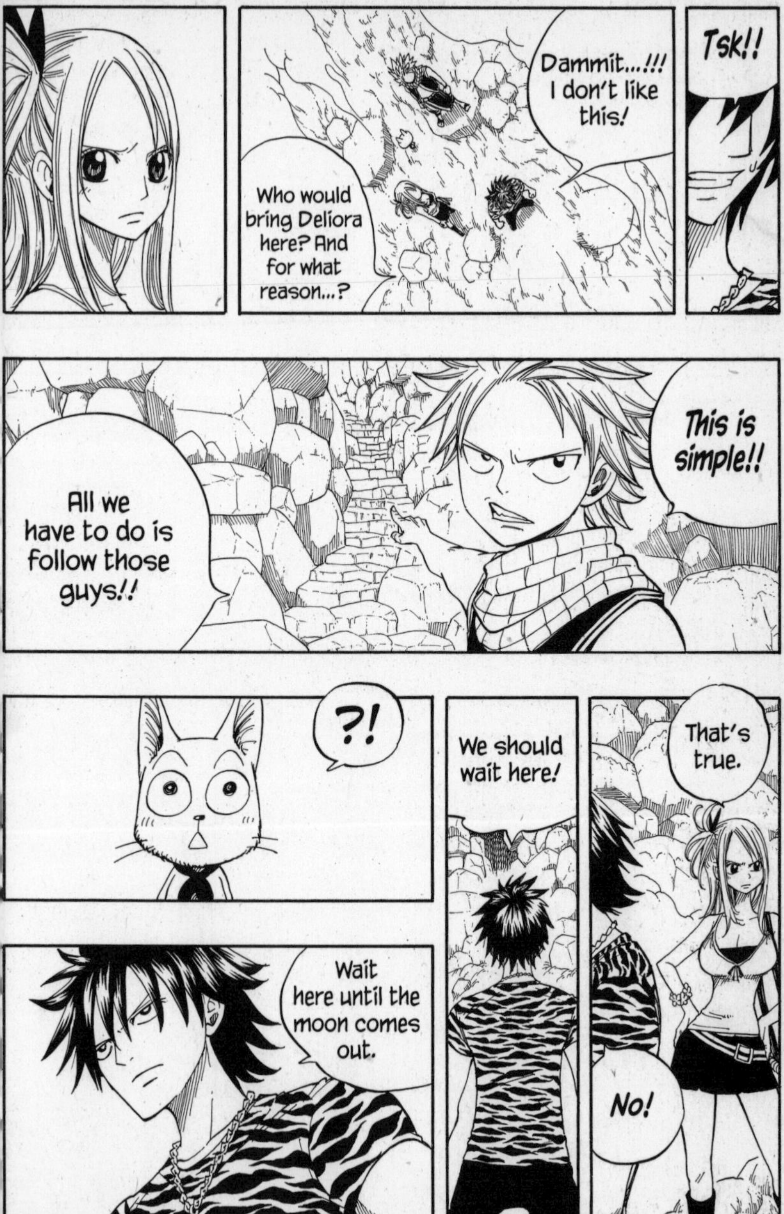

Tsk!!
Dammit...!!! I don't like this!
Who would bring Deliora here? And for what reason...?
This is simple!!
All we have to do is follow those guys!!
That's true.
No!
We should wait here!
?!
Wait here until the moon comes out.

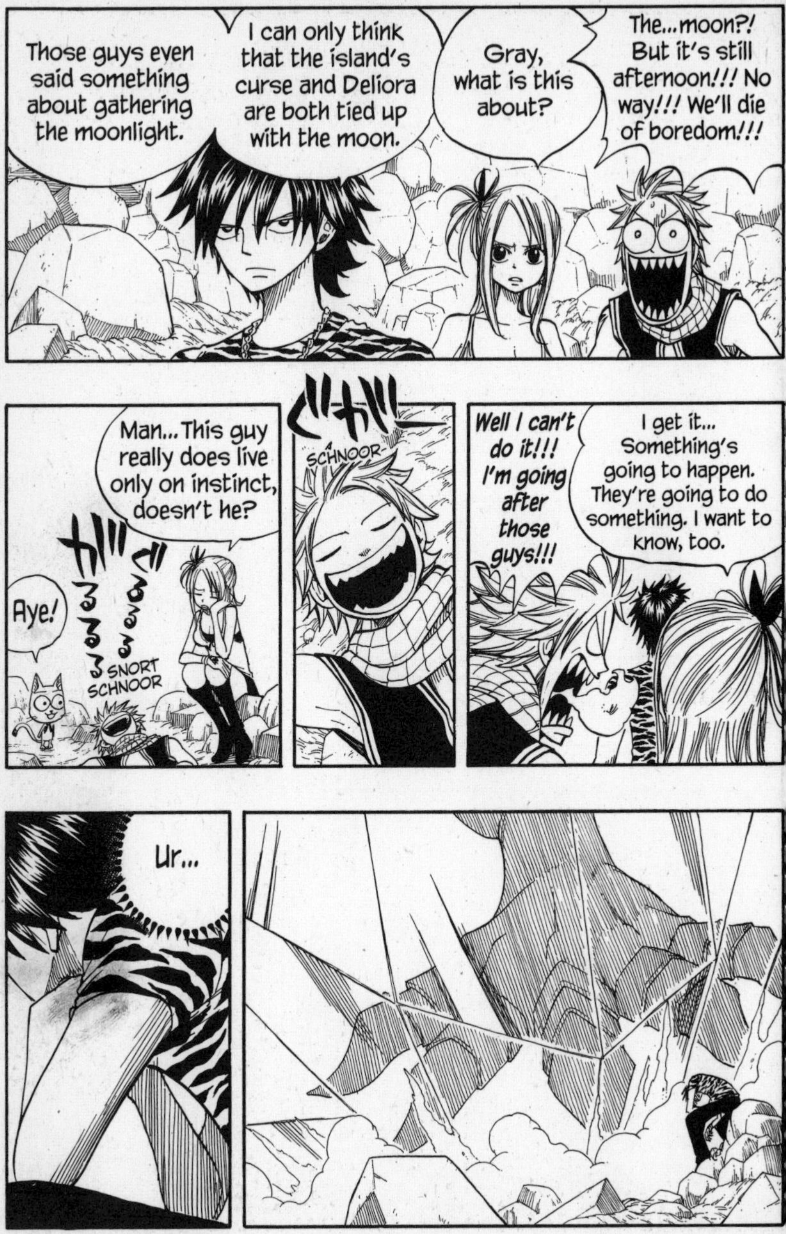

The...moon?! But it's still afternoon!!! No way!!! We'll die of boredom!!!
Gray, what is this about?
I can only think that the island's curse and Deliora are both tied up with the moon.
Those guys even said something about gathering the moonlight.
I get it... Something's going to happen. They're going to do something. I want to know, too.
Well I can't do it!!! I'm going after those guys!!!
SCHNOOR
Man... This guy really does live only on instinct, doesn't he?
Aye!
SNORT SCHNOOR
Ur...

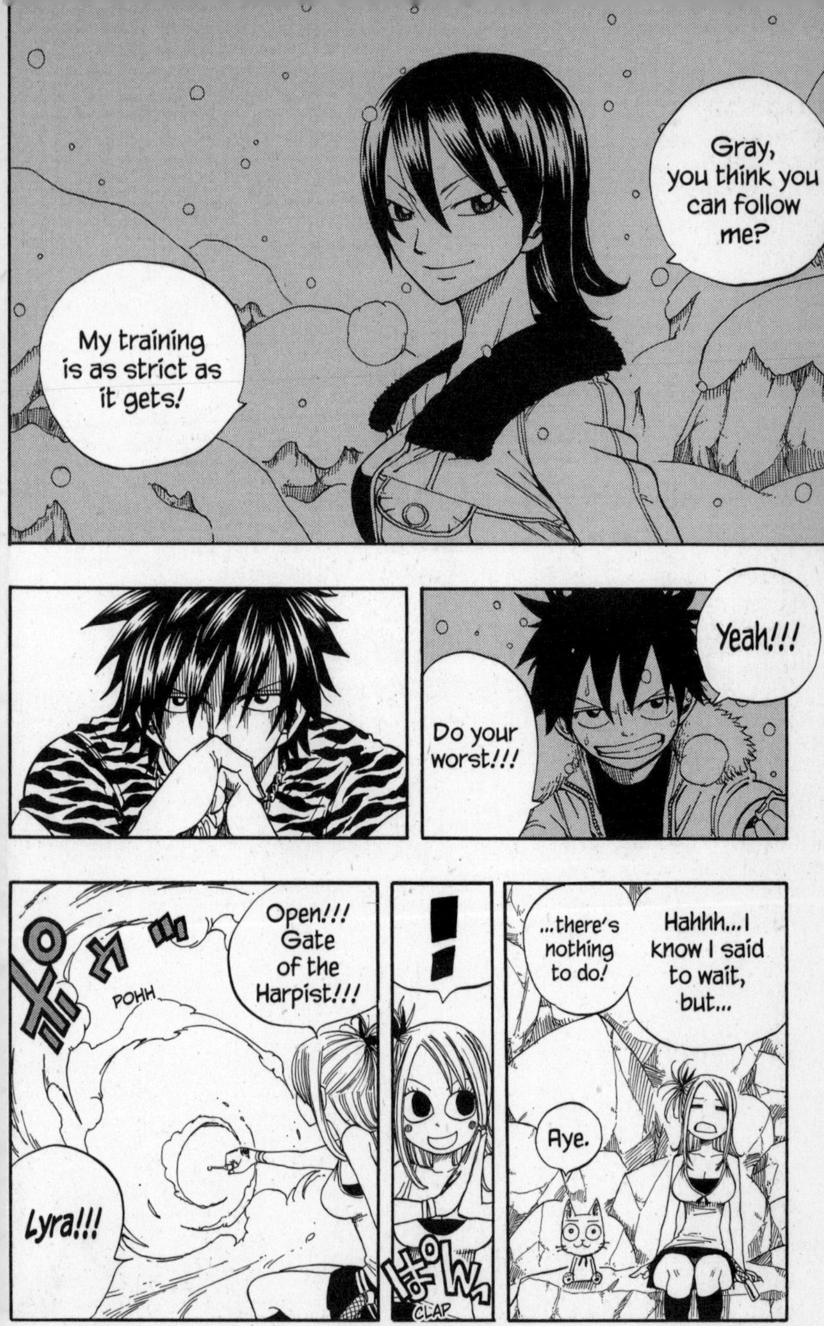
Gray, you think you can follow me?
My training is as strict as it gets!
Yeah!!!
Do your worst!!!
Hahhh...I know I said to wait, but...
...there's nothing to do!
Aye.
!
CLAP
Open!!! Gate of the Harpist!!!
POHH
Lyra!!!

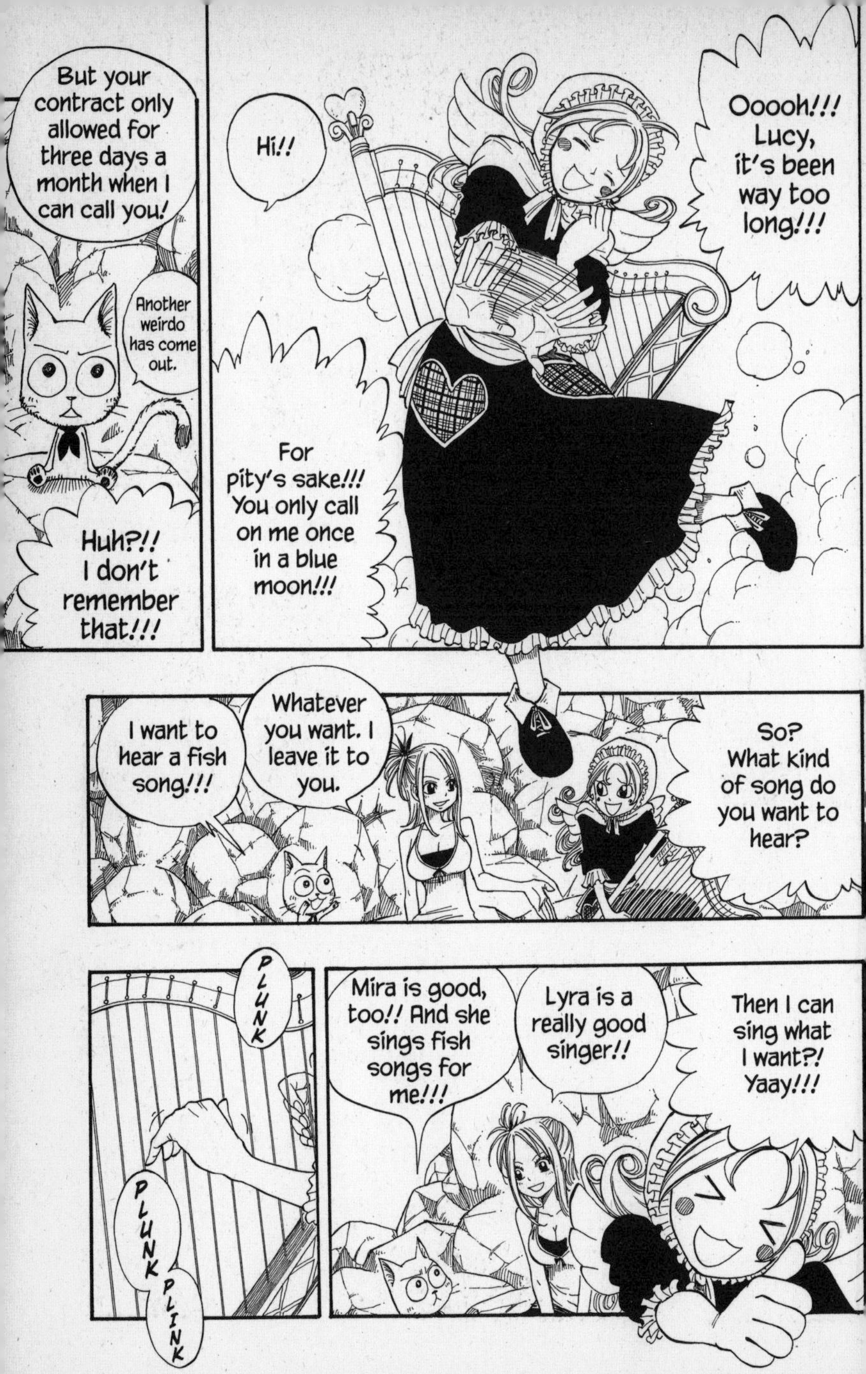
Ooooh!!! Lucy, it's been way too long!!!
Hi!!
For pity's sake!!! You only call on me once in a blue moon!!!
But your contract only allowed for three days a month when I can call you!
Another weirdo has come out.
Huh?!! I don't remember that!!!
So? What kind of song do you want to hear?
Whatever you want. I leave it to you.
I want to hear a fish song!!!
Then I can sing what I want?! Yaay!!!
Lyra is a really good singer!!
Mira is good, too!! And she sings fish songs for me!!!
PLUNK
PLUNK
PLINK

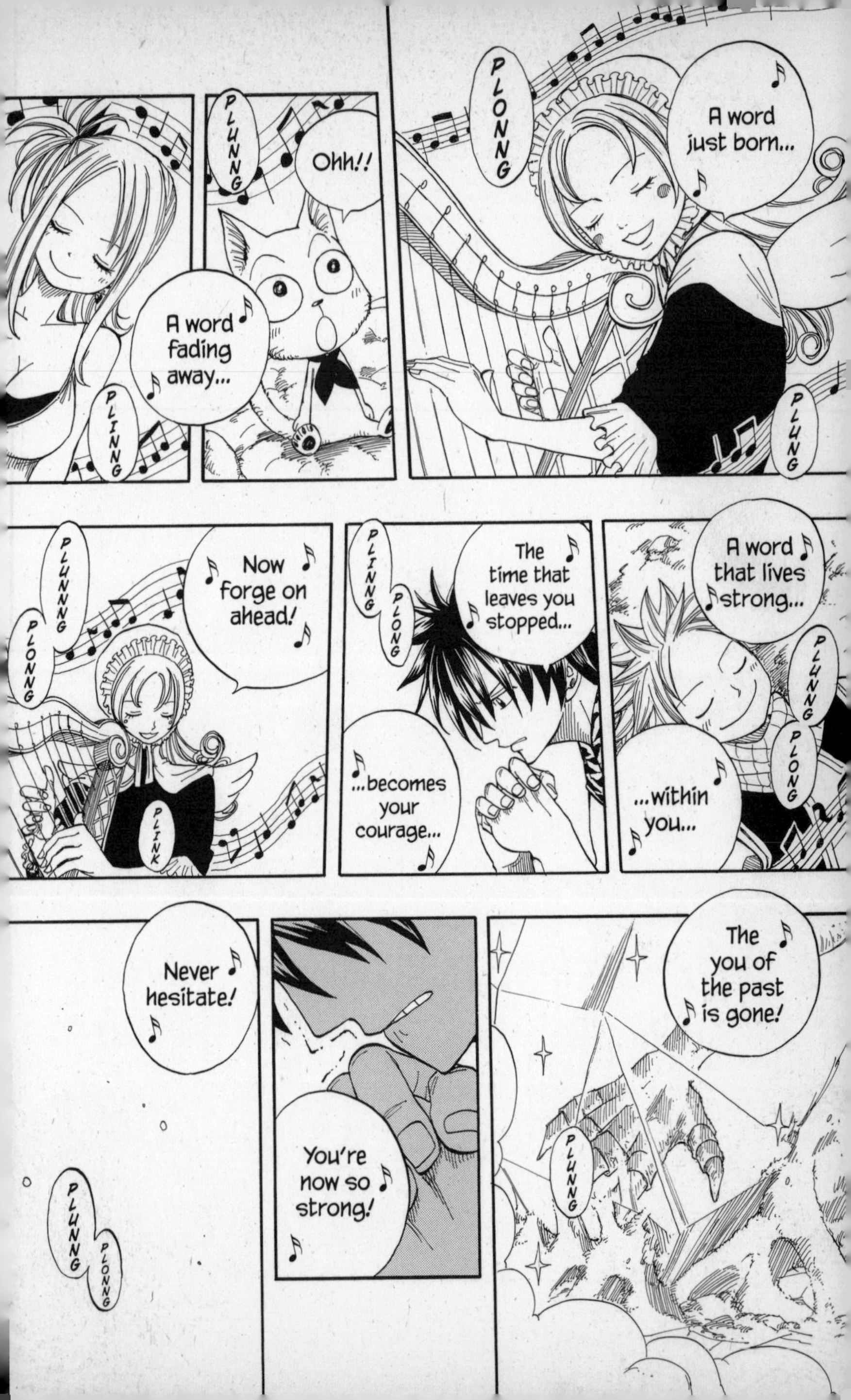
PLONNG
A word just born...
PLUNG
PLUNNG
Ohh!!
A word fading away...
PLINNG
A word that lives strong...
PLUNNG
PLONG
...within you...
PLINNG
PLONG
The time that leaves you stopped...
...becomes your courage...
PLUNNNG
PLONNG
Now forge on ahead!
PLINK
The you of the past is gone!
PLUNNG
You're now so strong!
Never hesitate!
PLUNNG
PLONNG

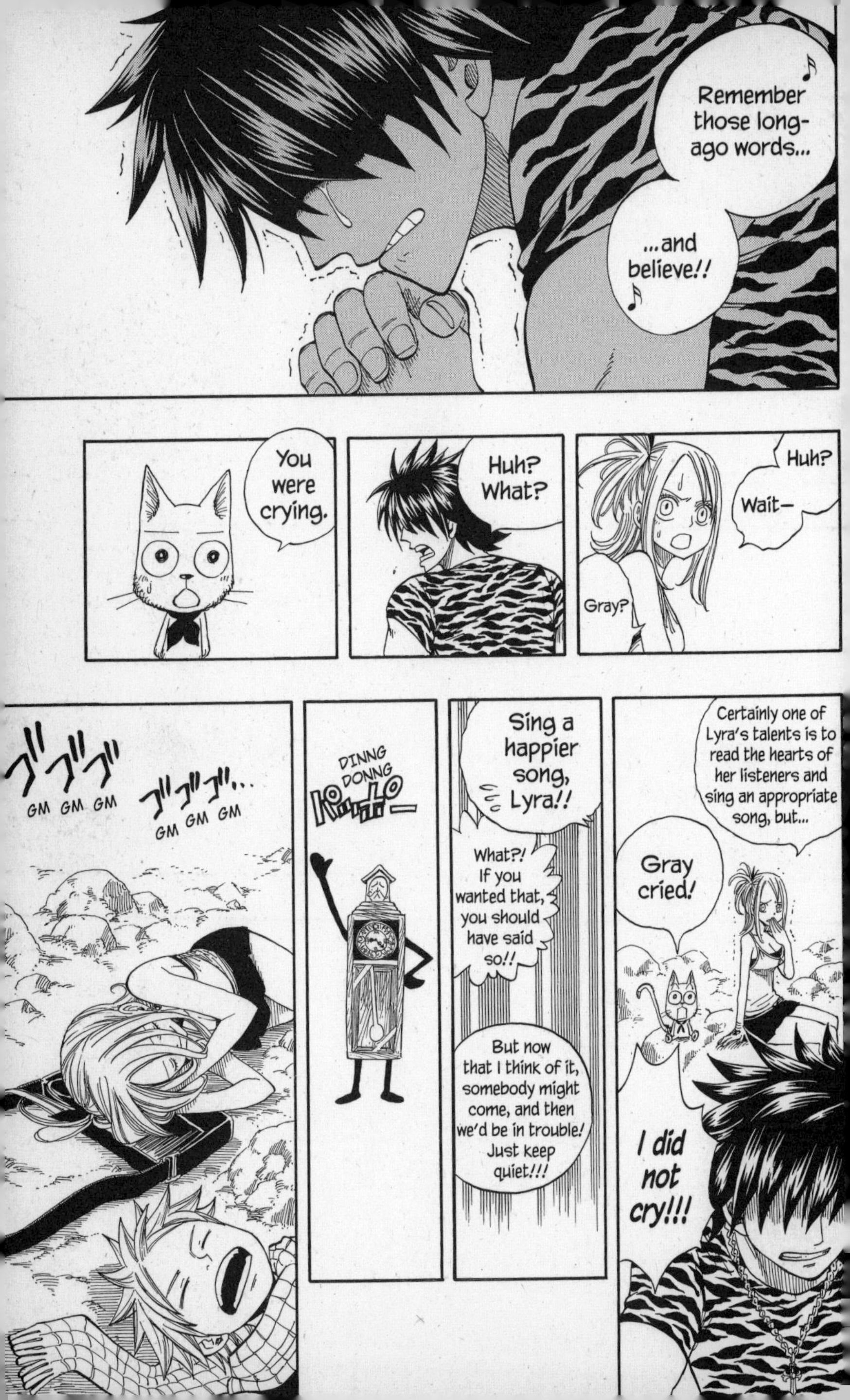

Remember those long-ago words...
...and believe!!
Huh?
Wait—
Gray?
Huh? What?
You were crying.
Certainly one of Lyra's talents is to read the hearts of her listeners and sing an appropriate song, but...
Gray cried!
I did not cry!!!
Sing a happier song, Lyra!!
What?! If you wanted that, you should have said so!!
But now that I think of it, somebody might come, and then we'd be in trouble! Just keep quiet!!!
DINNG DONNG
GM GM GM
GM GM GM

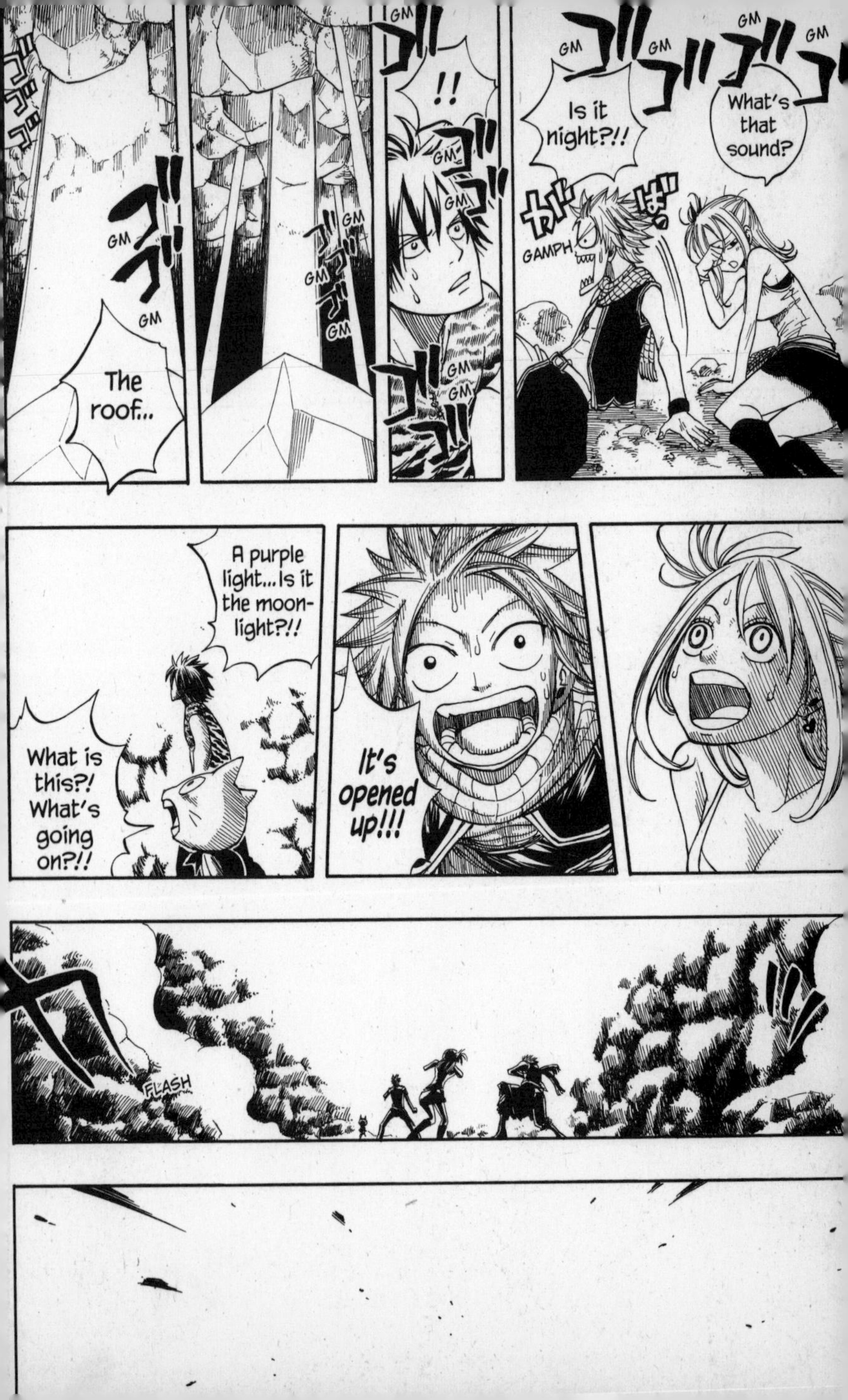
GM
What's that sound?
Is it night?!!
GAMPH
!!
GM
The roof...
It's opened up!!!
A purple light... Is it the moonlight?!!
What is this?! What's going on?!!
FLASH

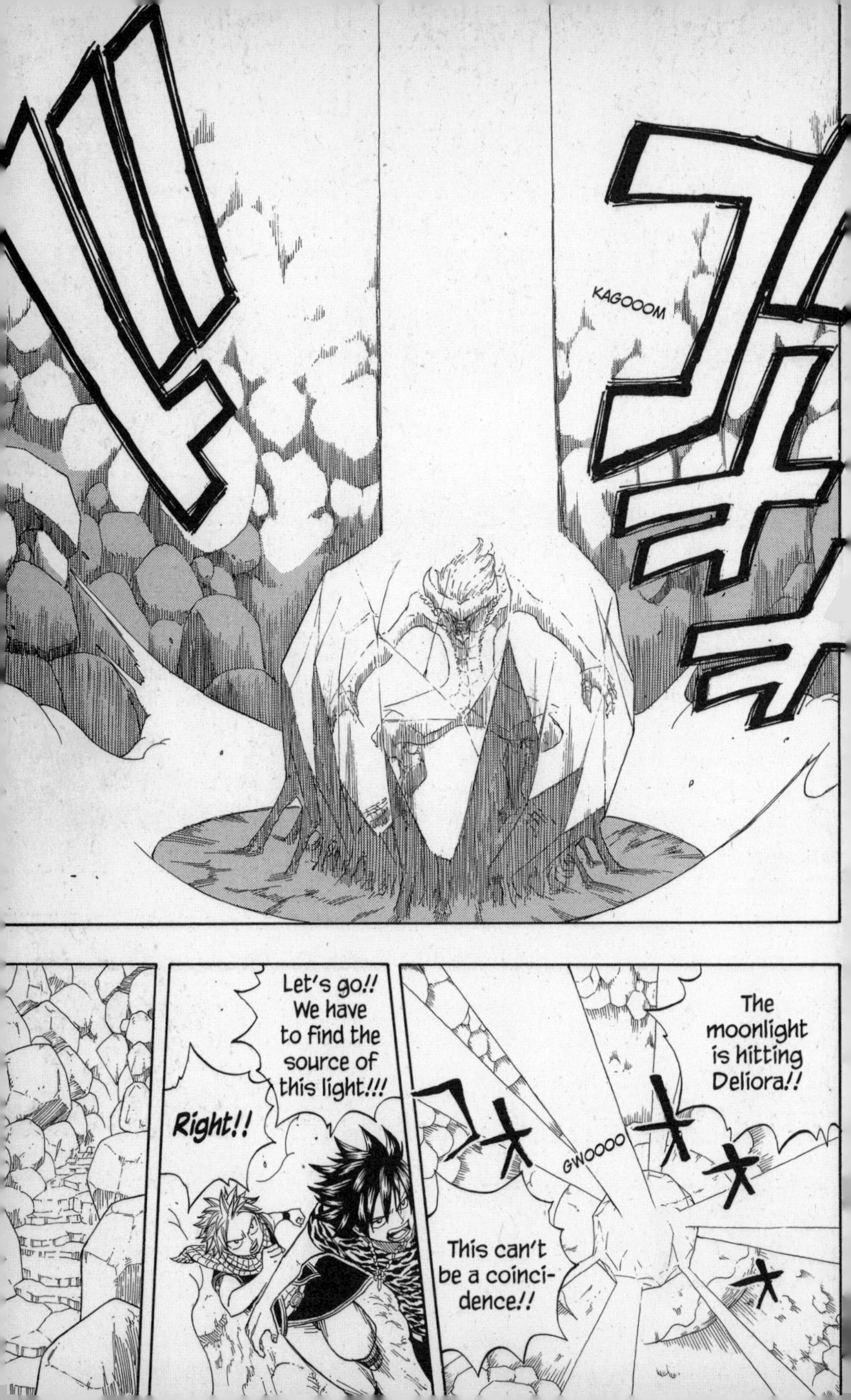
KAGOOOM
The moonlight is hitting Deliora!!
GWOOOO
This can't be a coinci-dence!!
Let's go!! We have to find the source of this light!!!
Right!!

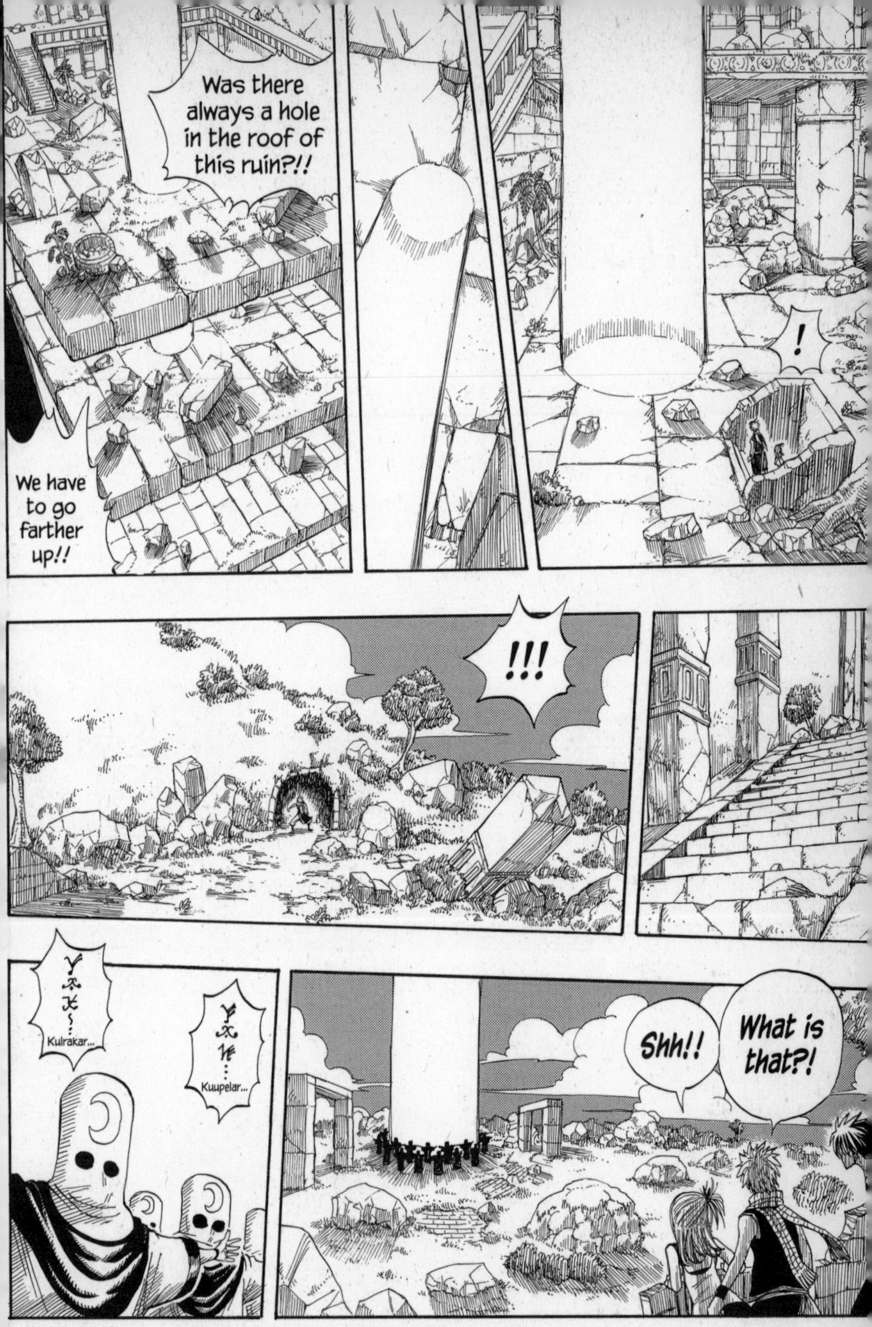
Was there always a hole in the roof of this ruin?!!
We have to go farther up!!
!
!!!
Kulrakar...
Kuupelar...
What is that?!
Shh!!

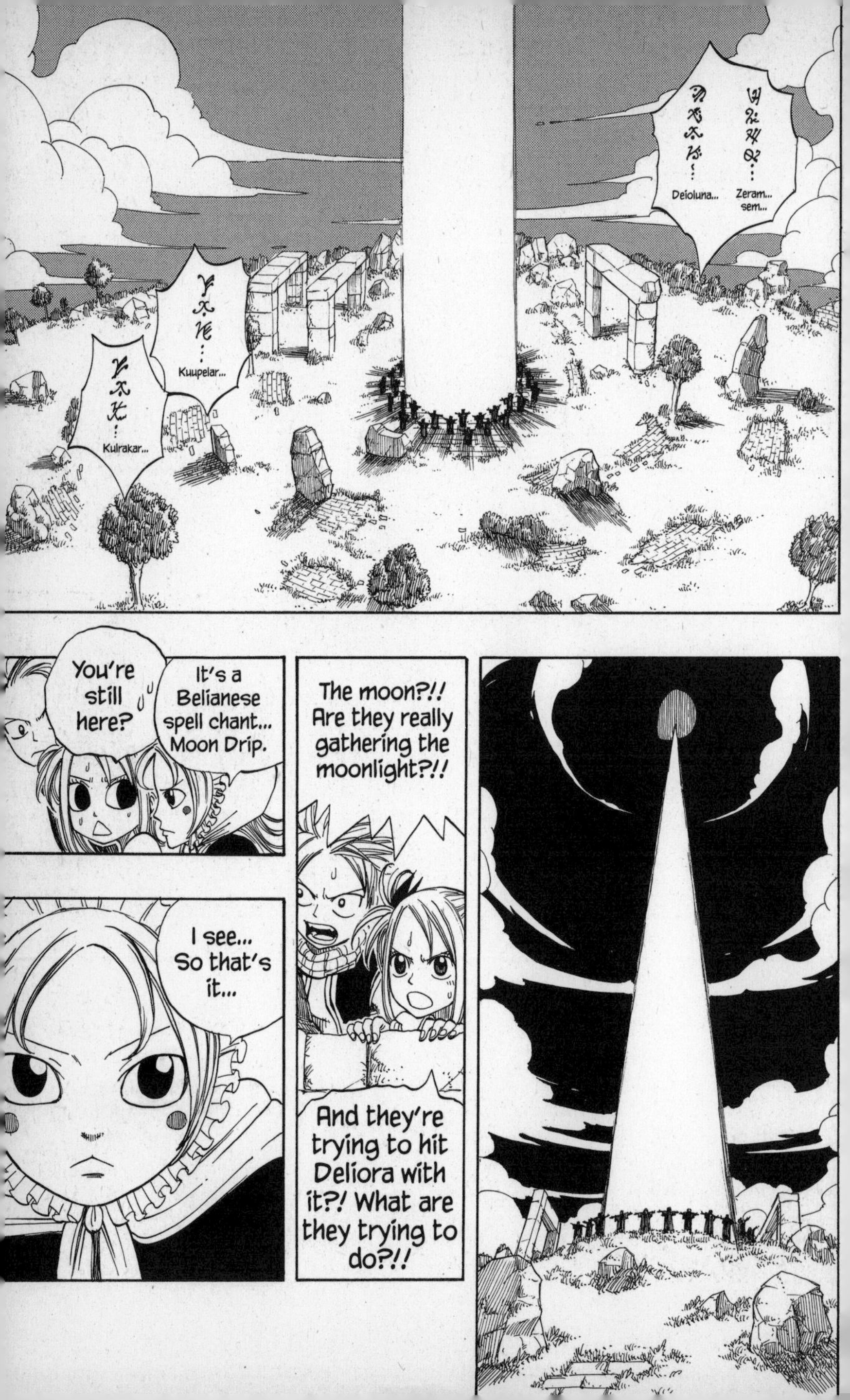
Zeram... sem...
Deioluna...
Kuupelar...
Kulrakar...
The moon?!! Are they really gathering the moonlight?!!
It's a Belianese spell chant... Moon Drip.
You're still here?
And they're trying to hit Deliora with it?! What are they trying to do?!!
I see... So that's it...

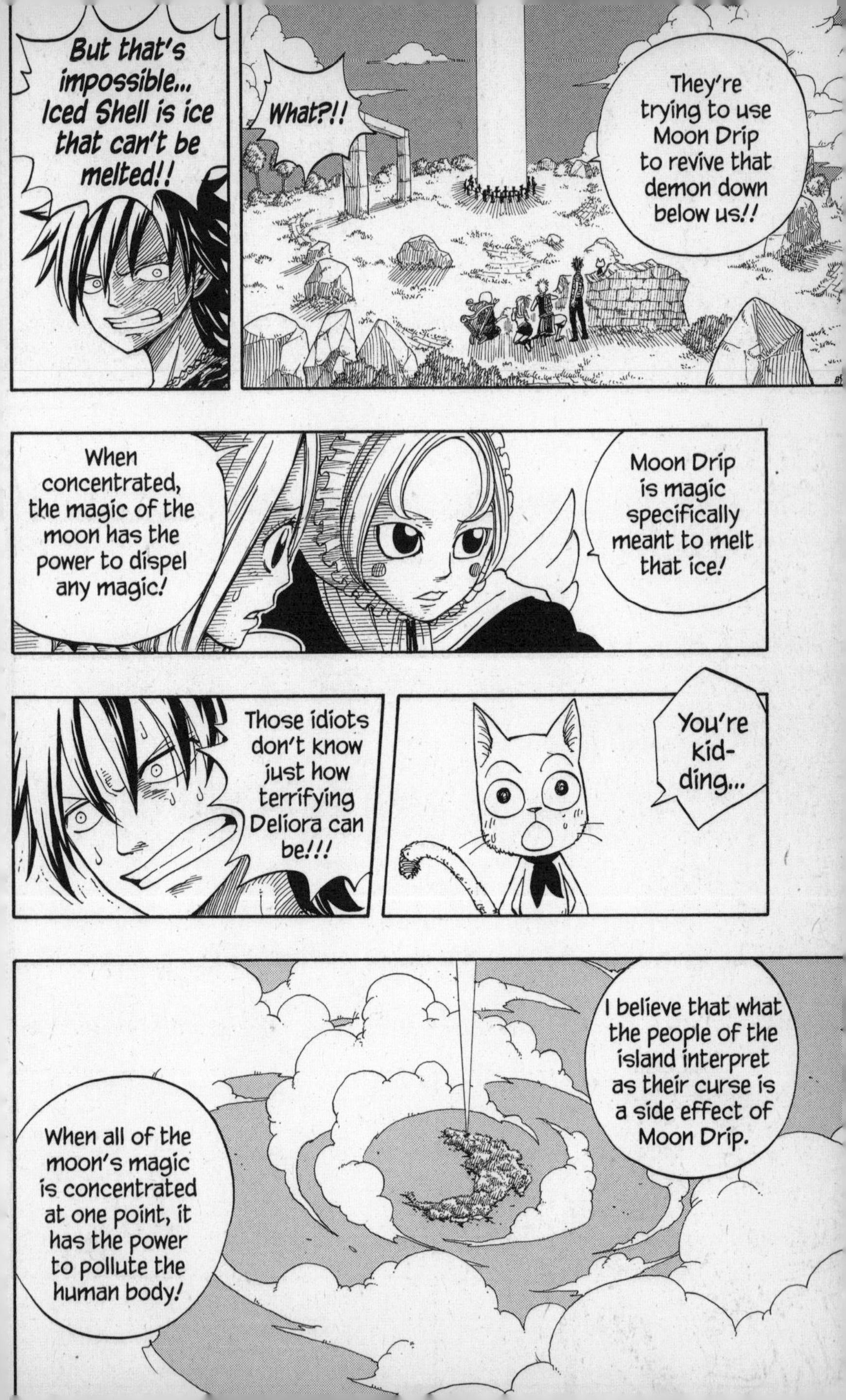
But that's impossible... Iced Shell is ice that can't be melted!!
What?!!
They're trying to use Moon Drip to revive that demon down below us!!
When concentrated, the magic of the moon has the power to dispel any magic!
Moon Drip is magic specifically meant to melt that ice!
Those idiots don't know just how terrifying Deliora can be!!!
You're kid-ding...
I believe that what the people of the island interpret as their curse is a side effect of Moon Drip.
When all of the moon's magic is concentrated at one point, it has the power to pollute the human body!

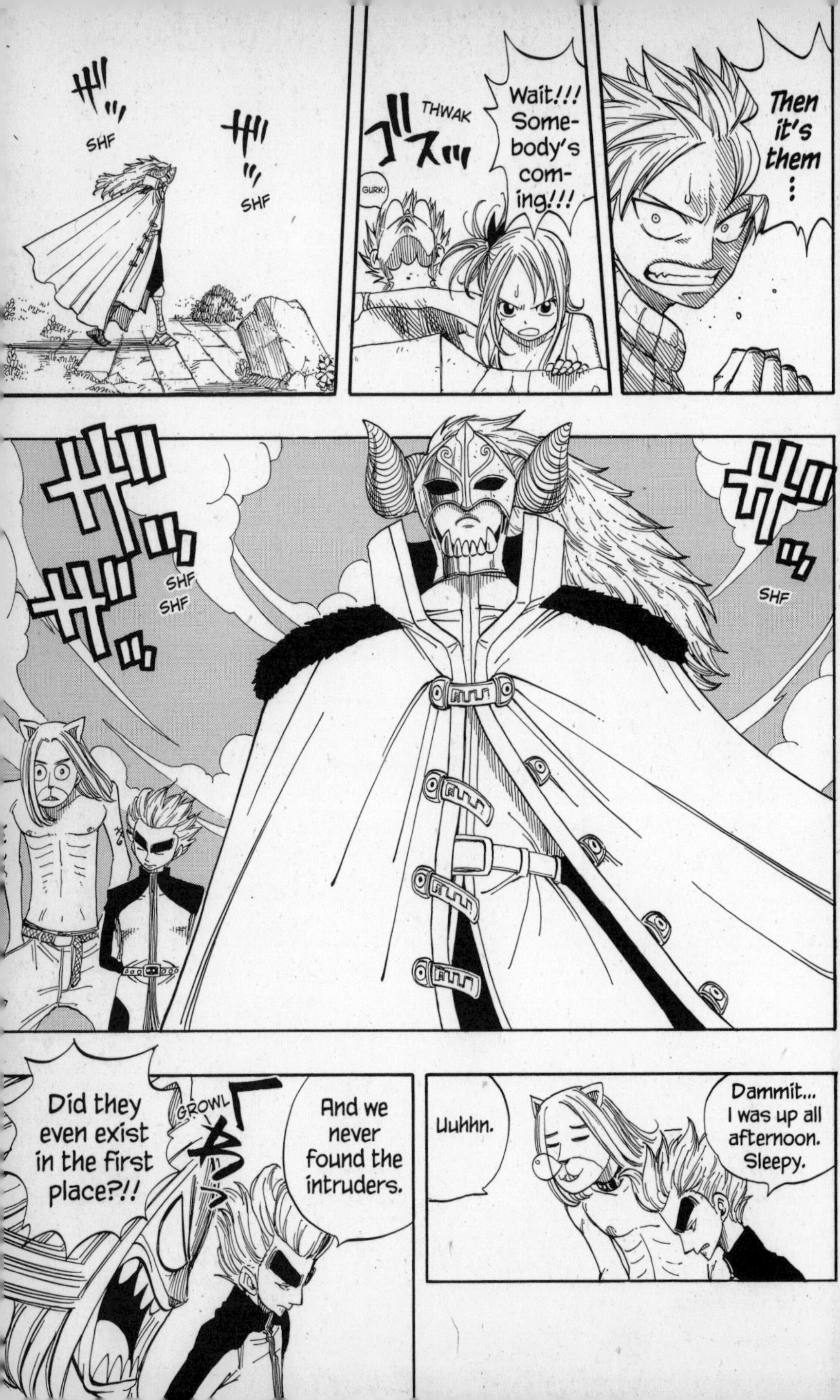
Then it's them...
Wait!!! Somebody's coming!!!
THWAK
GURK!
SHF
SHF
SHF
SHF
SHF
Dammit... I was up all afternoon. Sleepy.
Uuhhn.
And we never found the intruders.
GROWL
Did they even exist in the first place?!!

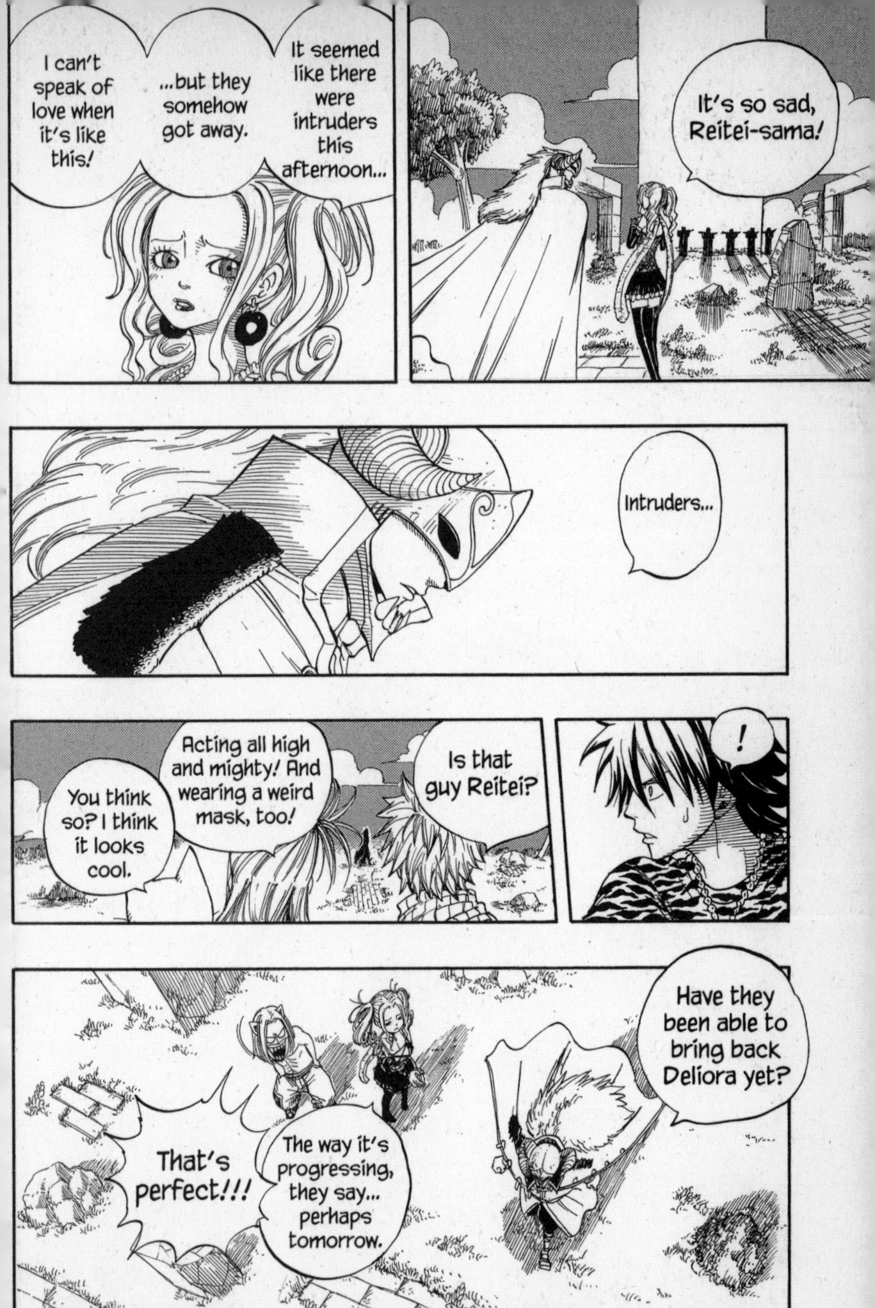

It's so sad, Reitei-sama!
It seemed like there were intruders this afternoon...
...but they somehow got away.
I can't speak of love when it's like this!
Intruders...
!
Is that guy Reitei?
Acting all high and mighty! And wearing a weird mask, too!
You think so? I think it looks cool.
Have they been able to bring back Deliora yet?
The way it's progressing, they say... perhaps tomorrow.
That's perfect!!!

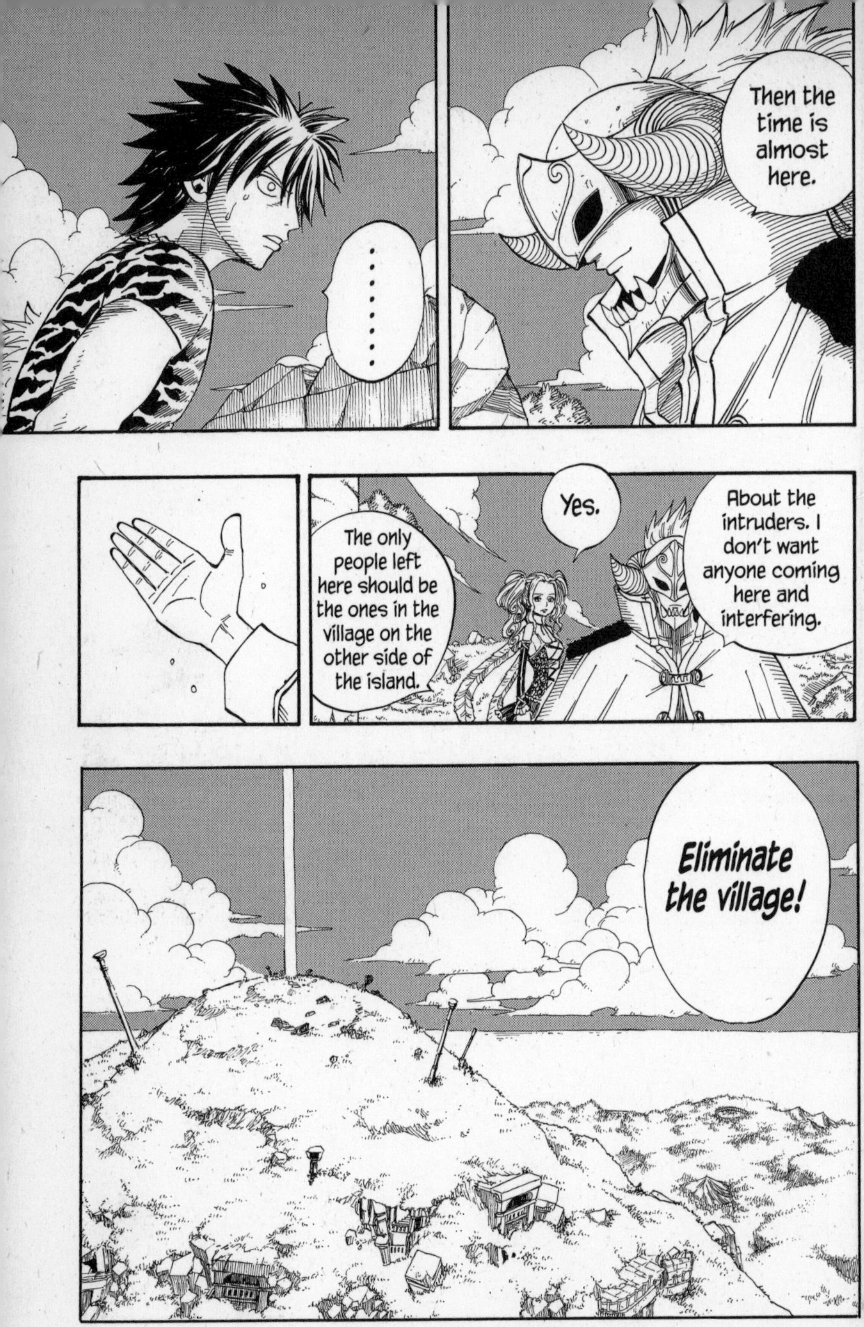
Then the time is almost here.
......
About the intruders. I don't want anyone coming here and interfering.
Yes.
The only people left here should be the ones in the village on the other side of the island.
Eliminate the village!

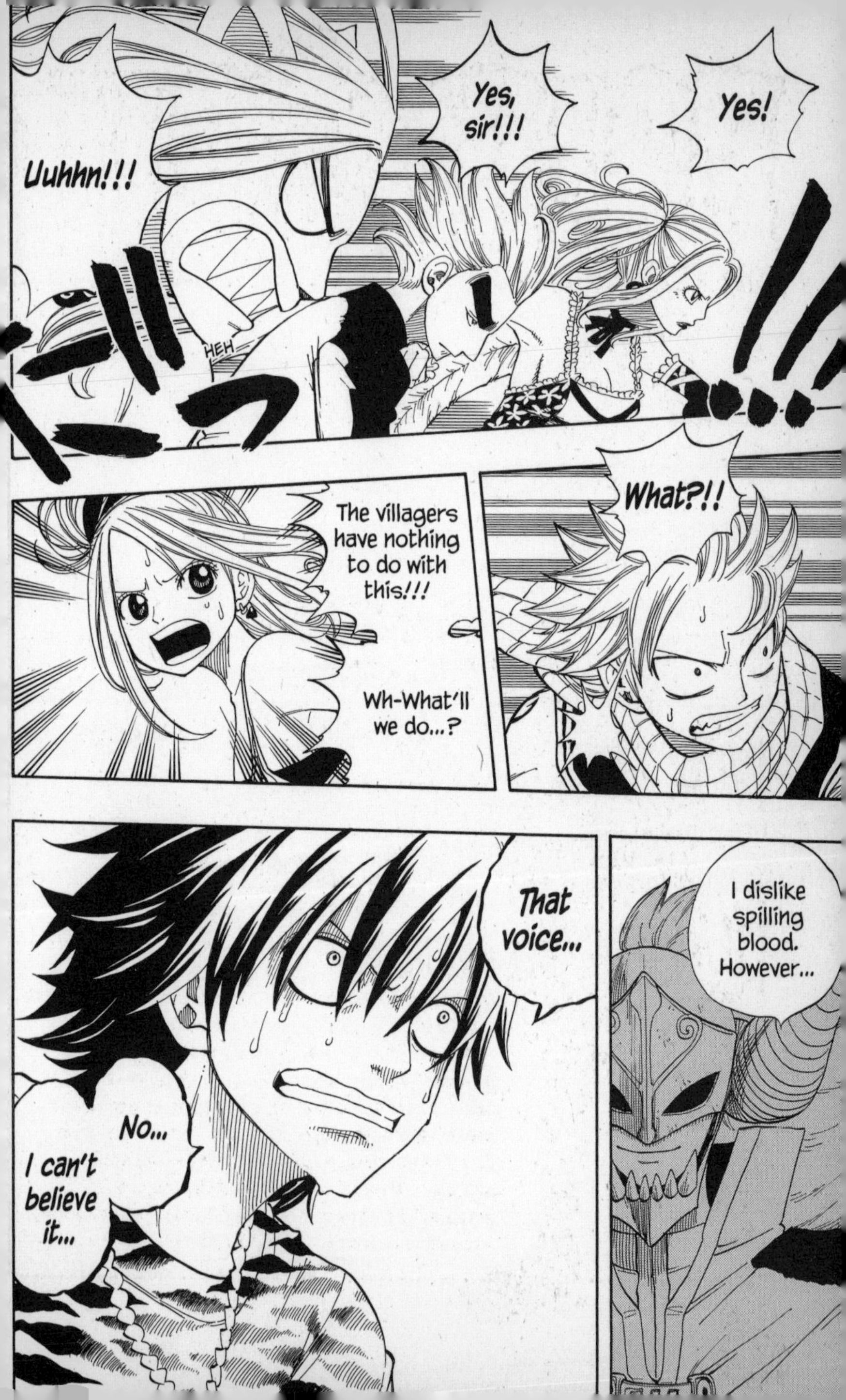
Yes!
Yes, sir!!!
Uuhhn!!!
HEH
What?!!
The villagers have nothing to do with this!!!
Wh-What'll we do...?
I dislike spilling blood. However...
That voice...
No... I can't believe it...

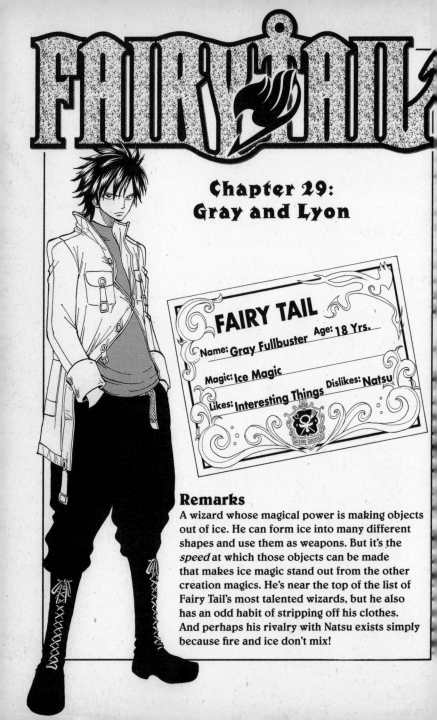

Chapter 29: Gray and Lyon

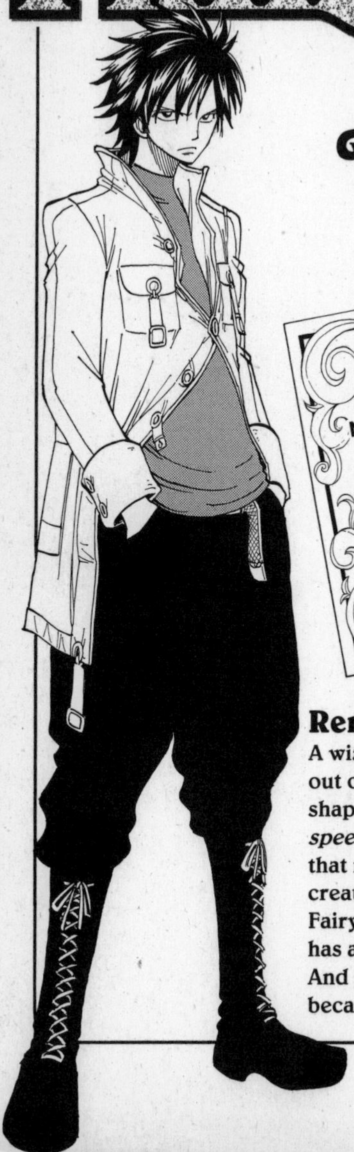

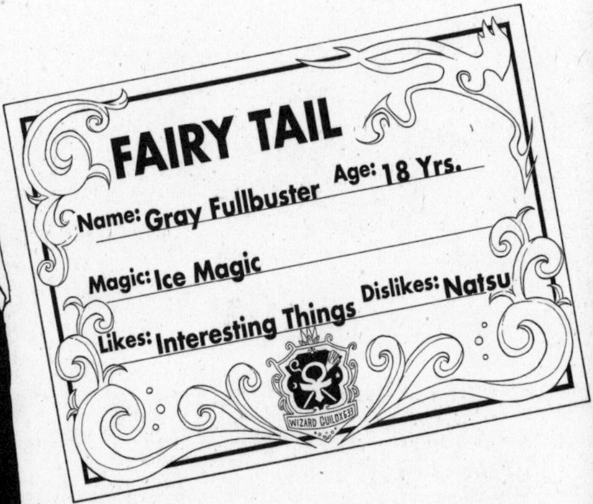
FAIRY TAIL
Name: Gray Fullbuster
Age: 18 Yrs.
Magic: Ice Magic
Likes: Interesting Things
Dislikes: Natsu
WIZARD GUILD X633

Remarks

A wizard whose magical power is making objects out of ice. He can form ice into many different shapes and use them as weapons. But it's the *speed* at which those objects can be made that makes ice magic stand out from the other creation magics. He's near the top of the list of Fairy Tail's most talented wizards, but he also has an odd habit of stripping off his clothes. And perhaps his rivalry with Natsu exists simply because fire and ice don't mix!

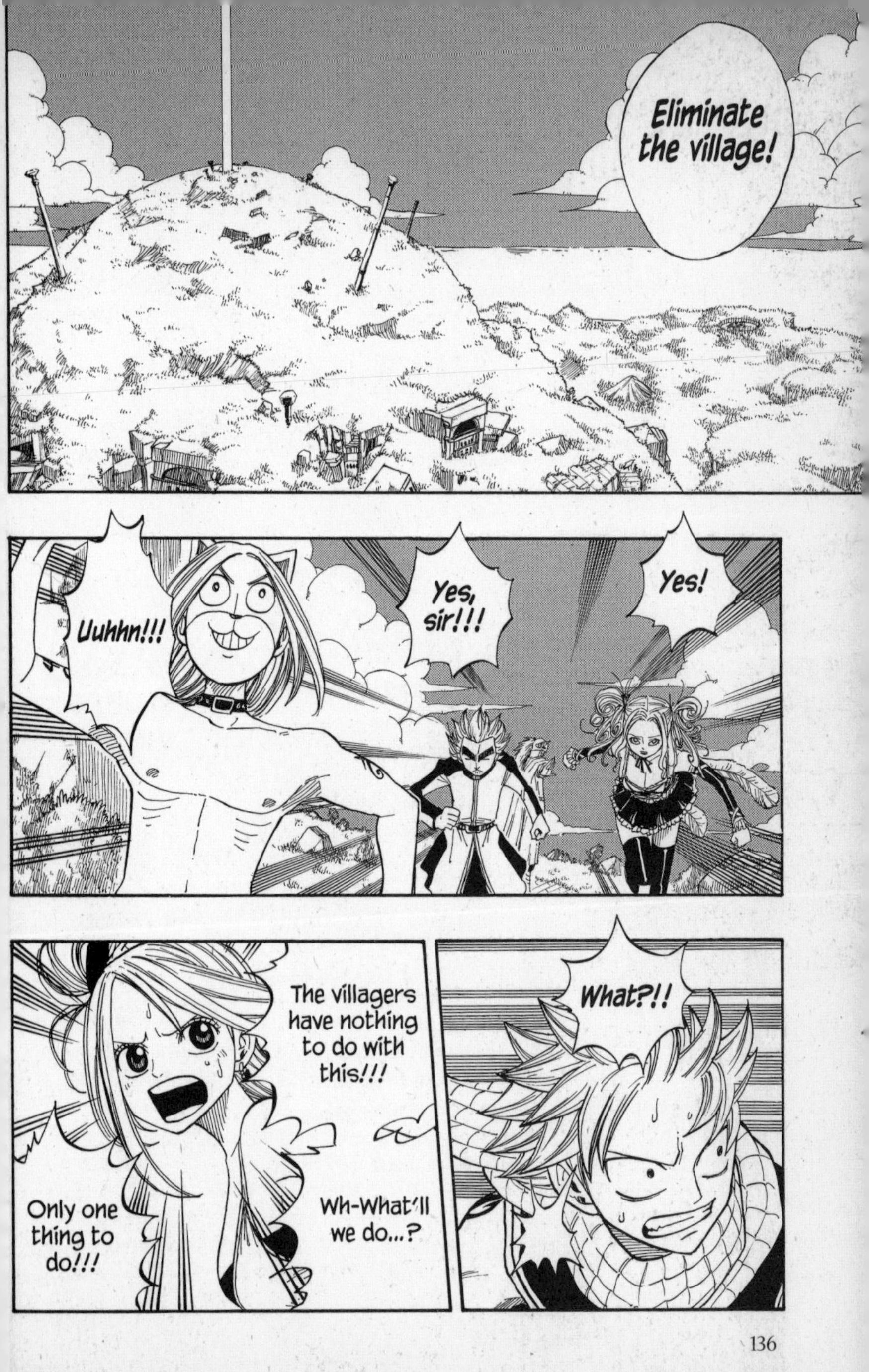

Eliminate the village!
Yes!
Yes, sir!!!
Uuhhn!!!
What?!!
The villagers have nothing to do with this!!!
Wh-What'll we do...?
Only one thing to do!!!

That voice...

No... I can't believe it...

I dislike spilling blood. However...

I'm just about fed up with all this hiding!!!

BWMM

FWOO

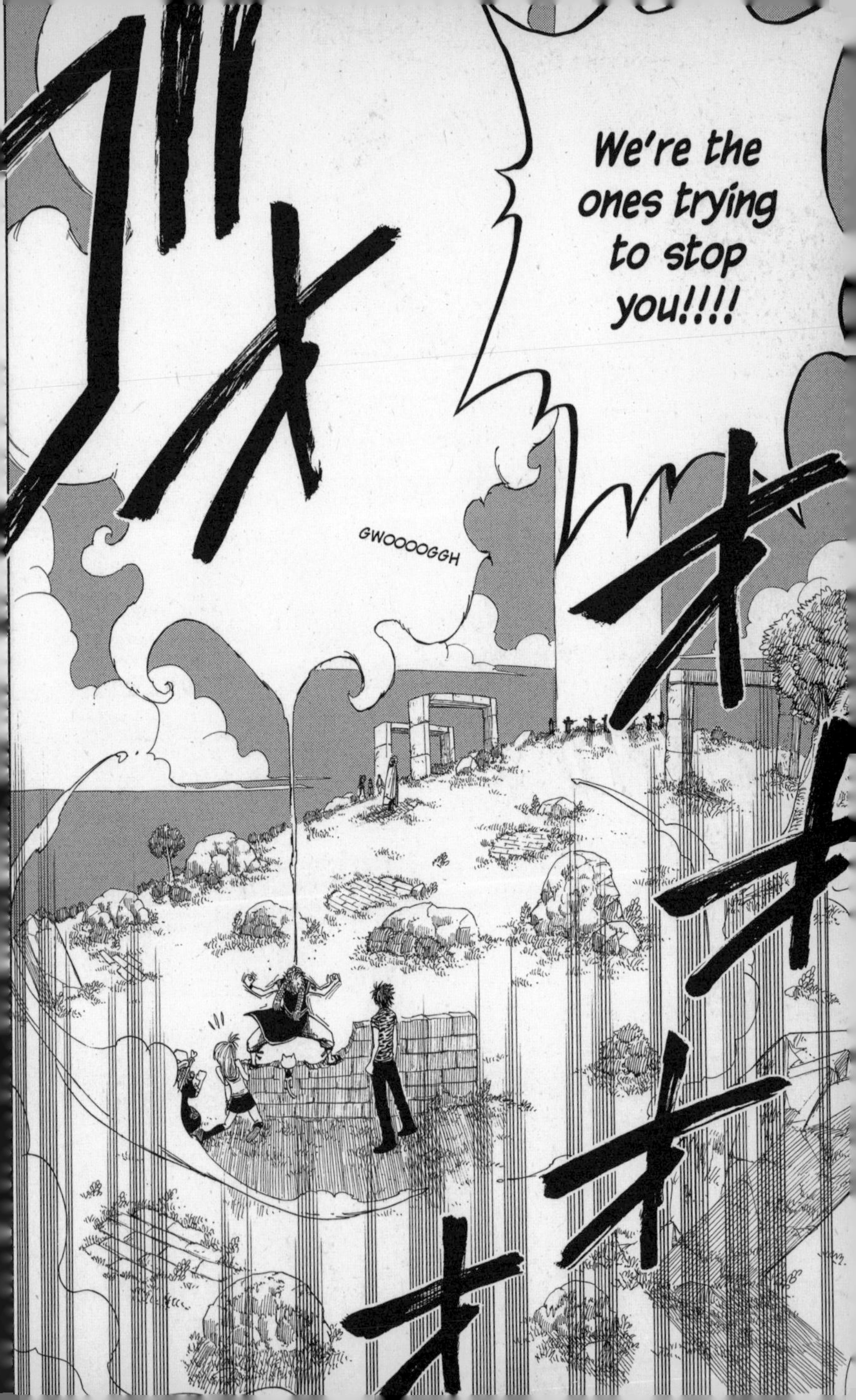
We're the ones trying to stop you!!!!
GWOOOOGGH

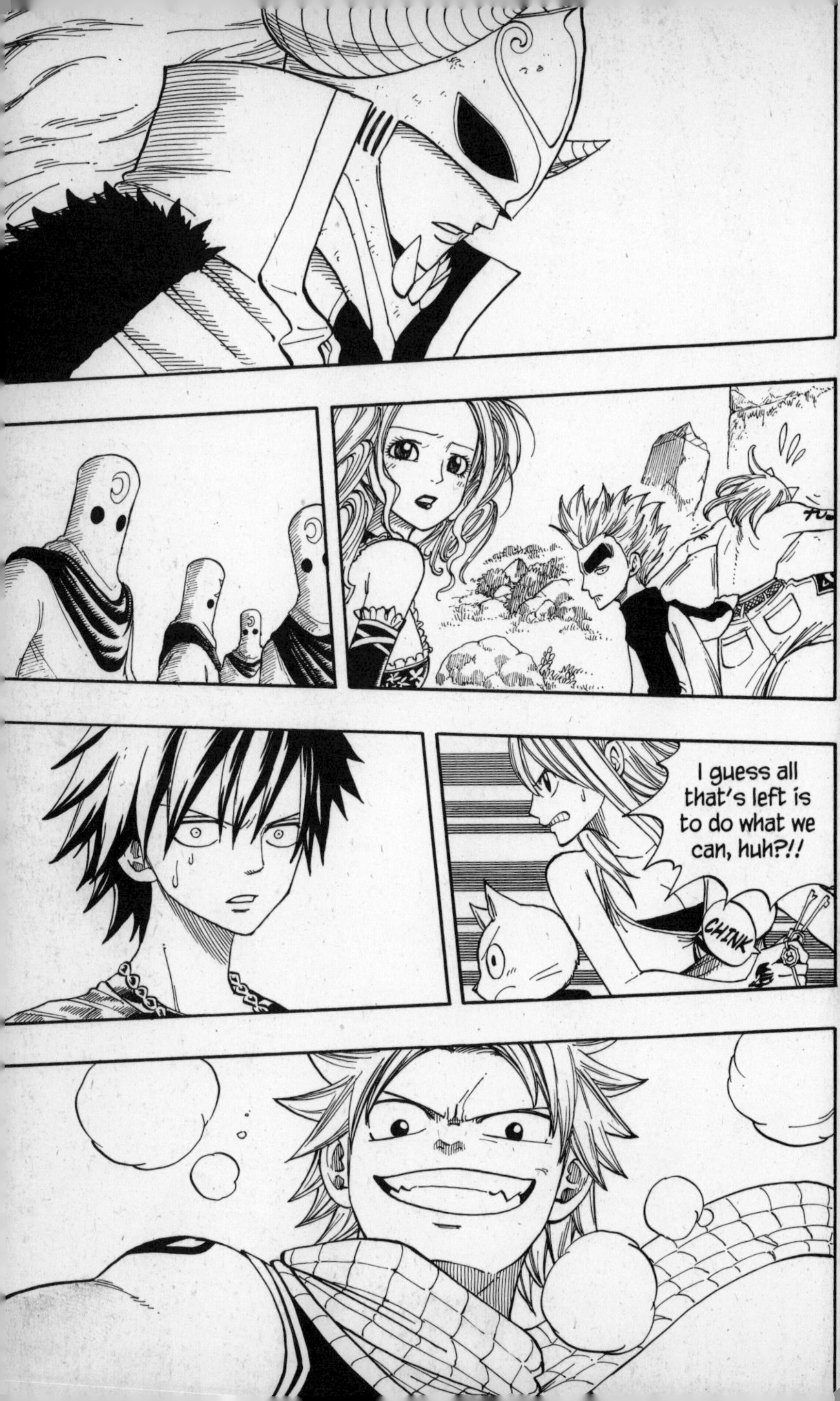
I guess all that's left is to do what we can, huh?!!
CHINK

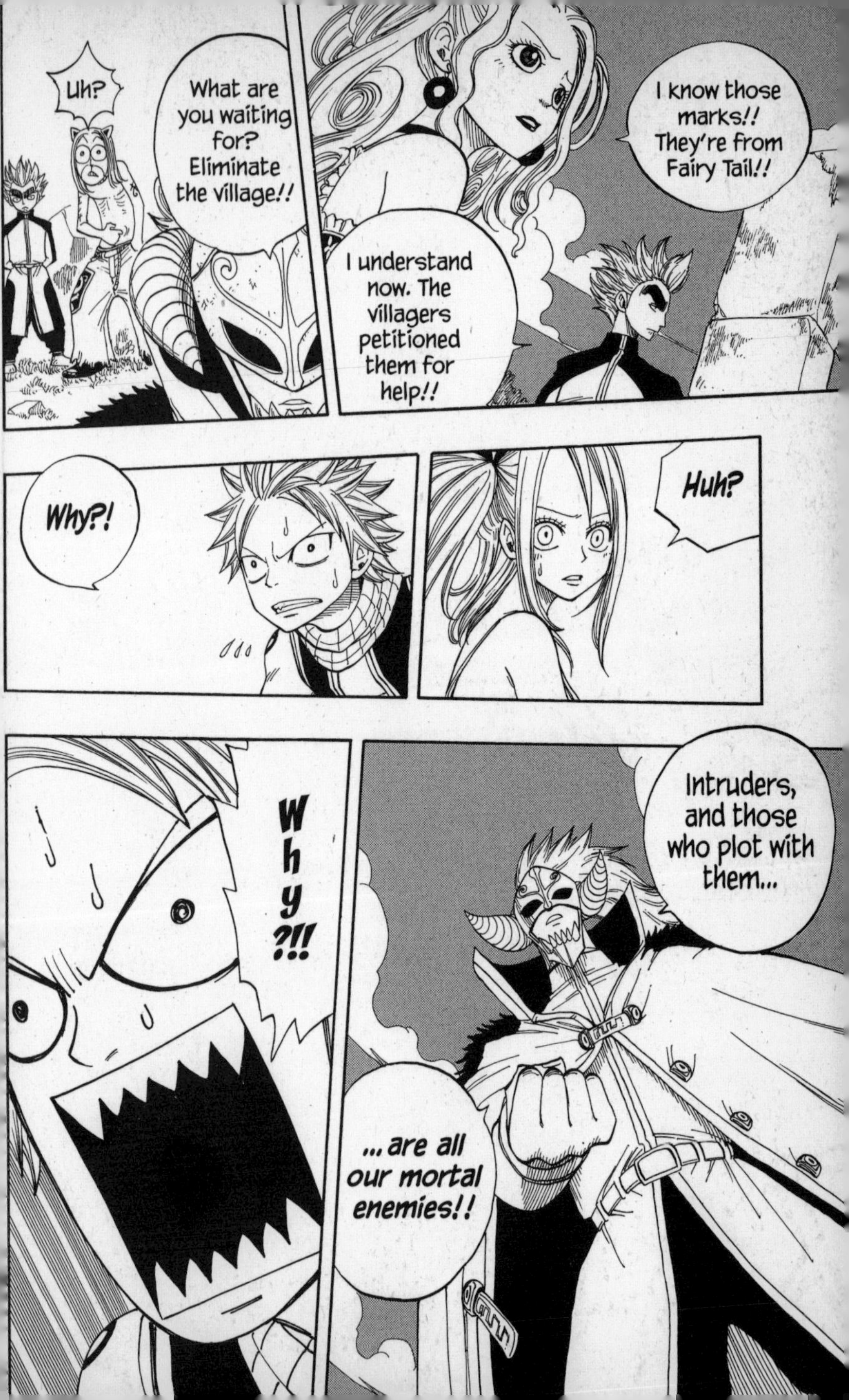
Uh?
What are you waiting for? Eliminate the village!!
I know those marks!! They're from Fairy Tail!!
I understand now. The villagers petitioned them for help!!
Why?!
Huh?
Why?!!
Intruders, and those who plot with them...
...are all our mortal enemies!!

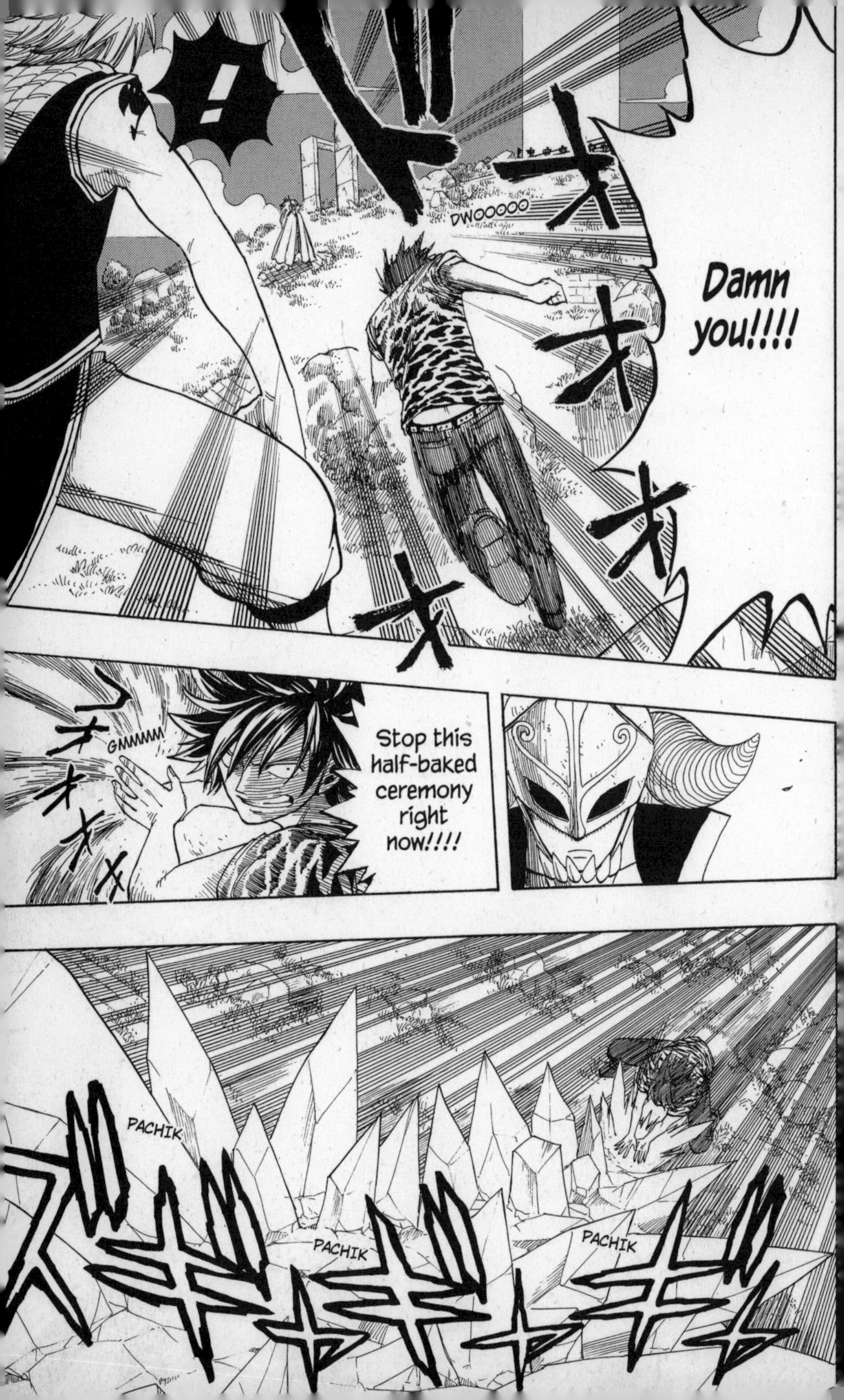

!
DWOOOOO
Damn you!!!!
GMMMMM
Stop this half-baked ceremony right now!!!!
PACHIK
PACHIK
PACHIK

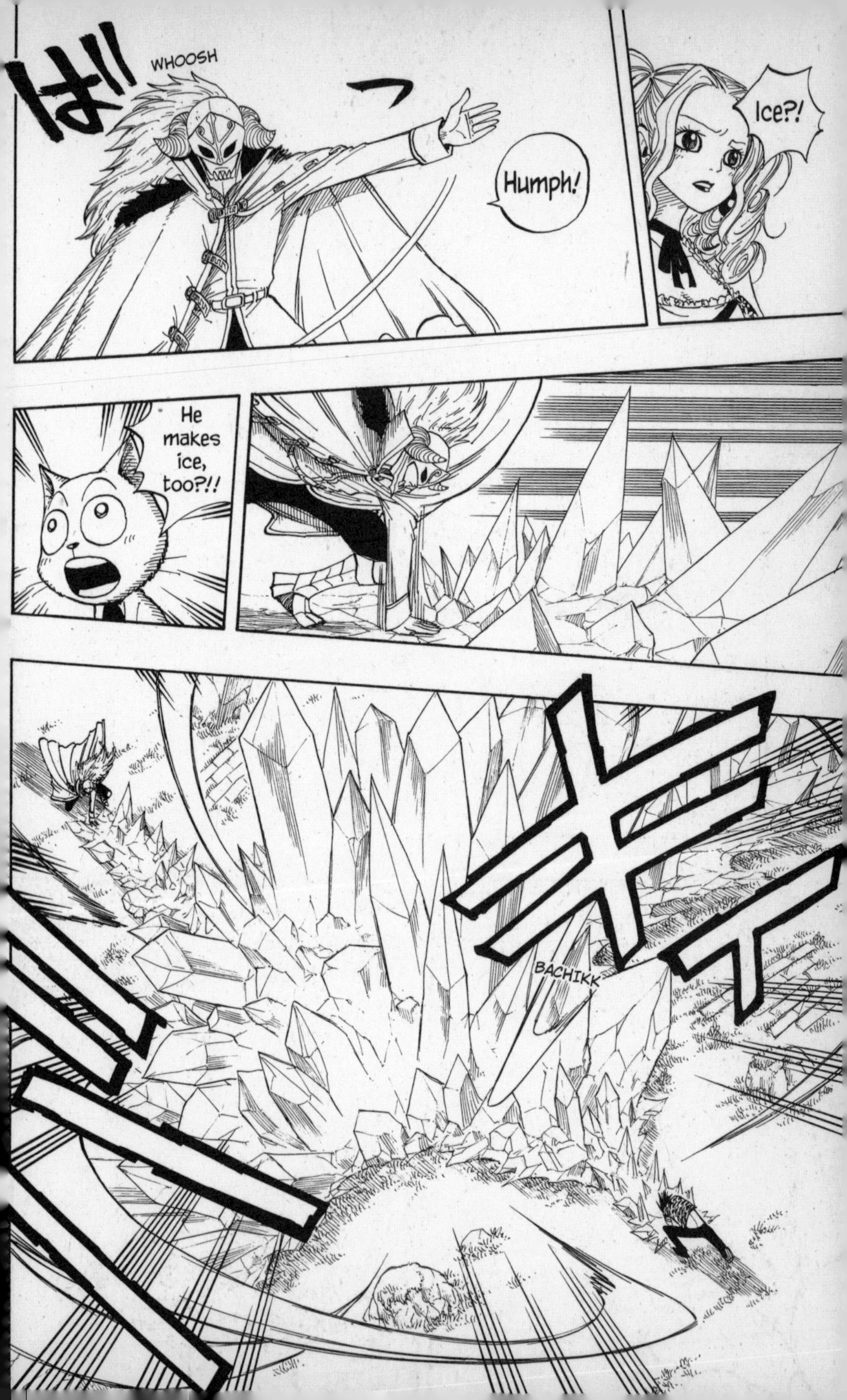
Ice?!
WHOOSH
Humph!
He makes ice, too?!!
BACHIKK

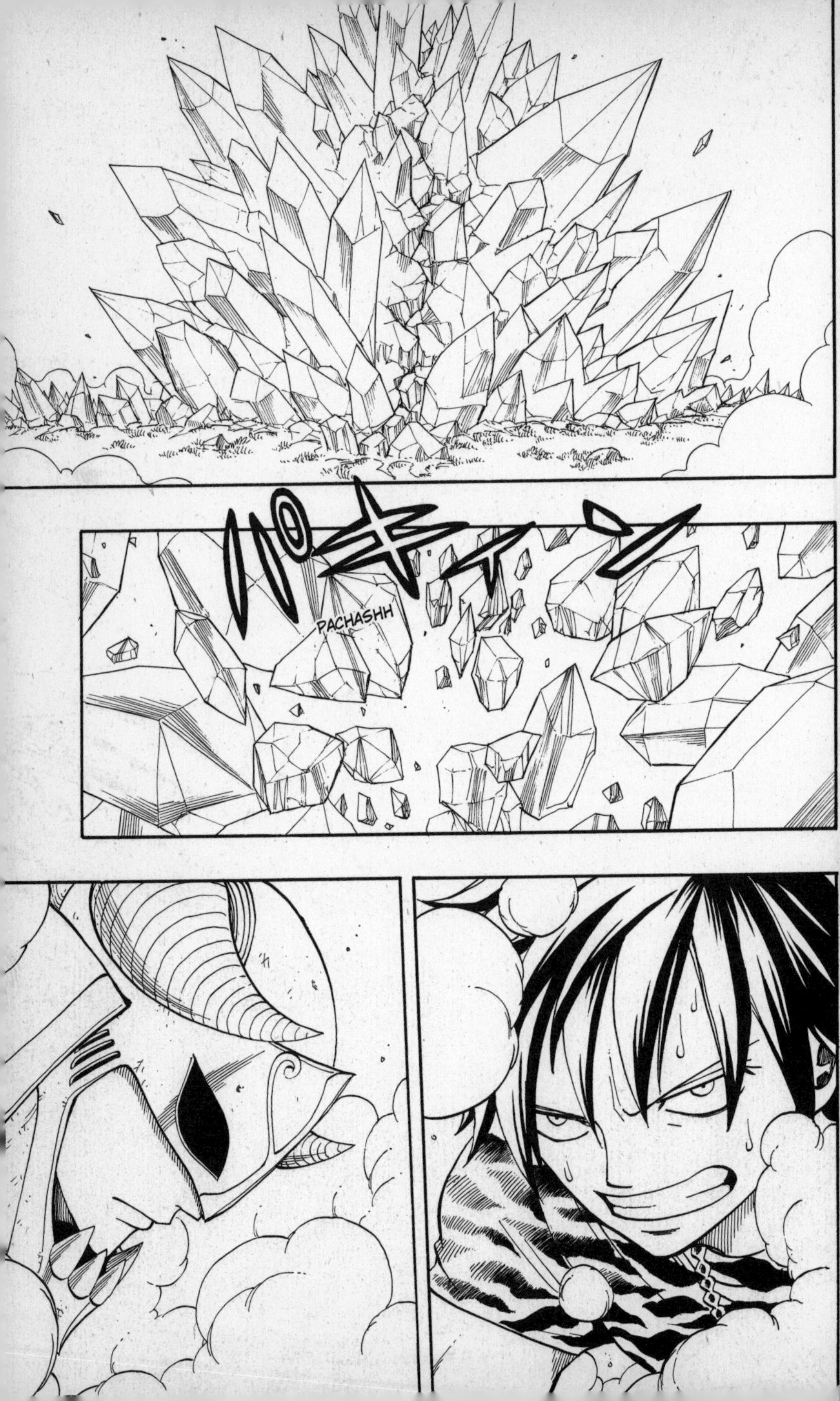
PACHASHH

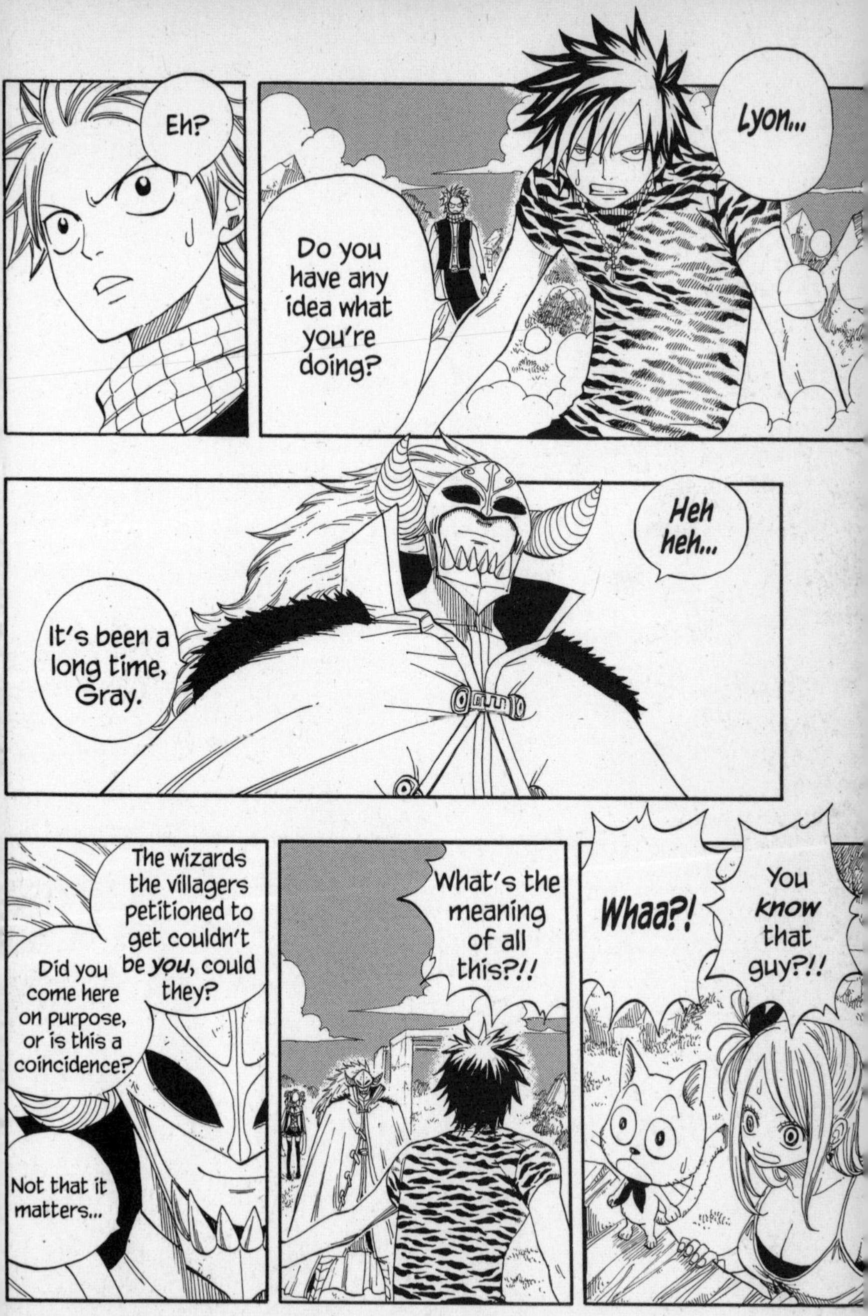

Lyon...
Do you have any idea what you're doing?
Eh?
Heh heh...
It's been a long time, Gray.
You *know* that guy?!!
Whaa?!
What's the meaning of all this?!!
The wizards the villagers petitioned to get couldn't be *you*, could they?
Did you come here on purpose, or is this a coincidence?
Not that it matters...

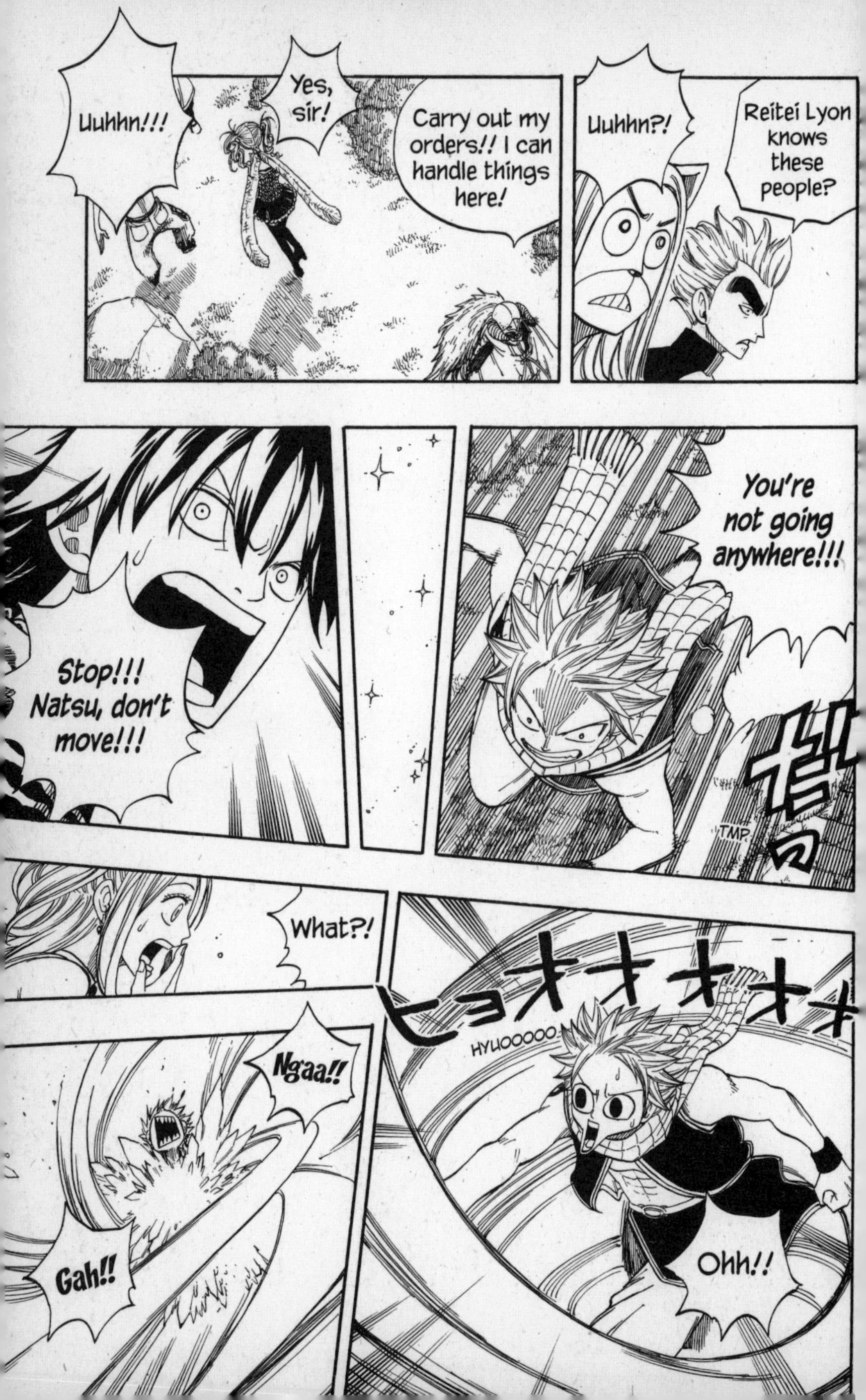
Reitei Lyon knows these people?
Uuhhn?!
Carry out my orders!! I can handle things here!
Yes, sir!
Uuhhn!!!
You're not going anywhere!!!
TMP
Stop!!! Natsu, don't move!!!
What?!
HYUOOOOO
Ngaa!!
Ohh!!
Gah!!

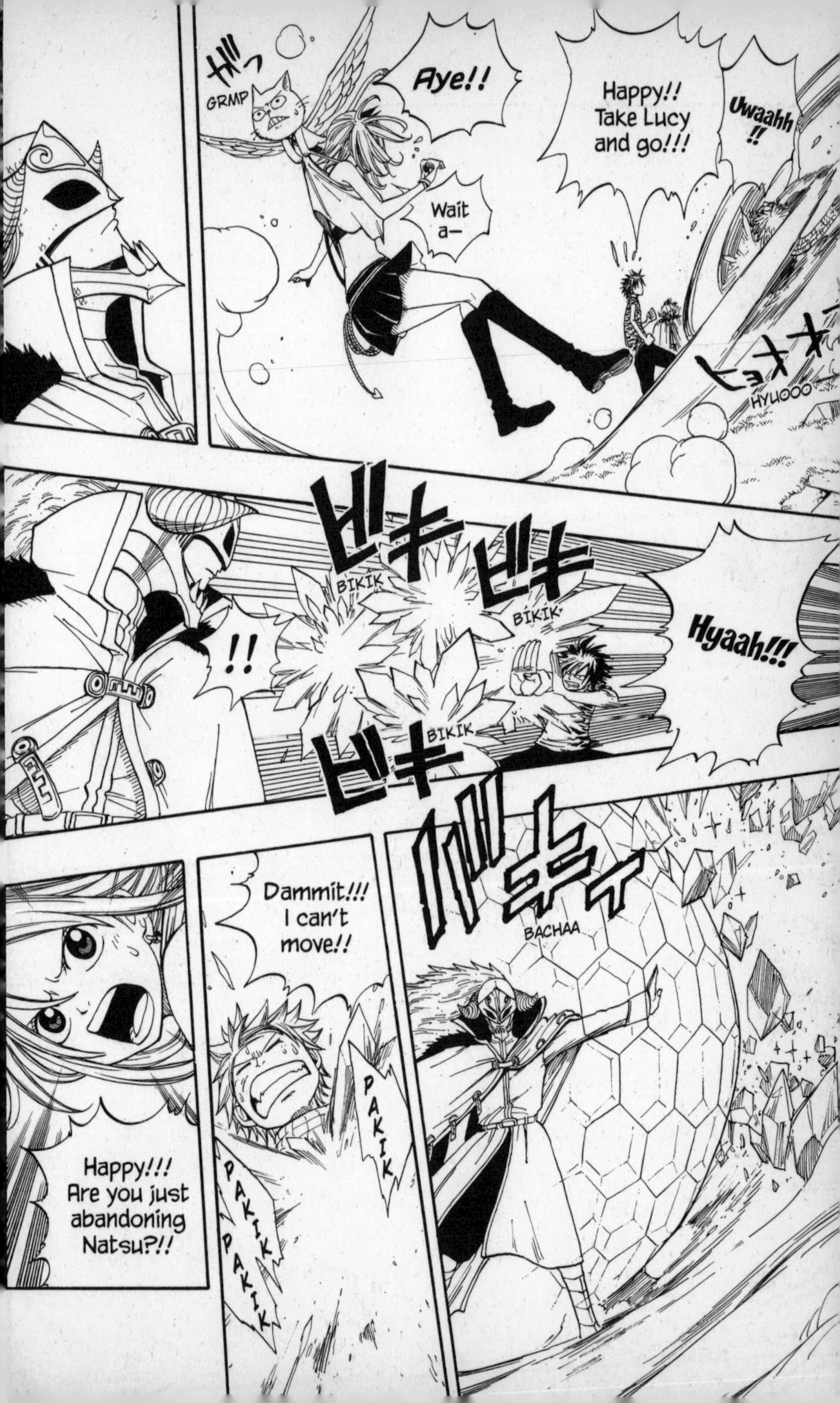

Happy!! Take Lucy and go!!!
Uwaahh!!
HYUOOO
Aye!!
GRMP
Wait a—
Hyaah!!!
BIKIK
BIKIK
BIKIK
!!
BACHAA
Dammit!!! I can't move!!
PAKIK
PAKIK
PAKIK
Happy!!! Are you just abandoning Natsu?!!

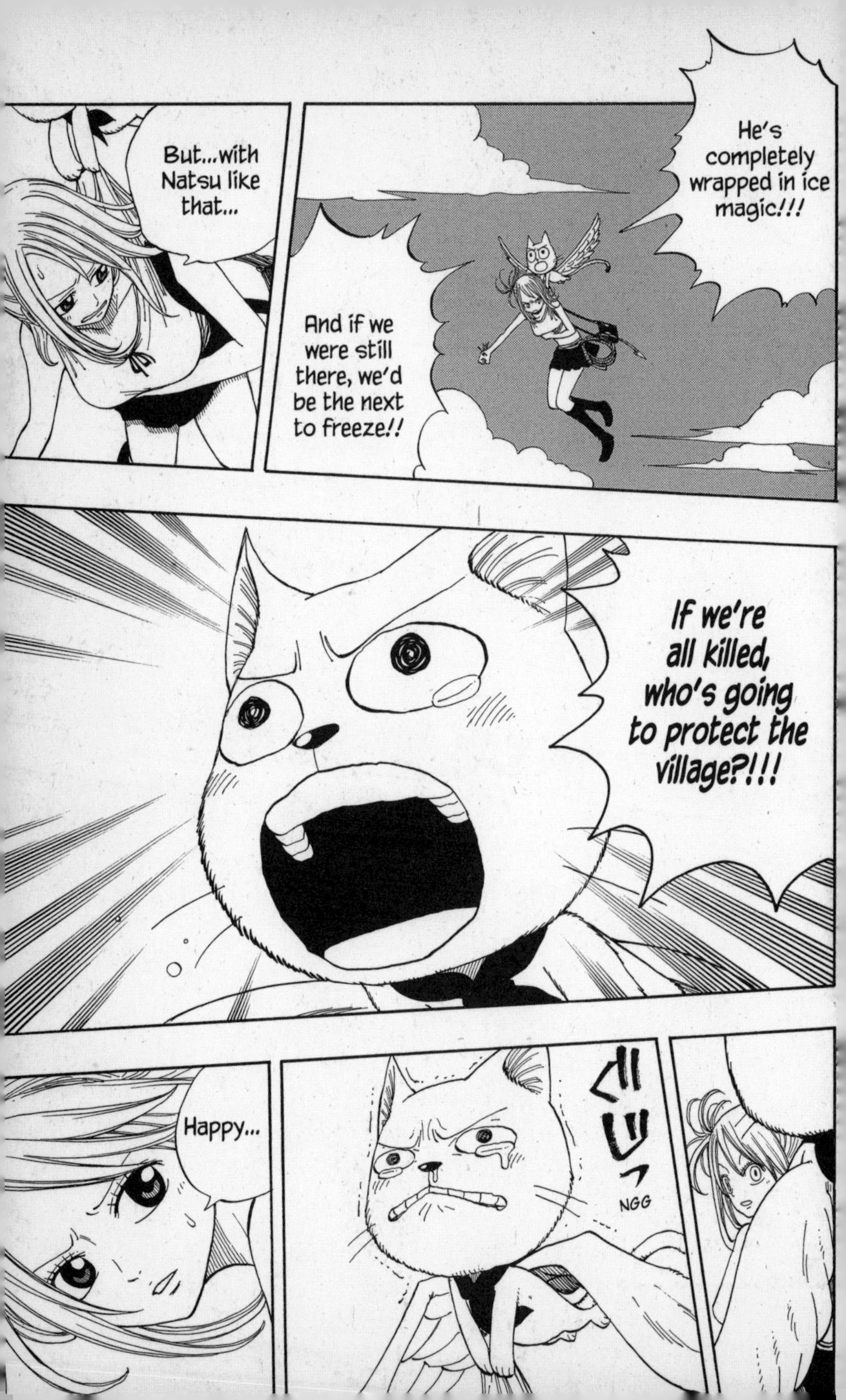
He's completely wrapped in ice magic!!!
And if we were still there, we'd be the next to freeze!!
But...with Natsu like that...
If we're all killed, who's going to protect the village?!!!
NGG
Happy...

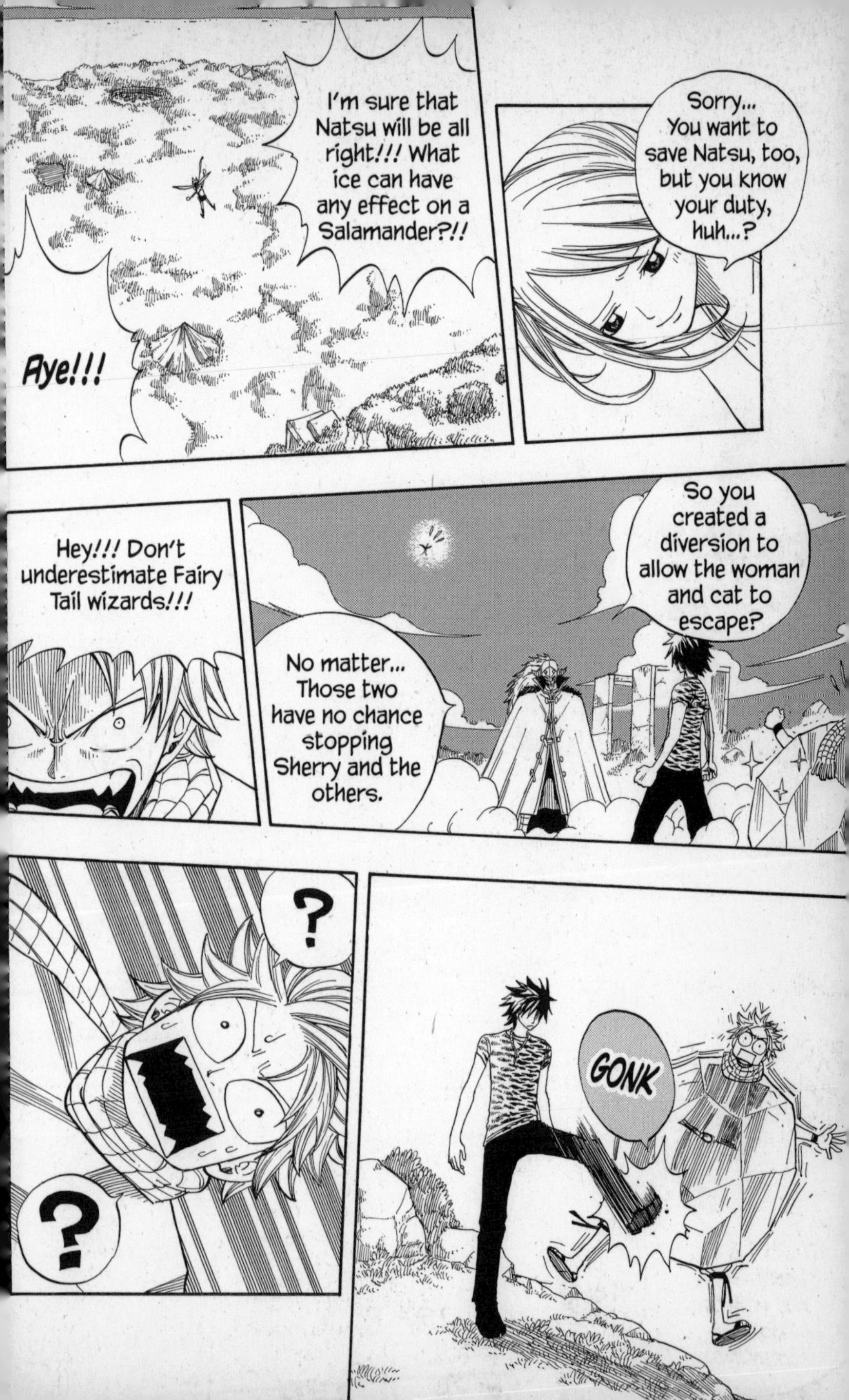
Sorry... You want to save Natsu, too, but you know your duty, huh...?
I'm sure that Natsu will be all right!!! What ice can have any effect on a Salamander?!!
Aye!!!
So you created a diversion to allow the woman and cat to escape?
No matter... Those two have no chance stopping Sherry and the others.
Hey!!! Don't underestimate Fairy Tail wizards!!!
GONK
?
?

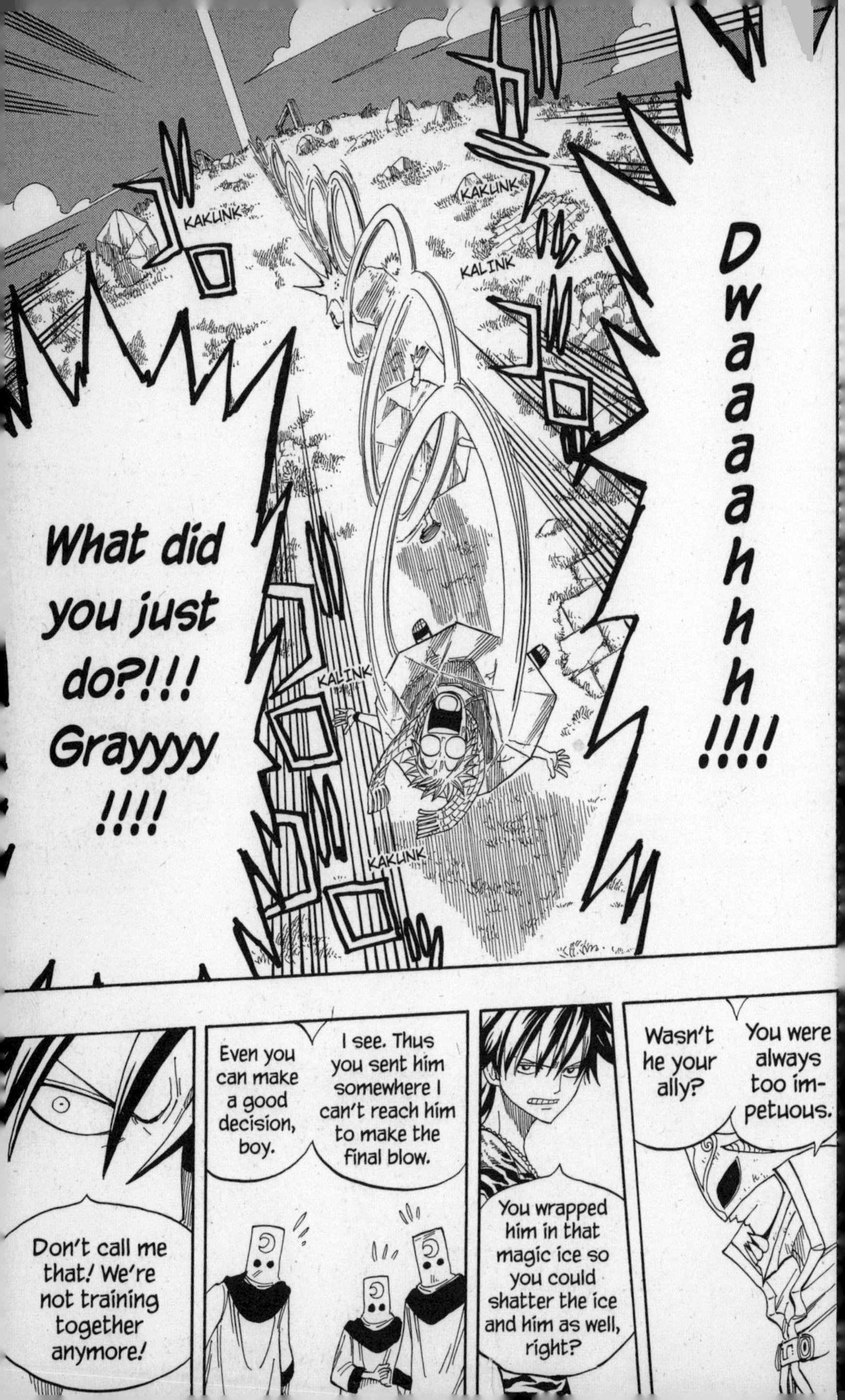
Dwaaaahhh!!!!
KAKUNK
KALINK
KAKUNK
What did you just do?!!! Grayyyy!!!!
KALINK
KAKUNK
You were always too impetuous.
Wasn't he your ally?
You wrapped him in that magic ice so you could shatter the ice and him as well, right?
I see. Thus you sent him somewhere I can't reach him to make the final blow.
Even you can make a good decision, boy.
Don't call me that! We're not training together anymore!

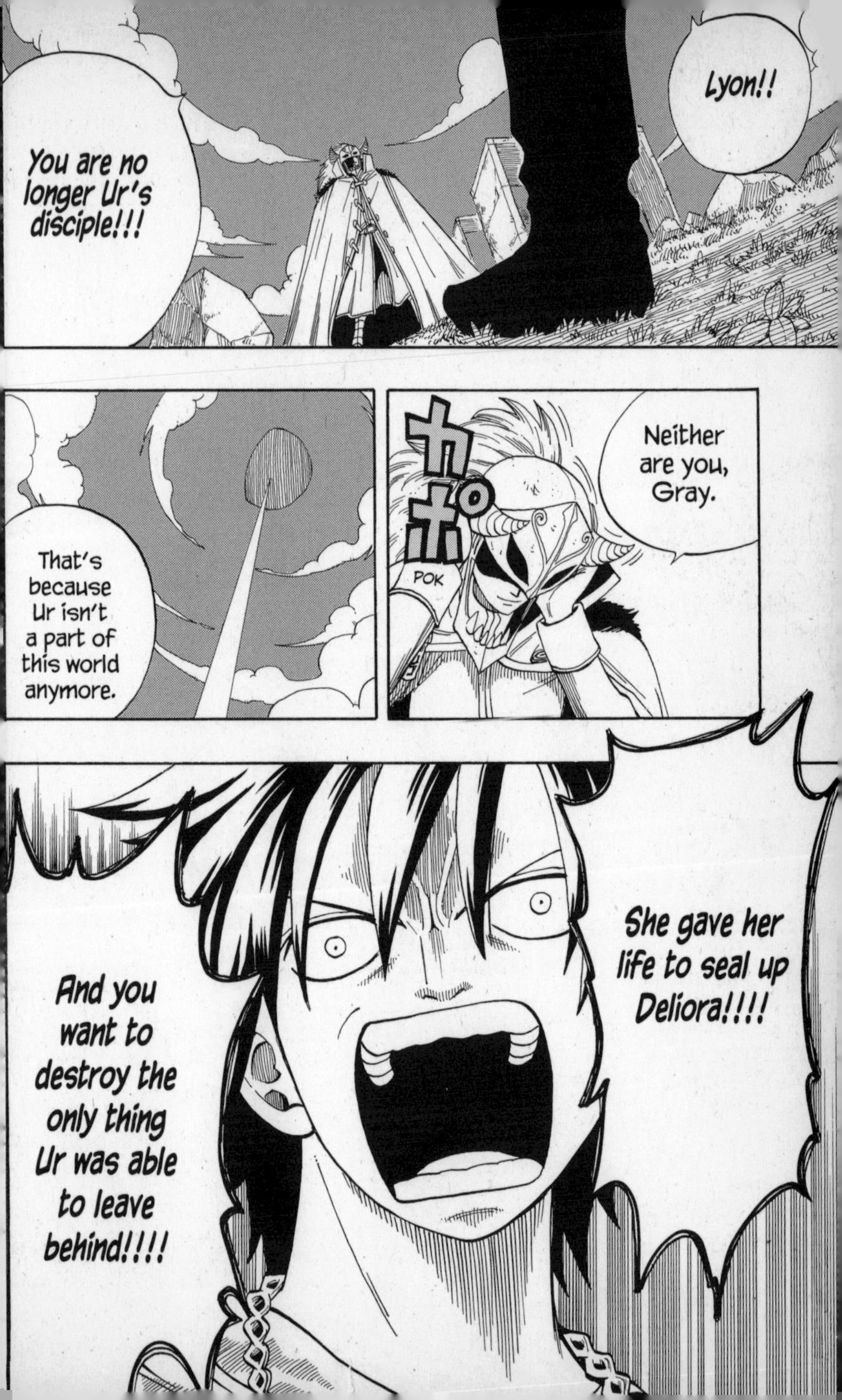
Lyon!!
You are no longer Ur's disciple!!!
カポ
POK
Neither are you, Gray.
That's because Ur isn't a part of this world anymore.
She gave her life to seal up Deliora!!!!
And you want to destroy the only thing Ur was able to leave behind!!!!

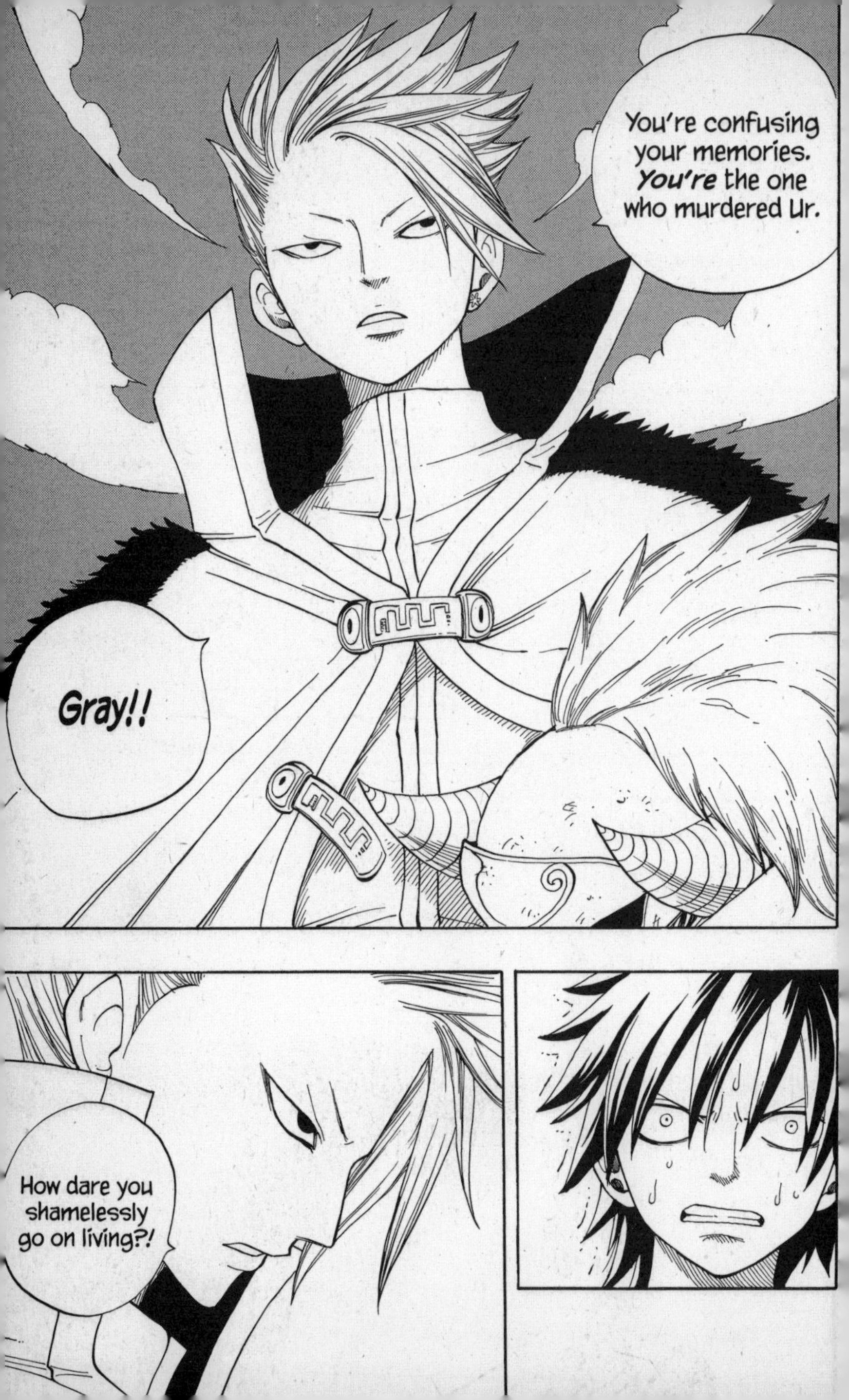

You're confusing your memories. *You're* the one who murdered Ur.
Gray!!
How dare you shamelessly go on living?!

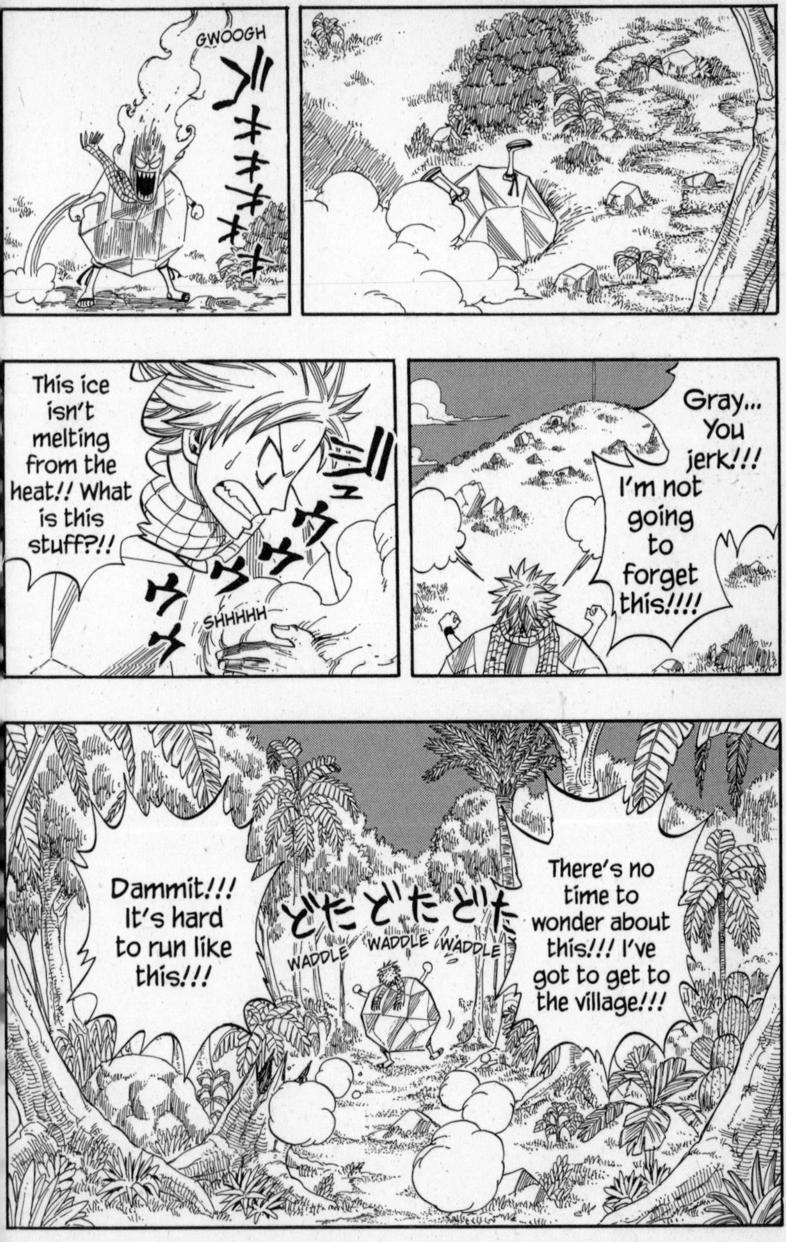
GWOOGH
Gray... You jerk!!! I'm not going to forget this!!!!
This ice isn't melting from the heat!! What is this stuff?!!
SHHHHH
There's no time to wonder about this!!! I've got to get to the village!!!
Dammit!!! It's hard to run like this!!!
どたどたどた
WADDLE WADDLE WADDLE

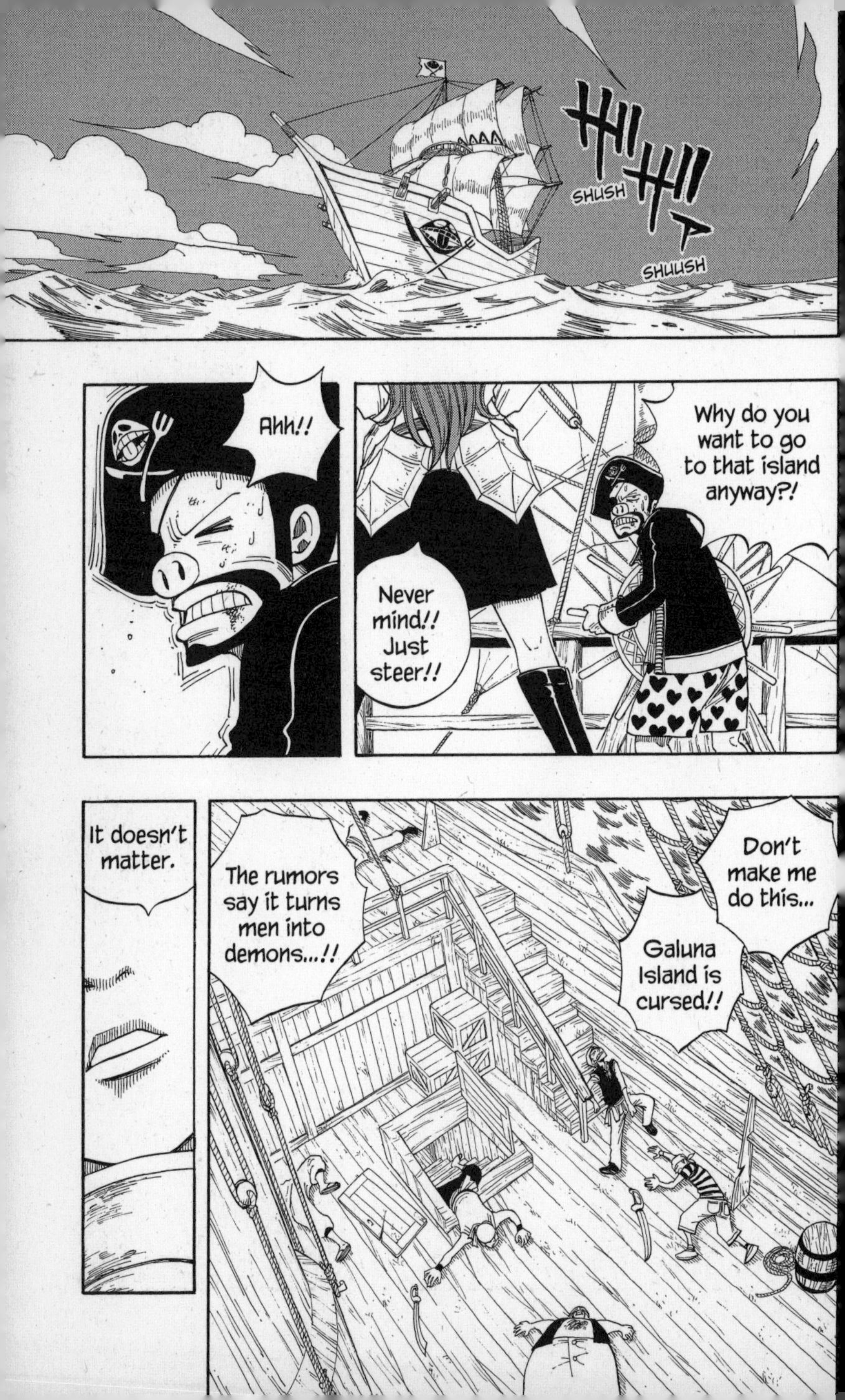
SHUSH
SHUUSH
Why do you want to go to that island anyway?!
Never mind!! Just steer!!
Ahh!!
Don't make me do this...
Galuna Island is cursed!!
The rumors say it turns men into demons...!!
It doesn't matter.

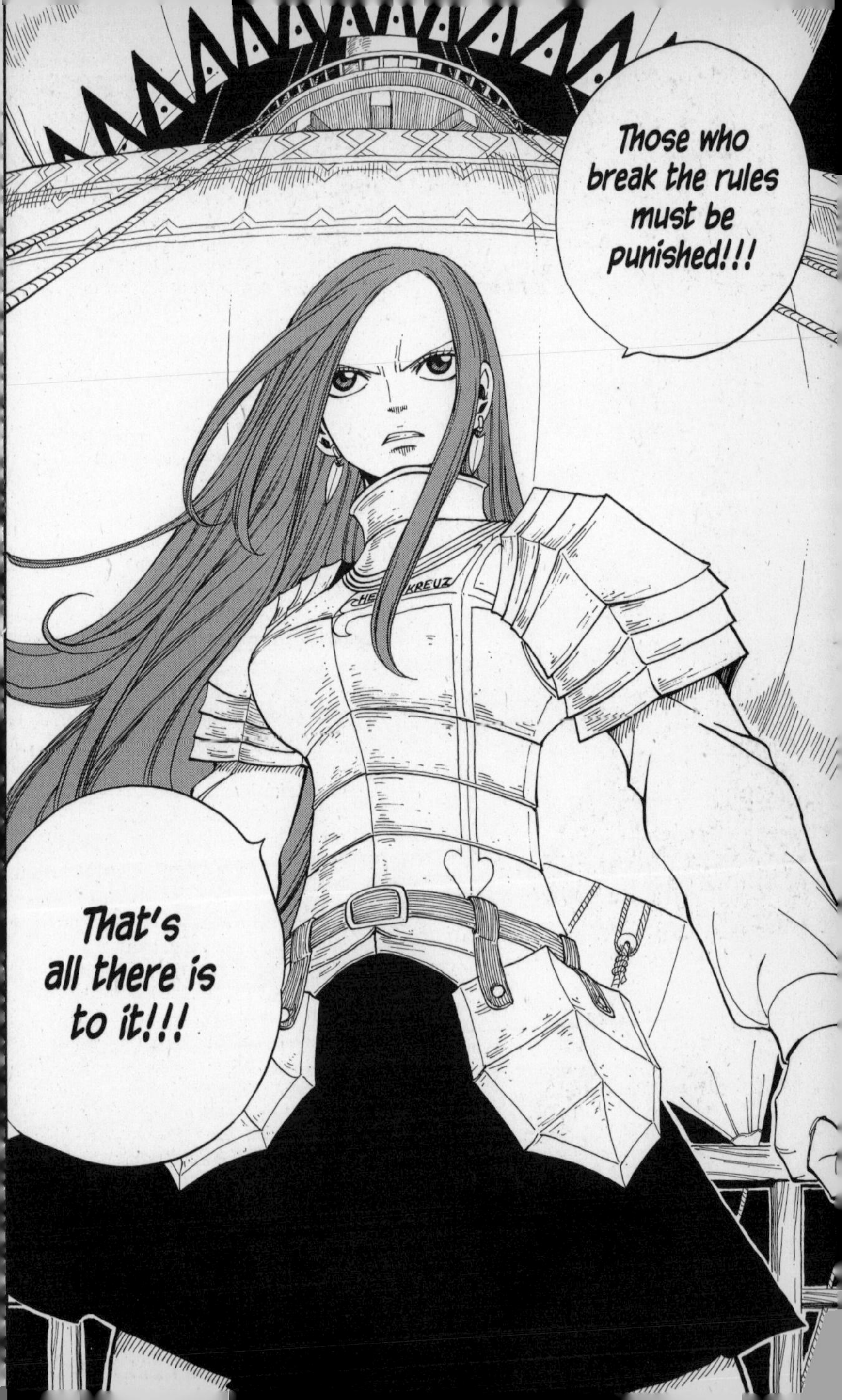
Those who break the rules must be punished!!!
That's all there is to it!!!

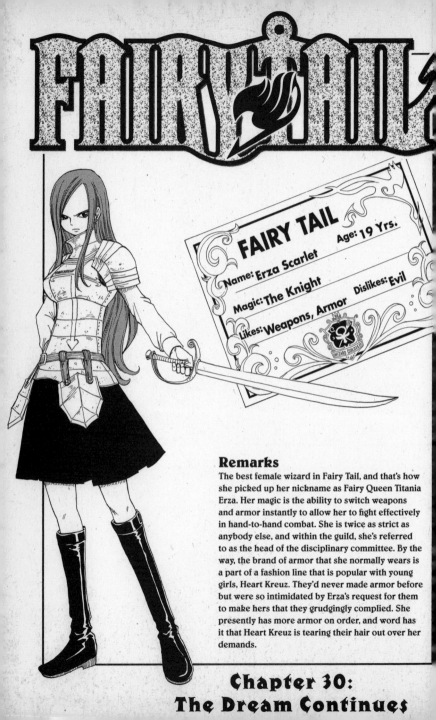

FAIRY TAIL

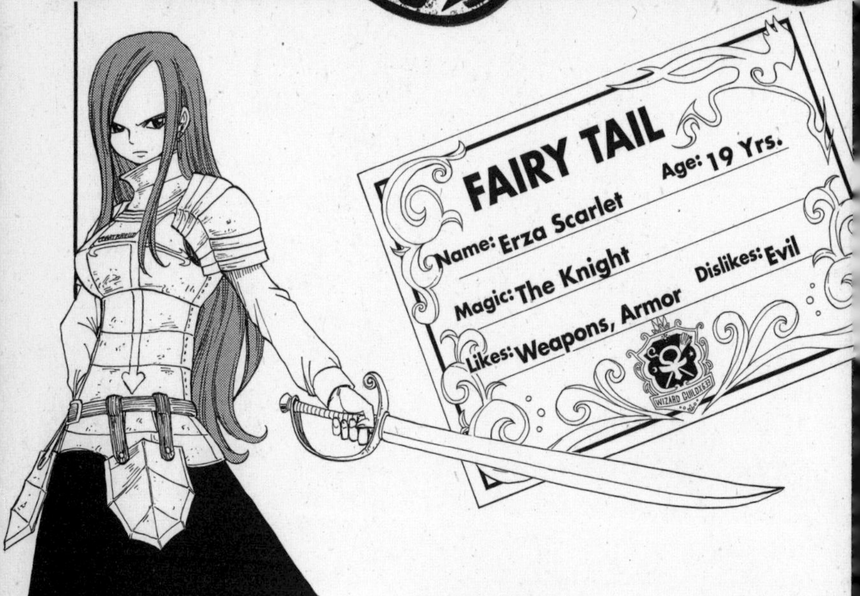

FAIRY TAIL
Name: Erza Scarlet
Age: 19 Yrs.
Magic: The Knight
Dislikes: Evil
Likes: Weapons, Armor
WIZARD GUILD

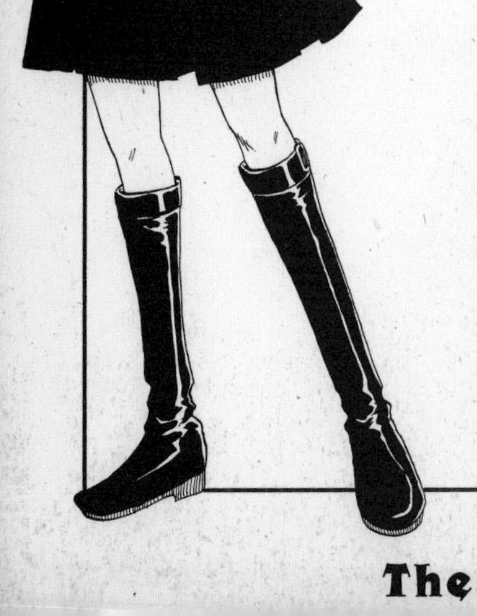

Remarks

The best female wizard in Fairy Tail, and that's how she picked up her nickname as Fairy Queen Titania Erza. Her magic is the ability to switch weapons and armor instantly to allow her to fight effectively in hand-to-hand combat. She is twice as strict as anybody else, and within the guild, she's referred to as the head of the disciplinary committee. By the way, the brand of armor that she normally wears is a part of a fashion line that is popular with young girls, Heart Kreuz. They'd never made armor before but were so intimidated by Erza's request for them to make hers that they grudgingly complied. She presently has more armor on order, and word has it that Heart Kreuz is tearing their hair out over her demands.

Chapter 30: The Dream Continues

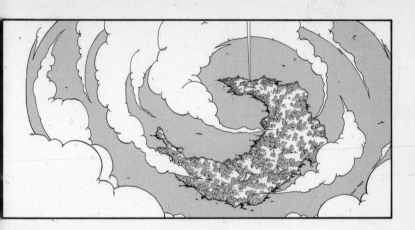

You're the one who murdered Ur.

Gray!!

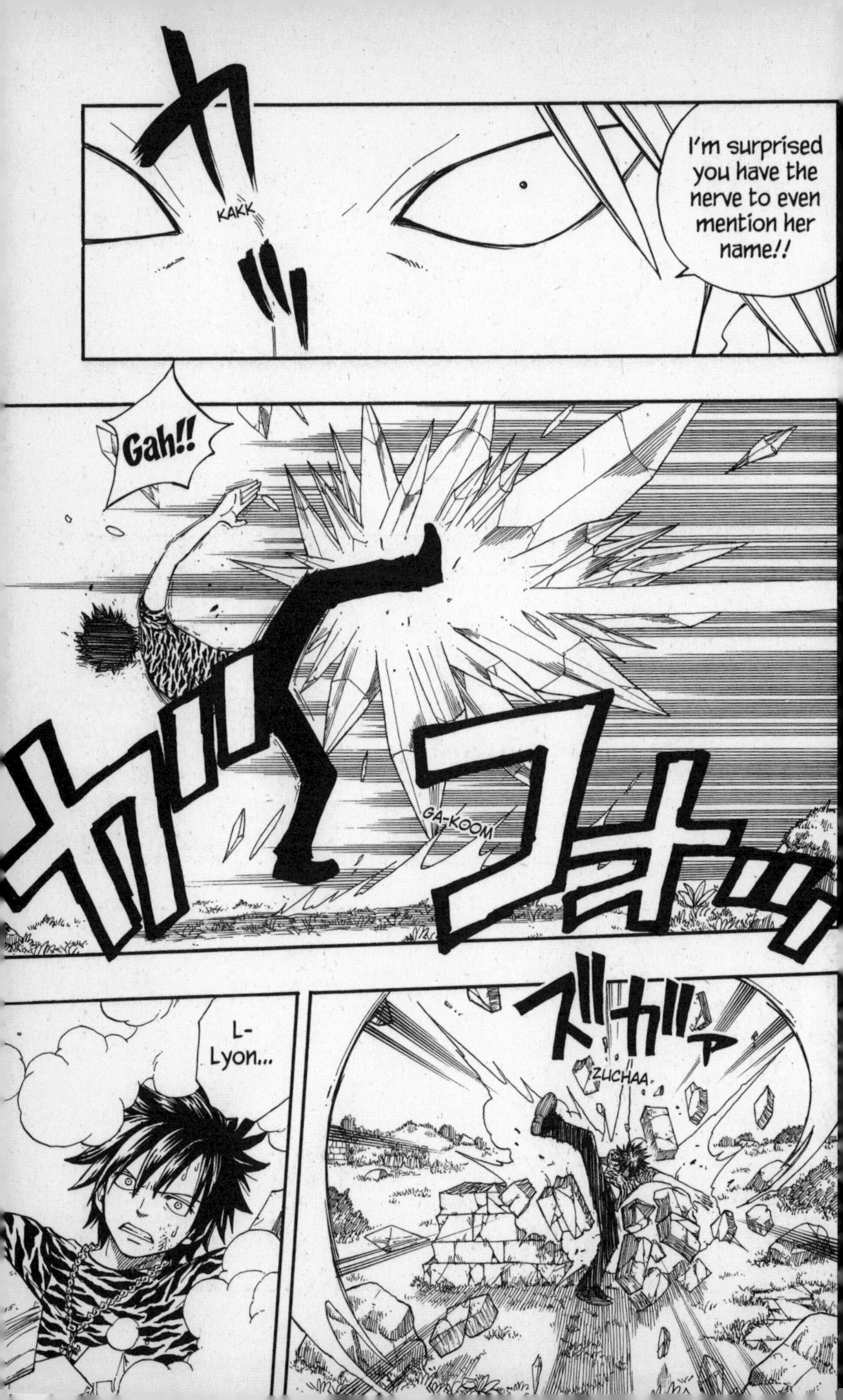
I'm surprised you have the nerve to even mention her name!!
KAKK
Gah!!
GA-KOOM
ZUCHAA
L- Lyon...

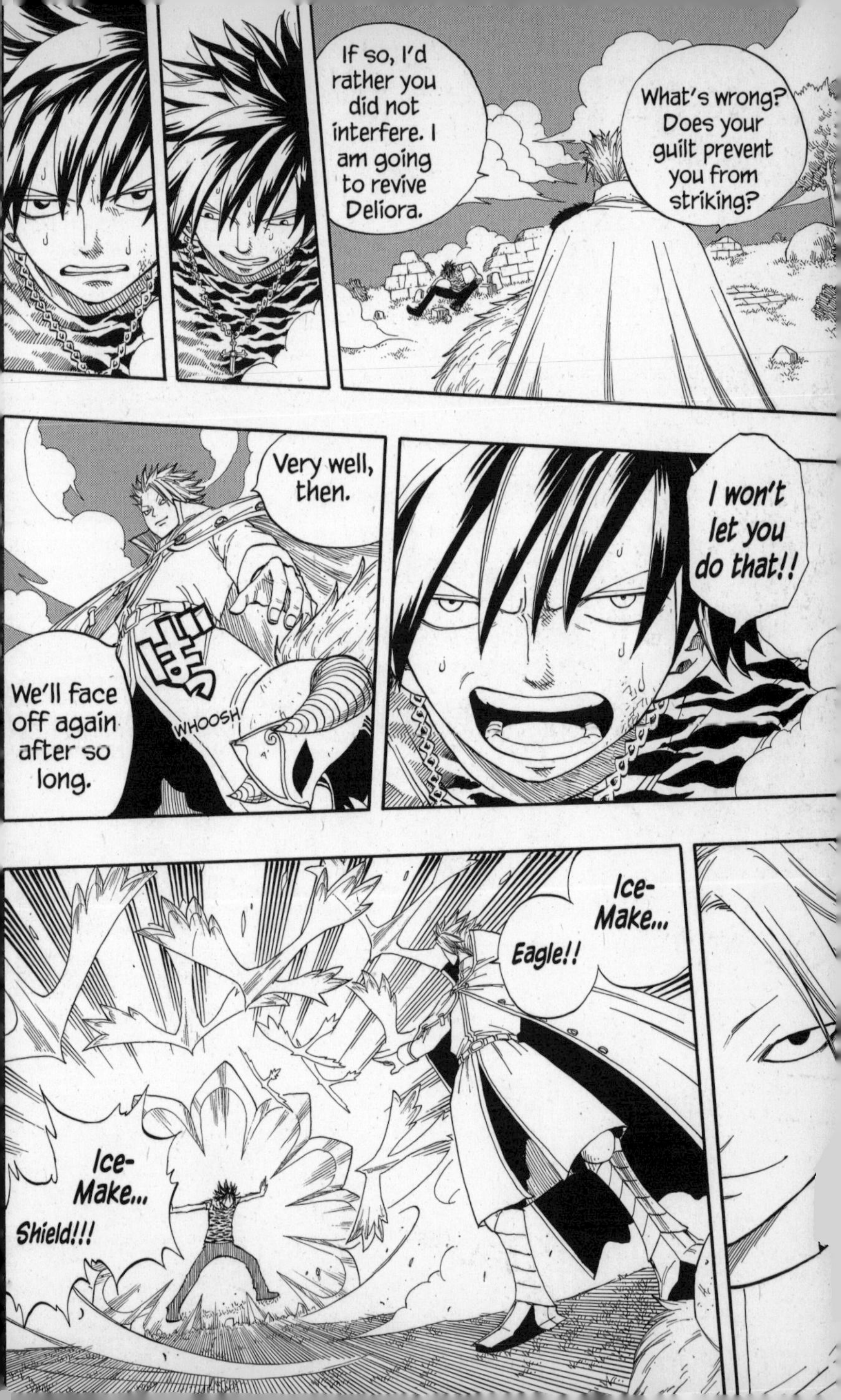
What's wrong? Does your guilt prevent you from striking?
If so, I'd rather you did not interfere. I am going to revive Deliora.
I won't let you do that!!
Very well, then.
We'll face off again after so long.
WHOOSH
Ice-Make...
Eagle!!
Ice-Make...
Shield!!!

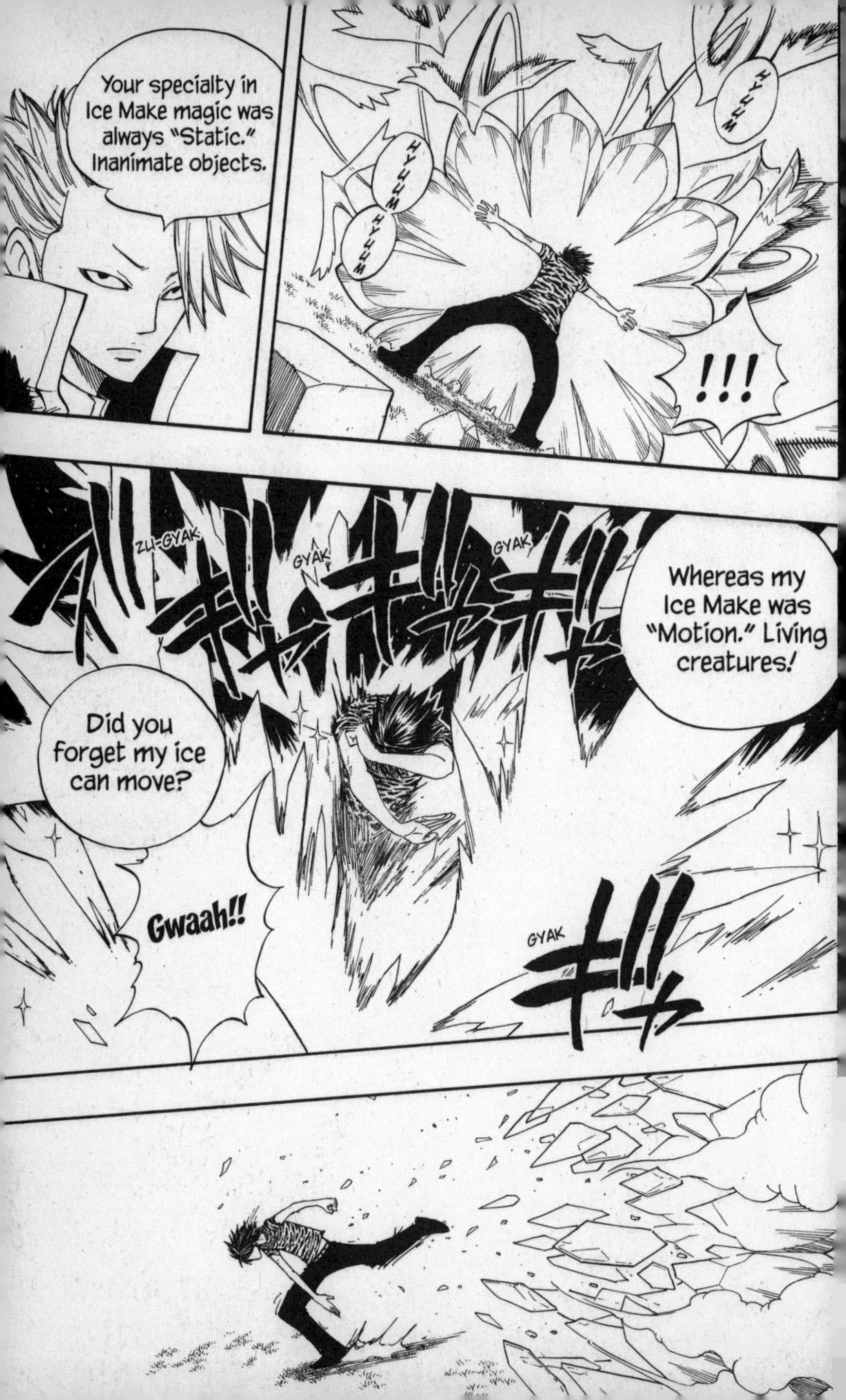
Your specialty in Ice Make magic was always "Static." Inanimate objects.
HYUUM
HYUUM
HYUUM
HYUUM
!!!
ZU-GYAK
GYAK
GYAK
Whereas my Ice Make was "Motion." Living creatures!
Did you forget my ice can move?
Gwaah!!
GYAK

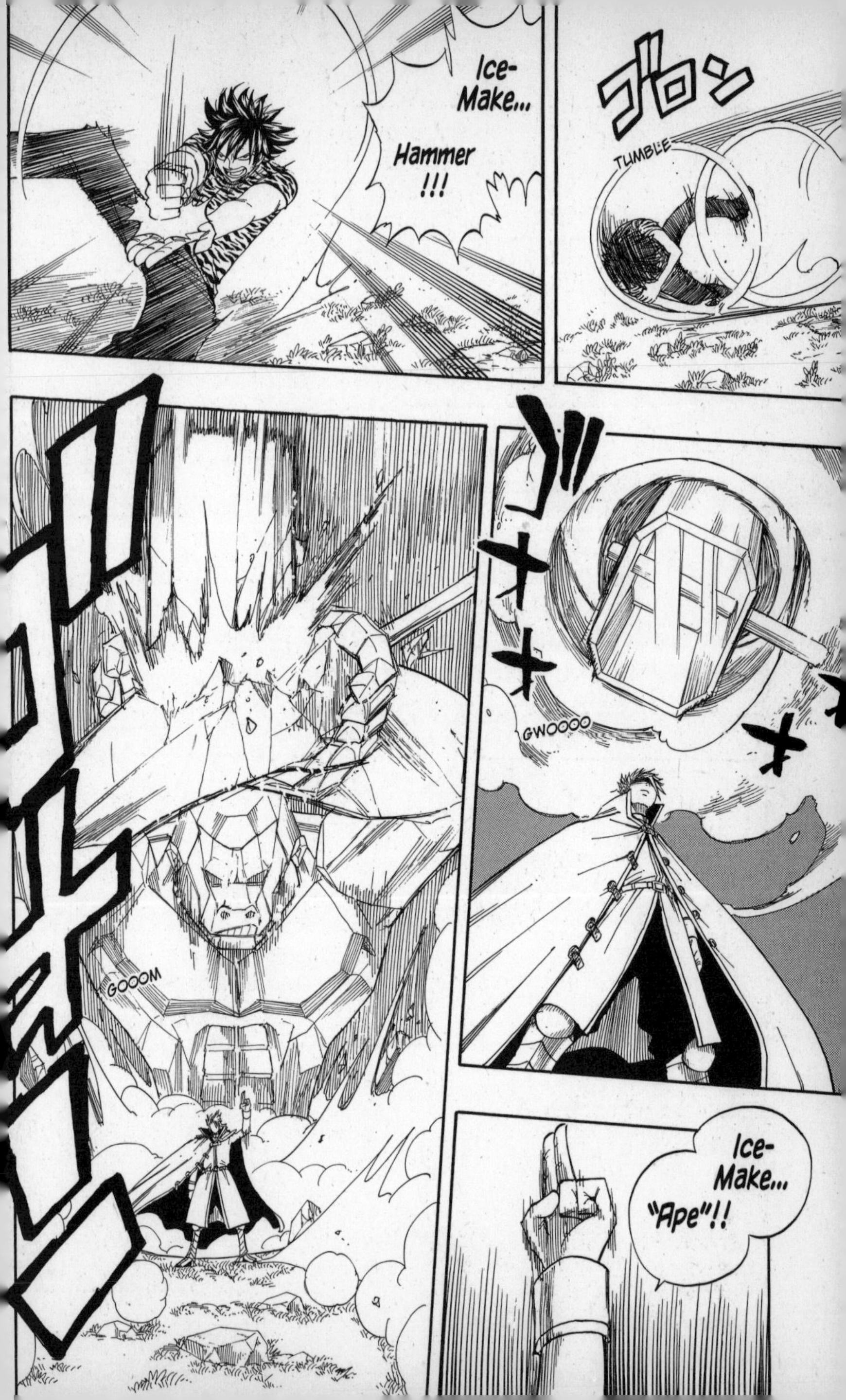
Ice-
Make...
Hammer
!!!
ゴロン
TUMBLE
ゴォォ
GWOOOO
ゴゴン
GOOOM
Ice-
Make...
"Ape"!!

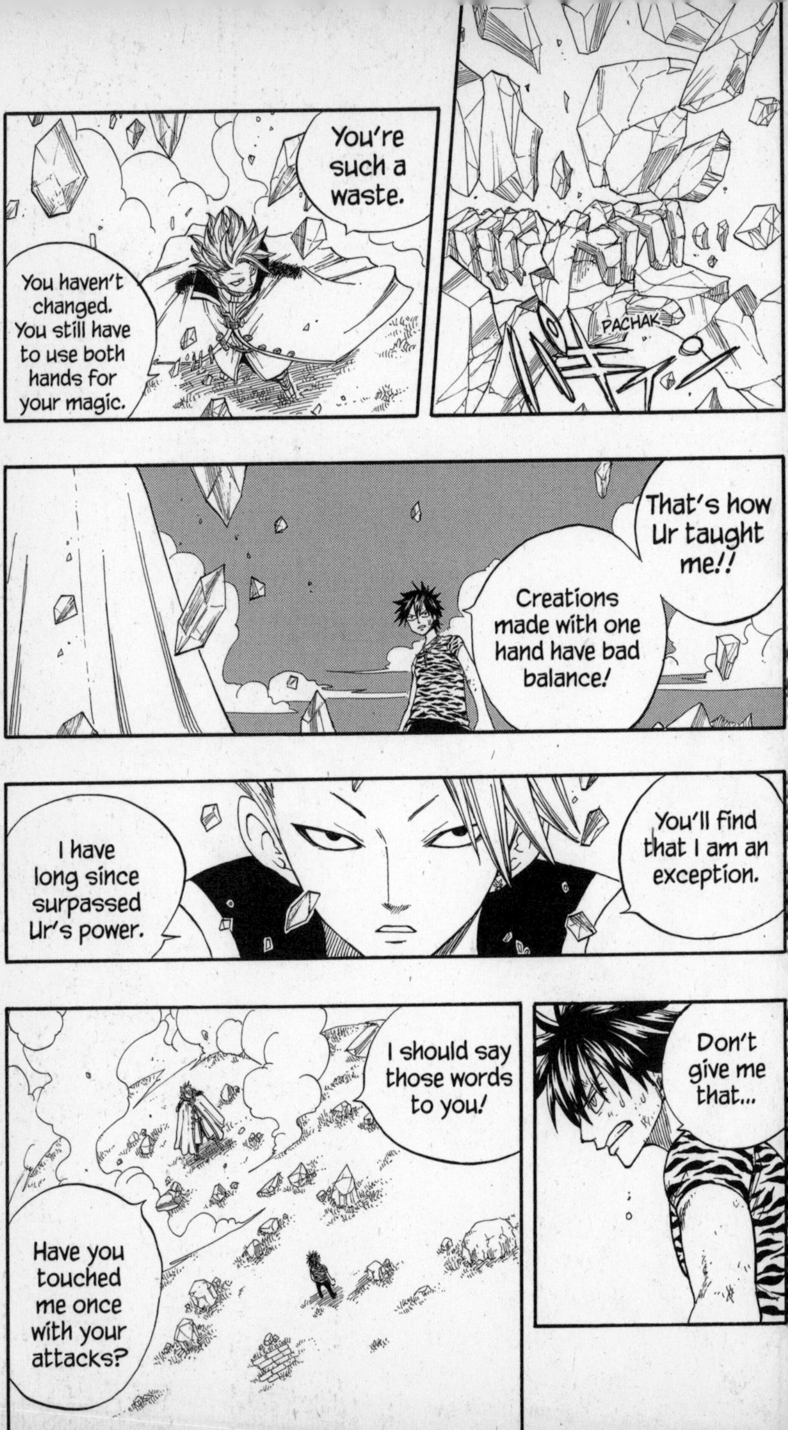
PACHAK
You're such a waste.
You haven't changed. You still have to use both hands for your magic.
That's how Ur taught me!!
Creations made with one hand have bad balance!
You'll find that I am an exception.
I have long since surpassed Ur's power.
Don't give me that...
I should say those words to you!
Have you touched me once with your attacks?

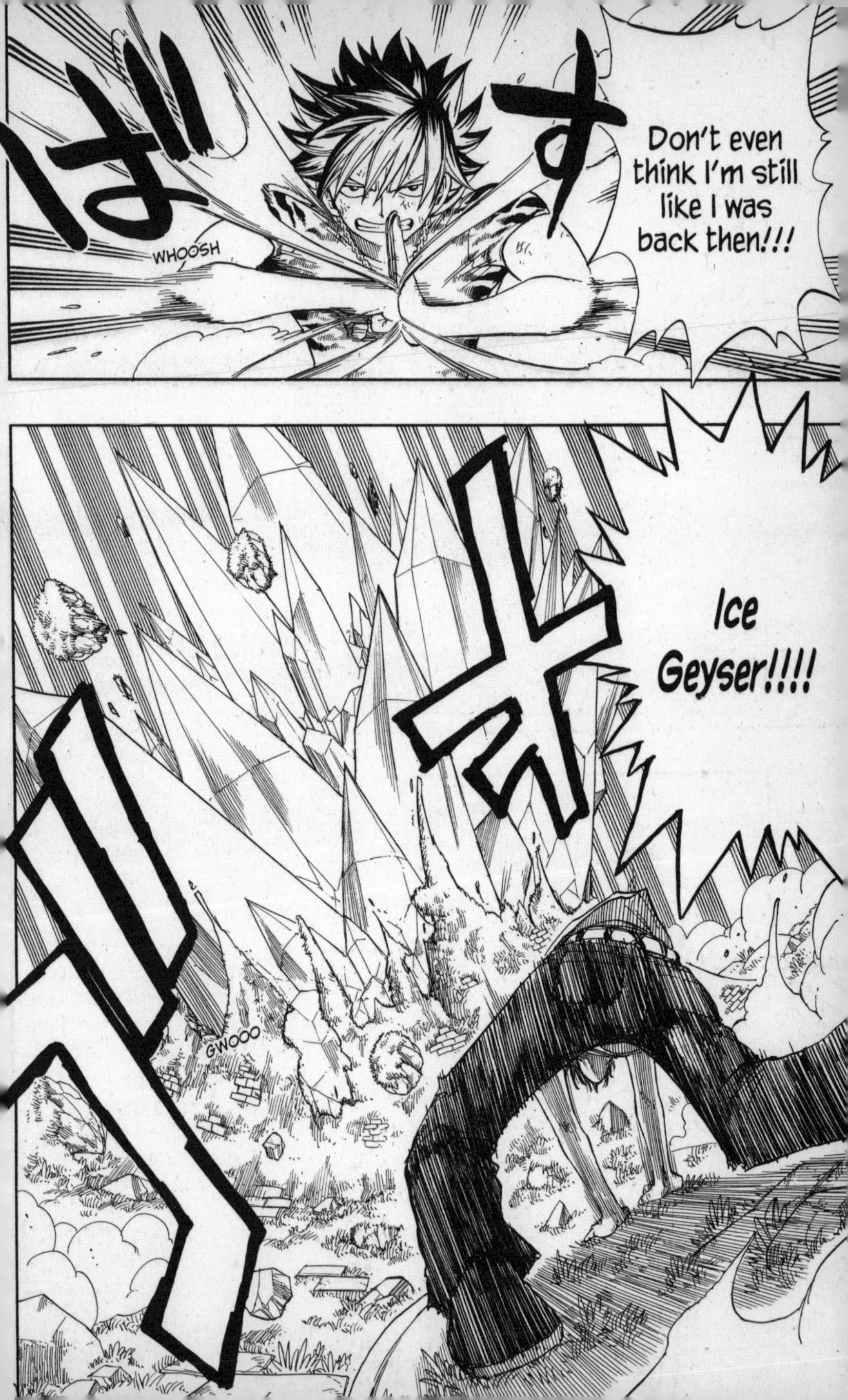
Don't even think I'm still like I was back then!!!
WHOOSH
Ice Geyser!!!!
GWOOO

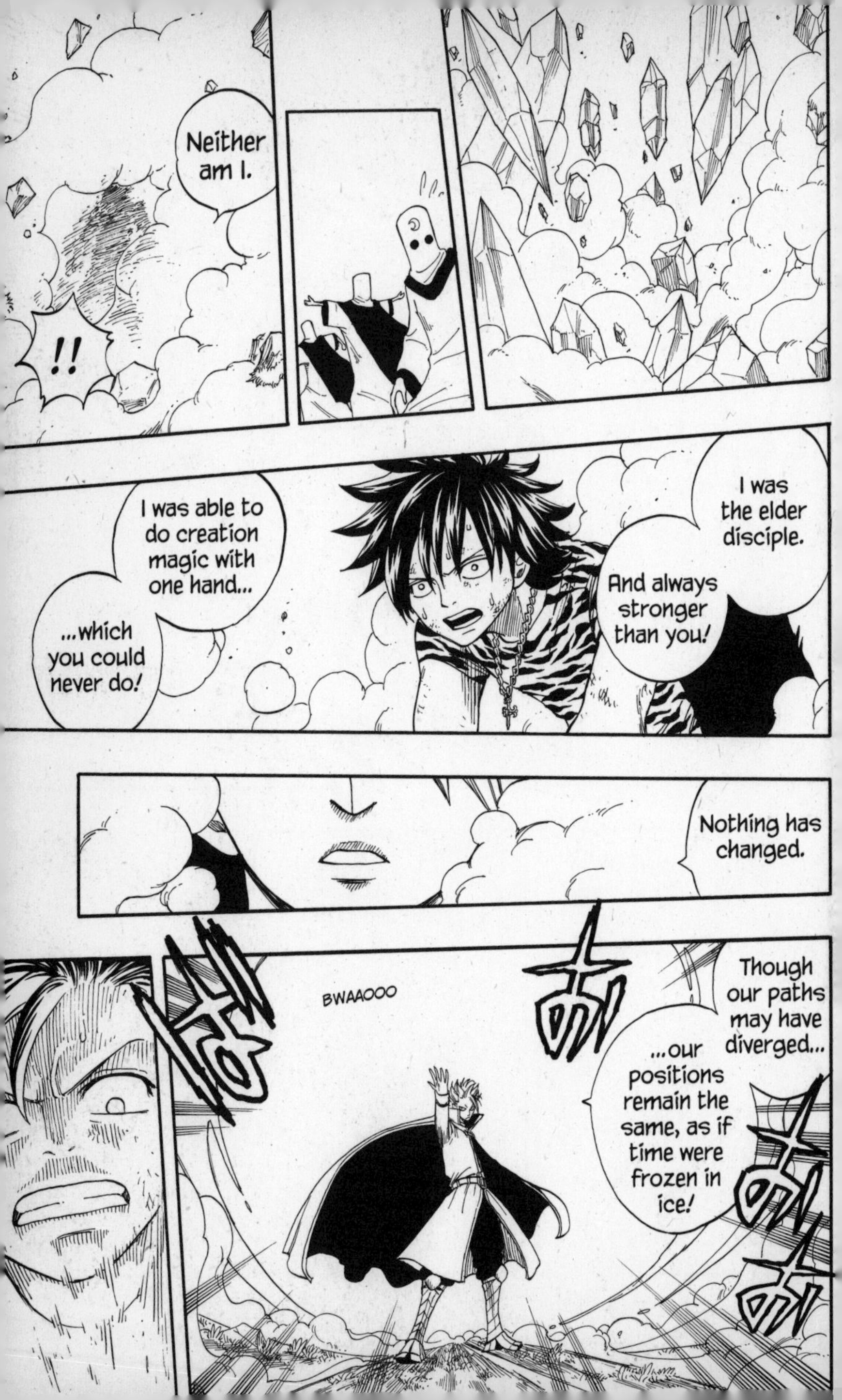

Neither am I.
!!
I was the elder disciple.
And always stronger than you!
I was able to do creation magic with one hand...
...which you could never do!
Nothing has changed.
Though our paths may have diverged...
...our positions remain the same, as if time were frozen in ice!
BWAAOOO

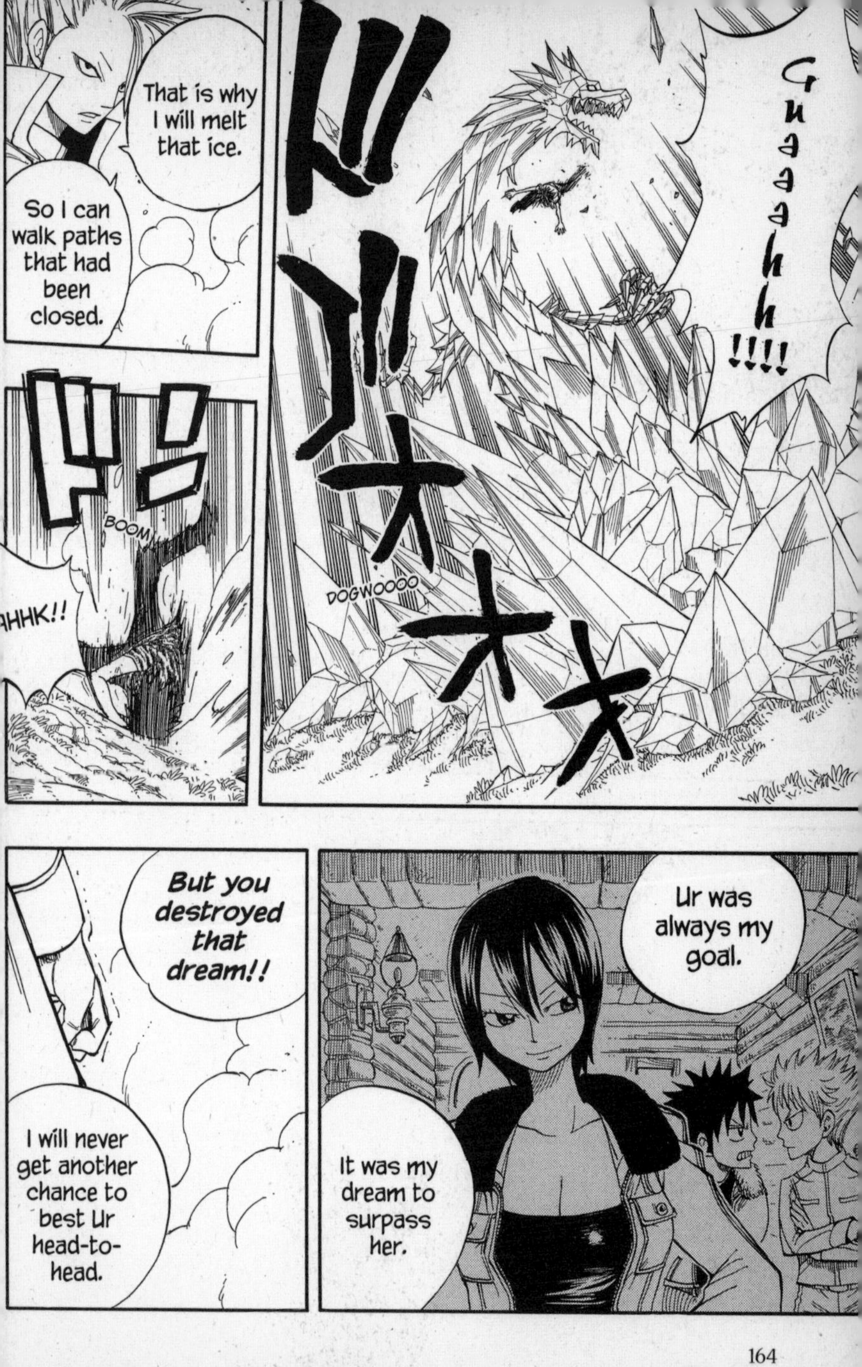

Guaaaahh!!!!
That is why I will melt that ice.
So I can walk paths that had been closed.
DOGWOOOO
BOOM
AHHK!!
Ur was always my goal.
It was my dream to surpass her.
But you destroyed that dream!!
I will never get another chance to best Ur head-to-head.

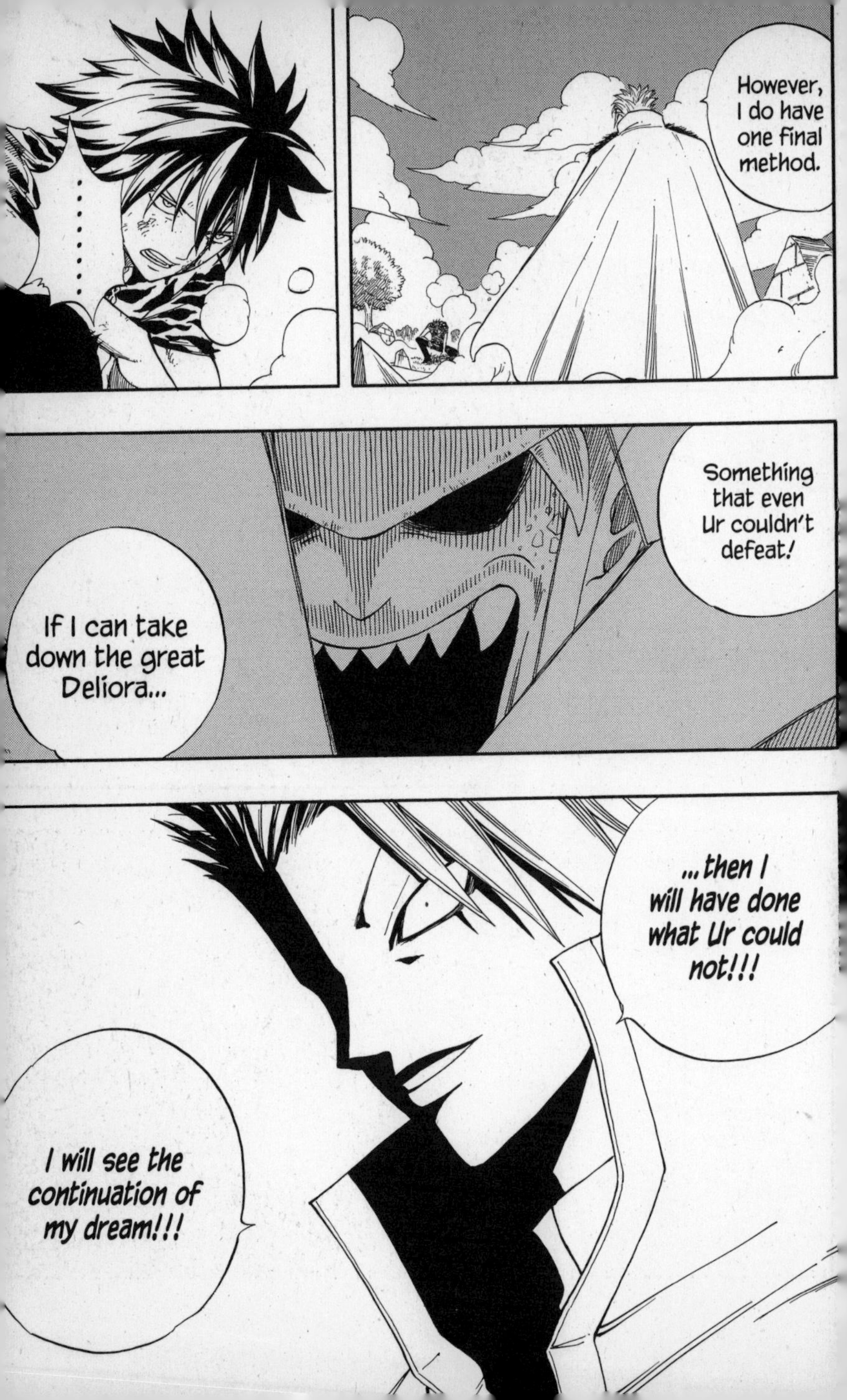

......
However, I do have one final method.
Something that even Ur couldn't defeat!
If I can take down the great Deliora...
...then I will have done what Ur could not!!!
I will see the continuation of my dream!!!

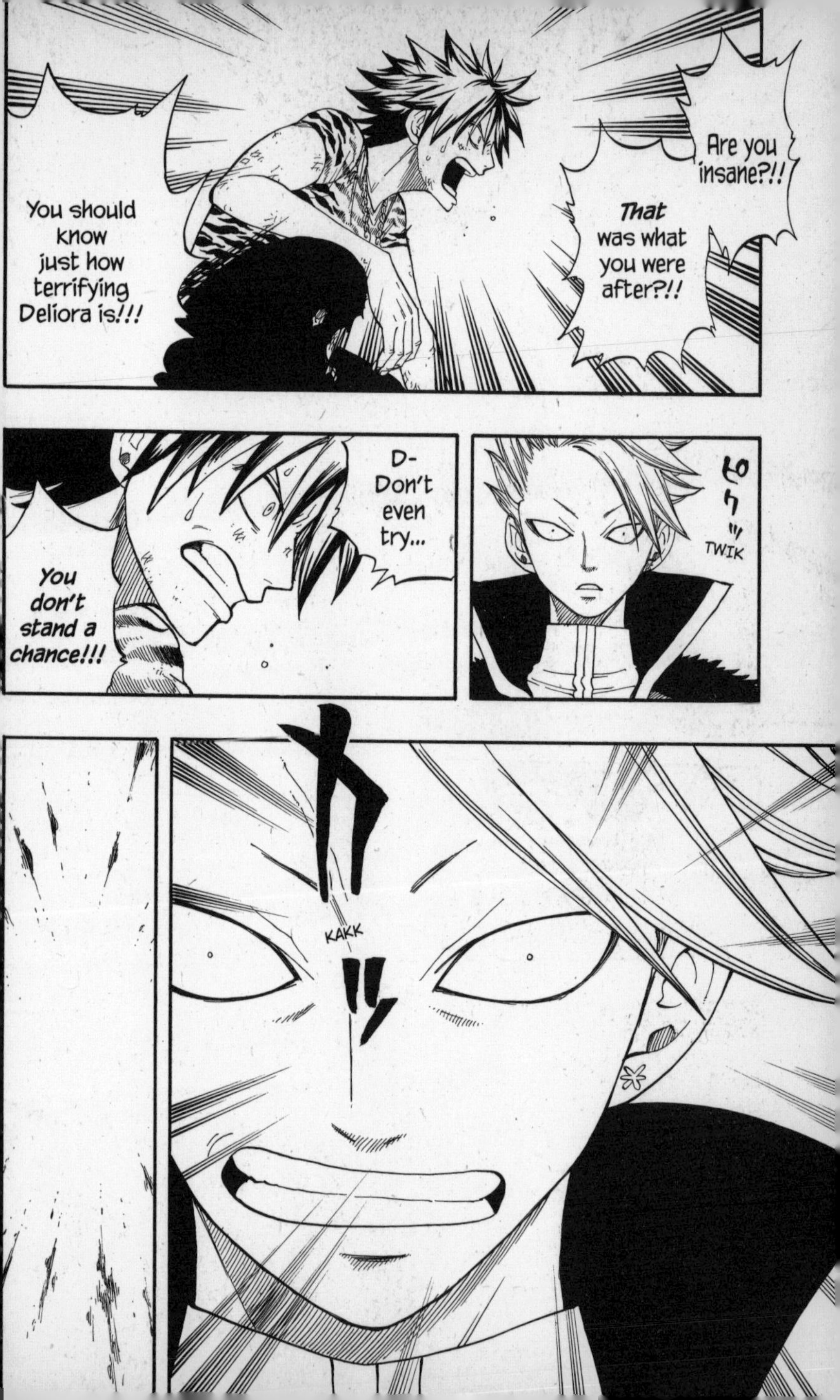

Are you insane?!!
That was what you were after?!!
You should know just how terrifying Deliora is!!!
ピクッ
TWIK
D- Don't even try...
You don't stand a chance!!!
カッ
KAKK

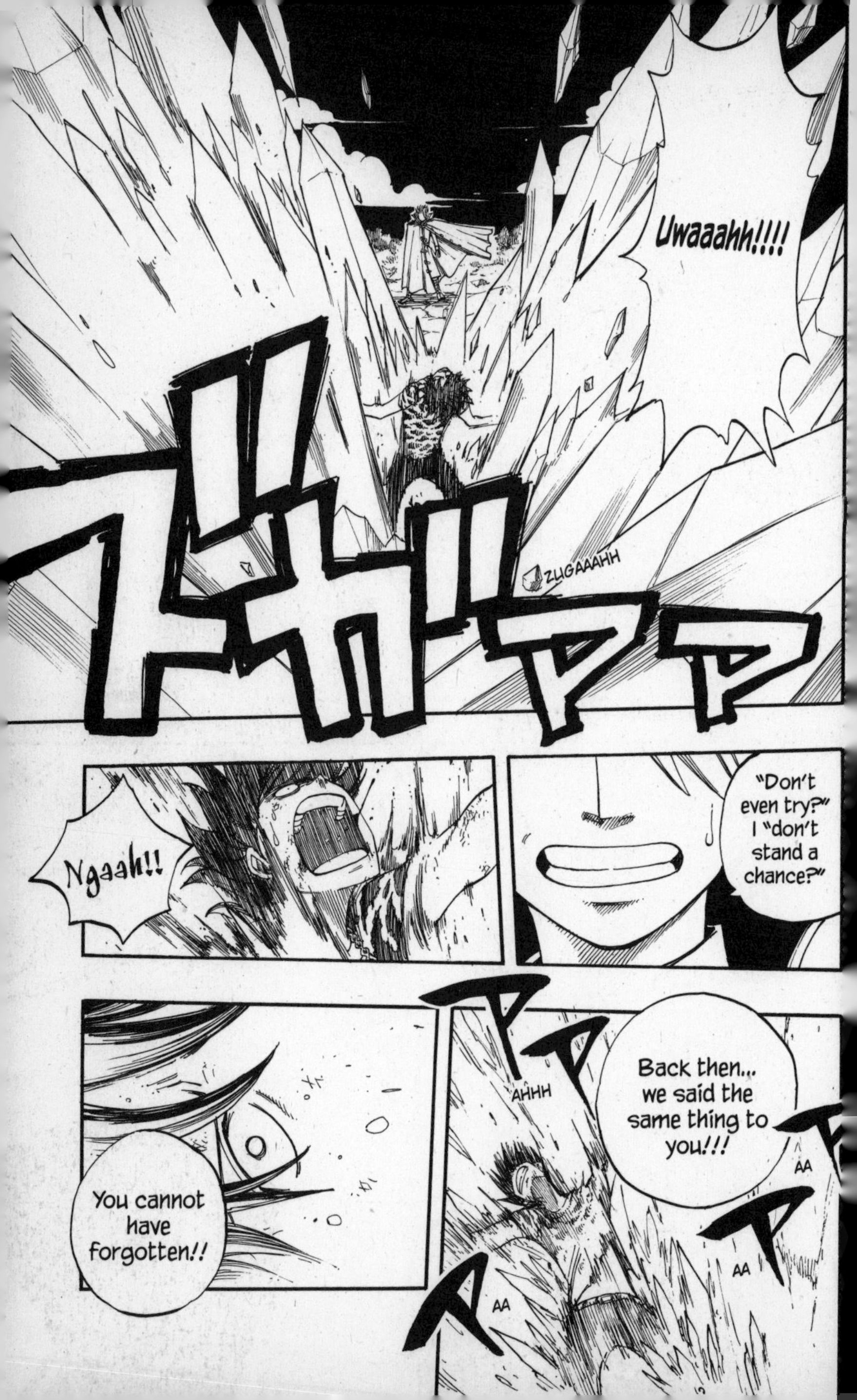
Uwaaahh!!!!
ZUGAAAHH
"Don't even try?" I "don't stand a chance?"
Ngaah!!
Back then... we said the same thing to you!!!
AHHH
AA
AA
AA
You cannot have forgotten!!

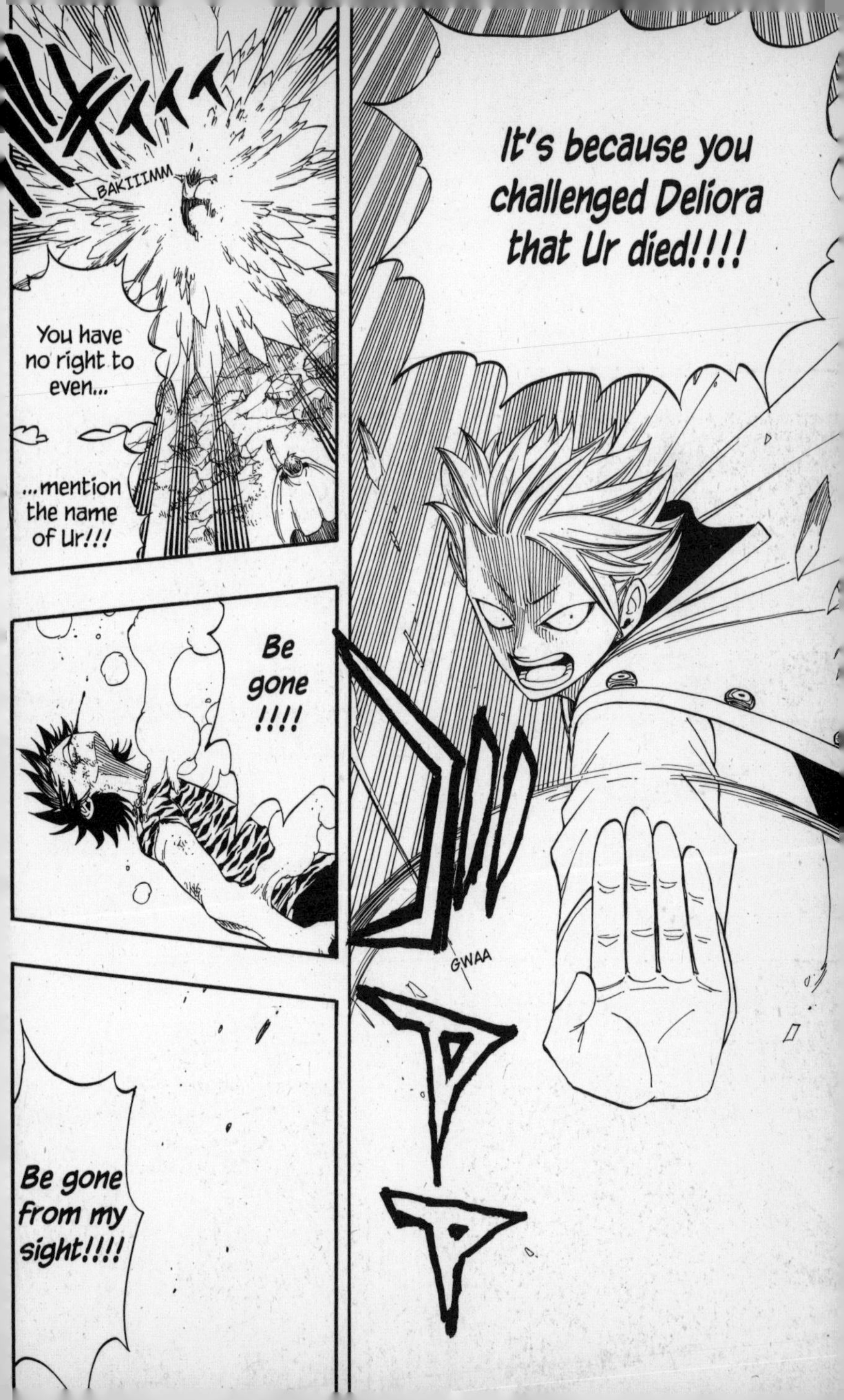
It's because you challenged Deliora that Ur died!!!!
GWAA
BAKIIIMM
You have no right to even...
...mention the name of Ur!!!
Be gone!!!!
Be gone from my sight!!!!

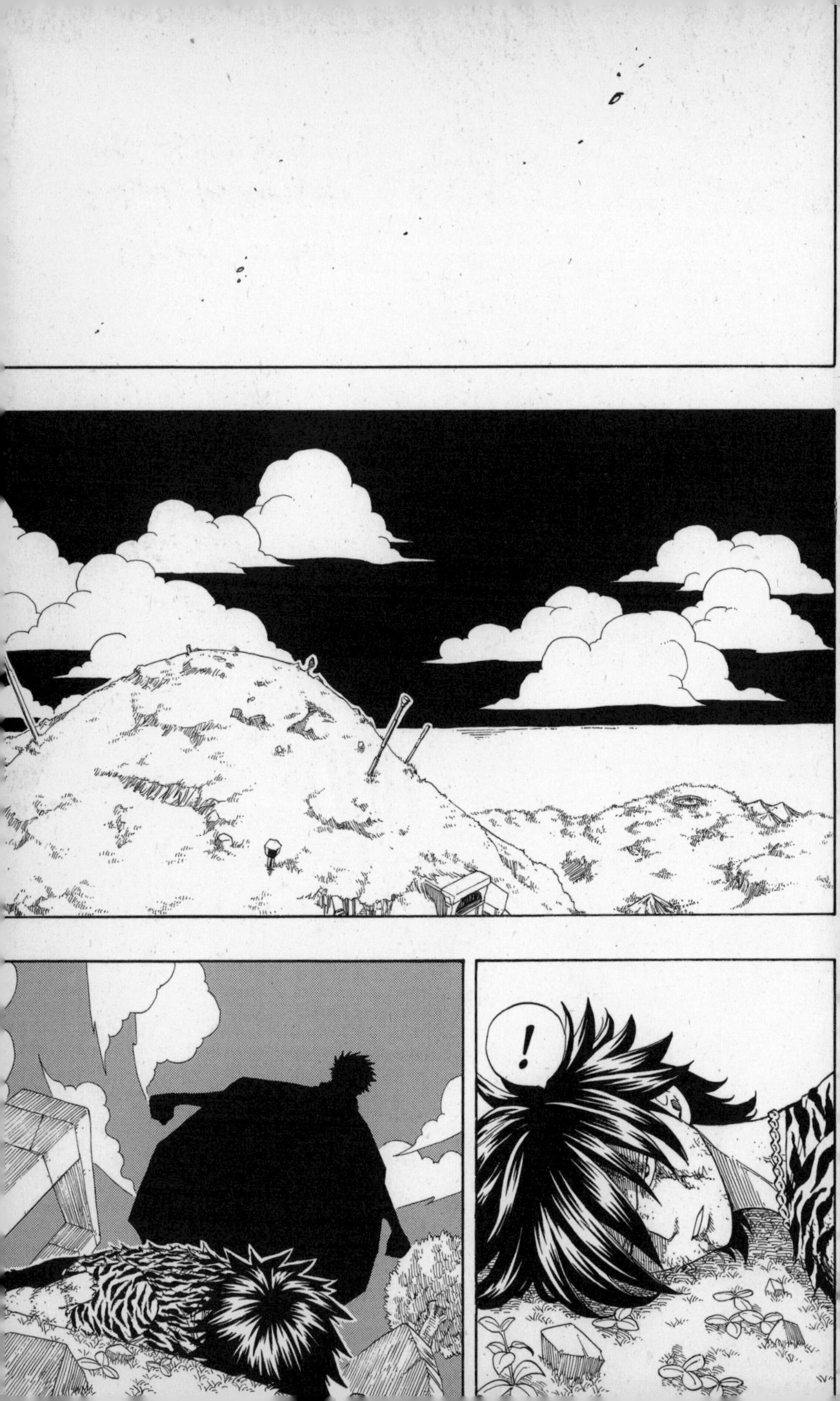
!

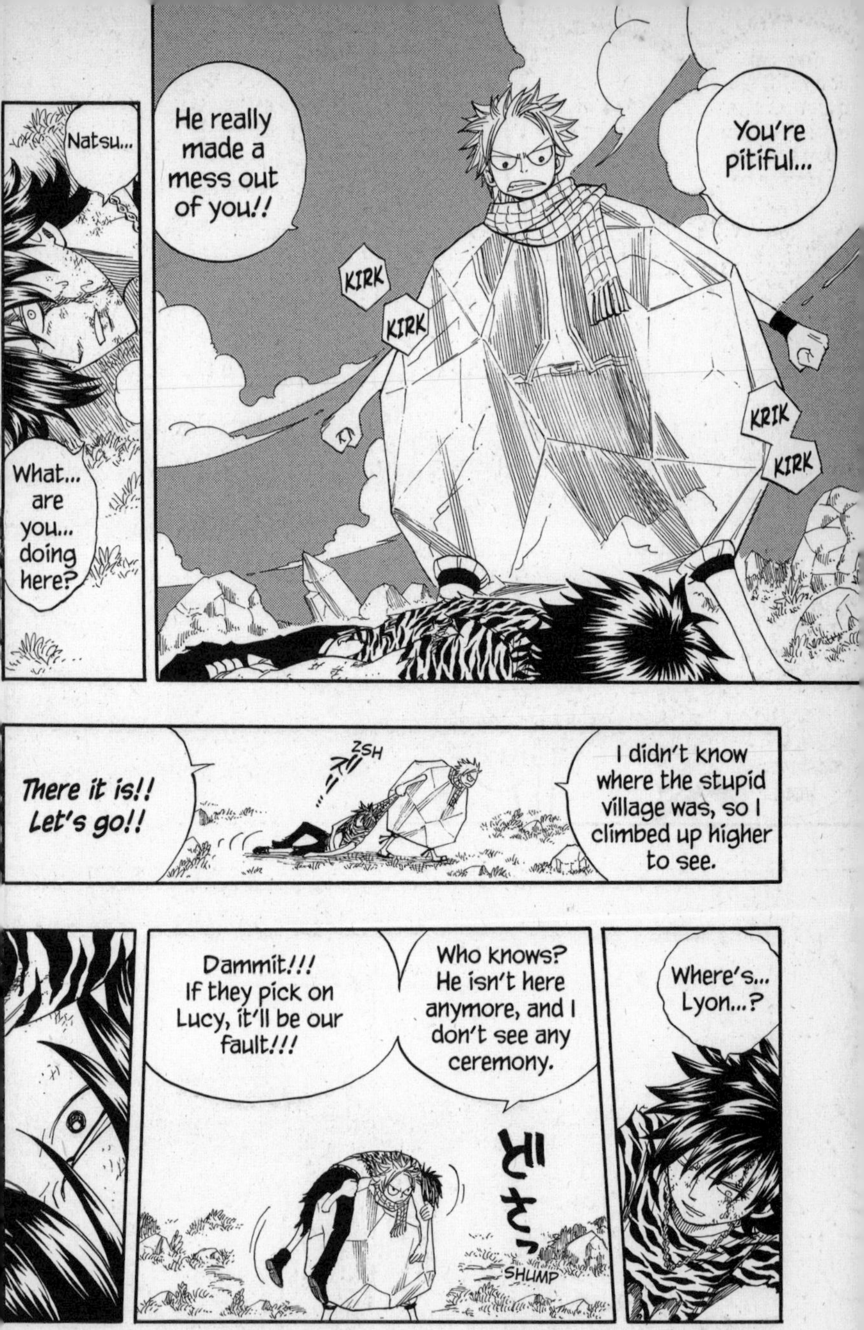

You're pitiful...
He really made a mess out of you!!
KIRK
KIRK
KRIK
KIRK
Natsu...
What... are you... doing here?
I didn't know where the stupid village was, so I climbed up higher to see.
ZSH
There it is!! Let's go!!
Where's... Lyon...?
Who knows? He isn't here anymore, and I don't see any ceremony.
Dammit!!! If they pick on Lucy, it'll be our fault!!!
どさっ
SHUMP

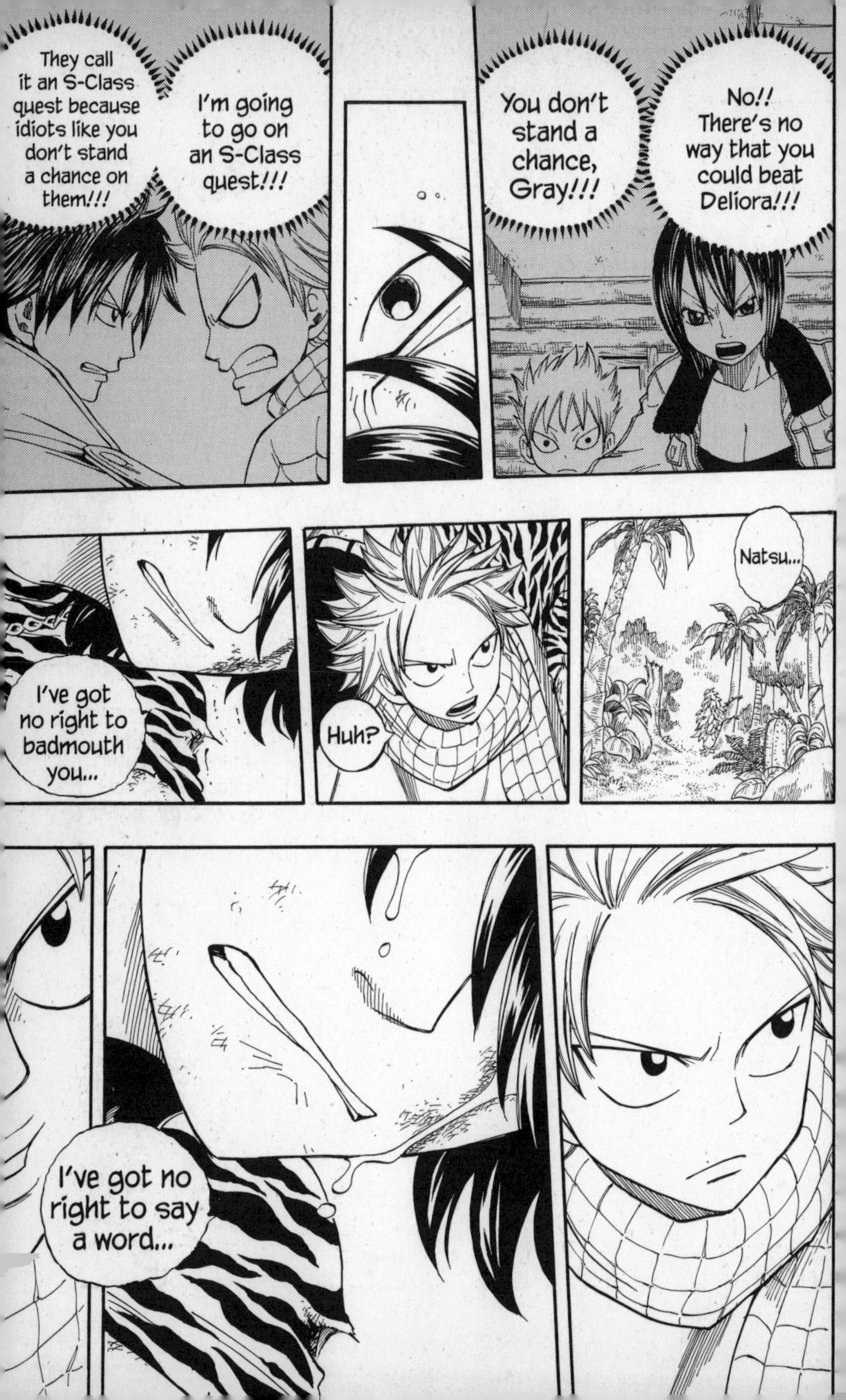
No!! There's no way that you could beat Deliora!!!
You don't stand a chance, Gray!!!
I'm going to go on an S-Class quest!!!
They call it an S-Class quest because idiots like you don't stand a chance on them!!!
Natsu...
Huh?
I've got no right to badmouth you...
I've got no right to say a word...

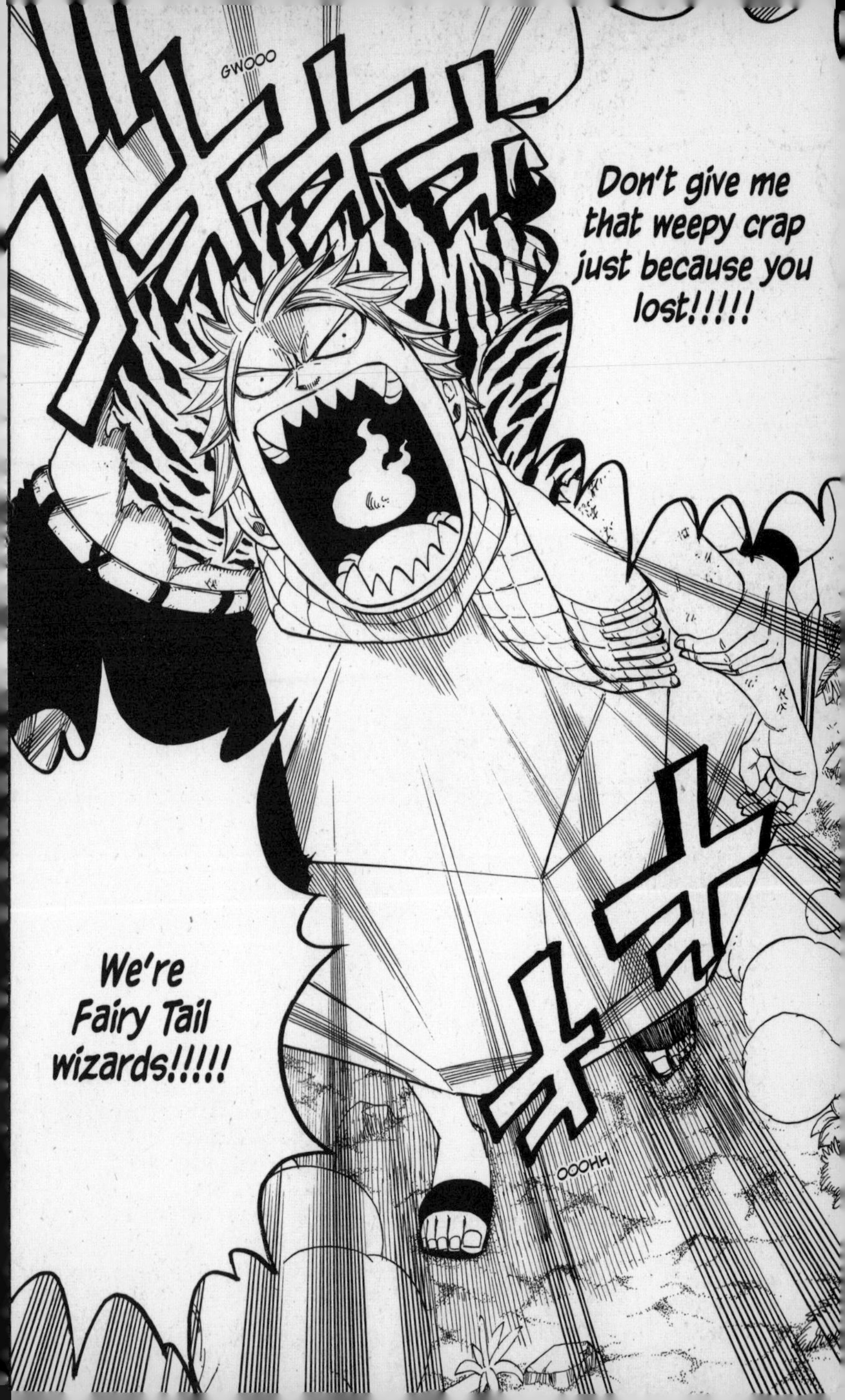
GWOOO
Don't give me that weepy crap just because you lost!!!!!
We're Fairy Tail wizards!!!!!
OOOHH

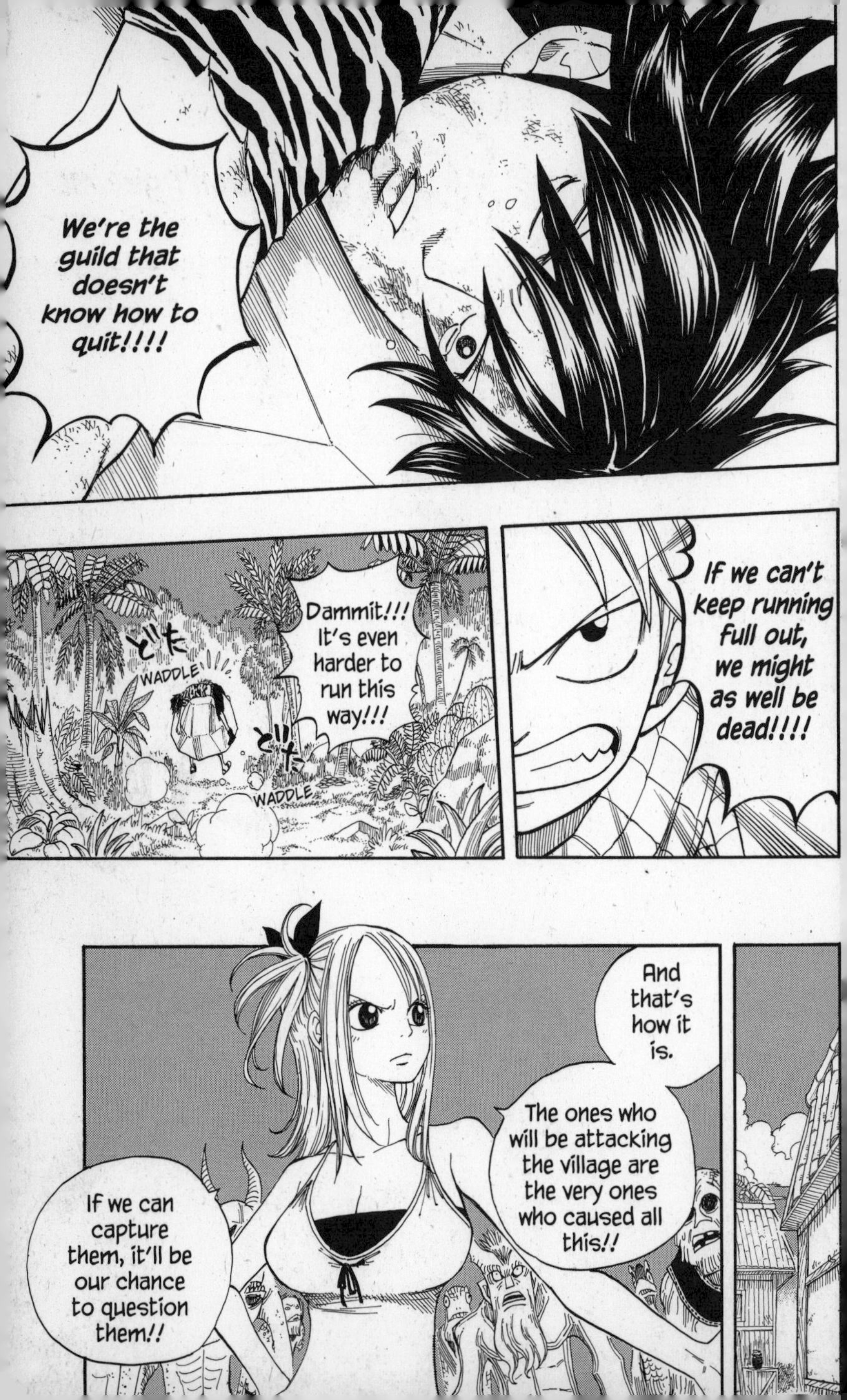
We're the guild that doesn't know how to quit!!!!
If we can't keep running full out, we might as well be dead!!!!
WADDLE
WADDLE
Dammit!!! It's even harder to run this way!!!
And that's how it is.
The ones who will be attacking the village are the very ones who caused all this!!
If we can capture them, it'll be our chance to question them!!

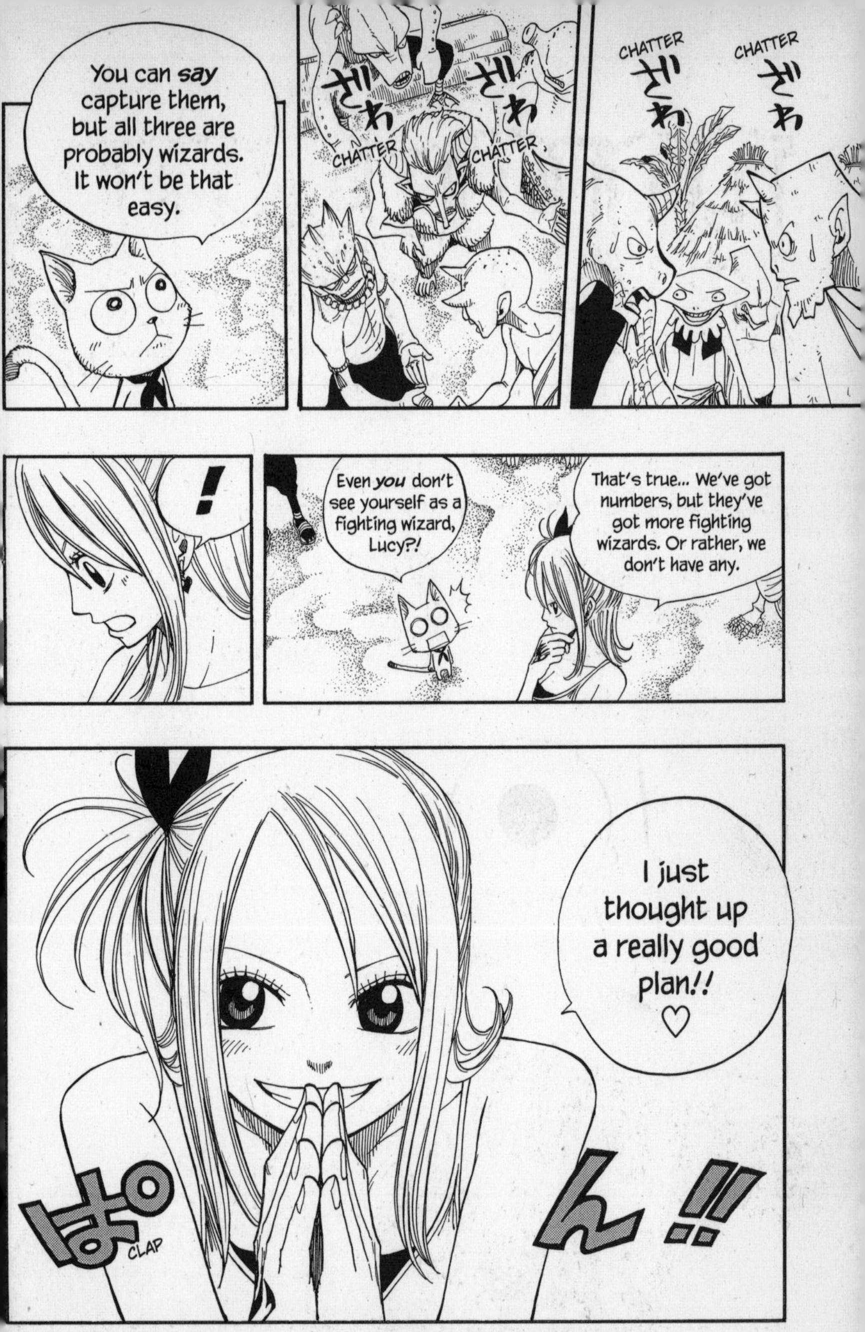
CHATTER
CHATTER
ざわ
ざわ
CHATTER
CHATTER
ざわ
ざわ
You can say capture them, but all three are probably wizards. It won't be that easy.
That's true... We've got numbers, but they've got more fighting wizards. Or rather, we don't have any.
Even you don't see yourself as a fighting wizard, Lucy?!
!
I just thought up a really good plan!! ♡
ぱ ん!!
CLAP

TO BE CONTINUED

FAIRY TAIL

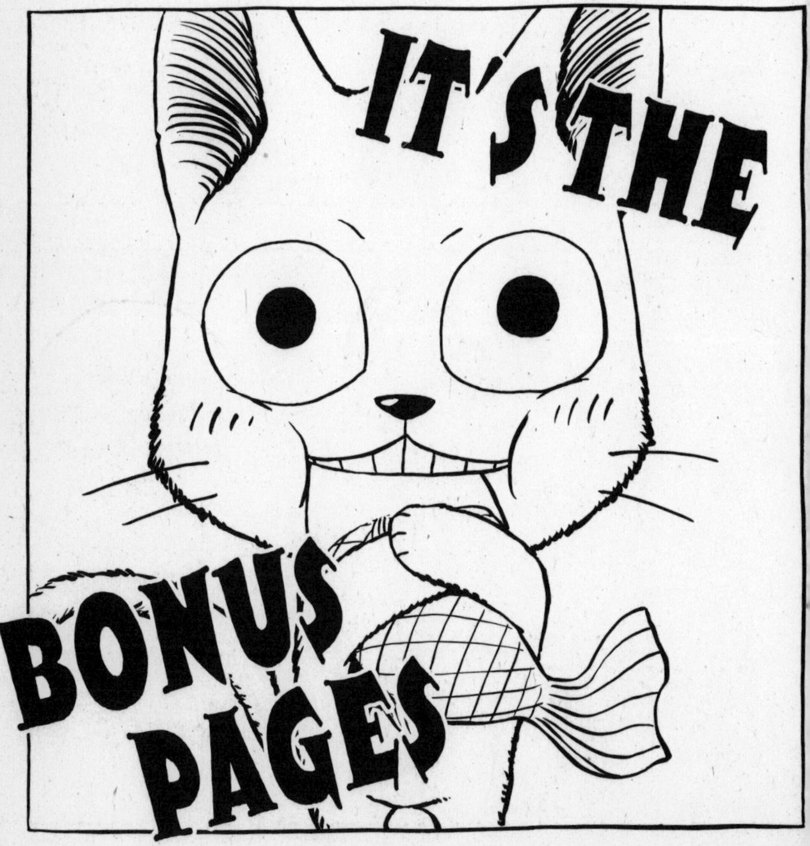
IT'S THE
BONUS PAGES

• A Rejected Splash Page •

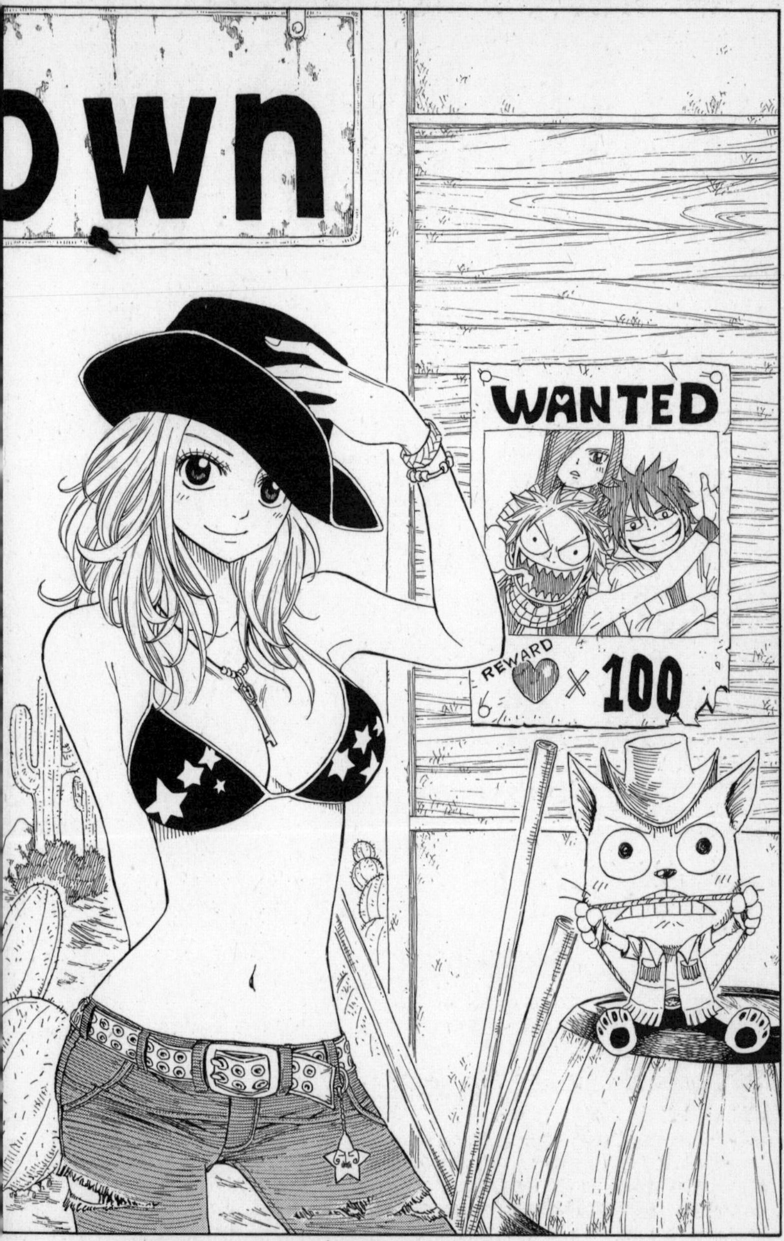

own
WANTED
REWARD
× 100

I guess I had drawn so many splash pages with Lucy that this one got shelved.

Introducing a Brand-New Four-Wheeled Magic Rental Vehicle!!

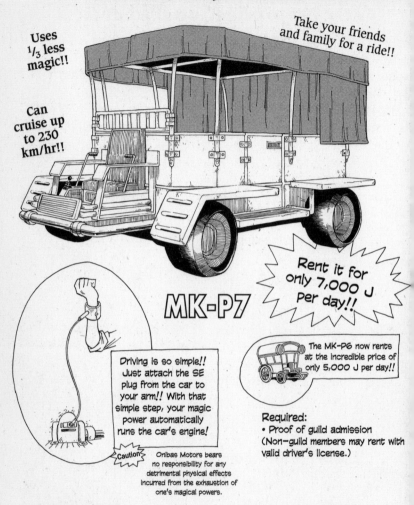

Uses 1/3 less magic!!

Take your friends and family for a ride!!

Can cruise up to 230 km/hr!!

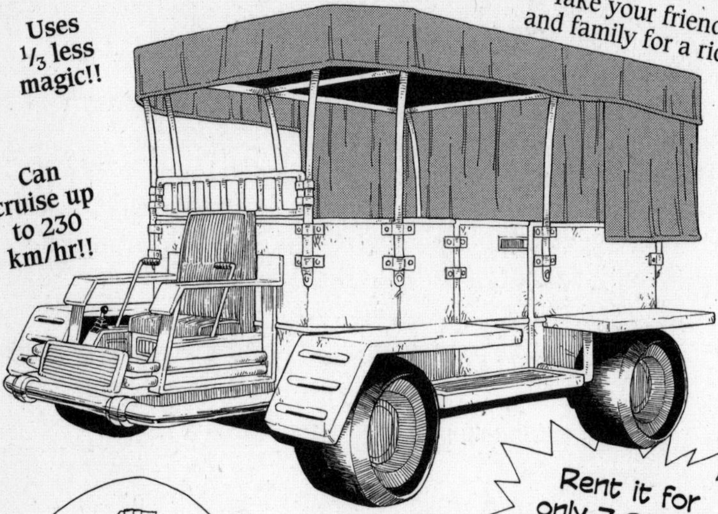

Rent it for only 7,000 J per day!!

MK-P7

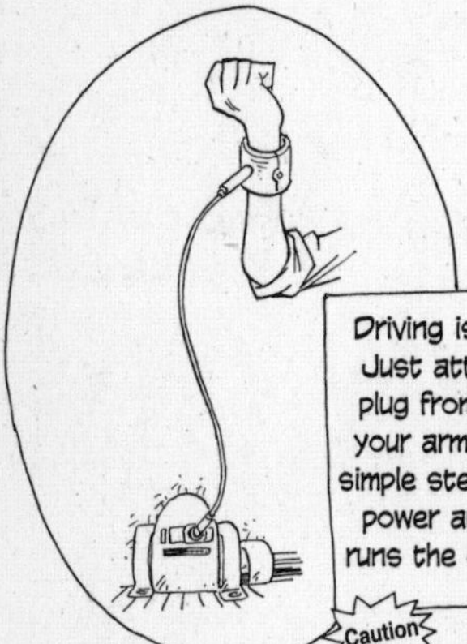

Driving is so simple!! Just attach the SE plug from the car to your arm!! With that simple step, your magic power automatically runs the car's engine!

Caution

Onibas Motors bears no responsibility for any detrimental physical effects incurred from the exhaustion of one's magical powers.

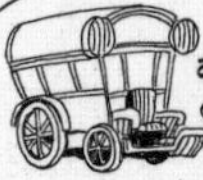

The MK-P6 now rents at the incredible price of only 5,000 J per day!!

Required:

- Proof of guild admission

(Non-guild members may rent with valid driver's license.)

A Message to Drivers

Four-wheeled magic vehicles will soon be available for purchase!!!

Up till now, they've only been available for rental, but we've heard the demands from customers who dream of owning their own vehicles!! Now our advancements in magic technology will make that dream possible!! The bottleneck presently preventing personal vehicle ownership is the problems caused by magic-power exhaustion. But Onibas Motors is developing a groundbreaking system that will solve that issue!! Buyers, your dreams will soon be fulfilled!!

—Onibas Motors

Early Preproduction Illustration

drew this to illustrate the feel of a guild. Since it was still very early in the con-ceptual stage, Happy-like cats have wings for arms. And there are two of them! That's Mirajane on the guitar, and I think that's supposed to be Natsu behind her, but both their hairstyles have changed. By the way, at the time of this drawing, the first chapter had a scene of Mirajane singing. I worked very hard on the lyrics, but the entire scene was cut. Well... still... it's allowed my ack of talent for creating lyrics to remain a closely kept secret.

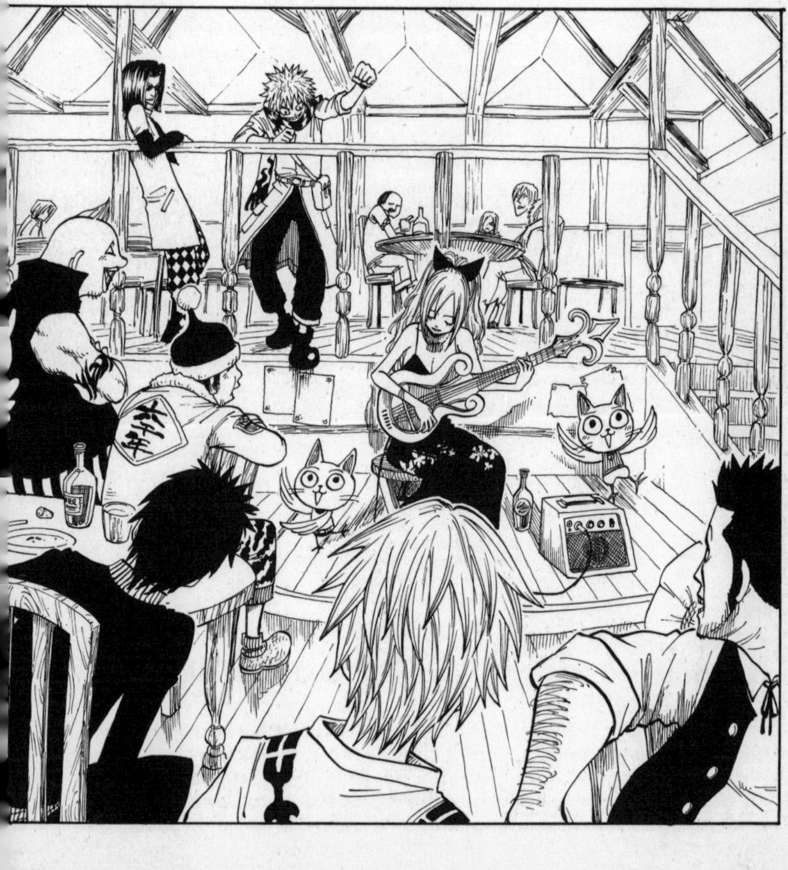

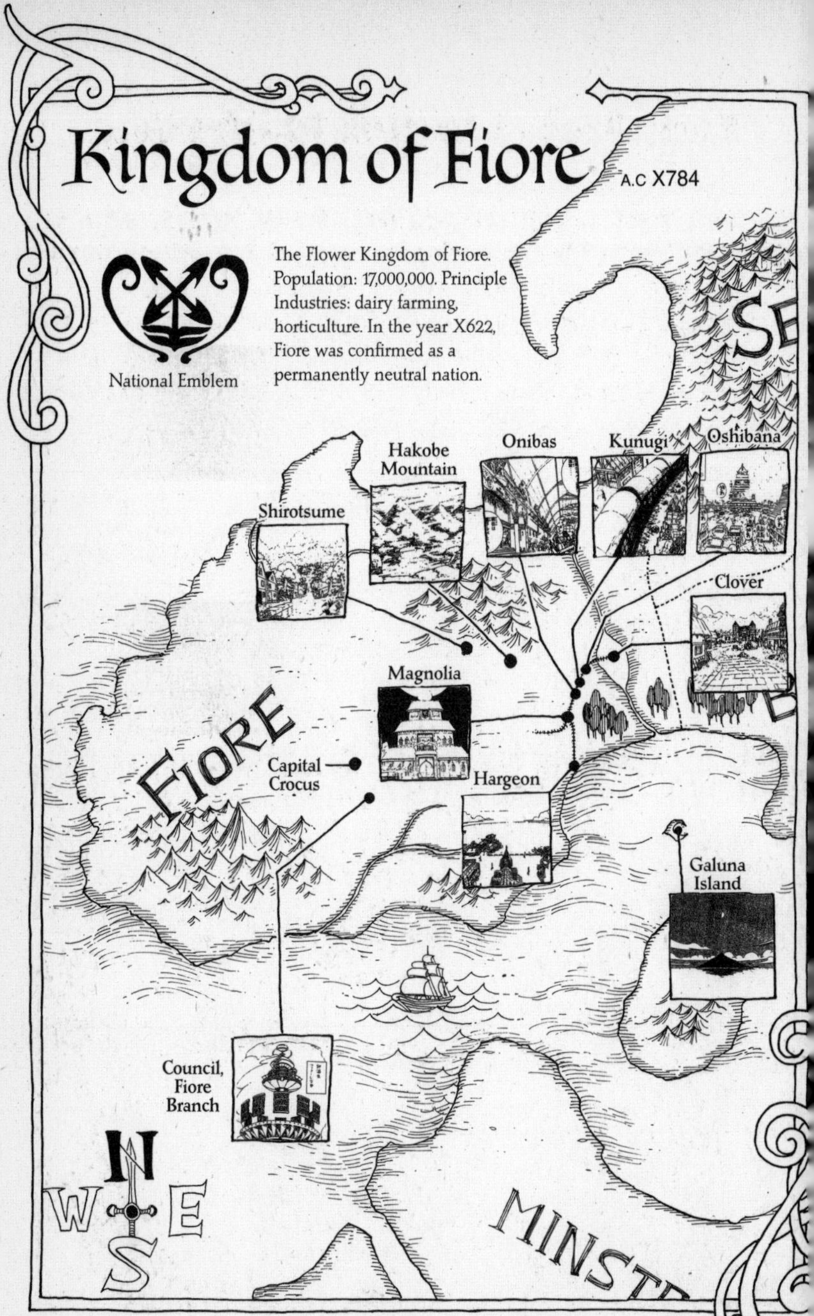
Kingdom of Fiore
A.C X784
The Flower Kingdom of Fiore. Population: 17,000,000. Principle Industries: dairy farming, horticulture. In the year X622, Fiore was confirmed as a permanently neutral nation.
National Emblem
Onibas
Kunugi
Oshibana
Hakobe Mountain
Shirotsume
Clover
Magnolia
FIORE
Capital Crocus
Hargeon
Galuna Island
Council, Fiore Branch
N
W
E
S

Erza's Magic Armor Collection

> If you must... Then you may see just a sample.

Heaven's Wheel Armor

An armor that allows her to wield a large number of weapons at once.

Attack Strength ☆☆☆★★
Defense Strength ☆☆☆★★
Speed ☆☆★★★
Range ☆☆☆☆☆

Hit me with everything you've got!!!

Fire Empress Armor

Anti-fire armor. Apparently it can halve Natsu's fire attacks.

Attack Strength ☆☆★★★
Defense Strength ☆☆☆☆★
Speed ☆☆☆★★
Range ☆☆★★★

Black Wing Armor

Armor that greatly increases the power of a single attack. It also enhances one's jumping ability.

Attack Strength ☆☆☆☆☆
Defense Strength ☆★★★★
Speed ☆☆☆★★
Range ☆★★★★

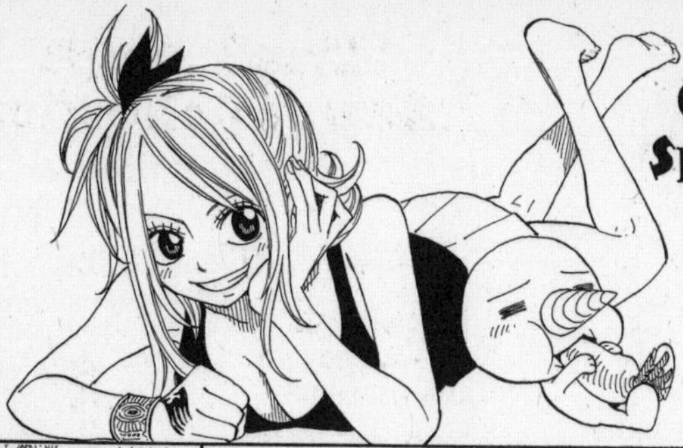

Celestial Spirit Data

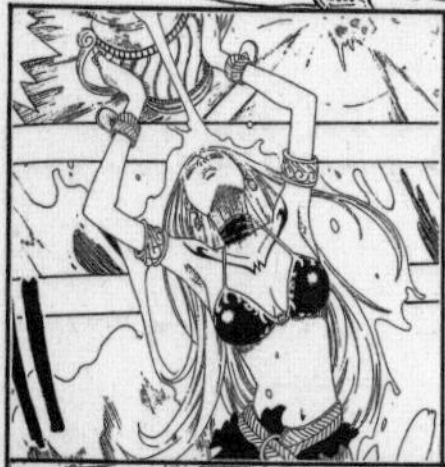

Aquarius of the Water Bearer Palace

One of the Twelve Golden Gates. Can create tidal waves that do not distinguish between friend and foe. Has great power, but is difficult to control. Can only be called in the presence of water.

Physical Power: 250
Attack Power: 388
Defensive Power: 275
Magic Power Expended: 100
Shift: Only on Wednesdays.

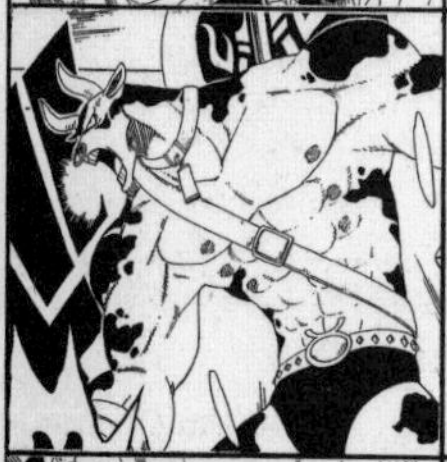

Taurus of the Golden Bovine Palace

One of the Twelve Golden Gates. Possesses Herculean strength, but tends toward sexual harassment with a fixation on breasts.

Physical Power: 160
Attack Power: 200
Defensive Power: 154
Magic Power Expended: 52
Shift: Monday, Wednesday, Friday, Saturday.

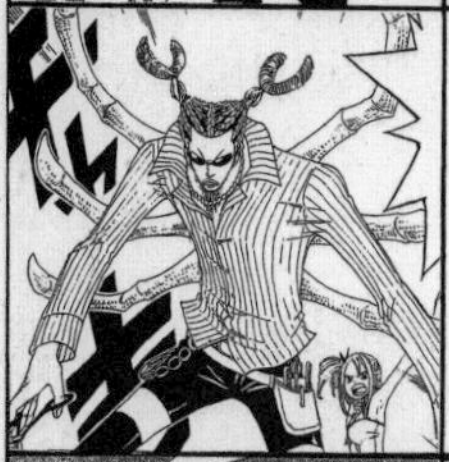

Cancer of the Great Crab Palace

One of the Twelve Golden Gates. His distinctive features are the inability to size up the situation and tacking on "-ebi" to the end of his sentences. He is in charge of Lucy's hair and makeup.

Physical Power: 147
Attack Power: 176
Defensive Power: 179
Magic Power Expended: 51
Shift: Wednesday, Thursday, Saturday, Sunday.

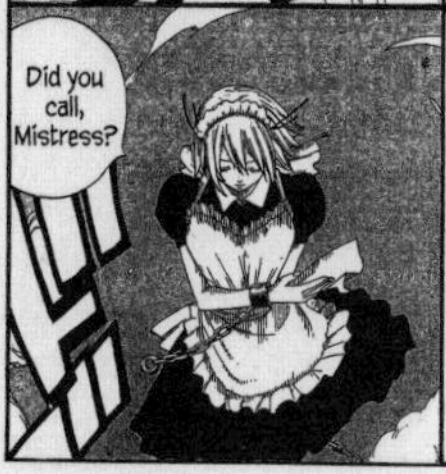
Did you call, Mistress?

Virgo of the Virgin Palace

One of the Twelve Golden Gates. Originally was under contract to Count Everlue but has switched to Lucy. She is especially good at digging holes.

Physical Power: 121
Attack Power: 164
Defensive Power: 84
Magic Power Expended: 43
Shift: Monday through Saturday.

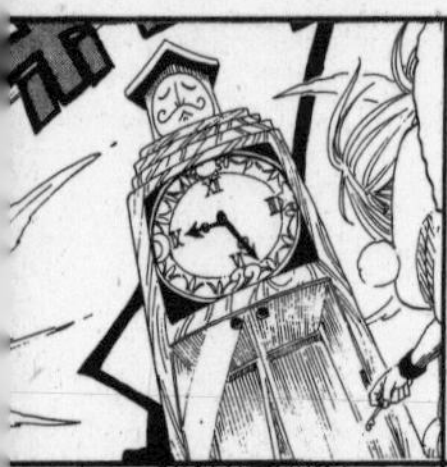

Horologium of the Hourglass Constellation

Can inform one of the time anywhere on the planet. When inside its workings, one can be protected from many outside influences, but since one's voice does not carry to the outside, Horologium must pass your messages on.

Physical Power: 85
Attack Power: 33
Defensive Power: 133
Magic Power Expended: 16
Shift: Monday through Saturday.

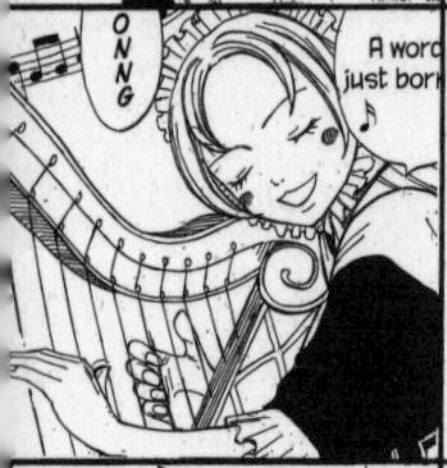

Lyra of the Harp Constellation

A skilled singer. Her singing voice is extremely beautiful, and her songs affect the hearts of her listeners. She is unexpectedly well informed.

Physical Power: 54
Attack Power: 62
Defensive Power: 81
Magic Power Expended: 18
Shift: Every second Wednesday and third Thursday and Friday of the month.

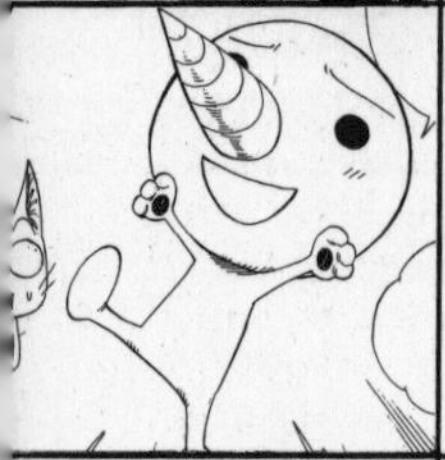

Nikora of the Canis Minor Constellation (Plue)

A pet spirit that for some reason always seems to be trembling. It is more or less doglike, but it takes some imagination to think of it as a dog.

Physical Power: 8
Attack Power: 2
Defensive Power: 3
Magic Power Expended: 1
Shift: Whenever. (Recently agreed to appear on Mondays, too.)

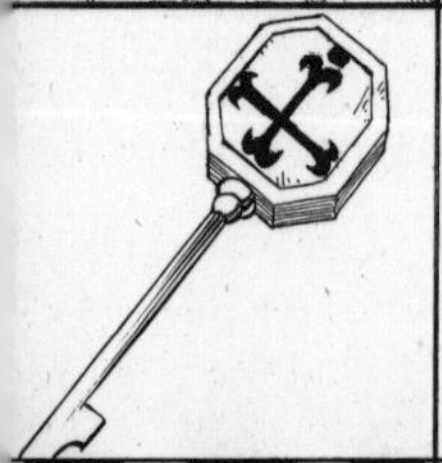

Crux of the Southern Cross Constellation

As yet unknown.

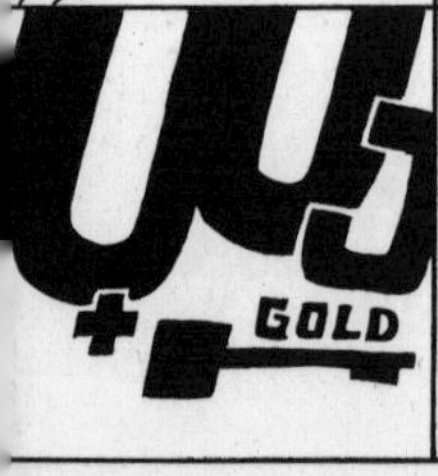
GOLD

Golden Key Reward for Services

Is most likely one of the Twelve Golden Keys, but details are as yet unknown.

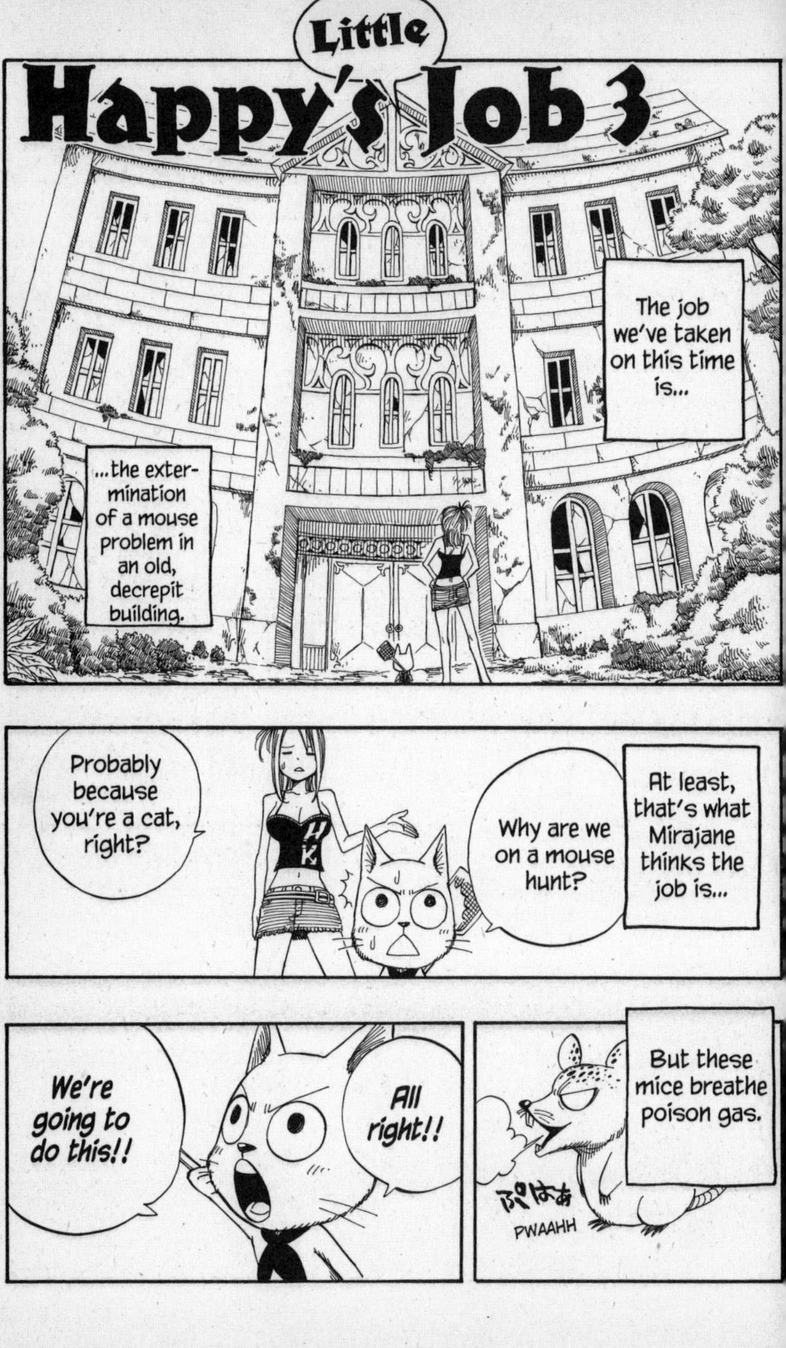
Little
Happy's Job 3
The job we've taken on this time is...
...the extermination of a mouse problem in an old, decrepit building.
At least, that's what Mirajane thinks the job is...
Why are we on a mouse hunt?
Probably because you're a cat, right?
But these mice breathe poison gas.
ぷはぁ
PWAAHH
All right!!
We're going to do this!!

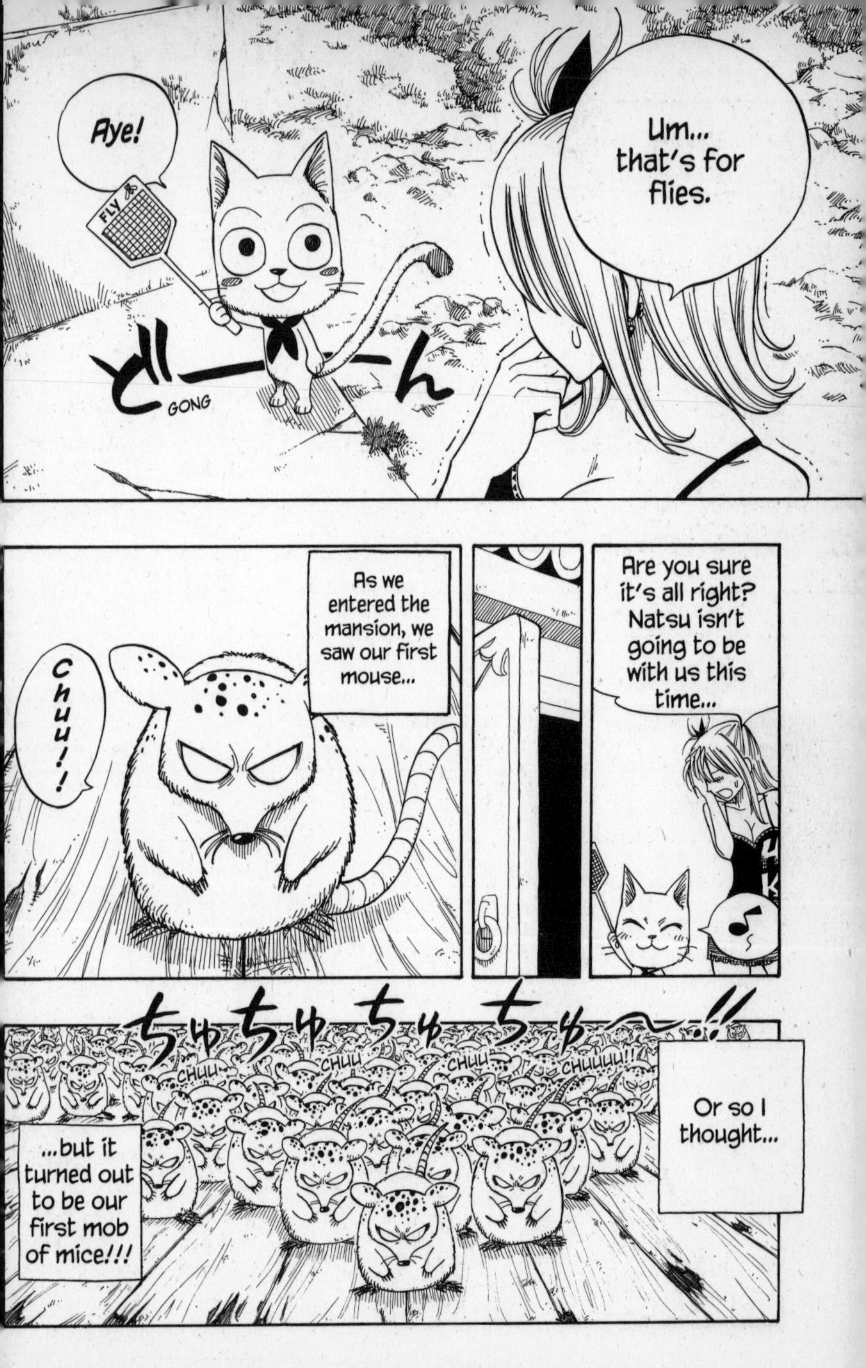
Um... that's for flies.
Aye!
FLY
GONG
Are you sure it's all right? Natsu isn't going to be with us this time...
As we entered the mansion, we saw our first mouse...
Chuu!!
CHUU
CHUU
CHUU
CHUUUU!!
Or so I thought...
...but it turned out to be our first mob of mice!!!

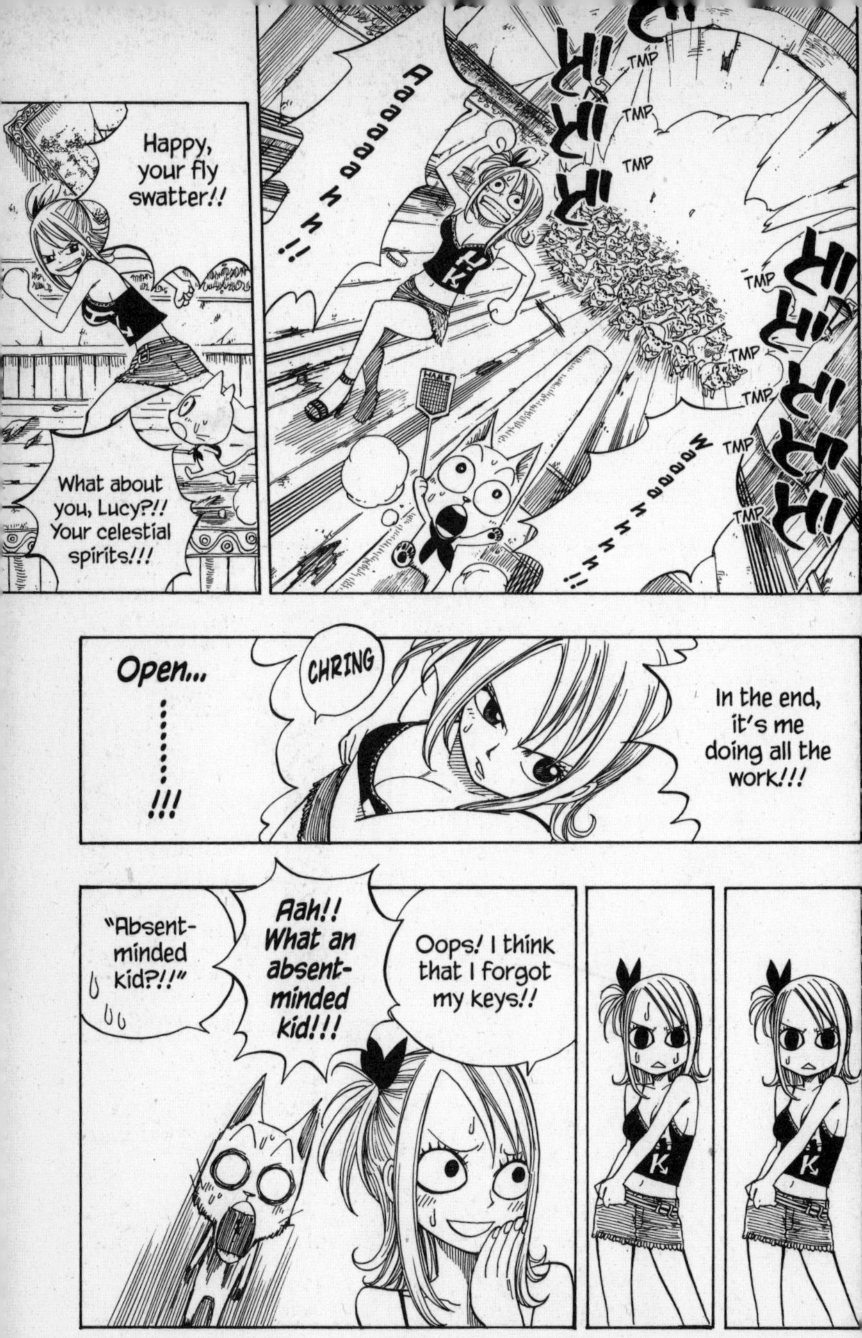

Gaaaaaahh!!
TMP
TMP
TMP
TMP
TMP
TMP
TMP
TMP
Waaaaahhhhh!!
Happy, your fly swatter!!
What about you, Lucy?!! Your celestial spirits!!!
In the end, it's me doing all the work!!!
CHRING
Open... ......!!!
Oops! I think that I forgot my keys!!
Aah!! What an absent-minded kid!!!
"Absent-minded kid?!!"

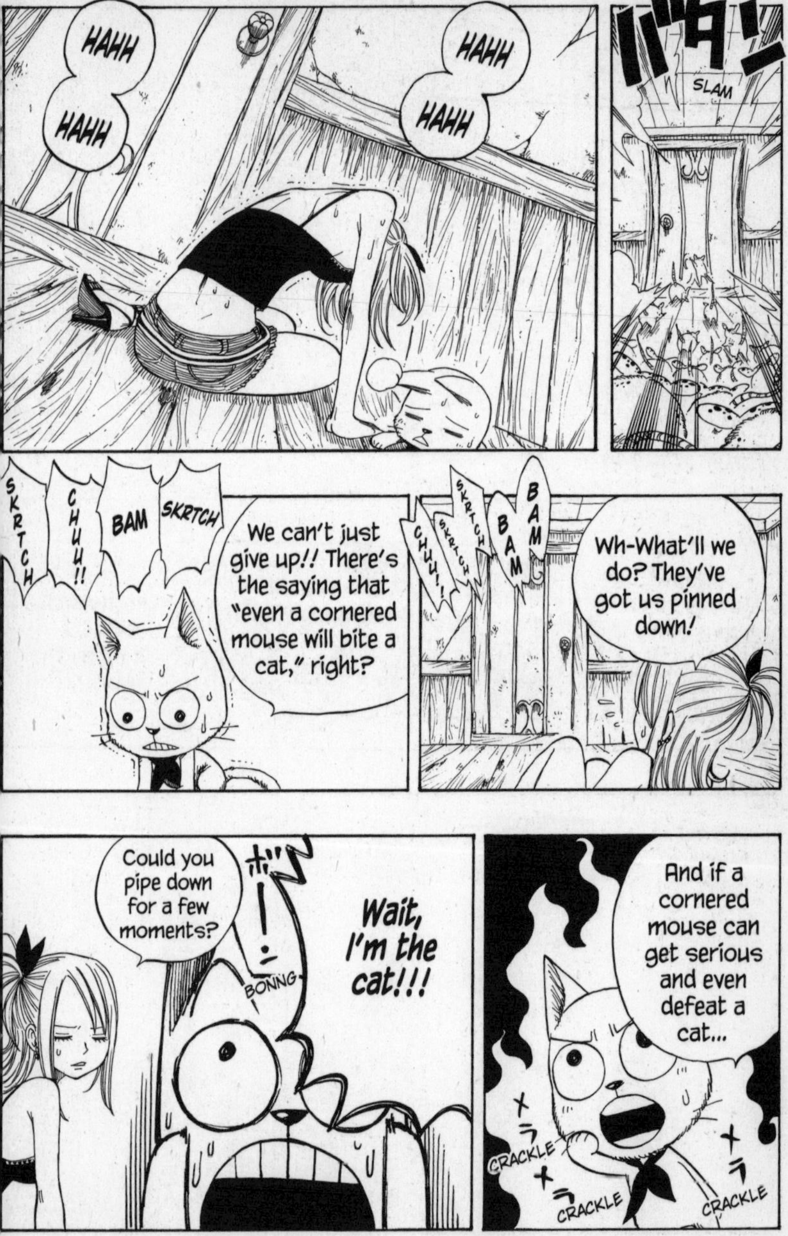
SLAM
HAHH
HAHH
HAHH
HAHH
Wh-What'll we do? They've got us pinned down!
BAM
BAM
SKRTCH
SKRTCH
CHUU!!
We can't just give up!! There's the saying that "even a cornered mouse will bite a cat," right?
SKRTCH
BAM
CHUU!!
SKRTCH
And if a cornered mouse can get serious and even defeat a cat...
CRACKLE
CRACKLE
CRACKLE
Could you pipe down for a few moments?
BONNG
Wait, I'm the cat!!!

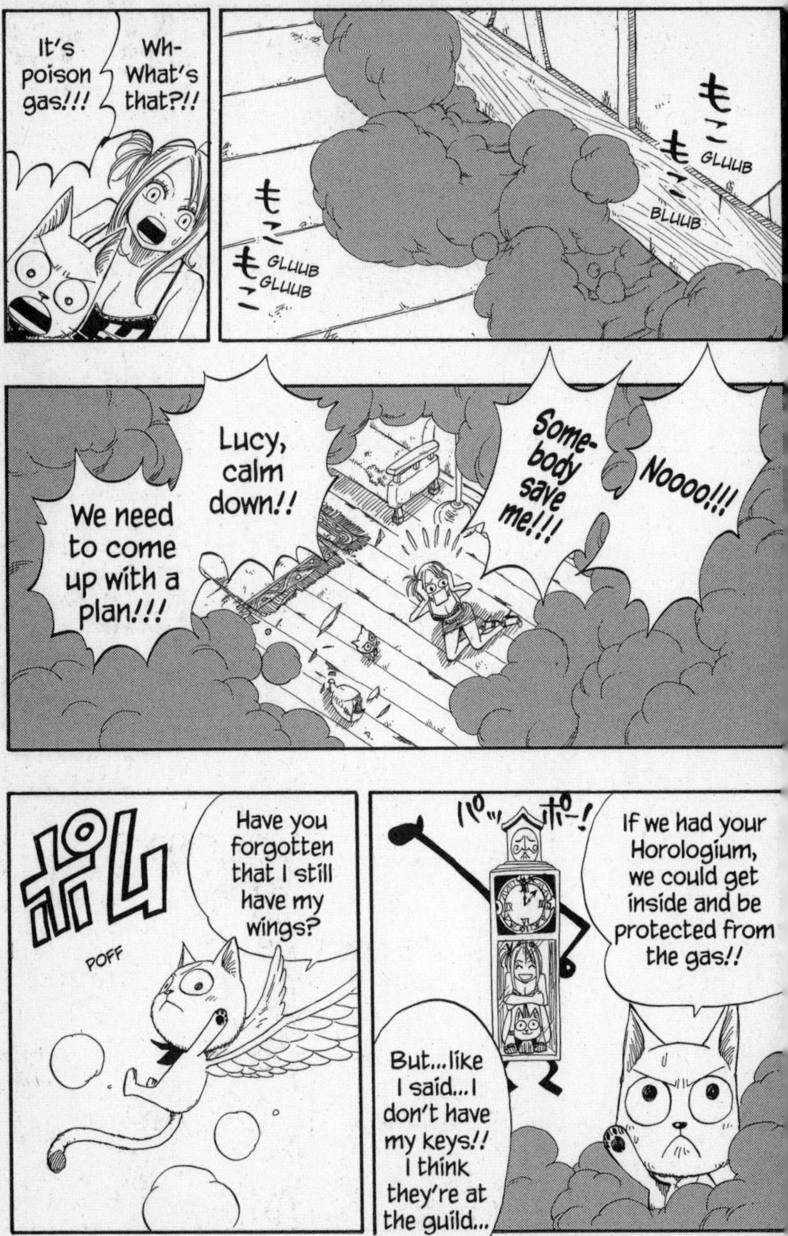

もこ
もこ
GLUUB
BLUUB
もこ
もこ
GLUUB
GLUUB
Wh- What's that?!!
It's poison gas!!!
Noooo!!!
Somebody save me!!!
Lucy, calm down!!
We need to come up with a plan!!!
If we had your Horologium, we could get inside and be protected from the gas!!
But...like I said...I don't have my keys!! I think they're at the guild...
ポム
POFF
Have you forgotten that I still have my wings?

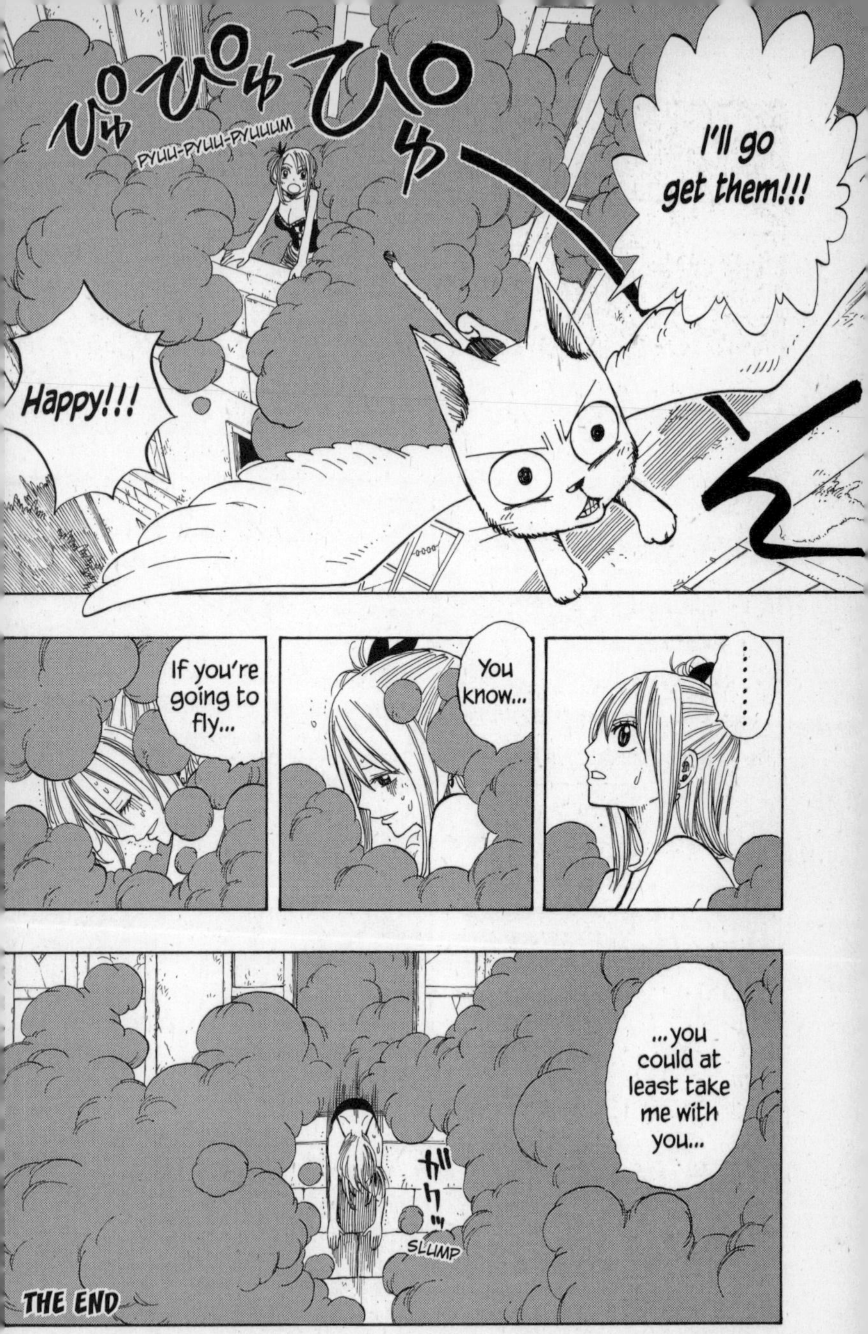
I'll go get them!!!
PYUU-PYUU-PYUUUM
Happy!!!
......
You know...
If you're going to fly...
...you could at least take me with you...
SLUMP
THE END

AFTERWORD

I introduced the "Guild d'Art" illustration corner in the last volume, and I got a huge load of postcards for it!! We're still putting together presents for those selected, so we'll publish them in the next volume — which means we're still accepting entries!!!* Below you'll find some rules we'd like you to follow when sending in your postcards.

1 • Only use standard postcard size. (Entries too big or too small will not be published.)

2 • Draw only with black pen. (Colored pens and pencil marks don't print very well.)

3 • Don't forget your name and address. (For those using a penname, include your real name as well.)

*This refers to the original publication in Japan in May 2007.

Send to ➡

Hiro Mashima
Kodansha Comics
451 Park Ave. South, 7th Floor
New York, NY 10016

While Kodansha Comics will make its best efforts to get your letters to Mashima-sensei, we cannot guarantee a reply.

Now to change the subject to this volume, S-Class quests! What does the S in S-Class mean? Well, it means Super. It means Special. It means *Soreya yabai-zo!!* (That's gotta be dangerous!!) Anyway, it means that there are a lot of amazing jobs! And Natsu and his group went and grabbed one of these high-level jobs without permission!! What's going to happen with them?! That's what this part of the series is all about! And the story is all wound up in Gray's past. **Why Gray?!** Well... Let's not think too much about that. I-It's got nothing to do with me seeing a lot of female fans out there!! Or rather, I don't really see many, so I hope to pick up more female fans.... Hopefully, that's the effect. Actually, Mirajane mentioned it a while back, but Fairy Tail's members have something in their pasts. Erza, Loke, and Elfman... I want to get their stories into the manga little by little. I'd like the readers to get the sense that every character has a deeper side. At least, that's what I want to attempt.

About the Creator

HIRO MASHIMA was born May 3, 1977, in Nagano Prefecture. His series *Rave Master* has made him one of the most popular manga artists in America. *Fairy Tail*, currently being serialized in *Weekly Shônen Magazine*, is his latest creation.

Translation Notes

Japanese is a tricky language for most Westerners, and translation is often more art than science. For your edification and reading pleasure, here are notes on some of the places where we could have gone in a different direction in our translation of the work, or where a Japanese cultural reference is used.

General Notes:
Wizard

In the original Japanese version of *Fairy Tail*, you'll find panels in which the English word "wizard" is part of the original illustration. So this translation has taken that as its inspiration and translated the word *madôshi* as "wizard." But *madôshi*'s meaning is similar to certain Japanese words that have been borrowed by the English language, such as judo (the soft way) and kendo (the way of the sword). *Madô* is the way of magic, and *madôshi* are those who follow the way of magic. So although the word "wizard" is used in the original dialogue, a Japanese reader would be likely to think not of traditional Western wizards such as Merlin or Gandalf, but of martial artists.

Names

Hiro Mashima has graciously agreed to provide official English spellings for just about all of the characters in *Fairy Tail*. Because this version of *Fairy Tail* is the first publication of most of these spellings, there will inevitably be differences between these spellings and some of the fan interpretations that may have spread throughout the Web or in other fan circles. Rest assured that the spellings contained in this book are the spellings that Mashima-sensei wanted for *Fairy Tail*.

Freedom!! page 24

Natsu shouts the English word here. American action movies are very popular in Japan, so the cry of "Freedom!!" from the movie *Braveheart* would certainly be remembered. However, on the popular stand-up comedy TV show *God of Entertainment*, the final act in every show features a young "blues singer" who sings new verses of his ironic "Freedom Blues" song each week, refreshing the meaning of the English word "freedom" in Japanese minds.

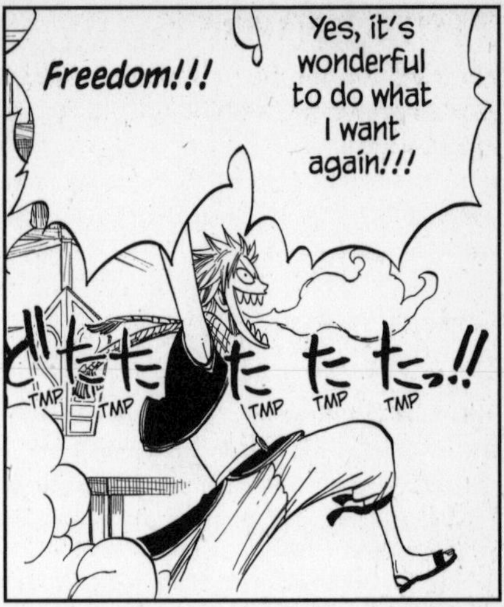
Yes, it's wonderful to do what I want again!!!
Freedom!!!
TMP
TMP
TMP
TMP
TMP

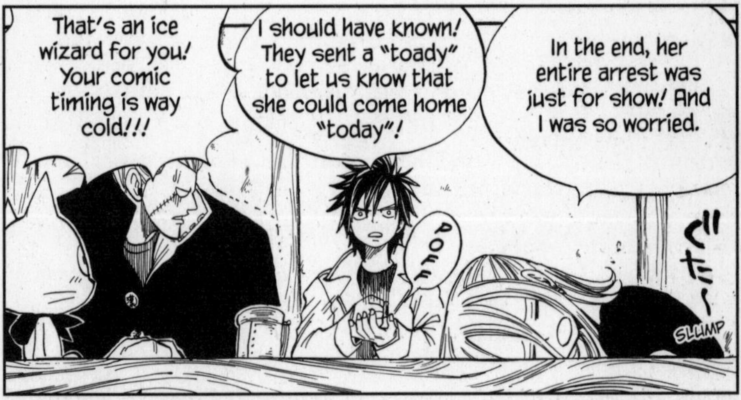
In the end, her entire arrest was just for show! And I was so worried.
I should have known! They sent a "toady" to let us know that she could come home "today"!
That's an ice wizard for you! Your comic timing is way cold!!!
POFF
SLUMP

Toady and cold, page 25

The Japanese version of Gray's pun was that the "frog" (*kaeru*) servant was a secret message that Erza would "come back" (also pronounced *kaeru*) very soon. Elfman's response that Gray, being an ice wizard, was "cold" played on the idea in Japan that a bad pun gives one the shivers. Fortunately there were handy puns in English that didn't change the meaning very much from the original.

Number kanji, page 31

The kanji for numbers used on this page are number kanji that were used in prewar Japan. They give a slightly archaic feel to Mystogan's countdown.

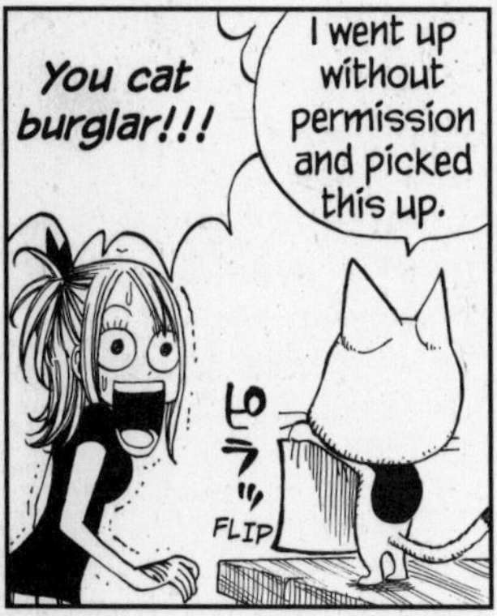
I went up without permission and picked this up.
You cat burglar!!!
FLIP

Cat burglar, page 44

The Japanese words translate directly to "cat thief" or "cat burglar."

Ahem, ahem, page 74

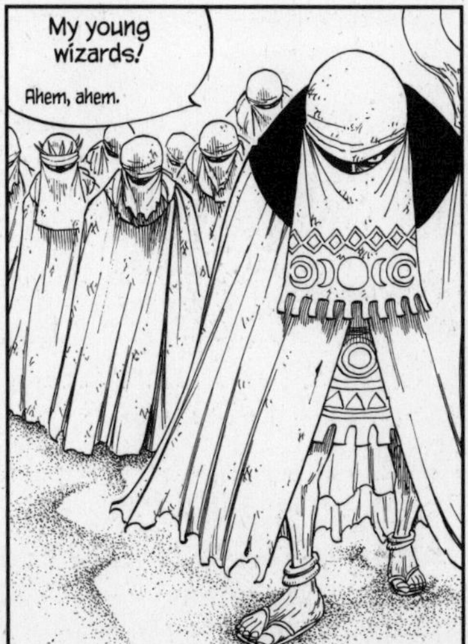
My young wizards!
Ahem, ahem.

In the original text, the onomatopoeia used was *hoga hoga*, which is the sound old men make when opening and closing their mouths trying to get their false teeth back in alignment. I couldn't come up with a sound that would convey that sentiment very well in English, so I went with the words "ahem, ahem"—the sound of clearing one's throat before a speech. Fortunately it fit the character of a village headman pretty well.

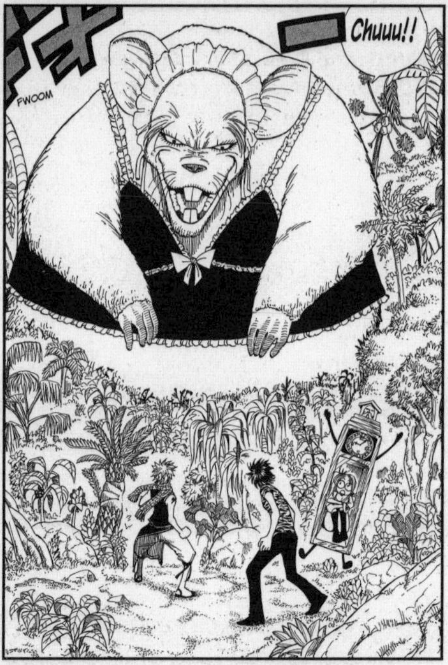
Chuuu!!
FWOOM

Chuu, page 92

The sound mice and rats make, as the Japanese hear it, is *chuu*. (Much like English speakers seem to hear mice and rats say, "Squeek.") There are many puns one can make using the sound, so this translation used the Japanese onomatopoeia on this page and at the back of the book in case Mashima wants to make comic use of the sound later in the series.

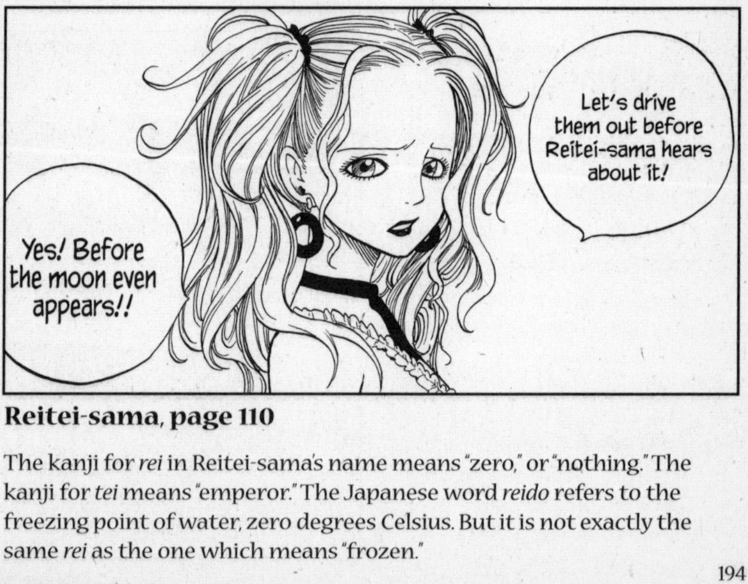
Let's drive them out before Reitei-sama hears about it!
Yes! Before the moon even appears!!

Reitei-sama, page 110

The kanji for *rei* in Reitei-sama's name means "zero," or "nothing." The kanji for *tei* means "emperor." The Japanese word *reido* refers to the freezing point of water, zero degrees Celsius. But it is not exactly the same *rei* as the one which means "frozen."

Lyra's lyrics, page 124

This translation makes no attempt to make the lyrics of Lyra's song rhyme. What's important here is the content: a direct translation of the lyrics best conveys why Lyra's song had such a profound effect on Gray.

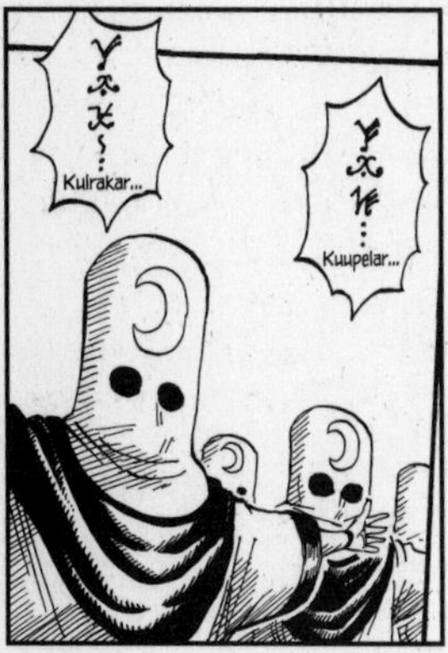
Kuupelar...
Kulrakar...

Chanting, page 128

The strange characters in this panel are not Japanese—they're a fictional language. In the original Japanese, an approximate Japanese pronunciation for each word was provided; here, we've provided the English approximation.

Splash page, page 176

In American comics terms, a splash page is the first page of a comic in which the entire page is taken up with one dynamic scene. Japanese usually have a splash page at the beginning of every chapter, called the *tobira peeji* ("door page"). Since they serve pretty much the same function, this translation interprets *tobira peeji* as "splash page."

Natsu's pose on the cover...
What the heck is he doing...?
Maybe the only reason for it is
that I wanted to draw a hand in
that shape. No matter how much
I wanted to draw it, the fact that
I couldn't draw it well is very
much like me. (laughs)
"That's it! I wanna draw that!!"
There are a whole lot of
examples of that kind of feeling
in this very volume, but the
final drawings never seem to
measure up to my mental image
of them....
I'll keep trying.

—Hiro Mashima

Honorifics Explained

Throughout the Kodansha Comics books, you will find Japanese honorifics left intact in the translations. For those not familiar with how the Japanese use honorifics and, more important, how they differ from American honorifics, we present this brief overview.

Politeness has always been a critical facet of Japanese culture. Ever since the feudal era, when Japan was a highly stratified society, use of honorifics—which can be defined as polite speech that indicates relationship or status—has played an essential role in the Japanese language. When addressing someone in Japanese, an honorific usually takes the form of a suffix attached to one's name (example: "Asuna-san"), is used as a title at the end of one's name, or appears in place of the name itself (example: "Negi-sensei," or simply "Sensei!").

Honorifics can be expressions of respect or endearment. In the context of manga and anime, honorifics give insight into the nature of the relationship between characters. Many English translations leave out these important honorifics and therefore distort the feel of the original Japanese. Because Japanese honorifics contain nuances that English honorifics lack, it is our policy at Kodansha not to translate them. Here, instead, is a guide to some of the honorifics you may encounter in Kodansha Comics.

-**san**:   This is the most common honorific and is equivalent to Mr., Miss, Ms., or Mrs. It is the all-purpose honorific and can be used in any situation where politeness is required.

-**sama**:   This is one level higher than "-san" and is used to confer great respect.

-**dono**:   This comes from the word "tono," which means "lord." It is an even higher level than "-sama" and confers utmost respect.

-kun: This suffix is used at the end of boys' names to express familiarity or endearment. It is also sometimes used by men among friends, or when addressing someone younger or of a lower station.

-chan: This is used to express endearment, mostly toward girls. It is also used for little boys, pets, and even between lovers. It gives a sense of childish cuteness.

Bozu: This is an informal way to refer to a boy, similar to the English terms "kid" and "squirt."

**Sempai/
Senpai:** This title suggests that the addressee is one's senior in a group or organization. It is most often used in a school setting, where underclassmen refer to their upperclassmen as "sempai." It can also be used in the workplace, such as when a newer employee addresses an employee who has seniority in the company.

Kohai: This is the opposite of "sempai" and is used toward underclassmen in school or newcomers in the workplace. It connotes that the addressee is of a lower station.

Sensei: Literally meaning "one who has come before," this title is used for teachers, doctors, or masters of any profession or art.

-[blank]: This is usually forgotten in these lists, but it is perhaps the most significant difference between Japanese and English. The lack of honorific means that the speaker has permission to address the person in a very intimate way. Usually, only family, spouses, or very close friends have this kind of permission. Known as *yobisute*, it can be gratifying when someone who has earned the intimacy starts to call one by one's name without an honorific. But when that intimacy hasn't been earned, it can be very insulting.

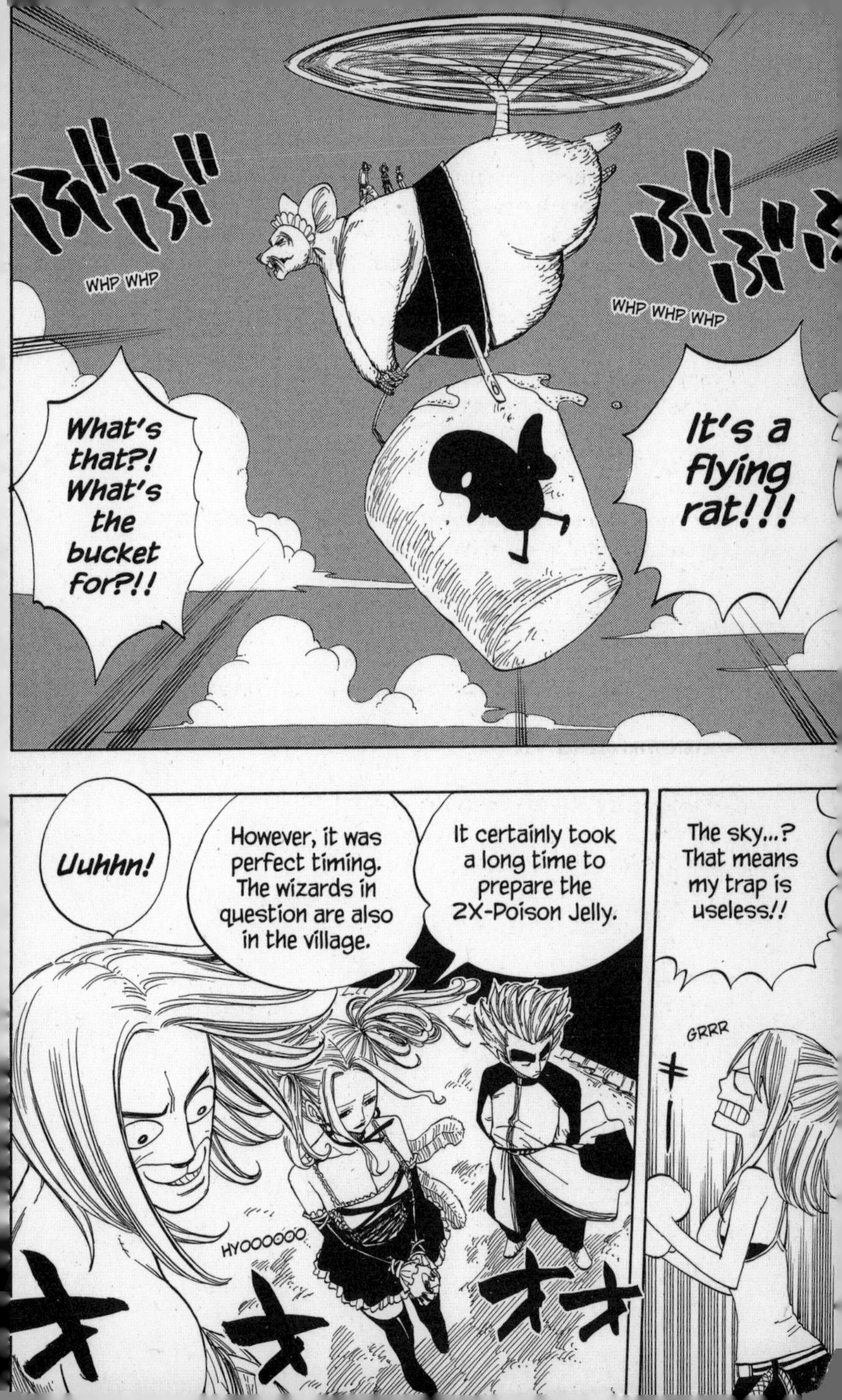

WHP WHP WHP
It's a flying rat!!!
WHP WHP
What's that?! What's the bucket for?!!
The sky...? That means my trap is useless!!
GRRR
It certainly took a long time to prepare the 2X-Poison Jelly.
However, it was perfect timing. The wizards in question are also in the village.
Uuhhn!
HYOOOOOO

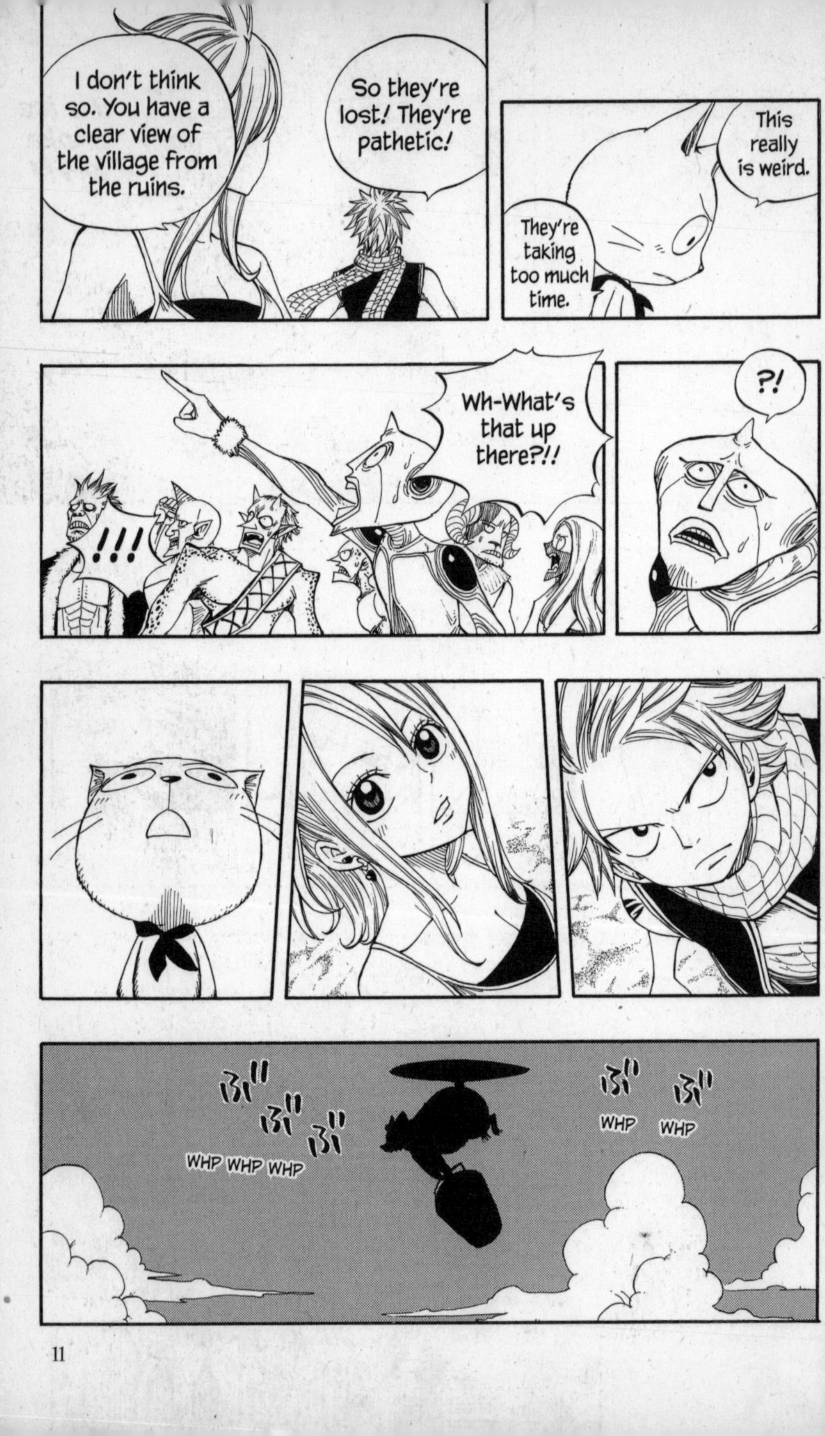

This really is weird.
They're taking too much time.
So they're lost! They're pathetic!
I don't think so. You have a clear view of the village from the ruins.
?!
Wh-What's that up there?!!
!!!
ぶ WHP
ぶ WHP
ぶ ぶ ぶ
WHP WHP WHP

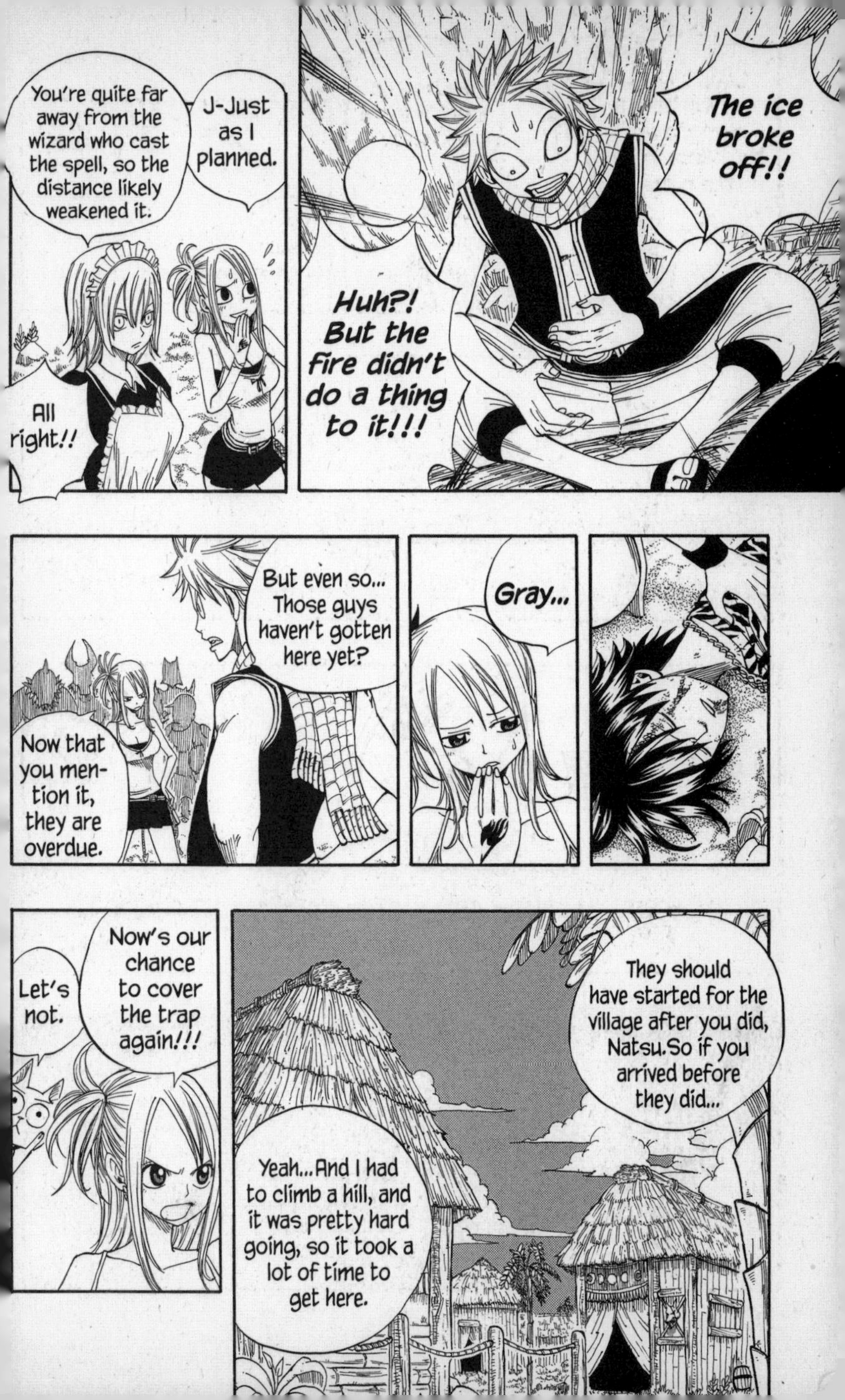
The ice broke off!!
Huh?! But the fire didn't do a thing to it!!!
J-Just as I planned.
You're quite far away from the wizard who cast the spell, so the distance likely weakened it.
All right!!
Gray...
But even so... Those guys haven't gotten here yet?
Now that you men-tion it, they are overdue.
They should have started for the village after you did, Natsu. So if you arrived before they did...
Yeah... And I had to climb a hill, and it was pretty hard going, so it took a lot of time to get here.
Now's our chance to cover the trap again!!!
Let's not.

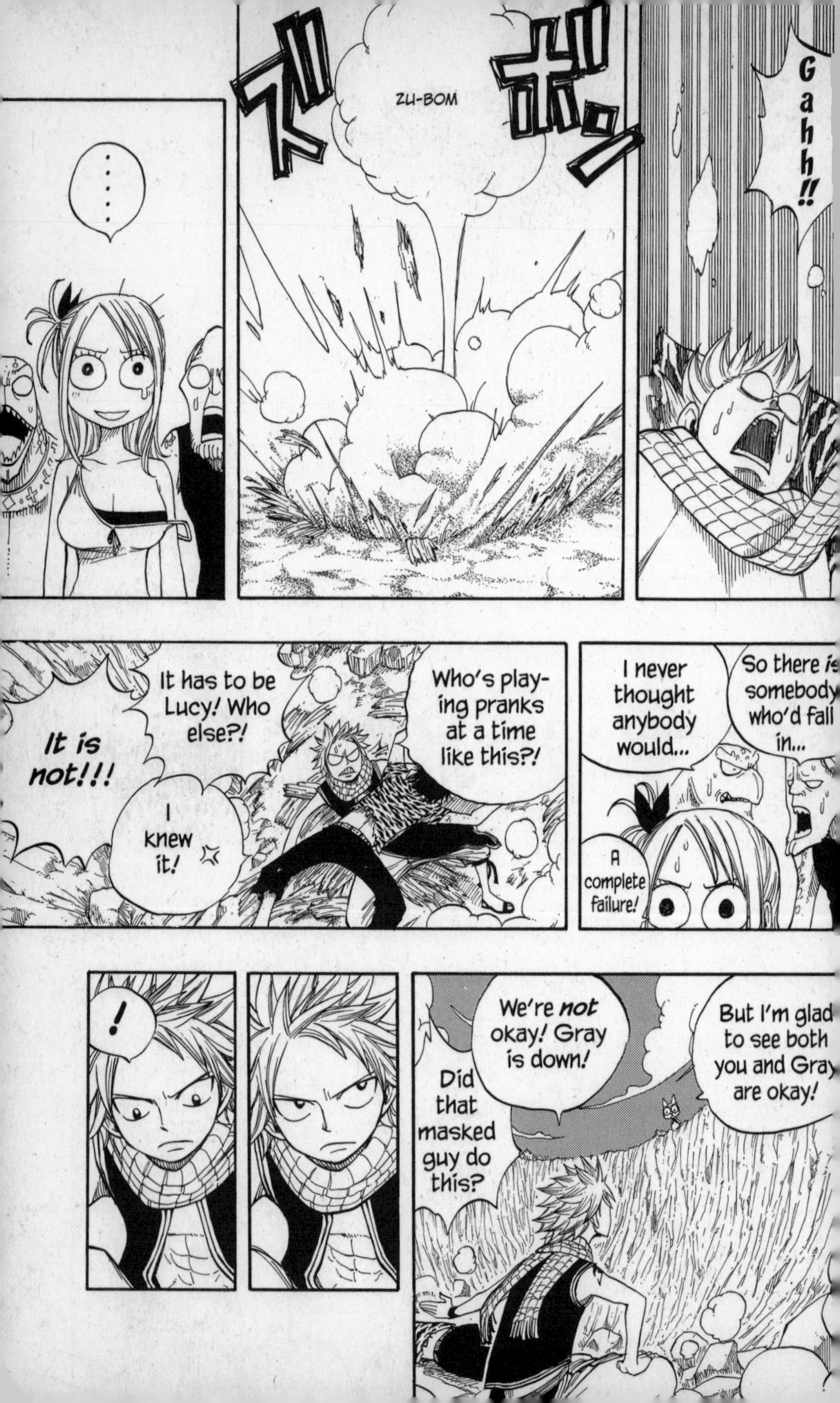
Gahh!!
ZU-BOM
.....
So there *is* somebody who'd fall in...
I never thought anybody would...
A complete failure!
Who's play-ing pranks at a time like this?!
It has to be Lucy! Who else?!
I knew it!
It is not!!!
But I'm glad to see both you and Gray are okay!
We're *not* okay! Gray is down!
Did that masked guy do this?
!

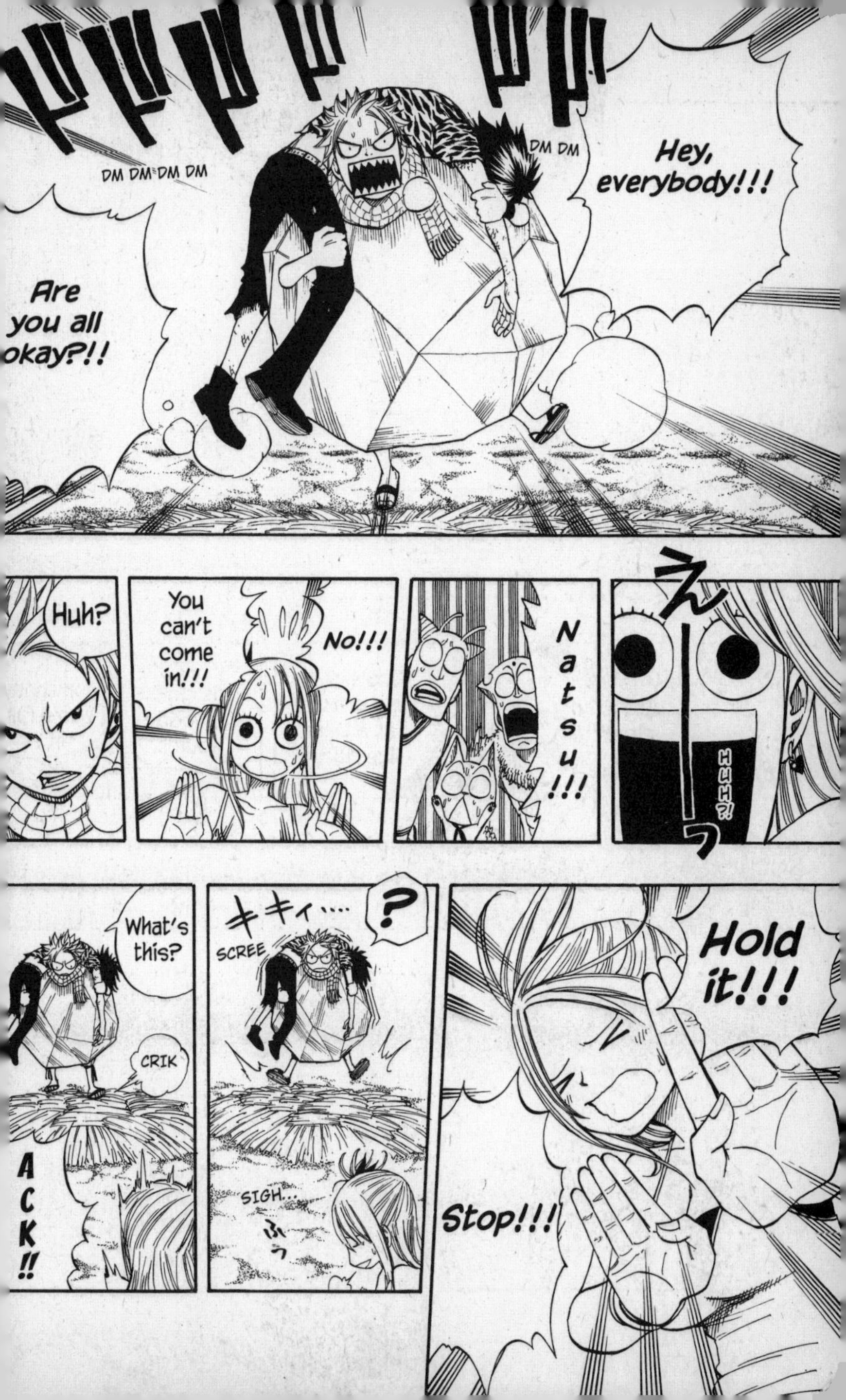
Hey, everybody!!!
DM DM
DM DM DM DM
Are you all okay?!!
えーっ
HUH?!
Natsu!!!
No!!!
You can't come in!!!
Huh?
Hold it!!!
Stop!!!
?
キキィ…
SCREE
SIGH...
ふっ
What's this?
CRIK
ACK!!

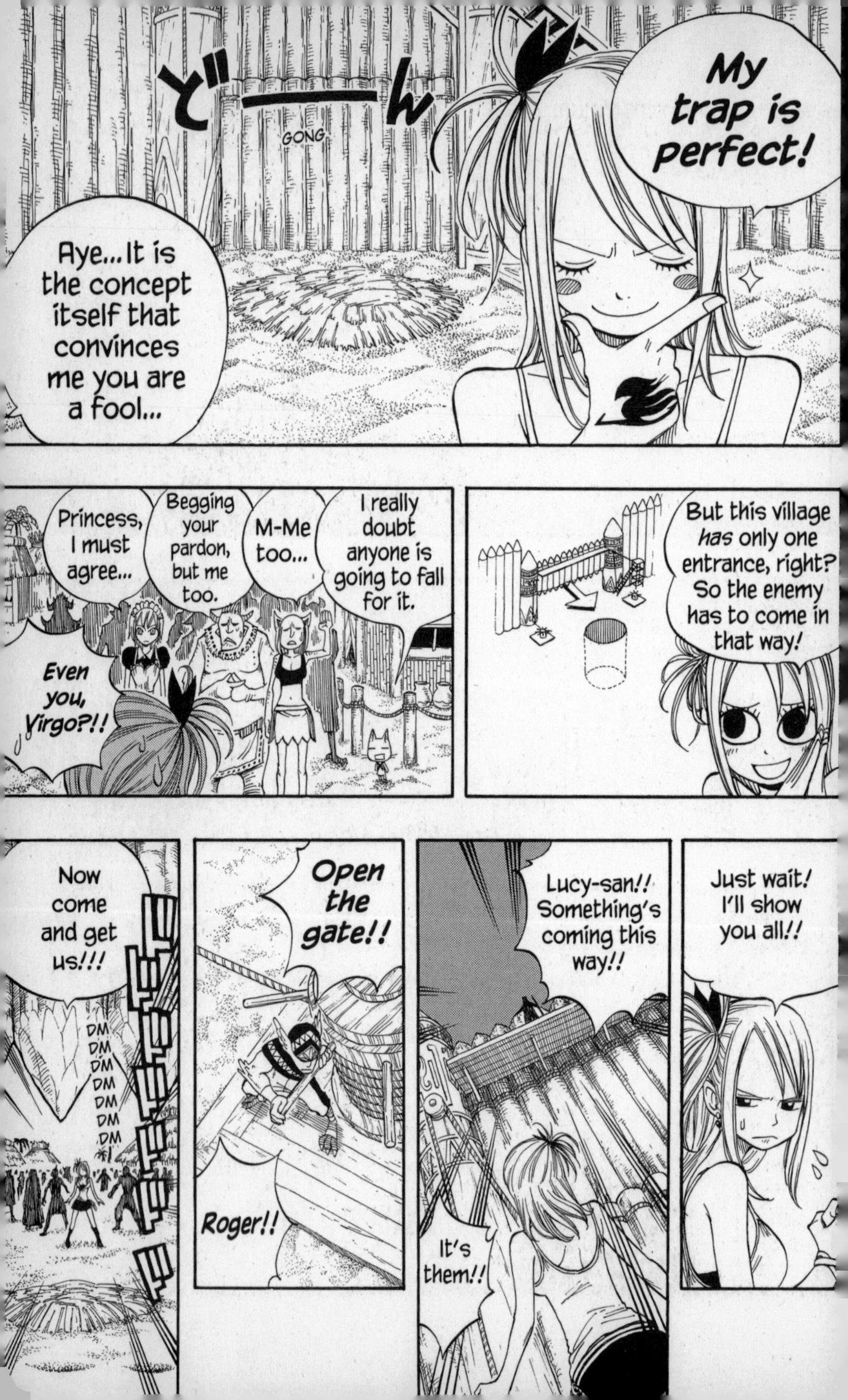
GONG
My trap is perfect!
Aye... It is the concept itself that convinces me you are a fool...
But this village has only one entrance, right? So the enemy has to come in that way!
I really doubt anyone is going to fall for it.
M-Me too...
Begging your pardon, but me too.
Princess, I must agree...
Even you, Virgo?!!
Just wait! I'll show you all!!
Lucy-san!! Something's coming this way!!
It's them!!
Open the gate!!
Roger!!
Now come and get us!!!
DM DM DM DM DM DM DM

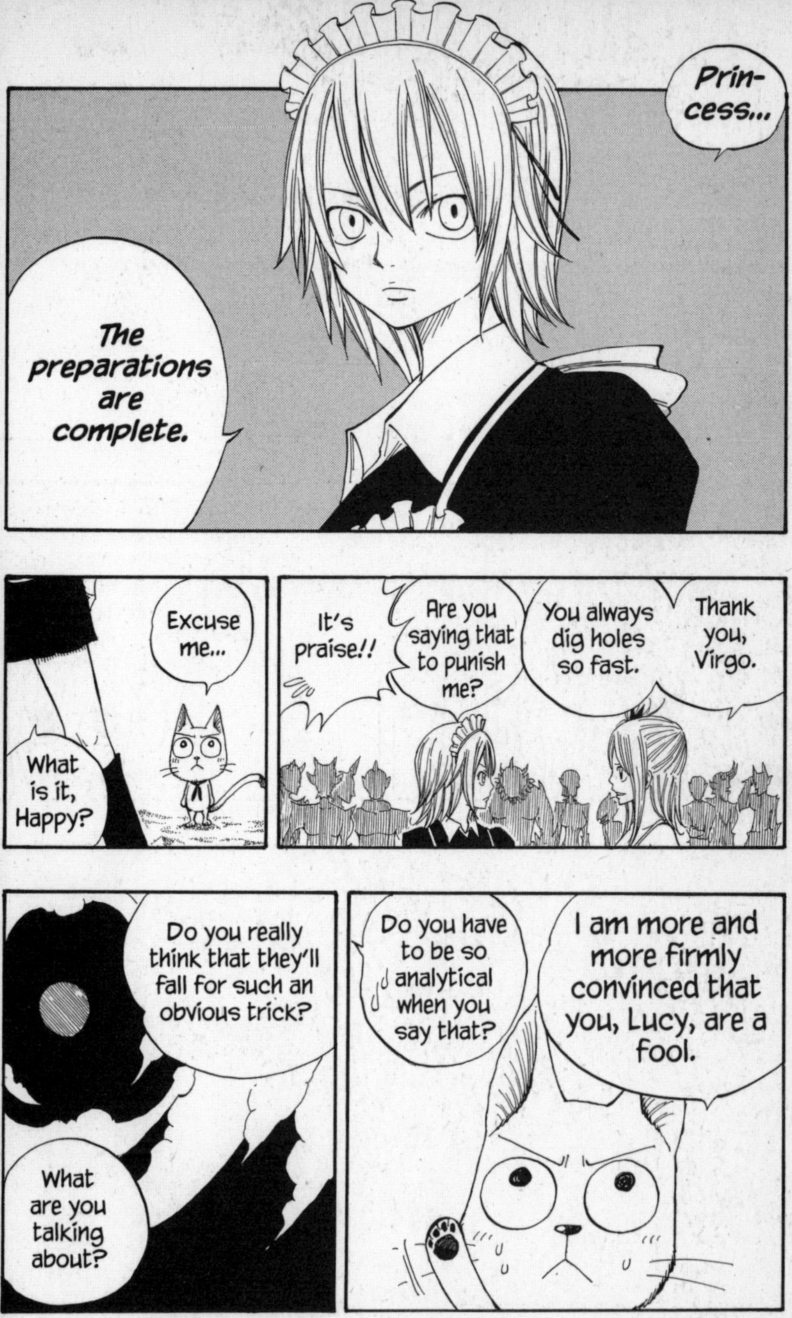
Prin-cess...
The preparations are complete.
Thank you, Virgo.
You always dig holes so fast.
Are you saying that to punish me?
It's praise!!
Excuse me...
What is it, Happy?
I am more and more firmly convinced that you, Lucy, are a fool.
Do you have to be so analytical when you say that?
Do you really think that they'll fall for such an obvious trick?
What are you talking about?

Preview of Volume 5

We're pleased to present you with a preview from volume 5, now available from Kodansha Comics. Check out our Web site (www.kodanshacomics.com) for more details!

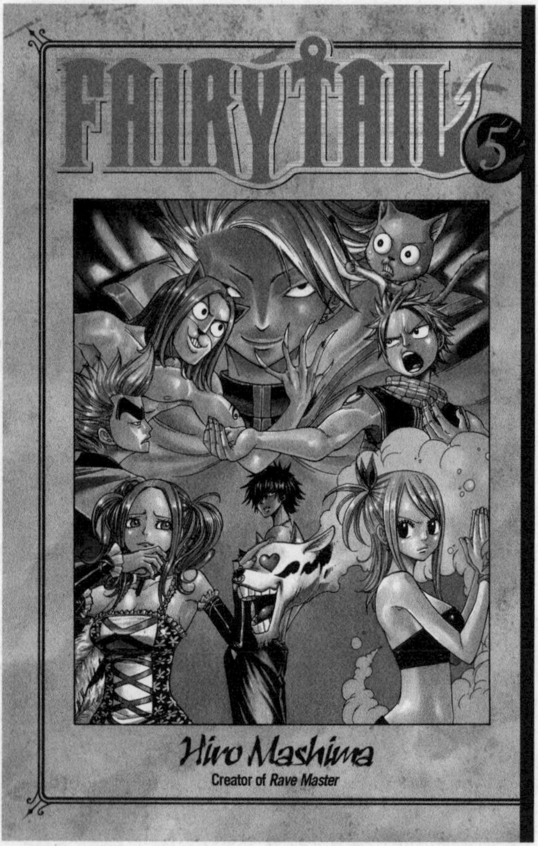

FAIRY TAIL
5
Hiro Mashima
Creator of Rave Master